REASONS FOR WELFARE

STUDIES IN MORAL, POLITICAL,
AND LEGAL PHILOSOPHY

General Editor: Marshall Cohen

REASONS FOR
WELFARE

The Political Theory
of the Welfare State

Robert E. Goodin

PRINCETON UNIVERSITY PRESS
PRINCETON, NEW JERSEY

Published by Princeton University Press
41 William Street
Princeton, New Jersey 08540
In the United Kingdom:
Princeton University Press, Guildford, Surrey

Library of Congress Cataloging-in-Publication Data
Goodin, Robert E.   Reasons for welfare.
(Studies in moral, political, and legal philosophy)
Bibliography: p.   Includes index.
1. Social justice. 2. Welfare state—Moral and ethical aspects.
I. Title. II. Series.
HM216.G564 1988   303.3'72   88–5822
ISBN 0–691–07766–5 (alk. paper)   ISBN 0–691–02279–8 (pbk.)

This book has been composed in Linotron Palatino

Clothbound editions of Princeton University Press books
are printed on acid-free paper, and binding materials
are chosen for strength and durability. Paperbacks,
although satisfactory for personal collections,
are not usually suitable for library rebinding

Printed in the United States of America
by Princeton University Press
Princeton, New Jersey

If one examines the two major ideological currents that have come down to us from the Enlightenment, liberalism and socialism, one finds that neither of them expresses any great yearning for social welfare policy— scarcely even so much, in fact, as the more patriarchical and religiously- tinged variants of the old feudal ideology of social estates and their duties.
—Gunnar Myrdal

CONTENTS

PREFACE   ix

ACKNOWLEDGMENTS   xiii

ONE. Introduction   3

Part I Against the Old Left

TWO. Needs   27

THREE. Equality   51

FOUR. Community   70

Part II Toward a New Theory

FIVE. Exploitation   123

SIX. Dependency   153

SEVEN. Discretion   184

Part III Against the New Right

EIGHT. Efficiency   229

NINE. Supply-side Policies   257

TEN. Desert   278

ELEVEN. Freedom   306

TWELVE. Self-reliance   332

Part IV Conclusion

THIRTEEN. Conclusion   363

REFERENCES   371

INDEX   411

PREFACE

The central aim of this book is normative rather than empirical. It is concerned not with the causes but with the reasons that can be offered for the welfare state. The two are not necessarily unconnected, of course. Sometimes people are moved by ethical arguments. Circumstances sometimes succeed in making abstract arguments personally compelling. Far from denying these truths, I actually take considerable comfort in them. They are what gives political philosophy some practical point.

Still, while such happy outcomes are always possible, they are never inevitable. It would be dangerously wrong to suppose that all welfare states now in existence have been brought into existence for "good reasons." Motives are characteristically mixed, and often bad. It would be folly to pretend otherwise.

So too would it be dangerously misleading to suggest that good arguments alone will suffice to bring a welfare state into existence or to protect one already in existence from those who would dismantle it. Moral philosophy, I am firmly convinced, is one form of political action. It is not the only one, however; and perhaps, pragmatically, it is not even the most important one. Various other forms of political activity will surely be required if we are to succeed in discharging what I hope to show are our clear moral duties to protect vulnerable and dependent members of our society from exploitation.

The phrasing of this book's title is positive, promising to offer "reasons for welfare." It is in the nature of such a crowded field, however, that nothing much positive can be accomplished without first clearing away a fair bit of underbrush on either side. The bulk of this book is, therefore, given over to largely destructive exercises.

My principal aim is to show that there are good reasons for us to favor an activist state promoting the social welfare of its citizens. But in the course of making that argument, I shall also be obliged to show that the New Right is wrong in thinking otherwise, and that the Old Left is wrong in thinking that the most fundamental reason for the most basic form of welfare state can be found in any of the standard justifications traditionally offered in defense of social welfare policies.

Between them, the concepts of need, equality, and community pretty well exhaust the catalogue of conventional Old Left justifications for the welfare state. None of them will suffice. On closer inspection, it turns out that we have no good, clearcut reason to give the task of "meeting needs per se" systematic priority over merely "satisfying desires." On closer inspection, it turns out that our commitment to equality per se, and for its own sake, is substantially weaker than we have long supposed. On closer inspection, it turns out that communitarian ideals lead us to enhance individual welfare only incidentally, if at all.

Each of those considerations points in the direction of a principle which, suitably reformulated, might have considerable moral force. Each of those principles might bear tangentially on questions of the justifiability of the existence of the welfare state. Each of them might even bear centrally on questions of the justifiability of the expansion of welfare-state programs, once they are in place. None of those principles itself provides the central justification for the existence of basic welfare-state institutions, however. Demonstrating the failure of all the standard Old Left arguments in this regard is the burden of Part I of this book.

To say that none of the standard justifications of the welfare state will suffice is not to say that the welfare state is without justification. It is merely to say that its justification must be sought elsewhere, in less conventional arguments. The one that I favor is couched in terms of the moral duties of the strong to protect the weak. I hesitate to call this a "new" justification. In a way, it is nothing more than noblesse oblige in modern guise; and in certain respects, its central tenets are already fairly well established in the practical political history and the rhetoric of the welfare state itself. When formally discussing the ethical foundations of the welfare state, however, both politicians and scholars alike tend to leave this crucial premise suppressed. It is my intention to put that premise at the center of the argument, where it belongs.

I shall say relatively little about the deeper philosophical arguments for the general proposition that we have a strong moral duty to protect those whose interests are particularly vulnerable to our actions and choices. I have argued for that more general proposition at some length in a companion volume, *Protecting the Vulnerable* (Chicago: University of Chicago Press, 1985). Those looking for philosophical foundations should search there. Here I shall confine myself principally to tracing the implications of that general proposition for the welfare state.

The essential function of the welfare state thus construed is to prevent the exploitation of vulnerable members of society. Put more positively, it is to protect the interests of those who are not in a position to protect them themselves. Tracing out the implications of such arguments is the business of Part II.

This analysis of the true moral foundations of the basic institutions of the welfare state lays the necessary groundwork for rebutting various attacks upon it mounted by the New Right. Those attacks are many and varied. But whether they are couched in terms of efficiency, desert, self-reliance, freedom, or supply-side logic, all those arguments eventually founder in one way or another on the ethical foundations laid in Part II. Showing that to be so is the burden of Part III.

Taken together, the various arguments and counterarguments of this book leave the welfare state's basic institutions safe against the onslaught of the New Right, without forcing it to fall back on the familiar arguments of the Old Left. The ethical foundations here revealed are, in my view, firmer foundations for the basic institutions of the welfare state than those on which they have for too long been forced to rely.

Wivenhoe, Essex
March 1987

ACKNOWLEDGMENTS

This book represents the culmination of my work with the Social Justice Project of the Research School of Social Sciences at the Australian National University, to which I was attached between 1982 and 1984. Some of the material in these chapters was written in anticipation of going there; much of it was written, or at least sketched out, while I was working there. My first and largest debt is therefore to my colleagues in that project (especially its director, Pat Troy, and its secretary, Norma Chin) and in the school more generally for their generous support, material and otherwise.

These arguments have been aired in a variety of venues, first around the ANU and then elsewhere. Among those whose incisive comments have contributed directly to one or more of these chapters, I should thank particularly: Michael Adler, P. S. Atiyah, Stanley Benn, Dorothy Broom, David Bull, Tom Campbell, John Chapman, Jerry Cohen, Darryl Dixon, Meredith Edwards, Jerry Gaus, Fred Gruen, Vinit Haksar, David Heald, Ken Judge, Des King, John Kleinig, Martin Krygier, Eric Mack, Stuart Macintyre, Don Moon, Max Neutze, Virginia Novarra, John Passmore, Carole Pateman, David Piachaud, John Pocock, Andy Reeve, Richard Rose, Don Rowland, Wojciech Sadurski, Sidney Sax, Peter Self, Jim Sharpe, Jack Smart, Paul Spicker, Richard Routley Sylvan, Tim Tilton, Pat Troy, Robert van der Veen, Jeremy Waldron, Steve Walt, Hugh Ward, and John Watkins.

Special thanks are due to a few close friends—many also sometime collaborators—whose influence extends over most of these chapters. Among them are Brian Barry, Diane Gibson, Julian Le Grand, Philip Pettit, Patricia Tulloch, Albert Weale, and Peter Wilenski (who actually co-authored parts of chapter 8). Others have done me the uncommon kindness of providing virtually line-by-line commentaries on earlier drafts of the manuscript as a whole. Allen Buchanan, Loren Lomasky, and David Miller deserve my special gratitude in that connection.

All are to credit, none to blame.

REASONS FOR WELFARE

O N E

INTRODUCTION

I

The welfare state is, first and foremost, a political artifact. As such, it is the product of historical accretion and political compromise. Different bits have been added, over the years, by different people with different purposes in mind. It is today supported by many diverse groups, for many diverse reasons. Each group of its supporters takes greatest pride in some slightly different one of its many, varied aspects; each tries to nudge its future development in some slightly different direction. Conversely, each of its many diverse groups of detractors finds in it some slightly different flaw.

The truth of that simple observation has important ramifications for any attempt at mounting an ethical defense of the welfare state. Basically, it means that the "welfare state" is not itself a single, unified, unambiguous entity. It is instead a ragbag of programs, only vaguely related and only imperfectly integrated.

As a historical proposition, "social assistance" (or "general assistance") programs aiding those demonstrably in need came first, followed by programs of contributory "social insurance" (or, in American parlance, "social security"), followed by noncontributory benefits, first categorical in form (e.g., old-age pensions, child benefits) and then universal (e.g., the U.K. National Health Service).[1] Where, in this progression, the "welfare state" makes its first appearance is unclear. At what point we have moved "beyond the welfare state" is also unclear.

As an analytic proposition, which programs are to be included in (and which excluded from) the "welfare state" category varies with time, place, and commentator. There is little doubt that

Material in this chapter is reprinted from Robert E. Goodin, "Reasons for Welfare," *Responsibility, Rights and Welfare: Essays on the Welfare State*, ed. J. Donald Moon (Boulder, Colo.: Westview Press, 1988) by permission of the editor and Westview Press.

[1] This pattern is revealed in comparative histories of the welfare state (e.g., Heclo 1974), and is shown to have wider cross-national validity by Cutright (1965).

health care provision such as the National Health Service in Britain or Medicare and Medicaid in the U.S. count as welfare state programs. Whether other public health measures (e.g., sanitation, water treatment) do is unclear. There is little doubt that preschool programs for disadvantaged children (e.g., Project Head Start) count. Whether the state educational sector as a whole does is unclear. There is little doubt that unemployment benefits count. Whether labor market policies more generally do is unclear.[2]

More serious than problems concerning the locations of the boundaries around the welfare state, however, are problems concerning the identification of its core. Which programs should be seen as the most central, defining features of the welfare state—its sine qua non—which it must be the primary task of any ethical defense of the welfare state to justify?

Here questions of how to define the welfare state and how to justify it seem to be uncomfortably, but inextricably, linked. It is only natural that how we set about justifying something should depend upon what we take its defining features to be. But the process becomes distressingly circular where, as here, what we think its defining features to be then turn out to depend upon how we propose to set about justifying it.

Yet clearly such circularity is involved in defining and defending the welfare state. Residualists put the ethical emphasis upon the public's duty to relieve palpable distress. Accordingly, they presume the core of the welfare state to be "social assistance"—paradigmatically, "indoor relief" (the workhouse and the poorhouse), but extending also to needs-tested (typically, in-kind) assistance. New Liberals such as Beveridge put the emphasis upon the state's duty to remedy market failures. Accordingly, they suppose the core of the welfare state to be "social insurance"—paradigmatically, workmen's compensation, health and unemployment insurance, but extending also to old-age pensions, perhaps. Socialists

---

[2] We can, of course, put labels on the above periodization: the "positive state," followed by the "social security state," followed by the "social welfare state," followed now by the "democratic corporatist state" (Furniss and Tilton 1977: chap. 1; Furniss and Mitchell 1984: 29–36), or some such. There may be good grounds for arguing for the distinctiveness of each of the state types picked out by such labels. But there are none for the labels themselves. So far as I can see, there is nothing that would allow Furniss and his collaborators to say what marks the beginning and what marks the end of the *real* welfare state, as opposed to what marks the beginning and end of that state type that they have, for expository convenience, somewhat arbitrarily labelled "the welfare state." I do not imagine that Furniss, his collaborators, or any other reflective promulgators of social typologies ever thought otherwise.

of one stripe put the ethical emphasis upon the ideal of social equality. Accordingly, they imagine the core of the welfare state to be redistributive "transfer" programs—paradigmatically, cash transfers, but also extending perhaps to state subsidies for public services used predominantly by the less well-off. Socialists of another stripe put the ethical emphasis upon the ideal of community solidarity. Accordingly, they suppose the core of the welfare state to be universal social services—paradigmatically, state education and the British National Health Service, but perhaps also extending to mass transportation and public housing.

This tendency for one's analysis of what definitionally constitutes the "core" of the welfare state to depend crucially upon one's analysis of how best to justify it is a dangerous one. The result is that advocates of alternative justifications talk past one another, each discussing something slightly different when considering arguments for or against "the welfare state."[3]

There is, so far as I can see, no easy way around this impasse. All one can do is to be as forthright as possible about which definition one is using, and why. Since the impasse still remains, however, it is important to try to make one's arguments about the proper way to justify the welfare state turn as little as possible upon moves of a purely analytic form. Given that other commentators advocating other sorts of justifications for the welfare state do not necessarily share one's own views as to what the welfare state "really" is, it would be foolhardy to rely too heavily upon arguments that certain justifications of the welfare state are right or wrong on the grounds that what those propositions justify is or is not "really" a welfare state at all.

In what follows, I shall be offering a definition of the welfare state that falls squarely into what I have above called the "residualist" camp. That is to say, programs of general social assistance to those in desperate circumstances will be taken to constitute the core of the welfare state. That is not necessarily to say that more extensive programs for promoting public welfare are not justifiable. Neither is it necessarily to say that those more extensive programs are not part of the welfare state. It is merely to say that

[3] A standard, and devastating, point in the critique of the positivist philosophy of science is that observations are theory-dependent: they do not, therefore, provide any independent point from which we can evaluate theories. What is involved here is an analogous problem: definitions, here at least, seem to be justification-dependent. Hence they do not provide any independent point from which we can identify institutions and practices, which we can then set about trying to evaluate and defend ethically.

those more extensive programs are peripheral rather than central to the basic institutions of the welfare state.

As an answer to this narrow question—what is central and what is peripheral to the basic institutions of the welfare state?—the residualist analysis seems indisputable. A state that did not even try to relieve distress when it was clearly within its power to do so simply could not credibly claim to constitute a welfare state. That fact alone makes "attempting to relieve distress" a sine qua non of the welfare state.

The same cannot plausibly be said of any of the other activities with which the welfare state is sometimes associated. A state that did not even try to promote equality or fellow-feeling even when it was clearly within its power to do so might not be a very good state in all sorts of ways. But it simply would not be true that, on account of that fact alone, it could not credibly claim to be a welfare state. Neither would the fact that it did not even try to remedy market failures not actually connected with distress.

Another way of putting the same point would be this. A state that is enormously sensitive to considerations of equality or fellow-feeling but utterly indifferent to the needy could hardly be said to constitute a welfare state; the converse is not the case. Those other non-welfare states might, morally, be better states. That is a separate issue. My point here is merely that, whatever else, they do not properly count as welfare states.

While "attempting to relieve distress" will serve as a sine qua non—as one necessary condition—of a welfare state in the definition that I shall offer below, it will not in and of itself constitute a sufficient condition. Were it to do so, then any attempt by the state at relieving distress would qualify that state for the status of a "welfare state." By that criterion, the Elizabethan Poor Law would qualify. Whatever else we want to say about the welfare state, we clearly do not want to say that it started in 1601.

The welfare state will be defined as one particular way of attempting to relieve distress. Various more detailed conditions will be laid down below. The most crucial among them, however, has to do with notions traditionally discussed under the heading of "welfare rights." As I shall argue in chapter 7, that label is slightly misleading. In the meanwhile, however, the term "welfare rights" might nonetheless serve as a useful placeholder for what seems to me to be the second sine qua non of a welfare state. The essence of that second element is just this: for a state to qualify as a welfare state, it must attempt to relieve distress in such a way that the agents of the state are bound by a legal duty to provide those in distress with certain resources that they need. Phrased negatively, the crux of the matter is that agents of a welfare state must have no discretionary power over those resources that the state allocates for the relief of people in distress. That is what distinguishes a welfare state from a poor-law state.

I I

A more formal way of fleshing out the definition of the welfare state just sketched is to ask what features distinguish the welfare state from other sorts of state, on the one hand, and from other modes of welfare provision, on the other. Answering the first part of this question is the task of section II.A. Answering the second is the concern of section II.B.

A

In distinguishing the welfare state from other sorts of state, we must first stipulate that: *(a) The welfare state is set in the context of a market economy.* The function of the welfare state is, as Briggs (1961: 228) says, to "modify the play of market forces" in various, limited respects; its function is not to supplant the market altogether. The welfare state "did not reject the capitalist market economy, but held that there were some elements in a civilized life which ranked above it and must be achieved by curbing or suppressing the market" in those areas (Marshall 1963: 298).[4]

Of course, planned economies do ordinarily contain a social security or social service sector. That is not the same as a "welfare state," though. The point of welfare state interventions is to remedy unplanned and unwelcome outcomes. The welfare state strives to produce a post-fisc distribution of certain goods and services that is preferable to the pre-fisc one. In a planned econ-

[4] Or, in Michelman's (1969: 32) terms, its operative premise is, "It is no justification for deprivation of a fundamental right . . . that the deprivation results from a general practice of requiring persons to pay for what they get." Thus, the market is supplanted, but only for purposes of satisfying a limited set of "just wants" or "fundamental rights." This is slightly different from the question, posed in the debate between Residual and Institutional models of welfare, of whether the welfare state should act as a first line of defense or merely as a second to be called upon when the first (i.e., the market) has failed (Wilensky and Lebeaux 1958: 138; Titmuss 1974). In the Institutional model, there are many things that are left to the market altogether, even if the welfare state takes "first line" responsibility, supplanting the market altogether for distributing the limited range of goods and services that comes within its purview.

omy, by contrast, all outcomes are the outcomes of planning. Not all are necessarily intended or welcomed outcomes, to be sure. But correcting planning errors is surely qualitatively different from correcting the market's unplanned perversities.

Many of the same (e.g., demographic) factors that force growth in the social service sectors of market economies may also force growth in the same sectors of planned economies. For certain purposes (empirical cross-national studies of public expenditures, perhaps), it might therefore make sense to lump together social service activities in both types of economy. For the normative purposes here in view, however, the differences clearly matter. The justification for public interventions in private economies will surely be different in kind from the justifications for public interventions in public economies.[5] So here I shall treat the "welfare state" as a public intervention in a private, market economy—and that alone.

The welfare state must, secondly, be distinguished from more thoroughgoing egalitarian regimes of either of two logically distinct sorts. The first strives to equalize everyone's share of consumption goods; the second strives to equalize everyone's share of productive resources. The welfare state as here conceived makes no systematic attempt at doing either.[6]

Consider first the contrast with the sort of state that gives everyone exactly equal shares of all consumption goods and services. Such a state may well thereby promote the welfare of its citizens.[7] But we would hesitate to say that it is (merely) a welfare state, when it goes so far beyond the sort of minimal provision for basic social needs that we think ordinarily characterizes a welfare state.

The characteristic function of the welfare state is to "limit the domain of inequality" (Tobin 1970), not to eliminate it altogether. Its task is to provide a "national minimum," in the words of the

---

[5] Rimlinger (1961) launches his comparative U.S./U.S.S.R. study of social security expenditures with an argument that the two are analogous, each being "a system of secondary income distribution . . . different in its distributive principles and primary objectives from the economy's functional income distribution." By the end of the article, however, it is clear that the differences between the two social security systems, their rationales, and their operative premises utterly swamp any such similarities. See similarly: Jouvenel 1960; Lowenstein 1960; Nove 1960; and Deacon 1983.

[6] Statutory guarantees of a certain future stream of income might, in effect if not in name, produce much the same result (Reich 1964). But backhandedness in this regard is itself a hallmark of the welfare state: if it does redistribute property, at least it tries to do so without being seen to do so.

[7] "May," because in a desperately poor country an equal division might leave everyone starving.

Beveridge (1942) report—a floor or social safety net. But above that, "individual effort must be free to create individual differences" (Marshall 1963: 295). Hence we can say that an important further feature of the welfare state is that: *(b) The welfare state limits its provision to certain basic needs.* The substance of those needs varies from society to society, but what remains relatively constant across all societies is the recognition of a category of "needs" separate from that of "mere wants."

Consider next the contrast between a welfare state and a state that strives to equalize productive resources.[8] Imagine a state which gives everyone exactly equal shares of capital—perhaps through public ownership of the means of production, or perhaps through market-socialist redistributions of finance capital to equalize the shares of all citizens. That sort of state, too, may well promote people's welfare (albeit less directly). Once again, however, we would be loath to say that a state that did that much was (merely) a "welfare state."[9]

The sorts of interventions that characterize what I have called the "central" or "core" features of the welfare state are much more modest than that. At the level of personal social service administration, the characteristically welfare-statist approach is to opt for in-kind transfers or nonfungible vouchers for specific goods or services, rather than for cash transfers. On the level of grand strategy, the characteristically welfare statist approach is to opt for readjusting final distributions, rather than altering the pattern of property rights in productive resources that gave rise to undesirable distributions in the first place.[10]

[8] Notice that Wilensky and Lebeaux (1958: 145–46) recommend a focus on "consumption" rather than "production" needs as a way of differentiating social welfare activities from those such as national defense, road-building, and soil conservation, which are all concerned with state servicing of producer interests.

[9] We would be similarly loath to call even the social security sector of such a state a welfare state. To do so would have this paradoxical consequence: The more successful the state is in promoting people's welfare by producing the right pre-fisc distribution, the less there is for the social security sector to do by way of patching up a better post-fisc distribution. But it is absurd to say that a state which does more toward (and succeeds better in) promoting people's welfare has a "smaller welfare state." Still, that is what we would be committed to saying, were we to regard the social security sector alone as the welfare state component of such a state.

[10] Or, as Cohen (1981: 14) more pejoratively puts it, supporters of the welfare state ("social democrats," in his terms) contrast with more radical "revolutionaries" who "find confiscation a more appropriate response to severe inequality of ownership than perpetual rearguard action against the effects of that inequality. . . . Social democrats are sensitive to the effects of exploitation on people, but not to

It would be wrong to stipulate any particular policy instrument (be it "in-kind benefits" or even "means-testing" itself) as being definitionally required in order for a state to qualify as a "welfare state." The defining feature of the welfare state, as analyzed above, is its attempt to relieve distress. A number of different policy options might be available for pursuing that goal. The choice of any one of those instruments as being pragmatically best-suited to that goal would be perfectly consistent with a state's being properly regarded as a "welfare state."

While it would be wrong to mandate definitionally the choice of any particular policy option, it would be right to say that welfare state interventions are defined by a certain policy style. This style might best be captured by saying that: *(c) The welfare state strives to meet people's welfare needs relatively directly, rather than indirectly.* The distinction between a relatively direct and relatively indirect approach to relieving distress is admittedly imprecise at the margins. Still, it does seem to mark an important difference.

For some examples, consider these contrasts. Suppose people are starving. One option is to give them food or food stamps; another is to give them a lump of capital or a guaranteed income stream against which they might borrow to buy food. Or, again, suppose people are in financial distress because they have lost their jobs. One option is to give them a cash unemployment benefit; another is to pursue certain macroeconomic policies with a view to reducing the overall unemployment rate, thereby creating jobs for them.

The characteristically welfare statist response is, in each case, the first option. What makes it so is not necessarily the fact that it is in-kind or even means-tested assistance: food assistance is both, the unemployment benefit neither. What makes those both characteristically welfare statist responses is, instead, the relative directness with which the benefits in each case respond to the precise sorts of distress being experienced. There is something curiously contorted and roundabout with increasing someone's income as a means of getting more food into his mouth, or with increasing general economic activity as a means of getting more money into any particular workman's pocket. There is something direct and straightforward, in comparison, about giving the hungry food (or food vouchers), and about giving those who are finan-

---

the fact of exploitation itself. They want to succor the exploited while minimizing confrontation with those who exploit them."

cially distressed due to unemployment the cash that they so desperately need. It is that directness of response to distress that is the hallmark of the welfare state.

Taken together, all three of these features of the welfare state reflect what might be called its "specific egalitarianism" (Tobin 1970). The welfare state supplants ordinary economic markets only in limited ways. Its interventions are characterized by a relatively great concern to limit the inequality of distribution of certain specific needed resources (food, shelter, health, etc.), and by relative indifference to the distribution of assets in general (be they income, wealth, or the means of producing or acquiring them).

Pulling together features a, b, and c, then, the first defining feature of the welfare state—that which distinguishes it from other sorts of state—can be rewritten as follows: *(1) The welfare state intervenes (a) in a market economy (b) to meet certain of people's basic needs (c) through relatively direct means.*

B

The welfare state must, secondly, be distinguished from other modes of welfare provision. State welfare provision should be distinguished, most especially, from private, voluntary, charitable provision. The Salvation Army, United Fund, or Catholic Benevolent Fund are simply not parts of the welfare state, great though their contributions to social welfare might be.

The reason is not just that they are private organizations, and not part of the state at all. In nations with established churches—England, Scotland, Sweden, Norway, etc.—the church *is* part of the state. Still, we would not want to say, on account of that fact, that the charitable activities of the Anglican, Presbyterian, or Lutheran churches in those places form part of the welfare state.

More importantly, such organizations are not part of the welfare state because their activities are voluntary—and doubly so. There is no compulsion, moral suasion apart, for donors to contribute to those charities. Nor is there any restriction upon who can (or who must) benefit from such charitable activities. Anyone can be included and anyone excluded from benefits, just as the benefactors please.

The latter feature was carried over even into pre-welfare state forms of poor relief.[11] Under the poor laws (both old and new),

---

[11] Notice that if the criterion of a welfare state were merely "formal organization," as Wilensky and Lebeaux (1958: 140) propose, then the poor law state would

public assistance was conceptualized as a "gratuity" the dispensation of which was, therefore, entirely at the discretion of the officials concerned. By virtue of such voluntariness, we can rightly regard such schemes as "public charity," distinguishing them in that way from the genuinely welfare state activities of the modern state.[12]

To distinguish the welfare state from other modes of welfare provision (private philanthropy or organized public or private charity) we must therefore stipulate: *(2) The welfare state is a system of compulsory, collective, and largely nondiscretionary welfare provision.*

Of course, no system of rules can ever be wholly nondiscretionary. There must inevitably be legislative discretion in deciding which rules to adopt in the first place; and there must inevitably be a certain amount of administrative discretion in bringing particular cases under general rules. While the welfare state cannot eliminate either sort of discretion entirely, it can and does minimize the impact of both.

The argument to be developed in part II is that it is discretion exercised at the point of service provision that is particularly objectionable. Voluntary benefactors (and, to a large extent, even poor-law guardians) can make up their own rules as they go along distributing their gratuities. In the welfare state, in contrast, rule-making legislative discretion is exercised at a safe distance from the point of service provision. Furthermore, in the welfare state, the administrative discretion of those charged with providing services is substantially hedged by legislatively mandated rules, rights, duties, etc., in such a way that the discretion of voluntary benefactors is not and by its nature cannot be constrained.

Thus, this second feature distinguishes state welfare provision from other modes of welfare provision. Combined with the first feature, which distinguishes the welfare state from other sorts of state, it uniquely identifies the welfare state form.

---

qualify, for the poor law administration was every bit as *organized* as welfare administration is today. It is the absence of discretion rather than the mere presence of organization that distinguishes welfare from charity, public or private.

[12] Those who, such as Obler (1986), want to argue for a return to "state charity" rather than "public duty" as foundations for public relief should reflect carefully upon the risks of exploitation that those models entail; see chapters 5 through 7 below. Even if the goal is merely to improve the political marketability of welfare programs (and there is much in the moralistic character of Obler's arguments to belie that benign official intention), the ethical cost of any such strategy is likely to be high.

III

Historically, residualists, New Liberals, and socialists of several stripes have all had a hand in creating and expanding the welfare state. At least some of the aspects of the welfare state that they have bequeathed to us reflect each of their slightly different intentions. All those values, and more, can be found lurking in the political history and institutional structure of modern-day social welfare programs.

None of this is in any respect unique to the welfare state, of course. The same is true, to some greater or lesser extent, of any long-standing public institution or policy. Most programs probably are the products of pragmatic convergence upon the same practical proposals of a number of diverse principles and interests.

Being in this way a product of historical accretion and political compromise, however, has an important further consequence both for the definition and for the ethical justification of the welfare state. We are often tempted to rely, for both purposes, upon an analysis of founders' intentions. Here, though, there was no single founder and no single set of intentions. Instead, we find ourselves faced with the handiwork of many successive groups with only partially overlapping members, some of whom intended one thing by the program they voted to enact and some of whom intended another altogether. What is the true "legislative intent" behind a bill that was passed by a coalition, half of whom had one thing in mind and half of whom had something else entirely? (MacCallum 1966). Still more, what sense can we make of the overall "intent" of the succession of legislatures, composed of different members and shifting coalitions, that have added to the programs over what is sometimes the best part of a century?

A

The upshot, for purposes of framing definitions, is just that the welfare state must be defined primarily in terms of the mechanisms that it employs, rather than in terms of the intentions and motivations that underlie it. Perhaps we cannot dispense with considerations of intentions altogether. After all, the very name "welfare state" implies that the institution was established with some specific goal or intention (viz., promoting social welfare) in mind. Drawing a distinction between the intentional pursuit of social welfare and the incidental promotion of it might, in practice, be the best way of distinguishing between genuinely social welfare programs and other activities, such as profit-making enterprises in a perfectly competitive economy, that produce much the same results but which we would nonetheless be loath to call "welfare programs" (Wilensky and Lebeaux 1958: 141–42). Furthermore, I have myself argued in section I above that a defining feature of the welfare state is its attempting to relieve distress; "attempting," in turn, implies the existence of a goal and the purposive pursuit thereof. So at some level, consideration of intentions in some form does indeed seem unavoidable.

The level at which consideration of intentions is appropriate, however, does not concern the particular intentions of the particular actors responsible for establishing or expanding any particular institutions. That Bismark *really* intended his social insurance scheme to purchase social peace, or that Beveridge *really* intended to give the British soldier a stronger motive for fighting, or that Roosevelt *really* intended to reflate the American economy, or that the Swedish socialists in the 1930's *really* just intended to stimulate population growth (Tilton 1986) does not make the institutions that they established any the less welfare states. At that level, at least, founders' intentions should rightly be regarded as irrelevant to the proper characterization of the institutions that they established.

The level at which the consideration of intentions does seem appropriate concerns not the particular intentions of the particular individuals that founded any particular institutions. Instead, it concerns the "conventional intentions" that ordinarily lie behind the employment of certain sorts of policy instruments. Just as we infer the meaning of words from the connotations that speakers conventionally intend by them (Barry 1965: chap. 2), so too should we base our classification of policy instruments on the conventional intentions that characteristically lie (or are said to lie) behind them.

Analyzed in these terms, a welfare state can be defined as a state that employs mechanisms that conventionally are intended to relieve distress.[13] What the more devious motives of such a welfare state's founders or backers might be is wholly irrelevant to the classification of that state as a "welfare state."

---

[13] Perhaps I should say "are conventionally—and, in this particular case, can at least plausibly claim to be." An interpretation that is perfectly plausible in the standard sort of case, around which conventional understandings are formed, might be wholly implausible in any particular case owing to some peculiar circumstances that surround it.

14

B

For purposes of framing an ethical defense of the welfare state, the upshot of the difficulties rehearsed above in surmising its founders' intentions is even more dramatic. Traditionally, those seeking an ethical defense of the welfare state approach that problem through an analysis of its history and its politics—which ordinarily comes down to an analysis of the intentions of its founders and its present proponents. Not surprisingly, given what has just been said about the difficulties in surmising the collective intentions of a large, shifting, disunited group of political actors, those who approach the task in that way see nothing but a bewildering plurality of only partially compatible values underlying welfare state arrangements.[14]

Now, of course, there is nothing necessarily incoherent about pluralistic value systems. All that rationality would strictly require is some systematic method of trading off these competing values for one another.[15] Neither, however, is there anything particularly "special" about the compromise solution picked out by any particular pattern of tradeoffs. Which solution is selected, on any given occasion, is just some arbitrary artifact of how the "possibility frontier" fell across the "indifference curves"—i.e., of how the options available to us on that particular occasion happened to match up with the various competing values we were trying to juggle simultaneously. What turns out to be the "right" compromise on one occasion is, therefore, not necessarily the right solution on any other (even very similar) occasion. Within pluralistic value systems, "the right" is always in this way negotiable.

None of that is to say that previous commentators are necessarily wrong to seek an ethical defense of the welfare state in the competing and partially incompatible intentions of the institution's founders. It is just to say that that strategy carries a very high cost. The ethical case for the welfare state that emerges from any such analysis must, of necessity, be precarious at best.

Here I shall pursue a different tack. I shall show that there is a set of tightly interlocking reasons for state welfare services. Those

[14] See, e.g., Robson (1976), Furniss and Tilton (1977) and Heclo (1981), building on arguments like those of Beales (1946), Marshall (1949), MacDonagh (1958b), Myrdal (1960: esp. chap. 5), Briggs (1961), Goldthorpe (1964) and Offe (1984: esp. chap. 6).

[15] Barry 1965: chap. 1. Arguably, liberalism as a whole is nothing more than one big set of just such tradeoffs; see Barry (1965), Rawls (1971: 34–40), Berlin (1978), and Macpherson (1985: chap. 4), for example, arguing this.

reasons have to do with older (perhaps almost feudal) notions of what the strong owe to the weak. They deal in the slightly out-moded terms of duties to protect—not to exploit—others who are dependent upon us.

That unified purpose, rather than the ragbag of other values suggested by an analysis of founders' intentions, is, I argue, what at root truly justifies welfare state activities. There may be good reasons for wanting the state to move beyond those minimal tasks of protecting the vulnerable. But in moving beyond those tasks, there is no good reason for states to abandon those tasks.

I V

This book is aimed at providing an ethical defense of what I have been calling the "basic institutions" of the welfare state. Given the analysis above of what constitutes the "central" or "core" features of those institutions, that amounts to a defense of what might rightly be regarded as a "minimal welfare state." I shall be offering a defense of policies aiming at "minimum protection" rather than "equal protection"; my arguments will be striving for a "vindica-tion of a state's duty to protect against certain hazards which are endemic in an unequal society, rather than vindication of a duty to avoid complicity in unequal treatment" per se (Michelman 1969: 53, 9).[16] Hence, a few words are in order to explain why I have chosen to defend a merely minimal welfare state rather than some-thing more grand.

In one way, providing an ethical defense for having at least a minimal welfare state might be seen as a small service. After all, the propriety of a minimal welfare state is conceded all around, by politicians and political parties of all stripes. Even President Rea-gan is a strong supporter—in words, if not necessarily in deeds—of a social "safety net" to protect the genuinely needy (Reagan 1981: 2; Goggin 1984).

In another way, providing an ethical defense of at least a mini-mal welfare state may be a very great practical political service in-deed. It may well be true that the legitimacy of such programs is, just now, effectively conceded by one and all. For many, however,

---

[16] Interestingly, Michelman finds that those were the concerns of the late Warren Court as well. In purely practical terms of American Constitutional litigation, it is important to add as Michelman (1969: 33 fn. 78) does that "I do not of course mean to forswear reliance on the equal protection clause [of the U.S. Constitution] as a textual base for litigation inspired or shaped by minimum-protection thinking."

those concessions seem to be deeply pragmatic and purely political. Among those who would roll back the welfare state, there seems to be no reasoned rationale for rolling it back to the safety net and then stopping. There is no reason, in principle, to suppose that the same arguments offered for rolling it back to the safety net will not later be used to justify rolling it right back through the safety net.

There is more than a little cause for such concern. Consider, for example, the closing chapters of Charles Murray's enormously influential book, *Losing Ground*—a book that is to Reagan's rollback of the welfare state roughly what Michael Harrington's *The Other America* was to the Kennedy-Johnson expansion of it. After presenting a thoroughgoing indictment of the effects of current welfare policies, Murray (1984: 195) asks, "But what should we *do?*" Of course, "the political system's tolerance for reform is extremely limited," so "the number of 'politically feasible' changes that would also make much difference is approximately zero." But setting political practicalities aside, and just considering what reforms in public welfare he would regard as "ideal," Murray (1984: 227–28) offers the following chilling vision as his first approximation:

> scrapping the entire federal welfare and income-support structure for working-aged persons, including AFDC, Medicaid, Food Stamps, Unemployment Insurance, Worker's Compensation, subsidized housing, disability insurance, and the rest. It would leave the working-aged person with no recourse whatsoever except the job market, family members, friends, and public or private locally funded services.

Of course, that is only his first approximation. But in subsequent refinements of that "ideal" vision, the only one of these programs that Murray (1984: 230) reinstates is Unemployment Insurance. Beyond that, all that would be left of the social safety net would apparently be old-age pensions and such poor relief as local communities might care to provide. While Murray's statement of this "ideal" is an uncommonly frank one, there is no particular reason to believe that his vision of the ultimate goal is altogether atypical of those arguing for a rollback of the welfare state.

When commentators on the New Right argue for a minimal welfare state, they are not really "arguing for a minimal welfare state" at all. This is true, first, because theirs are not arguments "for"— positively in favor of—a welfare state, minimal or otherwise. Such endorsement as social services, even of a minimal sort, receive in those arguments is backhanded at best. The positive argument of the New Right is basically for rolling back the frontiers of the state. If minimal welfare services are exempted from that general roll-back, it is not because there is anything positively desirable about them, so much as it is because they mark the point at which the general argument for rolling back the state begins to break down—or, anyway, the point beyond which New Rightists are politically unprepared, for the moment at least, to press their case. Second, New Right arguments are not arguments for a "minimal" welfare state. They are not arguments for minima at all; what they advocate are maxima, not minima. Their argument is not that the state should, at a minimum, relieve destitution. They argue instead that the state should do that *at most*.[17]

The argument to be developed in this book contrasts with standard New Right arguments in both these respects. It, too, offers a case for a minimal welfare state. Unlike the New Right's argument, however, it constitutes a *positive* defense for the minimal welfare state. It is an argument that the state *should* provide for people's basic needs. Furthermore, it is an argument that the state should do that much *at the very least*. There is nothing in the positive case for a minimal welfare state that I shall be developing (as

[17] Thus, for example, Hayek is remembered—by, among others, Brian Barry (personal correspondence, 1986)—as "having no quarrel with the proposition . . . that states (at any rate in affluent countries) should provide some sort of 'safety net.' " In one way, such recollections are accurate enough: Hayek (1960, 286) does say, in *The Constitution of Liberty*, that "up to the point" of compulsory (albeit nonstate) insurance for social hazards "the whole apparatus of 'social security' can probably be accepted by the most consistent defenders of liberty." But absent regulated rates and assigned risks—which Hayek shows no sign of accepting—this will stop far short of anything recognizable as a "social safety net." Furthermore, the arguments Hayek offers for allowing things to go this far constitute reluctant acquiescence in this state of affairs, rather than any positive support for it. It is, he writes, "only in the interest of those who require protection against acts of desperation on the part of the needy" to provide poor-law relief; and "the availability of this assistance will induce some [others] to neglect such provision against emergencies as they would have been able to make on their own" (Hayek 1960: 285–86). Or, again, he justifies old-age pensions, saying: "By failing to keep faith and not discharging their duty of maintaining a stable currency, governments everywhere have created a situation in which the generation going into retirement in the third quarter of our century has been robbed of a great part of what they had attempted to put aside for their retirement" (Hayek 1960: 295). Yet it is clear that the pension he contemplates would be very miserly, indeed, judging from the scorn he pours on the innocent Labour Party proposal that the pension should be adequate for retired people to "go on living in the same neighbourhood, to enjoy the same hobbies and to be able to mix with the same circle of friends" as they did before retirement: "It will probably not be long before it is argued that, because the retired have more time to spend money, they must be given more than those still at work" (Hayek 1960: 297). If this is the stuff of which the "pragmatic consensus" upon the social safety net is constructed, it seems to me a highly precarious consensus indeed.

there is in the New Right's negative case for a minimal welfare state) to debar the state from doing more than relieving the destitute. My argument will set a minimum task for the state, not a maximum one.

Furthermore—and following on from that—there is an important difference between my arguments and those of the New Right on the importance of targeting welfare benefits tightly on those in need. My concern, just like the New Right's (ostensible) concern, is principally to relieve distress among the neediest members of the community. Unlike them, however, I would have no principled objections to extending social benefits more widely than that, if doing so were pragmatically the best way to succor the truly needy. Empirical research reported elsewhere suggests that what I have there called the "beneficial involvement" of the non-poor in social welfare programs probably is, for one reason or another, largely inevitable (Goodin and Le Grand 1987: chap. 10). For the New Right, that would constitute a compelling reason for rejecting the welfare state. For me, it is a compelling reason for resigning myself to the non-poor benefiting and welcoming the welfare state in spite of it. Relieving those in distress is what really matters, in my view; relieving *only* those in distress is not (Goodin 1985a).

A final, crucial difference between my arguments and those of the New Right lies in the terms on which benefits would be conferred to those in need. The New Right proposes to go "back to the poor law" in the fullest sense, conferring benefits as a matter of wholly discretionary state charity. Welfare payments are, in their view, a public benefice, to which any number of strings might legitimately be attached. My arguments, in contrast, dictate aiding the needy through rule-bound systems of welfare entitlements, wherein those dispensing the benefits have minimal discretion to withhold or lay down conditions for receipt of benefits by those entitled to them. In my view, the crucial shift from the old poor law state to the modern welfare state lay in the emergence of welfare rights to supplant notions of public benefice. In that sense, the New Right's arguments truly do imply going "back to the poor law"; mine imply precisely the opposite.

V

It is the argument of this book that there is an especially compelling and interestingly different ethical case to be made for having at least a minimal welfare state. There may well be reasons for moving beyond the minimal welfare state, thus justified. But those will be *other* reasons, quite distinct from the reasons that can be (and here will be) offered to justify the minimal welfare state. They are not necessarily any the worse, or less compelling, for that. It is important, however, to realize that they are distinct.

One reason that it is important to recognize their distinctiveness is that, as we move beyond the minimal welfare state, these reasons for moving at least as far as the minimal welfare state do not drop away or somehow get preempted. The morally distinctive reasons for making sure that those minimal tasks get accomplished always remain, even in a more robustly interventionistic state. My case for having at least a minimal welfare state therefore remains relevant, even to those who would move beyond it.

The relevance of the moral distinctiveness of my arguments for having at least a minimal welfare state is even greater for those who want at most a minimal welfare state. Suppose that the arguments they offer against moving beyond a minimal welfare state were to prove politically compelling. Even so, the moral distinctiveness of the arguments here presented in favor of having at least a minimal welfare state means that the same counterarguments that had been successfully deployed against a more-than-minimal welfare state cannot (straightforwardly, at least) be used equally effectively as arguments against holding onto at least a minimal welfare state. Being morally distinctive, my arguments for having at least a minimal welfare state thus provide something of an ethical firebreak or backstop, preventing New Right arguments for rolling back the welfare state to the safety net from rolling it back through the safety net.

It is my thesis that there is a morally distinct reason for having at least a minimal welfare state. To succeed in establishing that thesis, I must show that there is some argument which will justify us in going as far as the minimal welfare state, but which will not itself justify us in going any further. Standard arguments for going that far (couched in terms of egalitarian or communitarian ideals) tend to overshoot. If they work at all, they tend to justify much more than merely a minimal welfare state. Standard arguments against going further (couched in terms of deserts or self-reliance, e.g.) typically also argue against going even that far. A distinctive pattern of argument is required to justify the precise set of practices that constitute the minimal welfare state.

Some empirical commentators, of course, deny that the welfare state is really anything distinctive at all. Some see it as just a failed attempt at bringing about a more thoroughly redistributive state; others see it as just a stalking horse for a more thoroughly redistributive state yet to come. As an empirical matter, either may well be correct. This book, however, is concerned with ethical justifications for the welfare state, not with the historical causes of it.

Transposed into the moral realm, the claim that the welfare state is "not distinctive" would seem to suggest that the welfare state as such—and still more the minimal welfare state—has "no independent justification." On this analysis, the most the welfare state might do is to bask in the reflected moral glory of some other social institution (be it one of former aspiration or future consequence). But the welfare state has no independent moral value, and derives its moral value instead wholly from its contribution (or its expected contribution) to some other cause. All of this can be—and has been—said of the welfare state in general, and of the minimal welfare state most particularly.

No one denies that the welfare state might serve many different goals, and act as a steppingstone to many different things. It may well be that we will want to go "beyond the welfare state" (Myrdal 1960), either in the sense of going beyond the narrow range of goods and services that the welfare state dispenses to its narrow clientele, or (more dramatically) in the sense of going beyond the boundaries of the nation-state itself to serve needs wherever they are found in the world. There may be good reasons for advocating a thoroughgoing redistribution of economic resources. Nothing I say here is meant to deny that there are, nor is anything I say here meant to deny that the welfare state (even the minimal welfare state) might make a useful start toward those ends.

What I want to emphasize is that those are not the *only* reasons for having a welfare state. There is another, morally distinctive justification that can be offered for having at least a minimal welfare state. This is an argument that justifies the minimal welfare state in and of itself, and not just as a contribution to some other, larger, worthier social cause.

V I

The central positive thesis of this book is simply stated. The problem to which the welfare state is the solution is the risk of exploitation of dependencies. Such exploitation could well occur in the course of interactions in ordinary economic markets. By removing a wide range of interactions from the market, the welfare state aims to prevent that form of exploitation. Similar exploitation could equally well occur in the course of interactions between benefactor and beneficiary in the context of old-style public or private charities. By tightly defining the legal rights and duties of welfare claimants and welfare dispensers, the welfare state aims to prevent that form of exploitation, too. Therein lies the distinctive style of moral justification to which the welfare state might aspire. But before that vision can be developed in part II below and defended against New Right attacks in part III, first it is necessary to establish the superiority of that vision over those offered by ostensible friends of the welfare state on the Old Left. It is to this task that I now turn.

Part I

AGAINST THE OLD LEFT

Broadly speaking, the Left has traditionally offered a choice of three distinct modes of justification of the welfare state and its constituent programs and policies.

One revolves around notions of "minimum standards," "poverty thresholds" and such like. The aim of the welfare state, its constituent programs and policies, is on this account to bring everyone up to some "social minimum," usually calibrated in terms of people's "needs." Such arguments are the subject of chapter 2.

A second distinct mode of justification revolves around notions of "social equality." The aim of the welfare state, its constituent programs and policies, is on this account to redistribute resources—ideally, until everyone is "equal," in some sense or another. Such arguments are the subject of chapter 3.

A third mode of justification revolves around notions of "fraternity," "community," and such like. The aim of the welfare state, its constituent programs and policies, is on this account to promote social solidarity. Such arguments are the subject of chapter 4.

The three chapters that follow conclude that none of these traditional leftist justifications of the welfare state is wholly satisfactory. The reasons for their failure vary. Sometimes the values in view are unclear or epiphenomenal; and sometimes, partly in consequence, there seem to be no good grounds for supposing that the values in question are quite as compelling, morally, as the arguments appealing to them need for them to be. Other times, the relationship between the values in view and the mechanism in view—the welfare state—is unclear or unproven.

My arguments against the Old Left style of justifications for the welfare state are, thus, many and varied. All point in the same ultimate direction, however: the traditional arguments for the welfare state will not in and of themselves, suffice. We must look elsewhere for the real moral supports for the welfare state, if we are to find them at all.

Where we should be looking, though, is very much in the ruins of the Old Left arguments for the welfare state. Chapter 2 shows that needs per se do not deserve the kind of priority that Old Left arguments accord them. But they do correlate with things that do. The positive defense of the welfare state that I shall be mounting in part II points to some of these. When people's needs are unmet, they are likely to be desperate, dependent, and hence exploitable. The welfare state is justified, I shall argue, as a device to guard against that possibility; and the way it does that is by meeting people's needs, thereby rendering them independent and nonexploitable. The value of satisfying people's needs is, on that argument, derivative rather than intrinsic. There is nothing about meeting needs, as such, that is morally particularly compelling, as the Old Left maintains there is. Still, it is right that there is *something* about meeting needs that is somehow morally important. Out of such partial truths, a cogent defense of the welfare state can indeed be built.

T W O

NEEDS

The central task of the welfare state, as depicted in Chapter 1, is to supplant ordinary market mechanisms for certain limited purposes. Individuals who would be left in "desperate circumstances" under the primary, market-based distribution are relieved through the nonmarket institutions of the welfare state. But it is not the place of the welfare state to remedy every shortfall between aspiration and attainment. Instead, it distributes a strictly limited sort of assistance to relieve "distress" of a very particular sort.

The first and most obvious place to look for a justification of the welfare state would thus seem to be in the peculiar characteristics of the goods and services which it delivers, or (equivalently) in some peculiar characteristics of the sort of "demand" which it satisfies. The conventional way of marking the distinction is to say that the market addresses itself to the satisfaction of "wants" or "desires" whereas the welfare state addresses itself to the satisfaction of "needs."

Drawing any such distinction between "needs" and "mere desires" is difficult enough, as will become apparent at various points in this chapter. But to justify the welfare state's supplanting of the market, it is necessary to go further still. It is not enough to show that "needs" and "mere desires" are conceptually distinct. Nor is it enough to argue that needs have some prima facie or ceteris paribus claims to satisfaction (Nielsen 1969: 193–94). For "wants," too, have some prima facie or ceteris paribus claim to satisfaction; and if needs and desires were equally compelling considerations, then how could we justify mechanisms for satisfying the one (welfare states) systematically supplanting mechanisms for satisfying the other (markets) wherever the two principles come into conflict?

Material in this chapter is reprinted from Robert E. Goodin, "The Priority of Needs," *Philosophy & Phenomenological Research*, 45 (June 1985): 615–25, by permission of the editors.

To justify the welfare state's supplanting of the market for distribution of those things that come within its purview, then, we require some further argument to the effect that the goods and services that the welfare state distributes (and the "needs" to which they speak) are morally more important than the goods and services which the market distributes (and the "wants" and "desires" to which they speak). Absent some argument, not just for the "distinctiveness" of needs and their prima facie claim to satisfaction but also for the "priority" of needs-claims over wants-claims, there could be no (needs-based) justification for the welfare state to supplant systematically the market in that manner.[1] Furthermore, to justify the state *systematically* supplanting the market in each and every instance in which people's needs are involved, that priority must be of a singularly strong sort.[2] The bulk of this chapter is given over to the search for arguments for some such principle—which I shall call a Principle of Precedence or a principle of the "priority of needs"—to tell us why meeting people's needs should always take absolute precedence or priority over satisfying their mere desires.

Intuitively, Principles of Precedence of this sort seem plausible enough. Most commentators, indeed, seem to assume that some form of that principle simply *has* to be correct. But finding precisely the right form proves surprisingly difficult. Part of the problem is that, if needs are going to enjoy priority over desires, people naturally strive to cloak almost all their claims in the sometimes implausible language of necessity. The upshot is that "the list [of putative needs] grows, so that one begins to wonder how anything is left over for wants" (Fried 1978: 122; cf. Braybrooke 1968). That, however, is not an objection to the Principle of Precedence as such, but rather to people's fraudulent misrepresentation of the nature of their claims.

Similarly, some needs turn out, upon further analysis, to be just desires at one remove. Suppose you need a hammer to build a

---

[1] I say nothing here to justify the presumption that the operations of ordinary economic markets are, ordinarily, justifiable morally. Still, advocates of the welfare state themselves grant it implicitly insofar as they argue only for the limited, not the thoroughgoing, supplanting of market outcomes by state intervention.

[2] Thus, it is not enough to argue for a priority rule that "attributes to needs only a quite minimal moral superiority over desires." To justify the welfare state, it is inadequate to appeal to a principle, like Frankfurt's (1984: 7), that "maintains no more than that when there is a competition between a desire and a need for the same thing, the need starts with a certain moral edge. . . . Meeting A's need is prima facie morally preferable to satisfying B's desire"; but like all prima facie demands, this one is liable to be overridden.

holiday home that you want but do not in any respect "need" to have. Then your need for the hammer is a "volitional need" (Frankfurt 1984), wholly derivative from your mere desire for a holiday home. Obviously, there is no reason for according those "volitional needs" any more precedence than we would accord to the "mere desires" from which they are derived. To cloak volitions in the language of necessity in this way, too, constitutes a subtle form of fraud.

It would be wrong to reject all needs-based arguments solely on the grounds that some—perhaps many—fraudulent claims are entered under that heading. In evaluating arguments for the priority of needs, we must try to bracket out those counterfeit claims of necessity and consider only the genuine article.

The real question is whether we can find good grounds for giving even genuine claims of need systematic priority over desires and wants. In this chapter, I shall argue that we cannot. Several possible arguments are considered; all are found to be fundamentally flawed. Needs do correlate, in a rough-and-ready way, with several other things which truly do deserve priority consideration. But there is no good reason for supposing that needs per se deserve such treatment. The priority we generally seem to accord to needs is thus seen to be purely epiphenomenal, and the purposes we serve by doing so could usually be better served through other avenues.

As the Principle of Precedence falls, so too does the needs-based justification for the welfare state. Needs-based considerations would provide good grounds for state interventions meeting people's needs to supplant systematically market distributions satisfying people's desires only if there are good grounds for supposing that needs should systematically trump desires. If the latter proposition is indefensible, then so too is the former—or at least the former proposition cannot be defended in terms of the latter, needs-based argument.

I

One good place to start this analysis is to note the basic form of argument employed by those who regard themselves as friends of the Principle of Precedence to deny fraudulent "volitional needs claims" any priority over mere desires. Here I shall show, as a preliminary to my larger argument, how precisely the same style of argument might be used to deny any such priority to genuinely "nonvolitional needs claims" as well.

"All necessities," Frankfurt (1984: 3) writes, "are . . . conditional: nothing is needed except in virtue of being an indispensable condition for the attainment of a certain end."[3] In the case of volitional needs, we need X for Y, and we desire Y. That is just the definition of a "volitional need." In the case of nonvolitional needs, we need X for Y, and we need Y. But for what? All necessities are conditional. We cannot "need Y" *simpliciter*. We can only need Y for some further end.[4]

With volitional needs, desires underlie needs. There is no more reason for us to provide people with what they need, in this sense, than there is for us to satisfy people's desires. That is why Frankfurt thinks volitional needs claims are so weak. That is why they should enjoy no precedence over desires.

But much the same is true of nonvolitional needs as well. What underlies them is not desires but rather the "further end" for which the needed need is an "indispensable condition." Just as there is no more reason to satisfy people's volitional needs than there is to satisfy the desires that underlie them, so too is there no more reason to satisfy people's nonvolitional needs than there is to promote the "further ends" that underlie them.[5] Nonvolitional needs, by an argument perfectly paralleling Frankfurt's own, must enjoy no precedence over the "further end" underlying them.

Whether nonvolitional needs deserve to enjoy systematic priority over mere desires thus reduces to the question of whether the "further ends" they serve should systematically take precedence over mere desires. I can find only one plausible reason for thinking that they should. Notice that nonvolitional needs, by definition,

[3] See similarly Barry (1965: 47–49) and White (1971: 105–6).

[4] "Need Y *for* some other end Z" is meant to straddle Y being a means to Z and Y being a part of Z. The latter sort of relationship is misconstrued by calling it "instrumental," as Miller (1976: 128) is right to protest (cf. Galston 1980: 162–63). But while not being "instrumental," his "intrinsic needs" and Wiggins' (1985: 154) "absolute needs" are nonetheless "conditional." They are conditional, motivationally, for the person concerned upon his wanting situation Z to come about; and they are conditional, morally, upon the premise that situation Z should come about.

[5] Anscombe (1958: 7) complains, "To say that [an organism] needs that environment is not to say, e.g., that you want it to have that environment, but that it won't flourish unless it has it. Certainly, it all depends on whether you *want* it to flourish! as Hume would say. But what 'all depends' on whether you want it to flourish is whether the fact that it needs that environment, or won't flourish without it, has the slightest influence on your actions." But it is precisely *that*—influence on our actions—that the Principle of Precedence is supposed to have.

promote ends that are in principle independent of (i.e., not necessarily derived from) the bearer's own desires.[6] Promoting those
ends must therefore be valuable in some objective sense, if it is
valuable at all. This is in contrast to the subjective values served
by satisfying people's desires.[7]

Perhaps, then, we give nonvolitional needs priority over mere
desires because we think that promoting objective values takes
priority over promoting subjective ones. That argument, if it goes
through at all, could quite plausibly give rise to a very strong form
of the Principle of Precedence. Satisfying objective needs would
indeed then enjoy absolute priority over satisfying mere wants.

The case for the welfare state is sometimes cast in precisely these
terms. The task of the welfare state, it is said, is to promote people's welfare; and that is to be understood as doing what is *really*
good for people rather than just what they think is good for them.
The welfare state, being concerned with people's objective needs,
thus has every right to trump markets that respond merely to people's subjective desires.

But that would end up justifying a much more thoroughgoing
supplanting of the market than the welfare state contemplates. To
say that the objectively needed should take precedence over the
subjectively desired is to say that the objectively good should take
precedence over the subjectively good. That, in turn, would imply
that we should institute a "command economy" that allocates to
people things that are objectively good, rather than tolerating a
"market economy" that allocates things to people merely because
they subjectively desire them.[8] Arguing in this way for the priority
of needs does not, therefore, constitute a justification for the wel-

[6] Of course, people may—and perhaps usually do—desire what they nonvoli-
tionally need. The point here is just that things do not cease being nonvolitional
needs just because the bearer of such needs happens to fail to desire them.

[7] Thus, Anscombe (1958: 7) analyzes "needs" as those things which are objectively required for something to "flourish"; Feinberg (1973: 111) and Miller (1976:
130ff.) analyze "needs" as those things which are objectively required for something to avoid harm; and Wiggins (1985) rests his analysis of objective "absolute
needs" on those precedents.

[8] Various stories could of course be told about how it is objectively good (or required, objectively, for human beings to "flourish") that people should frame and
pursue their own goals, projects, etc. But then the Principle of Precedence would
not be strong enough to justify the state's *systematically* supplanting the market:
satisfying objective needs through welfare state interventions and satisfying subjective needs through market transactions are both objectively valuable, on this
account; so there would seem to be no reason to suppose that one should enjoy
lexicographical priority over the other, rather than being traded off for one another
in the ordinary way (with one prevailing sometimes, and the other at other times).

fare state, after all. The welfare state, as described in chapter 1 above, is a system of public interventions supplanting ordinary market distributions for certain strictly limited purposes. The sort of state toward which the objective/subjective value distinction points would leave no such room for markets to govern the bulk of ordinary affairs.

I I

The welfare state, as its name suggests, strives to promote social welfare. One cluster of reasons for supposing that meeting needs should be accorded priority over satisfying mere desires derives straightforwardly from that fact. Perhaps it is simply the case that meeting needs makes a greater contribution to people's welfare than satisfying their mere desires. There are various ways this argument might run. None of them is wholly satisfactory.

A

One argument along these lines points to a distinction between being *harmed* and being *benefited*. It is standardly thought that the former matters—both morally and materially—more than the latter. This is at least part of what underlies the ostensible distinction between "acts" and "omissions" in modern moral philosophy (Glover 1977; Davis 1980; Bennett 1983); and it seems to be a particularly plausible part of that story, as I have argued elsewhere (Goodin 1982: 14–15).

Its plausibility derives from the particular way that "harm" and "benefit" are defined, conjoined with a particularly plausible postulate about "diminishing marginal value." It is ordinarily said in these contexts that, definitionally, "Being harmed has to do with becoming worse off than one was, while failing to obtain a benefit is more a matter of not becoming better off than before" (Frankfurt 1984: 6).

What is then needed to complete the argument about the priority of avoiding harm is simply a postulate to the effect that "making things better is, from a moral point of view, less important (measure for measure) than keeping them from getting worse" (Frankfurt 1984: 7). There are various ways to justify this postulate. One, following Hume (1739; 1777) is couched in terms of the moral importance of stable expectations. Another, more compelling argument is couched in terms of "diminishing marginal utility" (or, for those uncomfortable with "utility" language, a postulate about "diminishing marginal value," where "value" can be objective or subjective, moral or material). In its classic formulation, that postulate simply states that each unit of a good matters less to you than the last; from that, it would straightforwardly follow that the loss you would suffer if one unit were taken from your existing stock would be greater than would be the gain you would experience if one unit were added to your existing stock.

The principle of the priority of avoiding harm is standard—and, in that derivation, fairly uncontentious—in modern moral philosophy. What would be both nonstandard and much more contentious would be an attempt to derive from the priority of avoiding harm a priority of meeting needs.

Naively, there would surely seem to be some connection between the two. In any ordinary sense of the word, people certainly suffer "harm" when their needs are unmet; and meeting those needs would avoid their suffering those harms. Naively, it seems that avoiding harms in this way is precisely what the welfare state does, and that its justification therefore straightforwardly follows from the priority of avoiding harms. Even so subtle a philosopher as Frankfurt (1984: 7) is led by such logic to conclude that "allocating resources to meeting needs takes precedence over allocating them to fulfilling mere desires" because "the former aims at avoiding harm, while the latter aims only at providing unneeded benefits."[9]

That argument trades on a very different definition of "harm" than that which was used to ground the principle of the priority of avoiding harm, however. Implicitly, we are here being asked to think of "harm" as anything that causes someone to suffer. That is the sense in which someone whose needs are unmet is being "harmed." Intuitively, that is a perfectly plausible understanding of the notion.

Unfortunately, it is not the sense of "harm" that was used—and that *had* to be used—to generate uncontentiously the priority of avoiding harm above. On the definition used there, a person could be construed as "harmed" only if he was made worse off than he was before. That rather than the (in many ways more attractive) intuitive notion of "harm" is what we must use, if we are to derive the priority of meeting needs from the priority of avoiding harm.

[9] Feinberg (1973: 111) similarly argues that "to say that S needs X is to say simply that if he doesn't have X he will be harmed" (see also Bay 1968).

On that definition, the derivation will work only for that part of the population that is presently having its needs satisfied. The priority of avoiding harm, thus construed, means that we must give priority to preventing their needs from ceasing to be met. Those with adequate supplies of food, clothing, and shelter should, on that argument, be kept in food, clothing, and shelter. And so on.

Consider, though, the plight of the standard clients of the welfare state. Their needs are not presently being met: that is precisely why they find themselves needing to file a claim. On the principle of the priority of avoiding harm, where "avoiding harm" is construed (as it must be, to generate that priority) as "not being made worse off than at present," there is no reason to prevent those who are presently suffering from continuing to suffer. We must stop anyone *else* from coming to suffer, to be sure. But those who are presently suffering may be left to suffer. Those who are starving may be left to starve, those who are homeless left homeless, etc.[10]

More paradoxically, the principle of the priority of avoiding harm would accord the same priority to satisfying mere desires as to meeting needs. Suppose my desire to X and your need to Y are both being met at present. Then I would suffer the same sort of "harm," on the definition of "harm" needed to generate that priority rule, if my desire to X ceased being satisfied as you would suffer if your need to Y ceased being satisfied. Each enjoys the same priority as the other, but neither enjoys any priority over the other. That is not the Principle of Precedence of needs over wants as we know it. That is not the Principle of Precedence required to justify the welfare state's succoring of needs to take priority over the market's pandering to mere desires.

More paradoxically still, the principle of the priority of avoiding

[10] Frankfurt (1984: 7) anticipates this objection, amending his official definition of "harm" to say, also, that "the life of a person whose condition is bad becomes worse and worse as long as his condition does not improve, simply because more of a bad thing is worse than less of it." That allows him to say that a person is harmed by a continuing failure to meet his needs. But to say that, he needs some independent standard of what "a bad thing" is. Otherwise, the same principle would indict a continuing failure to satisfy someone's mere wants: the longer they go unsatisfied, the worse that too is for a person.

Another, more credible response to this challenge might be cast in terms of rectification. Our duty to relieve those who are presently starving might be found in our duty to rectify our past failure to prevent them from falling below the subsistence threshold in the first place. But that argument will work only for those who once in their lives were not starving. Those who have never had enough to eat— which are those whom the welfare state ought, surely, to help first and foremost— would deserve no protection under this principle.

harm would sometimes actually accord satisfying mere desires priority over meeting needs. Suppose my desire to X is presently being met, but your need to Y is not. Then on this definition, I would suffer "harm" if my desire were to cease being satisfied, but you would suffer none if your need continued being unmet; and, on the principle of the priority of avoiding harm, avoiding the former deserves priority over avoiding the latter. Far from generating any priority for meeting needs, then, the principle of the priority of avoiding "harms" thus construed might sometimes imply precisely the opposite priority rule.

Thus, the derivation of the priority of needs from the priority of avoiding harm is legitimate only in a very particular set of circumstances. We may legitimately equate "meeting needs" with "avoiding harm," thus defined, and "fulfilling mere desires" with "providing benefits," thus defined, if and only if: (a) our (nonvolitional) needs are presently being fully met and (b) our "mere desires" are not being met at all. Then and only then will not meeting our needs make us worse off than at present. Then and only then will not satisfying our desires merely fail to make us better off than at present. Needless to say, that is an extraordinarily rare state of affairs. Needless to say, it is not the standard—much less the only—state of affairs in which we would want a case for the welfare state to apply.

B

Another way of making the case that meeting needs matters more to people's welfare than satisfying mere desires does would point to the *relative urgency* of the two types of claim (Scanlon 1975; Galston 1980: 162–70). Relatively urgent claims are those which will be of substantially less value (and, in the limiting case, none at all) if met later rather than being met now. Relatively nonurgent claims are those which will be of approximately the same value if satisfied later as they would be if satisfied now.

Claims that are relatively urgent in this sense command a certain measure of priority over ones that are not. Failing to meet the former promptly means forsaking them forever; failing to meet the latter now merely means postponing them. This priority is far from absolute. One and the same resource might be required urgently to serve a perfectly trivial end, or nonurgently to serve a tremendously important one. Then we may well prefer to serve the more important end and forsake the trivial one forever. (We will be particularly inclined to do so if we suppose that this is a common occurrence, so the important would be infinitely postponed if we were to give priority to the urgent in each such instance.) But at the very least, urgent claims command a ceteris paribus priority over nonurgent ones, and that priority probably persists to some extent even where the importance of the ends served is not strictly equal.

That might seem to translate into a priority for needs over mere wants. In the paradigm cases that come most easily to mind, needs are more urgent than wants. One's needs for food, water, or shelter are of a "now or never" sort. It is pointless to postpone the claims of famine victims. If they are not fed this year, they will not be around next year to benefit from a food-aid program.

But, again, there is only a rough-and-ready correlation between urgency and needs. Some desires that are indisputably "mere desires" are every bit as urgent as needs. My desire to hear Pavarotti's farewell performance next week is one such urgent desire. And, on the other side, some needs are relatively nonurgent. The need of the cataract patient for treatment sometime over the next two years is one example. But the waiting lists of the U.K. National Health Service hospitals are full of other examples: they would not be eligible for NHS treatment unless there were a genuine need present, but they would not be on a waiting list unless theirs were nonurgent needs.

C

A final way of making the case for thinking that meeting needs contributes more to people's welfare than does satisfying their desires construes needs as goods, conditions, or circumstances that are *necessary preconditions* or instruments for the attainment of any and all particular ends which one might want to pursue.[11] Let us call this the "universally necessary instruments" analysis of needs.

This is, in my view, the most plausible general analysis of needs

[11] See, e.g., Nielsen (1969: 188), Miller (1976: 133–34; 1980), Weale (1978a: chaps. 4–5), Galtung (1980a), H. Shue (1980: chaps. 1 and 2), Doyal and Gough (1984: 14), Daniels (1985: chaps. 2 and 3), Plant (1985) and Sen (1985a, b). These build on, but depart in various important respects from, Hart (1955) on "natural rights," Barry (1965: chap. 10) on "interests," and Rawls (1971: 90–95) on "primary goods."
Talking in terms of "necessary instruments," incidentally, explains why people can be said to need some things without their actually wanting them: on this analysis, that merely means that they have not realized that (or readjusted their wants in light of the realization that) some particular instrument is necessary in order to accomplish what they want.

available. But the question before us here is not how best to construe the notion of needs. Instead, it is whether needs, however construed, deserve priority over mere desires.

Now, needs defined as necessary instruments inevitably have a kind of logical-cum-temporal priority over mere wants. By definition, you cannot get what you want until you have what you need: that is just what it means for something to be a "necessary instrument." But that in itself is not enough to expain why needs should enjoy the sort of priority that the Principle of Precedence claims for them.

To say that it is necessary to satisfy needs *before* wants is not to say that needs should be satisfied *instead* of wants. Jack's needs must, ex hypothesi, be satisfied before Jack's wants can be satisfied; but that provides no good reason for thinking that Jack's needs should be satisfied before, much less instead of, Jill's wants. Temporal priority does not translate automatically into value priority. The necessity of satisfying needs before wants can be satisfied does not imply that it is more important to satisfy needs than wants.

On the contrary, there are good reasons for supposing that the value of instruments—however necessary they may be—cannot exceed the value of the ends which they serve. If the value of an object (a ten-dollar bill, say) is purely instrumental to Jack, then the value of that object to Jack is just equivalent to the value of the most valuable thing he can use that object to obtain (a bottle of gin, say).

The same can be said of needs. If the value of needs is purely instrumental, then the satisfaction of Jack's needs cannot be any more valuable to or for Jack than is the satisfaction of the desires or other ends for which those needs are necessary instruments. The value of need-satisfaction, where needs are construed merely as necessary instruments, is thus wholly derivative from the value of want-satisfaction. The former cannot therefore take priority over the latter. Or at least it cannot claim priority on those grounds, anyway.[12]

To make out a case for the priority of needs over wants, what we must emphasize is not their role as necessary instruments but

[12] An exception to the claim of this paragraph would arise if we were to attach value to freedom of choice per se, over and above the value we attach to the wants that are satisfied through exercise of that free choice. But this principle of "respecting free choice" cannot justify giving needs priority over wants, for reasons laid out in section V below.

rather the *wide variety* of ends for which they are necessary instruments. That is what is so distinctive about "universally necessary instruments." That, likewise, is what is so distinctive about needs, thus construed.

As a first approximation, the argument for the priority of needs as universally necessary instruments would go like this. Granted, needs are no more than necessary instruments; and granted, the value of satisfying them is wholly derivative from the value of the ends which they are instrumental in producing. All this said, however, it may nonetheless be true that the value of satisfying any particular need always exceeds the value of satisfying any particular want because of all the other wants which satisfying that need also helps us to satisfy.

That argument as stated will not quite do. It confuses being a necessary instrument to any ends with being a necessary instrument to all ends. Some (perhaps most) resources, even if they are "universally necessary instruments," will diminish with use. Although the resource may well be a necessary instrument for attaining a wide variety of ends, once it is committed to the pursuit of any one of them it becomes unavailable for pursuit of any of the others. Money is a prime example. You need it for any of various purposes: to buy a house, or a car, or a yacht, or a color television. But the dollar spent on buying a house ceases to be available to you for buying a car. In such cases, it is simply incorrect to say that the value of the dollar to you is a function of its value in buying you a house *and* a car and so on. Instead, it is a function of the dollar's value to you in buying you a house *or* a car or so on.

The argument for the priority of needs over wants would fail were the reference to resources that are nonreusable in this sense. If a resource can be used to promote any of a variety of ends, but only one of them, then its value is wholly derivative from the value of that one end. It may be valuable to have more options rather than less where we are (temporarily) uncertain as to the relative value of the various ends which we may be asked to choose between in our use of the resource.[13] But that sort of uncertainty-based option value aside, the fact that the needed resource could have been used for any of a variety of other purposes does nothing

---

[13] I say "temporarily" because, if the uncertainty is not resolved (or at least diminished) by the time we are ultimately forced to choose which way to exercise the option, then we will have been no better off with the option than without it. The value of options is thus derivative from the value of postponement: their value is just the value of buying time.

to enhance its value, since at the end of the day it can only be used to pursue one of them.

Not all resources are like that, however. Perhaps the paradigm case of a reusable resource is health. It is a necessary instrument for the accomplishment of a great variety of goals. But unlike money it does not (ordinarily, anyway) diminish with use. Exceptional goals like scaling Everest aside, health functions rather like a chemical catalyst that enters into a reaction but then emerges at the end unchanged, available for reuse in exactly the same form and quantity as before.

Where need-statements refer to reusable resources of this sort, a certain measure of priority of needs over wants is justified. Of course, the value of satisfying needs is still purely instrumental and entirely derivative from the value of the various wants which those instruments help us satisfy. So it is inconceivable that needs, even of this sort, should take priority over the set of all wants taken as a whole. But needs for reusable resources might take priority over any *particular* want, because they are instrumental in (and hence derive value from their role in) satisfying various other wants as well as that one.[14]

This argument gives rise to a Principle of Precedence, but one which is doubly qualified. Firstly, priority is granted only if (and only insofar as) the needed resource is both *multipurpose* and *reusable*. If a resource is required for a single purpose, or exhausted with a single use, there is no reason on this argument to suppose that satisfying the need for that resource is any more important than satisfying the desire for that purpose to be accomplished. Secondly, this Principle of Precedence is qualified in the extent of priority it accords such needs over desires. Whereas any particular such need might enjoy priority over any particular desire, no such need (nor such needs taken as a whole) may enjoy priority over all desires taken as a whole.

Thus, even this best possible argument for the priority of needs over desires is qualified in important respects. Most importantly,

[14] This also explains why Frankfurt's "nonvolitional" needs enjoy priority over "volitional" ones. The problem is not, as Frankfurt (1984: 7) supposes, that the latter "have too little necessity in them." The problem is instead that they do not have enough satisfaction in them. Volitional needs may be necessary instruments, all right; but they are instruments to the satisfaction of only one particular desire. Hence they can claim no priority over the desire from which their own value is derived. Nonvolitional needs, being necessary instruments to the satisfaction of many different desires, can claim priority over any one of them by appealing to the value they derive from their role in satisfying all the others.

it extends only to certain classes of need-claims and accords them priority, once again, on the basis of features (reusability; serving multiple purposes) that are only contingently and imperfectly connected to the notion of a "need" per se.

I I I

Another style of defense of the Principle of Precedence would point to the fact that, with nonvolitional needs,"whether or not the harm ensues is outside the person's voluntary control." Mere desires and the volitional needs that flow from them, in contrast, "are voluntary, which means that the person need not have the needs at all" (Frankfurt 1984: 7).[15]

"Voluntariness" in this context might mean either (or both) of two things. One is that the desires were voluntarily adopted in the first place. The other is that the desires can be voluntarily renounced. Usually—but not always—desires are voluntary in both senses and needs in neither.

A focus on voluntariness-in-the-first-instance would surely be misplaced. Consider the case of someone suffering kidney failure owing to his own previous voluntary actions—a botched suicide attempt, say, or a drug overdose. That person's need for renal dialysis must surely count as a paradigm case of a nonvolitional need. He needs the dialysis machine to meet a need, not merely to satisfy a desire. The voluntariness of the previous acts that led him to need the machine does nothing to make his need for it any less of a need now.

Of course, we may well think that such a person's claim to scarce kidney dialysis units is less strong than that of someone who is not to blame for his own plight. We may want to give priority to satisfying claims with no voluntary aspects to their histories. The point here, however, is that that does not track perfectly with a rule to accord priority to satisfying needs. Some perfectly nonvolitional needs may indeed have just such a voluntary aspect to their histories.

"Voluntariness" can, alternatively, be understood as "alterability." This seems to be Frankfurt's preferred interpretation. When discussing "constrained volitional needs"—ones which deserve nearly as much priority as nonvolitional ones—Frankfurt (1984: 9) grounds their priority in the fact that they are "ineradicably per-

---

[15] Similarly, Wiggins (1985: 154) analyzes "need" as a "modal" notion implying, essentially, that "we have no real alternative."

sistent." The point, made by Rawls (1982) and Charles Taylor (1976) in addition to Frankfurt, is that if your mere desires are being disappointed there is something you can do to protect yourself from this disappointment, viz., alter your desires. Nonvolitional needs, by definition, are beyond any such volitional control.[16] And since there is no opportunity for people to protect themselves in this way where genuine needs are concerned, the social obligation to satisfy such claims is stronger than the social obligation to satisfy people's mere desires.

Again, we may well think it is more important for us to protect people the less able they are to protect themselves. But this translates only very imperfectly into a priority for needs over mere desires. It is simply not true that all nonvolitional needs are such that people cannot take any steps to protect themselves. True, they cannot protect themselves in the one particular way Frankfurt (1984) picks out, i.e., they cannot alter their needs in the way they can alter their mere desires. But altering them is one of many possible ways of protecting ourselves from the harm we would suffer. And it surely is the inability to protect oneself, rather than the inability to protect oneself in any particular way, that matters morally.

Consider the case of a particularly talented medical technician suffering kidney failure. Let us suppose that he could easily build himself a kidney-dialysis machine and operate it all by himself. The fact that he could protect himself does not make his need for kidney dialysis any less of a nonvolitional need. What it does show is that not all nonvolitional needs are beyond our control to protect ourselves from, and entitled to special priority on those grounds.

Or, again, consider the case of a desire that has given rise to a purely volitional need that the agent cannot now alter. I am a keen mountaineer, let us suppose. My desire to climb mountains gives rise to purely volitional needs for ropes and spikes. But once my desires have taken me onto the icy ledges of Everest, I can no longer by revising my desires extinguish my need for ropes and spikes.[17] One's inability to renounce one's volitional needs may,

---

[16] It is a consequence of this definition that the truly *compulsive* gambler's "mere desire" to gamble will be counted as a "nonvolitional need" to gamble, since that desire is beyond the agent's volitional control.

[17] That example may be an unduly dramatic one. For there it might be said that, once I am on the mountainside, my formerly volitional need for ropes and spikes suddenly becomes a nonvolitional one: I need that apparatus to survive; my desires no longer come into the matter. But much the same might be said of various

once again, make one more entitled to social assistance. But what it does not do is make volitional needs into nonvolitional ones. Thus, here too, according priority to inalterable claims fails to track perfectly with a rule according priority to nonvolitional needs.

The previous arguments suggest that nonvolitional needs are not "involuntary" in either of the two possible senses, taken singly. Neither are nonvolitional needs necessarily involuntary in both senses taken together. A talented medical technician who needs kidney dialysis because of his own botched suicide attempt would have a perfectly nonvolitional need for such a machine, though it would be one which was involuntary in neither of the two senses identified above.

In short, we may want to accord priority to claims that count as involuntary in either or both of the senses identified here. But that does not translate into a rule according priority to needs over mere desires, since needs are not necessarily involuntary and mere desires are not necessarily voluntary in either (or both) of those senses. If we are going to have a priority rule here, it should cue on things that matter (voluntariness) rather than on things that correlate only imperfectly with them (needs/desires).

I V

All of the arguments considered so far argue for the priority of needs over mere desires on the grounds that satisfying the former is, in some sense or another, *more valuable* than satisfying the latter. Another way of arguing for the Principle of Precedence takes precisely the opposite tack. Suppose we have no acceptable theory of value, or anyway none we would feel justified in imposing on others through social choices. Under those circumstances, need-satisfaction would once again prove to be preferable to want-satisfaction. This is not because it is seen to be more valuable. Without a theory of value, we can hardly claim that. It is instead because need-satisfaction is *more noncommittal*. In order to justify satisfying any particular desire, we require a theory of value guaranteeing that it is valuable to satisfy that desire. Since needs are indispensable instruments to a wide variety of ends, we do not have to be able to show that any one of them is particularly valu-

---

courses of action which, once initiated, you are bound (e.g., morally, contractually) to see through to their ends, even if your desires in the matter have changed midstream.

able in order to suppose that satisfying the need is nonetheless valuable.

A

There are various ways of running this value-skeptical argument. One—and probably the least interesting, philosophically—is essentially political in character. Much of the appeal of notions of "needs" in liberal democracies surely lies in the fact that, both politically and morally, they constitute a kind of least common denominator which proves enormously useful in building coalitions among diverse interests. Needs, like ambiguous phraseology, allow us to fudge all sorts of problems.

Like all fudges, however, this does not solve the problem but merely shifts it. While pretending to justify need-satisfaction without reference to any theory of value, this solution in fact inevitably appeals to just such a theory in a slightly different way. Arguments for need-satisfaction successfully avoid having to claim that any particular end is desirable. Since needs serve a wide variety of ends, we do not have to be able to show that any particular one of those ends is valuable in order to suppose that satisfying the need might be valuable. But we do have to have good reasons for believing that at least *some* of those ends are valuable. If needed resource R is instrumental to any and all of a hundred ends, but all of those ends are worthless, then the instrumental value of R itself is inevitably nil.

B

There is another variation on that value-skeptical theme. Suppose it is unclear what goods are truly "good," or how good they really are. Perhaps there is no objective standard of goodness: there are only subjective standards, and these diverge to a greater or lesser extent in their evaluations of the goodness of any particular good. Or perhaps there is a reliable, objective standard of goodness but that its concrete pronouncements vary wildly with the particular circumstances to or in which it is being applied.

Under such circumstances, it would be difficult for anyone trying to do good to know what to do. But whatever the difficulties of doing good in the private realm, they are compounded many times over in the public realm. For public policy, by its nature, will have to be applied to a wide variety of people with differing value systems and differing circumstances.

A state trying to do good will, once again, be driven back to the "least common denominator" of goodness found among its citizenry. The rationale this time is one of principle rather than political expediency: surely the state should devote the bulk of its efforts to providing goods that it has relatively more confidence are truly "good" for its people; and the only reliable grounds for such confidence would here be that most of its people (in light of their own value systems or circumstances) find those things to be good.[18]

This provides a rationale, of sorts, for the welfare state's meeting people's basic needs. The goodness of having one's basic needs met is minimally controversial, in this way. There are few circumstances and few value systems in which it would not be good for a person to have food, clothing, shelter, and so forth. The state can provide for such needs with substantial confidence that it is actually doing good. Beyond that, it cannot be nearly so sure. Indeed, it may even be doing harm—by imposing a false system of values upon people, or providing things they would do better without.[19]

Such value skepticism, if well founded, would indeed constitute a powerful argument for the state's meeting people's basic needs before the *state* took steps to provide other goods for people. That is to say, it is a good argument for a welfare state in preference to a command economy.

But value skepticism does not provide any similarly strong argument for the state's meeting people's basic needs rather than letting people pursue their *own* goods in ordinary economic markets. That is to say, it is not an argument for a welfare state in preference to a purely market economy. Yet that is precisely what we need the Principle of Precedence to justify: the state's overrid-

[18] Of course, these procedures will make sense only if the value skepticism is not of a really thoroughgoing sort: if it were, then no value consensus, however broad, could justify the conclusion that one good is more valuable (or more likely to be valuable) than another.

[19] Notice that theories that start by presupposing the existence of a valid theory of the good (Aristotle's, e.g.) would justify the Principle of Precedence by saying that needs are somehow *more valuable* than desires. Value-skeptical theories, starting from the presupposition of uncertainty about any valid theory of the good, justify it by saying that needs are *more certainly* valuable. But analyzing needs, as the value skeptic does, as the "least common denominator" among people's various conceptions of the good does not necessarily point to "higher values" at all. More likely, that will point to lower values—to sordid biological and psychological facts about the species, rather than to its highest aspirations. By giving priority to providing what we can be *more certain* are good things, the value skeptic ends up giving priority to providing what is likely to be *less good.*

ing ordinary market distributions with respect to a certain limited set of needed resources, and in that way to provide a justification for the central features of the welfare state.

The value-skeptical argument against the command economy is that, beyond the narrow range of basic needs on which there is broad consensus, state planners have no way of knowing what is good for people. That argument cannot, however, be easily transformed into an argument against (i.e., in favor of supplanting, even for limited purposes) the market economy. People may well know what is good for them, and be right in those judgments, without others necessarily agreeing with their judgments. That is particularly likely to be true if the variability of the good that leads to skeptical conclusions is in fact derived merely from the variability of the circumstances in, and to, which such value judgments are applied: people can attend to their own peculiar circumstances in a way that state planners cannot. The same is true even if the value skepticism derives, in some way, from the subjectivity of value judgments: whereas state action presupposes that state planners know what is good for everyone, the market allows each individual to pursue what is good for him. Hence, value skepticism offers a powerful argument against the state's forcing people to consume particular goods in a command economy. But that argument does not translate into an argument against the state's letting people consume such particular goods as they choose in a market economy.[20]

Perhaps that is not what is needed to justify welfare state interventions, of a certain sort, at least. Sometimes the welfare state does not intervene in the market, in the sense of allocating specific goods and services to people in need of them; sometimes, at least,

---

[20] Even if what an individual wants is not necessarily good, even in the minimal sense of being just good for him, it nonetheless remains true that private individuals do not have the same obligation to be "right" in their judgments of such matters as do state planners. The latter propose to substitute their judgment of an individual's good for that individual's own judgment of it; that can be justified only if the state planners have a high degree of confidence that they are more likely to be right in the matter than the individual himself. When making his own choices and taking his own chances, however, the individual bears no such heavy responsibility. Hence, the same degree of value skepticism cuts more heavily against state planners in a command economy than it would against private individuals in a market economy. The state's providing people with needed resources, which most people can agree are valuable, can thus be shown to be superior to the state's foisting upon people goods the value of which is contested. But, again, that does not translate into an argument for the superiority of the state's providing needed resources over people's pursuing such goods as they think to be good in a market economy.

welfare state interventions merely take the form of providing people with extra resources with which they can bid, in ordinary markets, for whatever they want.

Certainly it follows, from the value-skeptical argument, that *if*
the state is going to intervene in the market at all, then this form
of intervention is preferable to the other. The only question is
whether there is anything is the value-skeptical argument, in and
of itself, to underwrite that crucial antecedent. What reason is
there, in strictly value-skeptical terms, for the state to intervene to
redistribute basic resources?

The only argument I can find is this. Value skepticism implies
that we have no grounds for supposing that any person is better
than (or hence worth more, or hence deserves more resources)
than any other; and, by a sort of moral analogue of the Laplace
principle of insufficient reason, we should therefore presume
them to be equally worthy (and hence equally deserving of resources, and hence deserving of equal resources).

But why should either presumption be privileged here? Just as
we have no grounds for supposing that anyone is worth more
than anyone else, so, too, do we have no grounds for supposing
that everyone is worth the same as everyone else. Why should we
accept either of these two equally groundless propositions in preference to the other? Value skepticism cuts equally against both.[21]

V

One final variation on these themes traces the superiority of satisfying needs over satisfying wants to the value of personal autonomy. The argument would go roughly as follows. Needed resources, construed as "universally necessary instruments," can be
turned to any number of different uses. Hence, meeting people's
needs amounts to creating opportunities for them to exercise in a
variety of different directions, just as they please.

Notice, first, that this is not necessarily how the welfare state
works. Nor, more importantly, is it how the exponents of needs-
based arguments for the welfare state ordinarily say it should
work. Theirs is ordinarily very explicitly a program of "specific

[21] Indeed, value skepticism cuts against the whole notion of a presumption here
at all. If value skepticism (in some of its stronger forms, at least) is correct, then the
proper conclusion to be drawn is not that either of these presumptions about values should be privileged over the other. The conclusion is, instead, that no propositions about values are defensible. And presumptions about values are just as indefensible as any other proposition about values.

egalitarianism": if a person needs food, then he should (according to these arguments) be given food; he should not be given the money equivalent of food and be allowed either to spend it on food or not to spend it on food, just as he pleases. The only reason this person has any claim against us at all, these theorists would say, is that he has an unsatisfied need, and the claim can therefore extend only to such things as will end up in that need being satisfied. It is always possible, of course, that these exponents of needs-based arguments for the welfare state are misinterpreting their own arguments. But it is nonetheless significant that, according to their standard interpretation of those arguments, personal autonomy ought to be restricted in some ways. That rather suggests that maximizing personal autonomy tout court is not the value that truly underlies the priority of needs that the welfare state is said to embody.

Even if that objection were set to one side, however, the personal-autonomy argument for the priority of needs would still be subject to a further objection perfectly paralleling the one previously lodged against the value-skeptical argument. Considerations of personal autonomy might provide an argument for the state's providing people with needed resources (seen as "generalized means to any end") rather than the state's foisting particular goods (and, through them, particular ends) upon people. That is to say, the personal-autonomy argument might tell in favor of a welfare state over a command economy.

What the Principle of Precedence requires, however, is an argument for the state's meeting people's needs, rather than letting people pursue their own good with their own resources in ordinary markets. Then, and only then, will we have a justification for the welfare state's systematically supplanting the market economy in the distribution of needed commodities.

On the face of it, the personal-autonomy argument would be hard-pressed to justify any strong Principle of Precedence of that sort. Such a priority rule as that would require us to be systematically frustrating autonomously formed wants (either of the agent himself, or of others) in an effort to create yet further opportunities for autonomously formulating wants (for him or for others) by meeting his needs. Yet surely it is self-defeating to pursue a policy that creates opportunities for people to φ only by refusing to let them φ.[22]

---

[22] Or, as I put it in section I of chapter 11, negative freedom without positive freedom is worthless freedom.

Hence, it would seem that both the welfare state and the market—i.e., both meeting people's needs and satisfying their wants—can serve the cause of personal autonomy, each in its own way. In such circumstances, the proper relationship between the two would seem to be one of tradeoffs rather than one of absolute priority, as depicted in strong Principles of Precedence. Each set of considerations might prevail, depending on the particular circumstances of the case and the way that they impinge upon considerations of personal autonomy. Neither should be expected to prevail systematically over the other.

There is, of course, the important distinction between distributing and redistributing particular needed commodities, on the one hand, and distributing or redistributing basic resources that can be used to acquire any of a variety of different commodities, on the other. Of the two, the latter course of action leaves the recipient more room for choice and ought, on that account, to be preferred by advocates of personal autonomy.

But the point remains that resources allocated or reallocated to one person always have been taken from, or could alternatively have been made available to, some other person. Anything that enhances a person's autonomy when given to him must necessarily diminish a person's autonomy when taken from him. So those who would defend welfare state transfers of needed resources on grounds of personal autonomy must therefore face this challenge: they must show that the autonomy gains to the person who has gained the resource exceed the autonomy losses to the person who has surrendered the resource.

It may well be that resources have diminishing marginal payoffs, in terms of autonomy, just as they are standardly presumed to have in terms of utility. If so, that would provide an autonomy-based justification for transferring needed resources from those who have more of them to those who have less of them. But this is a justification for giving more priority to one person's needs rather than another's. It is not a justification for giving priority to anyone's needs over anyone's wants. That is what the Principle of Precedence dictates. For that, we still have yet to find any autonomy-based justification.

So far as I can see, the only way a strong Principle of Precedence according needs priority over mere wants could be justified in terms of personal autonomy would be by showing that the contribution to autonomy that is made by meeting people's needs is different in kind from that made by satisfying their mere desires. Unmet needs, it must be argued, impair agency in some way that unsatisfied desires do not. Meeting needs must be shown to be a "precondition of agency"—a precondition of the capacity to formulate and to act upon desires—that makes need-satisfaction far more fundamental to autonomy than mere desire-satisfaction in markets would be (Weale 1983: 35–37; Plant 1986).

This move is subject to an objection lodged against the model of needs as "universally necessary instruments" in section V above, however. Certainly it is true, for any given individual, that the preconditions for autonomy must be satisfied before he will be capable of exercising autonomy. But to say that Jack's needs must be satisfied before Jack's wants can be satisfied provided, in and of itself, no good reason for thinking that Jack's needs should be satisfied before, much less instead of, Jill's wants. Here, again, temporal priority does not translate automatically into value priority.

In an effort to show that meeting needs promotes autonomy in a way that is more "fundamental," not just in this logical-cum-temporal sense but also in a value-laden sense that morally matters, commentators ordinarily appeal to the nature of the moral-language game. The argument goes like this. Moral injunctions are by their nature addressed to—and in that way presuppose—agents who are capable of autonomy. Meeting people's needs helps to satisfy this precondition of the moral-language game by making people the sorts of autonomous agents to whom moral injunctions are addressed. (See, e.g., Weale 1983: 42–47; Plant 1986.)

There is, however, no reason to believe that all the background conditions presupposed by the moral-language game as we know it are themselves morally desirable. Consider this counterexample. Moral language as we know it also presupposes that humans are the sorts of beings capable of inflicting injuries upon one another. Were that not true, much of our moral language would make no sense. Yet it would be an indisputably better world, in some obvious respect, if that were not true—i.e., if that presupposition of the moral-language game as we know it were not satisfied. Hence, merely showing that something is presupposed by morality does not serve to show that it is necessarily desirable, morally.

Certainly I am prepared to concede that personal autonomy is a morally important value. (How exactly that argument could be grounded may be safely left to one side here.) All that I mean to query is the claim that creating autonomy is morally more important than exercising it—and, indeed, so much more important, morally, as to give the meeting of needs a strong, absolute priority over the satisfying of desires.

My position, in short, is this. I firmly believe that the welfare state contributes to personal autonomy; indeed, I devote chapter 11 to showing how the New Right is wrong to claim otherwise. I also firmly believe that personal autonomy is morally important. But I simply do not see, in considerations of personal autonomy, any good grounds for the sort of strong Principle of Precedence of needs over mere desires that would be required to justify the welfare state's systematically supplanting market-based distributions where needed resources are concerned.

V I

The central task of the welfare state, as analyzed in chapter 1, lies in meeting people's needs. Some commentators suppose that the moral justification of the institution can be read straightforwardly off that description of its central tasks. It has been the burden of this chapter to block any such swift move. None of the arguments here canvassed succeed in showing why needs per se deserve priority over mere wants. Consequently, none of the arguments succeed in showing why state provision should systematically supplant market provision where—but only where—needed resources are concerned.

T H R E E

EQUALITY

Many commentators claim that the most fundamental justification for the welfare state is to be found in principles of social equality. It is not difficult to see how the welfare state might have come to be regarded as an instrument of redistribution. Even if the welfare state were merely the device designed to relieve distress that it was depicted as being in chapter 1, so long as the required resources are drawn from those who are not themselves in distress the net effect of welfare state programs will be to transfer resources from those who are better off to those who are worse off. The end result, even of a minimal welfare state, is bound to be a reduction in overall social inequality, in some sense or another.

Various familiar problems immediately arise with that as the fundamental justification of the welfare state, however. The first is that the welfare state is not really *very* egalitarian—and it does not even really try to be. The welfare state, as characterized in chapter 1, redistributes only a certain strictly limited set of social resources; it is concerned with minimum standards, not thoroughgoing equalization; it is concerned to readjust final distributions, not basic holdings of productive assets, and so on. Now, of course, that characterization is itself contentious, and we must be wary of winning arguments purely by definitional fiat, but it is not *that* contentious. People may disagree over whether a state that does more than merely meet people's basic needs ceases to be (merely) a welfare state. But no one would deny that a state that did at least that much was indeed a welfare state.

If equality is the ideal that underlies such arrangements, then the welfare state is (or at least may be) a very imperfect realization indeed of that ideal. Other social arrangements would be vastly more egalitarian in their impacts than the welfare state; and they would therefore be morally superior to the welfare state, by its very own standards of moral goodness. All that may, of course,

Material in this chapter is reprinted from Robert E. Goodin, "Epiphenomenal Egalitarianism," *Social Research*, 52 (Spring 1985), 99–117, by permission of the editor.

be true. But if it is, then that is not a very strong justification of the welfare state. If that is all that can be said for the institution, then it is not much.

A second problem is that those who would justify the welfare state in terms of its contribution to social equality must face up squarely to the question, "Equality of what?" There seem to be three basic options: equality of status or respect; equality of resources or opportunities; and equality of welfare or "utility" or final results.[1]

Of these, the first option is a slender reed upon which to rest the whole of the case for the welfare state. It has more to do with symbolic gestures than material allocations; and while the former surely have implications for the latter (as I argue in chapter 8), these are not so strong and clearcut that the principal justification for the welfare state can plausibly rest upon them alone.[2] The second option would be attractive for those focusing upon the role of the welfare state in meeting people's basic needs, where those are seen (as in chapter 2) as a precondition of their pursuing any other goals. However, some welfare recipients (e.g., those suffering from special handicaps or "multiple deprivations") need *more* than equal resources if their opportunities, much less final accomplishments, are to be equal. Much of the work of the welfare state focuses upon giving special assistance to those with particularly intractable needs of just this sort. To justify those efforts, appeal to the third interpretation of the equality principle would be required. Yet this third interpretation obviously stands in conflict with the second. So before we can say that the welfare state is justified as an instrument of equality, we would have to come to some resolution of this conflict between the second and third versions of the principle—or at least to establish some properly ordered schedule of tradeoffs between them, offering clear guidance as to which prevails when.

In attempting to address that problem, I have come to the con-

---

[1] On the general philosophical themes, see: Dworkin (1978; 1981; 1985: chaps. 8–10); Plamenatz (1967); Rae (1981); Raz (1978); Roemer (1985a); and Sen (1980). For applications to the welfare state, see Le Grand (1982: 14–17) and Weale (1978a).
[2] Even Dworkin (1978: 133), keen though he is on notions of neutrality and equal respect as the ribbons that tie up the whole liberal package, cannot claim much at this point. Contemplating the way ordinary markets penalize the handicapped for having special needs, he writes: "No solution will seem perfect. The liberal *may* find the best answer in a scheme of welfare rights financed through redistributive income and inheritance taxes of the conventional sort . . ." (emphasis added). That is not very strong stuff from an author otherwise famous for robust egalitarianism and vigorous prose.

clusion that it is not true egalitarianism, in any form, that ultimately underlies the welfare state. Many of its practices may seem, at first blush, to be egalitarian. Upon further investigation, however, that apparent egalitarianism of welfare state practices turns out to be epiphenomenal. It reflects not so much the pursuit of equality for its own sake as it does the pursuit of equality as a means to other ends.

There are, of course, many ways in which egalitarianism might be epiphenomenal. Probably the most important goal which equality serves, in the welfare state context, is community; discussion of that argument is reserved for chapter 4. Another familiar and more formalistic argument runs through the notion of what differences between people are to count as "relevant" for purposes of determining different treatments. Whatever reason we have for treating people with a certain characteristic in a certain way, we have the *same* reason for so treating everyone presenting the same attribute. When acting on such reasons, we will end up treating people equally, not because we value equality per se but merely because the same reasons lead to the same action in the same circumstances.[3]

In the balance of this chapter, I shall explore a less formalistic

---

[3] See, e.g., Westen (1982); Dworkin (1981: 189); Miller (1982: 73–76); Raz (1978). Commentators sometimes try to give "relevance" an objective, naturalistic grounding by analyzing it as "instrumentally relevant to the purposes of the rule/practice in question." But we still need to input values, in the form of "purposes," to give that formula any practical meaning. And even where the purposes are worthy and the distinctions clearly relevant, we still sometimes balk at unequal treatment. Policemen enforcing undoubtedly "just" laws (against murder, rape, theft, etc.) develop all sorts of rules of thumb which are undeniably useful in catching criminals. Statistically, it simply *is* more likely that any given black is guilty of some crime than is any given white (Brown 1981: 111; Johnson 1983). Where veracity or criminality is at issue, " 'decent people' and 'bums' are not equal; 'studs' and 'working stiffs' are not equal; victims and suspects are not equal. . . ." (Wilson 1968: 36). Patrolmen regularly make those sorts of distinctions, and in one narrowly instrumental sense they should. Useful though such distinctions may be in curtailing criminal conduct, however, we dearly wish they would not act on them. Similarly with employer-sponsored retirement plans: the purposes of such schemes are undoubtedly desirable; and given those purposes, death rates are clearly relevant in setting premiums and benefit levels. But that would mean that women would have to pay higher premiums (and have less take-home pay in consequence) than otherwise identical workers who happen to be men, since women seem to live longer. Similarly, "actuarial studies could unquestionably identify differences in life expectancy based on race or national origin, as well as sex" (Stevens 1978: 709). Whether we want to allow those actuarial differences to shape the way we treat people—whether we want to regard them as "relevant"—is a matter of policy rather than a matter of technical instrumental rationality. See generally Tussman and ten Broek 1949.

and more complex way in which egalitarianism, especially as reflected in the welfare state, might be an epiphenomenon—and a
second-order one, at that. This argument proceeds in three stages.
First I shall show (in section I) that a rule of equality or uniformity
can act as a guarantee of impartiality. I go on to show (in section
II) that other things, such as uncertainty, can also guarantee impartiality; and that when these other guarantees are in place, we
no longer insist (or, anyway, not nearly so strongly) upon everyone being given strictly equal treatment. From this fact I infer that
we want a rule of equality largely (if not only) as a guarantee of
impartiality. But I proceed to point out (in section III) that we are
also prepared to tolerate unequal treatment on some occasions
even when there are no other guarantees of impartiality in place.
From this I infer that impartiality itself is not our ultimate value,
either. Examining the exceptions we allow, our ideal seems instead
to be one of "sympathy." The quasi-egalitarian aspects of the welfare state all seem often to be alternatively—and perhaps better—
interpretable under one or the other of these headings.

I do not claim that any of these reductions are wholly successful.
None completely empties the egalitarian ideal of its attractiveness.
But all seem largely successful, thus emptying the egalitarian ideal
of much of its independent attractiveness. My claim is not that,
after my argument in this chapter is finished, there is nothing left
to the egalitarian ideal; it is merely that there is not enough left in
it to ground anything so substantial as the welfare state on that
alone.

I

The first step in this argument is to show that a rule of equality or
uniformity may merely be serving as a surrogate—although admittedly an imperfect one—for a rule of impartiality. The basic
point is simple: where everyone must be treated the same, it will
prove impossible to display partiality or favoritism toward anyone.
Over the years, that is one of the most important reasons social
theorists have given for favoring systems of uniform collective
consumption arrangements. As Rousseau says (1762, bk. 2, chap.
4), under a rule of equality "one cannot work for someone else
without also working for oneself," and vice versa.

The force of this insight is widely appreciated. Le Chapelier ap-
pealed to it explicitly in a 1791 speech to the French Constituent
Assembly arguing against "mutual benefit societies" (akin to the

British "friendly societies") and in favor of national provision for the sick and unemployed (quoted in Bendix and Rokkan 1964: 84). Less predictably, and more exotically, the Maoist strategy of "moral incentives" was arguably no more than implementation of Rousseau's dictim—by rigging the payoff structure in such a way as to impose a regime of equal, collective consumption upon all the members of a commune, officials forced everyone to pursue impartially the common good (Riskin 1975; V. Shue 1980). Western theorists, too, are quick to notice that "one way of making it hard for officials to be corrupt, or partial, is to insist that large classes of people be treated the same" (Mirrlees 1981: 82). Arguably, some such insight informs the Equal Protection Clause of the U.S. Constitution. Justice Jackson, explicating its logic, writes that

> there is no more effective practical guaranty against arbitrary and unreasonable government than to require that the principles of law which officials would impose upon a minority must be imposed generally. Conversely, nothing opens the door to arbitrary action so effectively as to allow those officials to pick and choose only a few to whom they will apply legislation and thus escape the political retribution that might be visited upon them if larger numbers were affected . . . Courts can take no better measure [therefore] to assure that laws will be just than to require that laws be equal in operation. (Jackson 1949: 112–13; see also Ely 1974: 735, and Tussman and ten Broek 1949: 343–44)

Milton Friedman (1962: 175) couches his case against progressive taxation in identical terms: "A proportional flat-rate tax . . . would avoid a situation where any large numbers could vote to impose on others taxes that did not also affect their own tax burden." And so on.

Particularly significant, in the present context, is that just such arguments are sometimes offered to justify the universalistic practices sometimes adopted by welfare states. The basic aim of the welfare state, as described in chapter 1, is to relieve distress among the needy. On the face of things, that would seem to imply targeting programs tightly upon the poor. It is a commonplace, however, that a service that is reserved for the poor is a poor service. The middle classes, knowing that they will not use the service, refuse to vote funds for it to the extent that the demand or need for the service really warrants. Thus, politically, the best way to provide for the needy may well be through universalistic services and programs available to all. The refusal to means-test everything from the British National Health Service and public transport subsidies to the Child Benefit and old-age pensions has been justified on these grounds (Goodin and Le Grand, 1987: chap. 10).

Of course, equality in some sense (indeed, in the sense that surely matters) suffers in the process. Giving everyone strictly equal welfare benefits merely preserves the antecedent inequalities between rich and poor. But while equality in that sense suffers, impartiality is guaranteed. The uniformity of the service or program across all income classes means that the only way the middle classes can get more for themselves is to vote more for the poor as well.

Now, a regime requiring equal treatment of everyone guarantees impartiality, and impartiality has long been regarded as the hallmark of justice. But equality is, as I say, an imperfect surrogate for impartiality. The reason is simply that it provides more than impartiality strictly requires—it guarantees impartiality, and then some.[4] In the process of precluding partiality, any rule of strict equality also prevents us from discriminating on the basis of some considerations which impartiality would surely allow. It would doubtless prove possible to offer a perfectly impartial argument for allocating more resources to those with expensive needs (Vlastos 1962: 41); yet this would be precluded by requirements to give people equal resources. It would be perfectly possible to produce impartial arguments (couched in terms of diminishing marginal utility and equalization of sacrifice) for taxing richer people at higher rates; yet that, too, would be precluded by a regime of strictly equal tax treatment. It may even be possible to offer impartial arguments for allowing some people to enjoy more welfare than

[4] What this "then some" is might best be described as "neutrality" between people, lifestyles, etc. (Benn 1967; Dworkin 1978; Ackerman 1980: 15–17). "Neutrality" is often thought synonymous with "impartiality." Actually, it is not only analytically distinct but also far stronger. "To be neutral in any conflict is," according to Montefiore (1975: 5), "to do one's best to help or to hinder the various parties concerned in equal degree." A neutral will refuse to sell warplanes to either side, and in this way treat them "equally"—even though one side might *need* them far more. That is the sort of regime of strict equality which I have been discussing. And that is distinct from the notion of "impartiality," which is more akin to "indifference" (having "no personal preferences one way or the other") or, better yet, "detachment" ("setting aside . . . whatever personal preferences one may happen to have" when choosing between competing claims). As Grote (1870: 94–95) observes, "Because a judge is impartial, it does not follow that he will divide the thing in dispute equally between the parties. Impartiality between two parties means, the not allowing any considerations to contribute to the judgment formed which ought not to do so . . ."

others, in a way that would be prohibited by a strict rule of welfare equality.

In another way, however, these excesses of the rule of equality can themselves be traced to our quest for scrupulous impartiality. If we are to allow some people more than equal resources in order to equalize their welfare, we would obviously have to examine closely the goals, preferences, and life-plans of all the various individuals concerned. Any argument for allowing some people more welfare than others would, presumably, turn even more heavily upon such considerations.

It might be just barely possible to make such arguments on a purely impartial basis. There is, however, an enormous temptation in such deliberations for us to be biased toward one or another type of goal, preference, or life-plan. Selective Service Boards learned this lesson during the Vietnam war (Wamsley 1969). Policemen are reminded of it daily.

> Unless he is extraordinarily detached, a patrolman, whether he likes it or not, will be drawn into the situation. This may mean outright sympathy for one of the participants, but more often it engenders disdain, disgust, and resentment at the pathos of people's lives and their personal weaknesses. Attitudes toward cleanliness, drinking, and work, and prejudices based on race and sex enter into and shape the response.

For this reason, the rules of the force require policemen "to act impersonally in what is a highly personal set of circumstances" (Brown 1981b: 206).

Social workers, administering welfare law, also encounter such problems with distressing regularity. Consider, for example, the British scheme for giving Supplementary Benefits to claimants on the basis of "exceptional needs." It is standardly said that officials charged with administering this scheme behave in a "coercive" manner, letting their judgments as to who is in need and therefore qualified for benefits to be influenced by their views as to how claimants should be leading their lives (Handler 1973; see also chapter 7 below).

Anyone who strongly internalized the principle of impartiality, and who always acted upon it, would encounter none of these problems. But not everyone fully internalizes that value; and some who do not are bound to be in crucial positions in framing or implementing the policy in question. And not everyone who internalizes the value is sufficiently strong-willed always to act upon it.

57

For those reasons, it seems that some of the distinctions which impartiality might in principle permit us to make are, in practice, better omitted altogether. Rules of strict equality might thus be construed as protections against those hazards—which liberalism regards as the worst hazards, morally (Ackerman 1980; Dworkin 1978)—of second-order partiality for goals, preferences, and life-plans.

I I

Still, unequal treatment sometimes seems permissible. As a first step toward understanding why, notice that there are other ways of guaranteeing precisely the kind of impartiality that is secured by rules of strictly equal treatment. Uncertainty is one such guarantee. If people really were behind a veil of ignorance (rather than just playing a Rawlsian game of Let's Pretend), then they would be forced to consider the interests of all types of individuals impartially, because they might end up being in any of their positions (Goodin 1976: chap. 6).[5]

Such radical uncertainty might become pervasive—extending across all members of society, and all issues they have to consider—only in very exceptional circumstances. The uncertainties of distant futures associated with constitution-framing might be one example (Brennan and Buchanan 1986). Those associated with war might be another example with more practical significance (Titmuss 1950; 1976: chap. 1; Dryzek and Goodin 1986). But even in fairly settled times, there are pockets of social policy characterized by some such uncertainty—comprehensive health insurance coverage being, perhaps, the prime example. In cases such as these, the uncertainty itself is an adequate guarantor of impartiality, and rules of strictly equal treatment can therefore be relaxed.

This emerges most clearly, perhaps, in the distinction we intuitively draw between "identifiable" and merely "statistical" deaths. There is abundant evidence, anecdotal (Calabresi 1965: 716; Schelling 1968: 129; Fried 1969; 1970: chap. 12; Zeckhauser 1973a: 165ff.) and psychometric (Tversky and Kahneman 1981) alike, that some such distinction guides our thinking. We will spend thousands of dollars rescuing a single trapped miner, while refusing to spend

---

[5] That is the force of the assumption of "approximate equality" in the state of nature as depicted by Hobbes (1651: chap. 13): to show that each is as likely to benefit from restraint of the war of all against all as any other (or, equivalently, that over the long haul all are bound to benefit).

even a fraction of that on road repairs which would save many more lives. Surely this is irrational: if the life of the miner is worth $10,000, why is the life of the traffic victim not worth $100? Doubtless there are several strands to the answer.[6] But one important difference seems to be that the former involves the death of a specific, named individual, whereas the latter are just "statistical deaths." Certain though we may be that there will be a hundred fatalities next year due to road conditions, there is no way of telling ex ante which of the millions of drivers passing over those roads will turn out to be the unlucky ones. That matters, in turn, because of the crucial role of probabilistic reasoning in underwriting impartiality. At least no one could reasonably accuse us of willing the death of any particular individual killed on dangerous roads, in a way they could should we fail to aid the particular individual trapped in the mine.

A great many of the inequalities we are prepared to tolerate are ones whose incidences were, ex ante, uncertain. For example, we *know* that even coal-fired electricity generating plants emit a certain amount of low-level radioactivity (McBride et al. 1978); and we know, further, that some people (e.g., children, or the chronically ill who have already had more exposure through medical X rays) are more susceptible than others to getting cancer from such exposure (Shrader-Frechette 1980: 34–35). But even if it were possible to say with absolute certainty that ten percent of children or the chronically ill will contract cancer as a result of exposure to a given level of radiation, we would still be inherently uncertain *which* ten percent that would be. The risks from exposure to radiation are higher for some segments of the population than for others; but the damage is still only a risk rather than an absolute certainty for each person falling in even the most vulnerable class.

---

[6] Part of the answer is that people simply react irrationally to low-probability risks, underestimating the chance that they will be in a tight corner, overestimating their own skill at getting out of it, and inadequately appreciating what it would feel like to get caught in the squeeze (Goodin 1982c: chap. 8). Another part has to do with notions of "responsibility." Once the miner is trapped and we have the "last clear chance" to save him, we are in some sense responsible for his death if we fail to do so. In the case of merely "statistical deaths," we tend to presume that other causal factors will intervene after we have decided not to repair the road but before the accident, thereby lifting responsibility for the deaths off our shoulders. But this will not always be true. Of course, *something* further must always happen to transform statistical deaths into real ones. Such intervening factors can shift responsibility, however, only if they are attributable to moral agents. If, instead, it were just some random or natural factor that picked out victims (e.g., black ice no driver could have seen nor anticipated), then that could hardly absolve us of responsibility for not straightening out a curve that, combined with black ice, kills people.

Similarly, it is impossible to say very far in advance which people will benefit most from various social welfare programs, like schools or hospitals. People with high-IQ parents or a history of illness might stand a rather better chance, but the outcome is far from being fully determinate. The less certain we are who will gain or lose, the less scope we have for displaying favoritism or bias; and hence the less we need to insist upon strict equality of final distributions as a guarantee of impartiality.

Such arguments explain why we are so much more comfortable in making one kind of allocative decision than another. "Micro-allocations" are hard. Presented with the task of deciding which among dozens of worthy patients are to receive kidney dialysis on the single machine available, we regard it as a "tragic" choice (Calabresi and Bobbitt 1979). "Macro-allocations," in comparison, seem easy. We hardly recoil in moral horror when asked to decide whether the marginal tax dollar should be spent on sports rather than hospitals, even though a choice in favor of the former naturally means more "tragic" choices in the latter. Part of the explanation might, as Calabresi and Bobbitt (1979) suggest, be simply that we thereby fool ourselves into believing that we are not making any choices at all. The more important reason that "macro-allocations" are so much less morally troublesome than "micro-allocations," however, has to do with their impersonality. "Although the decision-maker [deciding how many kidney dialysis units to buy] may be acutely aware of the practical effect of his choice upon the lives of many persons, he is seldom conscious of the consequences upon an identified patient" (Anon. 1969: 671–72). Nor, indeed, could he be. That the decision-maker is necessarily blind in this way provides a sufficient guarantee of impartiality, and thus excuses the inequality of the final result—some renal patients living while others die (Fried 1975: 244).

Perhaps of most importance in the field of social policy, the same sort of argument might also explain our fondness for equalizing opportunities and our relative indifference to equalizing final results. There can be no doubt that races which start out equal will end up unequal. Were we fond of equality for its own sake, equalizing outcomes would be of paramount importance, and equalizing opportunities would be no more than an imperfect instrument for achieving that aim. If, however, equality is desired merely as a means of assuring impartiality, that would not be necessary. The crucial point, from this perspective, is that we have no way ex ante of knowing how any particular individual or groups of individuals will fare in the final outcome of a fair race; and the uncertainty that intervenes between opportunities and outcomes is itself a sufficient guarantee of impartiality. The end-states that ultimately result might contain great inequalities. But they cannot plausibly be attributed to favoritism or bias. Impartiality is achieved, even if equality is not.[7]

Similar arguments also underlie debates over alternative military conscription arrangements. Where "the number of persons needed in the armed services is smaller than the physically eligible population," strictly equal treatment of all is either impossible or else highly impractical. Some people must serve, while others stay home.[8] In these circumstances, the standard recommendation is for a lottery (Ginzberg 1966; Fienberg 1971). That is sometimes offered as "the only egalitarian device available . . . in these circumstances" (Tobin 1970). Any appearance of equal treatment is, however, largely illusory. While ex ante everyone stood an equal chance of being drafted, inequality reasserts itself where it really matters—ex post, some serve, others do not (Pauley and Willet 1968: 65–68). What is important about the device of a lottery is not that it assures equality, but rather that it assures impartiality. Randomizers are constitutionally incapable of playing favorites.[9]

I I I

The previous section has canvassed the argument that equality is valued largely as a guarantee of impartiality. When other factors

[7] The upshot of this argument is that Rawls' (1971: secs. 15 and 77; 1980) thesis that justice requires equality of opportunity is more plausible than—or, anyway, derivable independently from—the sort of Kantian egalitarianism upon which Rawls himself supposes it to be based.

[8] Universal national service would not fit the bill. Those who go into the armed forces would risk their lives; those opting for other forms of community service merely sacrifice their time. Neither would a volunteer army, so long as inequalities of income and wealth remain—those with less rewarding alternative employments do not have the same opportunity to decline the offer of a military salary. As Tobin (1970) says, "A volunteer army is subject to the same objections on egalitarian grounds as a free market in negotiable military obligations. It is just a more civilized and less obvious way of doing the same thing, that is, allocating military service to those eligible young men who place the least monetary value on their safety and on alternative uses of their time." The only method for strictly equal treatment would be through a system of short enlistments. But such rapid turnover would be so inefficient as to "make it impossible for the armed services to accomplish their missions" (Tobin 1970).

[9] In his searching discussion of the ethics of "Selecting People Randomly," John Broome (1984: 55) reluctantly concludes that that may be "the only merit" of such procedures.

61

such as uncertainty can guarantee the same sort of impartiality, we are often prepared to drop our demand for equality. But we are prepared to drop it in other cases as well. Uncertainty as a co-guarantor of impartiality does not account for all the instances in which we are prepared to tolerate unequal treatment.

This is especially clear in the way we feel we should give special treatment to people with special handicaps, although they are fully identifiable ahead of time. The handicapped cannot hide behind the cloak of anonymity provided, in many of the other examples, by uncertainty. The same may be true also in the case of radiation-emitting power plants. While we do not know which *particular* child will contract cancer as a result of radioactive emissions from electricity-generating plants, we do know that on the whole children are more likely to suffer than are ordinary adults; though uncertainty prevents us from displaying bias against any individual, we could still display a bias against a whole class of individuals, viz., children in general. In neither of these cases does uncertainty provide any very good guarantee of impartiality. Yet in neither do we insist upon an ironclad rule of equality as a guarantee of it: American courts do not demand a "child-blind" society (Tribe 1975: 9), etc.

The reason we do not insist upon special guarantees of impartiality in these cases seems to be that we assume (perhaps wrongly) children or the handicapped to be the objects of natural sympathy (Benn 1967: 69, 71). We insist upon special guarantees only where we fear that people might otherwise discriminate *against* someone on account of his personal characteristics, preferences, goals, etc.[10] This, perhaps, is the case with the individual with an extraordinarily expensive lifestyle. We insist upon giving him an equal share of social resources (or maybe just an equal opportunity to acquire them), no more and no less, for fear that if people were allowed to discriminate in such cases they would be likely to discriminate *against* a snob on account of his taste for caviar. There is thought to be no such danger where children or the handicapped are concerned. If allowed to discriminate where they are concerned, it is presumed to be unlikely that many of us (or, hence, society as a whole) would use that discretion to their disadvantage.[11]

---

[10] Thus, the Supreme Court holds discriminatory outcomes unconstitutional only if there is evidence of "invidious intent" (White 1976).

[11] That presumption may, of course, be in error. There is a fair bit of evidence to

Strict impartiality, of course, would disallow discrimination of either sort—against particular individuals or groups or in favor of them, either. Insofar as we are willing to permit especially favorable treatment of identifiable individuals or groups, without extending the same favors to all who are similarly situated, we are deviating from the requirements of both equality and impartiality. The conclusion I would draw is that strict impartiality is *itself* merely a means, rather than being our ultimate moral value (Grote 1870: 94). In the ideal world, it seems, our true goal would be "sympathy." We would dearly like to make social policy on the basis of a sympathetic response to the claims of each individual in society, based on a full and vivid awareness of what it would be like to lead his life (having both his experiences and his values, goals, and preferences). Our ideal would seem to be one of universal empathy.

But that is easier said than done. Most of us cannot help feeling revulsion rather than sympathy when confronted with the claims, preferences, and values of a mass murderer. Or, for a less dramatic example, social workers constantly remind us that the individuals with the greatest needs often also arouse the least sympathy.[12] It often seems terribly difficult to be sure that our response to the plight of particular others is not shaped, at least in part, by our own experiences and values rather than by a wholly sympathetic appreciation of their own. The ever-present fear must be that, in trying to respond sympathetically, we might (explicitly or implicitly) respond negatively rather than positively to the peculiar circumstances of individual cases. Much of the case for welfare states to place "greater reliance on the impersonal forms of social services"—tax relief, tax credits, subsidized public services and the like—"rather than the personal social services" is predicated precisely upon this fear (Pinker 1981: chap. 4). The best general rule for guarding against the possibility of negative discrimination seems to be one requiring us to take an attitude of detached im-

suggest that it is, at least where the mentally handicapped (and, especially, mentally handicapped newborns) are concerned.

[12] As Passmore (1981: 33) observes: "The aged, the physically handicapped, the insane, the chronically or mortally ill, the unemployed, share one characteristic. They are all of them extremely unpopular. Their very existence is resented. They are seen as a burden, they are feared as exemplifying a fate which any of us may have to endure but which we prefer as far as possible to forget." Advocates of "children's liberation" suppose the same is true of our attitudes toward children—we all (subconsciously) resent our own past weaknesses—and ground their case for strictly impartial rules on that presumption. See more generally Baer 1983: esp. chaps. 7–9.

partiality when adjudicating claims, except in those rare instances where we can be *really* confident that our response will truly be a sympathetic one.

This arrangement represents something of a compromise. In it, the requirements of impartiality—operationalized (however imperfectly) for ordinary cases by the rule of equality—sets the baseline for entitlements. No special treatment is allowed if it is likely to entail the exercise of negative discrimination, pressing people below what they could expect on that basis. Thus, the caviar-lover continues to receive his equal share of social resources, rather than being penalized for his ostentatious tastes. But special treatment is allowed if, owing to the effects of natural sympathy, it is virtually certain to entail the exercise of positive discrimination. Thus, the handicapped are allowed to receive an unequal—a more than equal—share of social resources.

Similarly, a doctor is expected to spend a certain amount of time on each of his patients, a teacher on each of his students, and a social worker on each of his clients. If, having given each his due, the doctor, teacher, or caseworker then chooses to spend more time on the case or child of a friend, then that deviation from impartiality would be judged morally laudable (Blum 1980: 48). Even in courts of law, judges and juries may be obliged to try cripples and blind beggars impartially according to the strict letter of the law when assessing the facts of the case. But when sentencing convicted cripples, it is perfectly proper for judges to respond sympathetically to their special hardships. Here, too, "extenuating circumstances" can only work to the advantage of the accused. "Discretion" in arrest and sentencing policies "is basically ameliorative, i.e., a discretion to impose upon individuals less restraint than the law authorizes" (Kadish 1962: 906).

This effectively describes the present practice among our social service agencies. Social security laws fix a baseline of equal treatment for all those who fall within each benefit class. Every eligible claimant should receive at least that much. There are various devices for increasing benefits, according to the circumstances of particular cases, above that baseline; there are none for reducing them below it. In both Britain and Australia, these upward adjustments are formalized in procedures for paying supplementary benefits to especially needy claimants.[13] Similar procedures seem to have

[13] As one British Minister of Health and Social Security says, it is the job of Supplementary Benefit officers to "unerringly distinguish between the men to whom sympathy and help and understanding should be extended and one who is trying

emerged informally among American caseworkers. According to one recent study of an American welfare agency (Goodsell 1981), all clients receive their statutory entitlement. Even those the caseworker dislikes intensely get scrupulously fair treatment, following the letter of the law.[14] Insofar as discretion is exercised at all, it comes in the form of special favors to especially sympathetic clients such as the old and disabled.

Or, for a more contentious example, consider the problem of reverse discrimination. The long and heated debates on this issue often neglect the distinction, which on this argument would be the crucial one, between discriminating *against* someone and discriminating *in favor of* someone.[15] Advocates on both sides of this debate labor under what might be an illusion of symmetry. Opponents of affirmative action suppose that both types "must stand or fall together. They believe that it is illogical . . . to condemn Texas for raising a color barrier against Sweatt [a black], and then applaud Washington for raising a color barrier against DeFunis [a white]" (Dworkin 1977: 229; see also Douglas 1974, and Powell 1978: 294–95). Even its advocates concede that discretion in favor

to get away with something," though, of course, even unsympathetic souls are nonetheless entitled to the basic pension (quoted in Briggs and Rees 1980: 46). Such practices seem to date at least back to the Great Depression, at which time the Unemployment Assistance Board was reporting that "in not less than 20 per cent of cases, the officers of the Board have used their authority to grant allowances above the normal provided for in the Regulations, and many instances have come to the knowledge of the Board of personal service given by officers, or secured by them, for households with which they are in touch."

[14] Similarly, Blau's (1963: 86) study of an unemployment agency shows that in a department that regularly dealt with unsympathetic clients a strictly detached, "impersonal orientation did indeed prevail." The same seems to be true of police behavior. As Skolnick's (1966: 84) study of the behavior of warrant officers suggests, "It is possible for him to be accorded wide decisional latitude; to be racially prejudiced; and to carry out his work relatively even-handedly." Attitudinal studies consistently show American policemen to be highly prejudiced toward blacks, yet participant-observer studies show they rarely act upon those prejudices. "In fact, . . . blacks were more likely to be treated *impersonally* than whites" (Brown 1981a: 116; Black and Reiss 1967: 138). One reason policemen so conscientiously "go by the book" when dealing with blacks may well be that they are self-consciously guarding against their own prejudices.

[15] Day (1981: 56), for example, insists that the two are analytically equivalent: "to discriminate against Fs is to favour not-Fs." Others acknowledge the distinction, but mistake its true moral importance. In the *Bakke* case, for example, the opinions of both Powell (1978) and Brennan et al. (1978) are at pains to emphasize that the intent of Title VI of the Civil Rights Act of 1964 was to eliminate discrimination *against* blacks, not to prohibit discrimination in their favor. But both are merely concerned to establish that the law, while outlawing negative discrimination, might permit positive. Neither opinion reveals any appreciation of what, if any, moral importance might attach to this distinction.

of blacks can be equivalently described as discrimination (albeit justifiable) against whites. Wasserstrom (1977: 621–22), for example, says that in light of existing "social realities," such discrimination can hardly be called "racist." Ely (1974: 727) says "it is not 'suspect' in a constitutional sense for a majority, any majority, to discriminate against itself." But all concede that discrimination in favor of blacks amounts to discrimination against whites.

The two may well, in their material effects, be strictly equivalent. The crucial difference, however, on the present argument would be this: the *intention* of affirmative action programs is to help blacks, not to hurt whites.[16] Philosophers are accustomed to assessing intentions for purposes of fixing credit or blame for actions. That is not the purpose in this context. Here, the idea is instead to assess the quality of the will from which an action proceeds merely in order to determine what sort of special measures (e.g., rules requiring impartial—or perhaps even strictly equal—treatment) might be required to protect those who might otherwise be victimized.

In cases of negative discrimination such protections are clearly required. Intentional discrimination *against* someone proceeds from malice, envy, or some other form of ill will; we are anxious to prevent those sentiments from influencing policy. Positive discrimination is another matter altogether. Singling out for especially favorable treatment certain people who are generally disadvantaged is a manifestation of sympathetic impulses which we wish to welcome rather than to protect against.[17]

Ideally, of course, everyone should have their claims judged equally sympathetically. But the human psyche being what it is, that ideal is beyond our reach; and moral principles must adjust themselves to people's psychological capacities (Urmson 1958; cf. Brandt 1976). Few people are psychologically capable of responding sympathetically to the claims of Caligula. Indeed, most people are incapable of offering any ironclad guarantee that their re-

---

[16] Thus, one distinguished jurist (White 1980) argues for "color-conscious remedies" to undo the damage that has resulted from "color-blind" theories. Of course, programs ostensibly offered to benefit one group might *actually* be intended to harm another (Brennan et al. 1978: 359–60). Questions of intention—especially of the collective intentions of a legislature as a whole—are notoriously difficult even to analyze, much less to resolve. Still, the courts are prepared to try to do so, and perhaps philosophers should be likewise.

[17] Advocates of strictly equal or impartial treatment demand that "racial factors do not militate against an applicant or on his behalf" (Douglas 1974: 336). Dworkin (1977: 235), similarly, would ignore altruistic preferences as well as malicious ones in excluding "external preferences."

sponse to the claims of most of their fellows will be a truly sympathetic one. The best we can usually expect is a detached, impartial response. But in a few, rare cases, people *can* do better. In such cases, it might be thought, there is no reason not to allow—indeed, to expect—the ideal of mutual sympathy to be realized. The fact that we cannot respond sympathetically to the claims of Caligula should not prevent us from responding sympathetically to those of Helen Keller.

The practical manifestation of this sentiment is that our lives are partitioned into various compartments, some of which require impartiality and others of which permit the exercise of nonuniversal sympathies. Role requirements—such as those of the doctor, teacher, social worker, policeman, judge, etc.—are institutionalized so as to guarantee everyone a certain level of care, whether or not others genuinely care. Those role requirements must be satisfied completely impartially (Blum 1980: 48). But anything left over after all those claims have been honored counts as discretionary resources. These may perfectly properly be distributed according to the (very partial) sympathies of those involved. When a doctor or a teacher or a social worker gives some of his *own* time to a friend's child, no one else has any right to complain.[18]

I V

The argument developed in this chapter suggests that such egalitarianism as we see in welfare state practices might be only a second-order moral epiphenomenon. Working backward from the actual practices and the way that they work, it rather seems that they are predicated on something like the following assumptions. (1) The ideal rule would be one enjoining mutual sympathy; that is often psychologically impossible, however. (2) Second-best would be a rule of disinterested impartiality, to be applied where sympathy proves impossible; but the same difficulties that arise in trying to legislate the ideal sort of attitude (sympathy) arises once again in legislating the second-best attitude (impartiality). (3) So we fall back upon a third-best system of practical mechanisms to

[18] John Stuart Mill (1848: bk. 5, chap. 11, sec. 13) recommends a division of labor between public and private charity along roughly these lines: "The state must act by general rules. It cannot undertake to discriminate between the deserving and the undeserving indigent. It owes no more than subsistence to the first, and it can give no less to the last. . . . Private charity can make these distinctions; and in bestowing its own money, is entitled to do so according to its own judgement." See similarly Paine (1969: 521) and Fried (1970: chap. 12).

guarantee behavior (if not attitudes) that conforms to the demands of impartiality; rules of strict equality are one such device.

Indeed, if all that is right, then equality may come even lower still in the pecking order of moral principles. There are other devices—such as uncertainty—that are capable of producing the same sort of impartial behavior that equality, on that interpretation, is designed to produce. They may even do a better job of it. If that is generally true, then the rule of equality would be a fourth-best arrangement, which we should fall back upon only when it proves impossible (or highly undesirable, for other reasons) to introduce sufficient uncertainty to preclude bias and favoritism.

Nothing that I have said here should be interpreted as implying that the value of equality is *wholly* epiphenomenal. Neither of the reductions performed above is wholly successful. Equality is not desired *just* as a guarantee of impartiality. A lottery can remove many—but not all—of our objections to ex post inequalities. Consider these two food distribution schemes. In scheme A, everyone is provided with identical calories per day, and these are sufficient to prevent anyone from starving. In scheme B, there will be a lottery: everyone has the same statistical expectation ex ante as in scheme A; but ex post of the lottery, some people will have lots of food while others will starve. The ex ante uncertainty as to who will win and who will lose scheme B's lottery would hardly suffice to remove our objections to its ex post inequality.[19] Impartiality, apparently, is not *all* that we want a rule of equality to guarantee for us.

Likewise, it does not necessarily follow that, if it is best to treat everyone sympathetically, then it must be second best to treat more people sympathetically rather than fewer. That proposition falls afoul of the general theory of second best (Lipsey and Lancaster 1956). If we cannot treat everyone sympathetically, it might be better to treat none in that way: universal impartiality might be preferable to partial sympathy. That would quite likely be true wherever one person's gains impose real costs on those who are passed over (Sen 1983).[20] It would also be likely to be true when

[19] Maybe that counterexample works only because basic needs and vital interests are at stake; perhaps our objection is not really to the ex post inequality at all, but merely to the ex post starvation.

[20] Giving one person a benefit that could have been given to another instead will always entail an opportunity cost, from the second person's point of view. Thus, the condition must be phrased in terms of a "real" cost and not just opportunity cost.

our sympathy extends only to those who are already greatly advantaged. Suppose it were true that apartheid policies in South Africa, although clearly working to the advantage of whites rather than blacks, were motivated by mutual sympathy among whites rather than by any malice whatsoever against blacks. Even if that were true, and even if those laws did not make blacks worse off than they would otherwise have been, we still would surely not be prepared to tolerate partial sympathy working so powerfully to the further advantage of an already greatly advantaged group in that way. Thus, it would appear that the elimination of mean motives is not *all* that we want rules of impartiality or equality to guarantee for us.

Even if these reductions do not wholly succeed, however, they do point to some important reasons for favoring egalitarian social welfare policies. Insofar as those are our reasons (and to a large extent they seem to be), the egalitarianism embodied in such policies is to that extent merely epiphenomenal. There may be more to our attachment to the equality principle than just impartiality and mutual sympathy. But if the equality principle is to be defended, much less defended well, these confounding factors must be filtered out. When that is done, egalitarianism is a much less plausible basis for the welfare state. Most of the egalitarianism of the welfare state seems to be epiphenomenal, deriving from these other sources.

F O U R

COMMUNITY

Certain writers on the soft left and the romantic right converge on an essentially communitarian justification for the welfare state. For them, the justification for social welfare programs lies principally in terms of the contribution such programs make to the integration of everyone—benefactors and beneficiaries alike—into the life of a single, unified, caring community.

Such themes have always been politically potent. In Britain, New Liberals such as Hobhouse (1911) relied upon them to defend turn-of-the-century steps toward the welfare state. Distinguishing those innovations from the old poor law tradition, one New Liberal of the era firmly emphasized, "Poor relief's . . . concern is with men and women who are at the best failures . . . [Our] proposal of old-age pensions starts from a totally different principle. It is a recognition . . . of the *solidarity of society* . . ." (quoted in Freeden 1978: 203; see similarly Vincent and Plant 1984: chap. 5). In France, this notion of "solidarity" has figured even more explicitly, and even more consistently, in justifications for social welfare programs from the nineteenth century forward (Hayward 1959; Lynes 1967: chaps. 4–6). And in the U.S., too, Franklin Roosevelt's welfare programs arguably were, and Lyndon Johnson's indisputably were, informed by a vision of a Great Society,

> a united nation, divided neither by class nor by section nor by color, knowing no South or North, no East or West, but just one great America, free of malice and free of hate, and loving thy neighbor as thyself. I see America as a family . . . [that] takes care of all its members in time of adversity. . . . I see our nation as a free and generous land with its people bound together by common ties of confidence and affection, and common aspirations toward duty and purpose. (Johnson, quoted in Schambra 1985: 32; cf. Holt 1975)

Philosophically, such themes are most powerfully developed in the works of modern socialists such as Tawney (1932/1971), Crosland (1956) and Walzar (1980; 1982; 1983: chap. 3). For them, "The purpose of socialism is quite simply to eradicate the sense of class, and to create in its place a common interest and equal status. This will require not only more measures on the economic plane, directed to the greater equalization of living standards and opportunities, but also measures on the socio-psychological plane" (Crosland 1952: 62–63). For socialists of this stripe, "socialism is not about distribution but about human relationships. . . . The right distribution is necessary to and made possible by the right relationships but it is morally of subordinate importance" (Barry 1973: 168; see likewise Wright 1984). The chief virtue of the welfare state, for such writers, lies in its propensity to create such desirable psychic states—"a certain civic spirit, a sense of mutuality" (Walzer 1982: 11)—and patterns of behavior that naturally follow from them.

Central though the notion of "community" thus obviously is, both in political rhetoric and political philosophy, there has been precious little analytic work done, either on the value itself or on its possible connections with the welfare state. Instead, all these issues are ordinarily run together in larger debates about "What is socialism?" or "What is the good life?" Big questions drive out little ones. All opportunity for precise thinking about the exact links between component parts of those larger ideals is lost.

Showing that socialism or the good life implies both community and welfare state services is ordinarily thought sufficient to establish a quasi-analytic link between the two. But of course it is not: even if there are good reasons for us to value both community attachments and welfare states, it does not necessarily follow that the same reason leads us to value both. Still less does the fact that we should value both suffice to prove that there is any causal connection between the two.

Most of the analytic work on these issues, then, remains yet to be done. Here I can hope to do no more than to make a start. After first discussing briefly the concept of "community" and the sort of social ideal toward which it points (section I), I shall canvas four versions of the communitarian case for the welfare state. As I shall show in section II, the stronger, quasi-analytic claims of the first two models are untenable, and the weaker, empirical claims of the second pair are weak indeed. Finally, in section III, I call into question the more general model of diffuse altruism that underlies the communitarian justification of the welfare state.

In assessing each of these claims, I take the communitarian ideal as being of unquestioned value. My only query here will be to what extent the existence of welfare state institutions constitutes a contribution to the realization of that ideal, and to what extent therefore they can be justified in terms of that ideal.

I

Disputes over definitions are notoriously nonproductive. This is nowhere more true than with respect to the notion of "community." In a 1955 essay, George Hillery reported discovering ninety-four definitions then extant in the sociological literature; the only point of agreement between them was that they all had to do with "people" in some way or another. The intervening quarter of a century has done little to clarify matters.

In addition to all the ordinary difficulties in framing a watertight definition of anything, there is yet another deriving from the role that the definition of "community" is meant to play in subsequent empirical sociological research. Analytic questions about what it *means* for a group to constitute a community are systematically confused with empirical ones about the *causes* and *consequences* of such an entity's existing. Failure to distinguish clearly between these two sorts of questions has helped to make a great many theories about community (among them, theories about the relationship between community and the welfare state) true, but true very largely by definitional fiat.

Naturally, with so many definitions to choose between, one's empirical theories about community development cannot help being influenced by one's choice of definition of "community." Still, that influence should be minimized as far as possible. To do that, the most general definition available ought to be adopted. Insofar as a definition is sufficiently general as to embrace all other definitions (and their correlative empirical theories), then it is not biased as between any of them.

For the purposes of this analysis, therefore, a social grouping will be said to constitute a "community" if and only if it embodies (1) a sense of solidarity and (2) a sense of significance for all those who are within the group (Clark 1973: 403–404). That is a very bare-bones definition indeed, and it can be fleshed out in any number of different ways (Plant 1978: 86 ff.). It is so stripped-down, in fact, that it is rarely found explicit in any more specific analyses of community: few bother to mention anything so basic as this. Still, that much at least should be common ground to all analysts of community—as, indeed, it has historically been to Althusius, Grotius, Pufendorf, Rousseau, and their latter-day followers (Friedrich 1959).

The essence of the communitarian case for the welfare state can often prove quite elusive. When trying to trace a distinctively communitarian strand in the argument, we often find that there is nothing much distinctive in it at all. Speakers (for it is in rhetorical appeals—speeches and pamphlets—that this happens most often) appeal almost indiscriminately to values of community, equality, dignity, alleviating distress and so on, without any reflection upon how, if at all, these might be related to one another.

Such rhetorical appeals are rarely forthright about underlying values, and sometimes are downright misleading. Consider the famous debate over selectivity versus universality of social welfare benefits (Deacon and Bradshaw 1983). The standard communitarian argument for universal benefits is that means-tested, selective benefits are stigmatizing. Now, there is no denying the proposition that if the selectively benefited group is defined according to some already degraded description, then social degradation will indeed follow when one receives such benefits; and there is no denying that, in our own societies, income-testing of social benefits does just that (Handler and Hollingsworth 1969; 1971: chap. 7; Rainwater 1982; Spicker 1984). But there are other ways of selectively targeting benefits that might actually *enhance* the status of recipients, as compared to others in the community. That was the essence of David Lloyd-George's (1908/1986: 54) argument for a "character" or "industry" test on old-age pensions, for example:

> I think it is highly important that the receiver of the pension should be regarded as quite honourable . . . ; and if every man, without distinction of conduct—if men who have never done an honest day's work in their lives—receive this pension in common with men who have really worked hard, I think that the receiver of the pension will be regarded in the same light as he who is actually known to be of that stamp which we wish ruthlessly to exclude, as they ought to be. In order, therefore, to raise the character of the gift . . . we [should] eliminate the loafer and the wastrel from among the recipients of the bounty of the State.

Similarly, veteran's benefits are awarded only to those who have served their country; but selectivity in awarding benefits on the basis of a meritorious attribute such as this could hardly be considered to be stigmatizing (Rainwater 1982: 40). Or, for another example, where (as in the U.S.) unemployment benefits are earnings-related it is surely a source of pride rather than shame that you had a sufficiently good job to qualify for a larger rather than smaller payment. In all these ways, the communitarian claim that selective benefits are necessarily stigmatizing (as compared to universal ones) is patently false.

If communitarians would still lodge a principled objection to selectively targeted benefits, as I believe they would, then the principle in view cannot be one of stigma-avoidance, as they claim it to be. It must instead be that communitarians are arguing most fundamentally for a single-status moral community. Pointing to cases where selective benefits necessarily demean their recipients is the most dramatic way of putting their point, perhaps. But that disguises their real point, which is that selective benefits necessarily set their recipients apart from the rest of the community. The communitarian goal is best described as "mainstreaming," i.e., bringing everyone into the mainstream of community life (Schorr 1986: 28–34). By that standard, selective benefits that raise the status of their recipients over that of others in the community would be as bad as ones that lowered their recipients' status. Either way, they set some people off from others in the community. It is that to which communitarians really object.[1]

---

[1] Note, similarly, Le Chapelier's 1791 speech in the Constituent Assembly of France, drawing upon Rousseau (1762: bk. 2, chap. 3) to argue against mutual benefit societies: "The bodies in question have the avowed object of procuring relief for workers in the same occupation who fall sick or become unemployed. But let there be no mistake about this. It is for the nation and for public officials on its behalf to supply work to those who need it for their livelihood and to succour the sick. . . . It should not be permissible for citizens in certain occupations to meet together in defense of their pretended common interests. There must be no more guilds in the State, but only the individual interest of each citizen and the general interest. No one shall be allowed to arouse in any citizen any kind of intermediate interest and to separate him from the public weal through the medium of corporate interests" (quoted in Bendix and Rokkan 1964: 84).

A modern variation on the "single-status moral community" theme is that welfare recipients should not be exempted from the ordinary requirements binding on all members of the community—specifically, they should not be exempted from the requirement (forced upon the rest of us by market discipline) that we should give or do something in exchange for any goods or services we receive. Neoconservatives interpret this as an argument for "workfare" (i.e., compulsory community service for welfare recipients) rather than "welfare"; see Mead (1982), Goggin (1984: 82–84) and Kirp (1986), picking up on themes from Tocqueville's 1835 "Memoir on Pauperism," reproduced in the neoconservative organ, *The Public Interest* (1983: 113–14). Among an earlier generation of writers on the welfare state, similar principles were interpreted more generously as implying a system of social insurance, wherein an individual paying his premiums did *something* (albeit, actuar-

But it is not just a single-status community—not just everyone's being part of one and the same *abstract* whole—that communitarians seek. The commitment they demand of people is not to abstract principles, either in the form of an "abstract love of humanity" (Crick 1984: 22) or in the form of an abstract idea or ideal of "community" (Gaus 1983: 88–101). Fraternity is what they are seeking. And that entails a commitment to particular other people with whom one is "working . . . towards common ends" (Crick 1984: 22; see further Finnis 1980: chap. 6).

The sort of social ideal which values of community tend to evoke builds most fundamentally upon a certain widespread romantic-cum-populist vision (Pinker 1983). "Historically, the idea of solidarity had a juridical point of departure" in the principle of Roman law that imposed "co-proprietorial obligations of mutual assistance and collective responsibility within the Roman extended family or 'Gens,' each member of which was held responsible for the payment of the whole of the debt contracted by any member, and had the right to receive payment of debts owed to the collectivity" (Hayward 1959: 270). Residues of this tradition of assimilating social groups to natural families are found in the very name of the principle, "fraternity," and more especially still in the forms of address ("brother, sister") that self-styled "fraternal organizations" adopt in dealings with one another (Hobsbawm 1975). By extension, a village society is taken to be a kind of "extended family," and pre-industrial village society of a certain, idealized sort is thus standardly taken to represent the paradigm of a "community" among modern communitarian theorists.[2]

The crucial elements in this idealization are the twin presumptions, first, of the organic solidarity of the group constituting the community, and, second, of the way in which this gives rise to a deep empathy between all members of the group thus constituted. Consider, in this connection, the depiction of a Hampshire village quoted so approvingly by John Dewey (1927: 40–41) in his discussion of *The Public and Its Problems*:

Each house has its center of human life with life of bird and beast, and the centers were in touch with one another, con-

---

ially, not enough) to earn his subsequent benefits; see Beveridge (1942: para. 9) and Brown (1956: 3; 1960), e.g.

[2] See, e.g.: Maine 1871; Kropotkin 1914; and Taylor 1982. The latter two authors argue that similar phenomena can be found—and should be further encouraged—in industrial and post-industrial society, respectively. This is the sort of "unitary" community that Barber (1984: chap. 9) contrasts with the sort that he hopes to promote through "strong democracy."

nected like a row of children linked together by their hands; all together forming one organism, instinct with one life, moved by one mind, like a many-colored serpent lying at rest, extended at full length upon the ground. I imagined the case of a cottager at one end of the village occupied in chopping up a tough piece of wood or stump and accidentally letting fall his heavy sharp axe on to his foot, inflicting a grievous wound. The tidings of the accident would fly from mouth to mouth to the other extremity of the village, a mile distant; not only would each villager quickly know of it, but have at the same time a vivid mental image of his fellow villager at the moment of his misadventure, the sharp glittering axe falling on to his foot, the red blood flowing from the wound; and he would at the same time feel the wound in his own foot and the shock to his system. In like manner all thoughts and feelings would pass freely from one to another, though not necessarily communicated by speech; and all would be participants in virtue of that sympathy and solidarity uniting the members of a small isolated community. (Hudson 1921: 110–12)

That ideal may well be an illusory one, either because it is impossible or else because it is ultimately undesirable. It may well be that no traditional village was ever quite like that, or that no modern (or post-modern) society can ever be like that again. Or it may well be that communities thus construed would be claustrophobic places, destructive of other equally important values of individuality, liberty, and autonomy (Benn 1982; Pinker 1983; cf. Taylor 1982). Those are larger issues that I do not intend to discuss at this point (although I shall return to some aspects of them in chapters 6 and 7). For now, I propose simply to take the value of "community" thus construed as an unquestioned good. Here I shall be asking merely how, if at all, that value might be promoted by—and hence be used to justify—the welfare state.[3]

The significance of theories of community of this sort for theories of the welfare state lies in their distinctive analysis of what motivates members of such communities to assist one another in times of need. It is altruism in the deepest sense: an internalization of others' pains and pleasures, as if they were your own. In the

[3] In the writings of Mill, Green, and Hobhouse, justifications of social assistance appeal both to principles of social solidarity and to principles of self-development (see Gaus 1983: 243–50 for a survey). Here I shall focus on the former alone.

words of one approving commentator, "The most obvious thing a doctrine of community tries to do is to determine what sympathetic social relations would look like and thus to describe the political equivalent of love" (Unger 1975: 261).

The institutional arrangements that follow from this empathetic identification of self with others, and hence constitute this "political equivalent of love," are institutions of "mutual aid" and "reciprocal altruism." Describing those arrangements, Hobsbawm (1975: 471, 473) writes,

> Fraternity is, at bottom, a certain type of social cooperation [the] main characteristic [of which is] this relation of voluntary mutual aid and dependence, which implies that each member can expect the unlimited help of every other when in need. . . . For obvious reasons, the relations between close kin have been regarded as the models for all such relations, and have produced a variety of artificial "brotherhoods." But the essence of the relationship is not kin but certain bonds of mutual support.

Such sentiments find particular expression in the preambles to the rules of British "friendly societies" dating from the early years of the nineteenth century: "Man is formed a social being . . . in continual need of mutual assistance and support"; "Interwoven in our constitutions [are] those humane and sympathetic affections which we always feel at the distress of any of our fellow creatures . . . " Accordingly, the aim of members of the friendly society is stated as being to produce "a sure, lasting, and loving society" (quoted in Thompson 1968: 461).

These arrangements are usually described as "mutual aid" or "reciprocal altruism" (Kropotkin 1914; Taylor 1982), and in certain respects those descriptions are perfectly apt. The essence of the arrangement is that everyone is prepared to—and fully expects to—aid and be aided in turn by everyone else, as the need arises. In another sense, however, those phrases are apt to mislead. Talk of "mutuality" and "reciprocity" rather suggests (or at least admits of the interpretation) that the reason that one person helps others today is to secure assistance from them tomorrow. Communitarians see no role for any such cynical "insurance" or "investment" logic in their mutual-aid arrangements. What motivates members of a *true* community to render assistance to a neighbor in distress, they would say, is not any expectation of future return on their investment but rather a genuine, empathetic concern for the plight of the needy neighbor (Hobsbawm 1975: 471; Miller 1976: 230–36).

The image of the welfare state that emerges from such discussions is as a kind of mass-society analogue of these village-society mutual-aid arrangements, motivated by a deep caring and concern for all members of the (now, national) community by all members of the community. "In short, mutual aid systematically developed would be the basis of a fraternal society" nationwide (Hobsbawm 1975: 473).

The welfare state, seen in this light, would amount to a form of "institutionalized altruism"—in Titmuss' (1971) felicitous phrase, the very embodiment of the "gift relationship." How to evoke a sense of community sufficiently strong to accomplish that result is, perhaps, unclear. In Britain, at least, it seems to have taken the shared traumas of the Second World War to do so, even on Titmuss' (1950: 506–508) own account.[4] But the end in view, once a proper community has indeed emerged, is clearly this altruistic merging of self with others, of which the welfare state is the institutional embodiment.

Such fraternal feelings and generalized altruism have both consequentialistic and nonconsequentialistic moral value. Good results flow from them. The starving are fed, the homeless sheltered, etc. To that extent, communitarian justifications of the welfare state point to consequentialistic concerns. Beyond all that, however, fraternal feelings and generalized altruism are morally desirable character traits. They betoken moral virtues that are good in and of themselves, whether or not any further good results flow from them.

Fraternal feelings and generalized altruism thus constitute at least the historical core of the communitarian case for the welfare state. There may of course be other—perhaps more compelling— reasons for living in a community than that. A recent argument, owing especially to Sandel (1982), is that one's community attachments give meaning to one's life and contribute crucially to one's sense of self. Insofar as they do, life completely outside any com-

---

[4] On the closing page of his blueprint for the postwar British welfare state, Beveridge (1942: para. 460) similarly writes: "The prevention of want and the diminution and relief of disease—the special aim of the social services—are in fact a common interest to all citizens. It may be possible to secure a keener realization of that fact in war than it is in peace, because war breeds national unity and readiness to sacrifice personal interests to the common cause, to bring about changes which, when they are made, will be accepted on all hands as advances, but which it might be difficult to make at other times." For an alternative explanation of the influence of war on social policy, see Dryzek and Goodin 1986.

munity at all would be not only morally impoverished, but virtually incoherent and devoid of meaning or purpose. This is not the place to enquire into the larger question of whether, or to what extent, such claims may be true. Rather, I confine myself to the narrower question of whether, if true, they would entail (or hence justify) a welfare state.[5] The arguments to be offered in section II, at least, will tell equally against this as the other, more familiar version of the communitarian justification of the welfare state.

I I

Having set out rather uncritically the communitarian ideal and its ostensible connections with the welfare state, I next turn to con-

[5] There is a very strong—and very implausible—form of this claim on which it would be true. Sandel's (1982: 150) assertion is that talk of "community" refers to "a mode of self-understanding partly constitutive of the agent's identity"; and that insofar as it does, "to say that members of a society are bound by a sense of community is not simply to say that a great many of them profess communitarian sentiments and pursue communitarian aims, but rather that they conceive their identity . . . as defined to some extent by the community of which they are a part." Imagine, now, the extreme case of this: people identify *so* strongly with one another (or with their community as a whole) that they are literally incapable of distinguishing themselves and their interests from others and their interests—they just cannot tell the difference. Then distinctions between altruism and egoism will be meaningless. People will promote the interests of others not because they care about others' happiness or well-being but rather because they cannot tell the difference between others and themselves, others' well-being and their own. There is some discussion of such models among sociologists (Jencks 1979: 64); something like this is suggested in MacIntyre's (1968: 466) *Encyclopedia of Philosophy* essay on "Egoism and Altruism"; and the point was explicitly raised in connection with the welfare state by Benjamin Barber's reply to David Miller's (1986) paper to the Poverty, Charity, and Welfare conference at Tulane University, New Orleans, La., February 1986 (see similarly Barber 1984: xv). In a very few, very special cases, it is conceivable that some such strong identification and merging of self and other just might occur. One example might be that of a mother and child, as Barber's comments suggested. Another might be an old-fashioned servant of an aristocratic master, who according to Tocqueville's (1840: vol. 2, chap. 5) analysis, "ends by losing his sense of self-interest; he becomes detached from it; he deserts himself, as it were, or rather he transports the whole of himself into his master's character; . . . he takes pleasure in identifying himself with the wealth of those whom he obeys; he glories in their fame, exalts himself by their nobility, and constantly feeds on borrowed grandeur. . . ." While such rare mergings of self and other do undeniably occur occasionally, I must join Jencks (1979: 65) in his judgment: "I find it hard to believe that any society is completely"—I would say, even largely—"successful in doing so" on a large scale. It seems to me utterly implausible to suppose that Barber's "enlarging of the self" could ever occur to such an extent as to embrace any very large body of people. I may well define myself *in relation to* my neighbor, even in a large body of people (the weak version of the Sandel thesis); but defining myself in relation to him, I can still tell the difference between him and me, his interests and mine (contrary to the claims of the strong version of that thesis).

sider whether or not that alleged link really does exist. In this analysis, two further distinctions will prove important, though they are rarely recognized in previous writings on the subject.

The first distinction concerns the direction in which the arrow (be it causal or logical) is thought to run. Welfare rights might be the cause of community attachments, or they might be the consequence of such attachments. Welfare rights might imply community attachments, or they might be implied by such attachments.

In neither case, however, would the mere existence of the arrow be quite enough to allow us to say that the welfare state is fully justified by communitarian principles. Suppose first that the arrow runs from the welfare state to community membership, so the welfare state causes or implies community attachments; and suppose a sense of community is morally important (as it is here presumed to be). Then the welfare state might appear to be justified as a means toward a morally important goal, in the perfectly ordinary way. But the welfare state might not be the only—or even the best—way of achieving that goal. The moral importance of the goal can impart moral importance to the means only if those are the best (or best feasible, or only) means to that end.

Suppose next that the arrow runs in the opposite direction, so it is the sense of community that leads to (causes or implies) welfare rights. Then the welfare state would no longer be a means to a morally important communitarian goal. Instead, the welfare state would be seen merely as a corollary or consequence of that morally important goal. But surely not all the corollaries and consequences of achieving a morally desirable goal are themselves morally desirable—or even morally acceptable. For that to be so, it must be the case that they are *necessary* consequences or corollaries of attaining that goal, i.e., *unavoidable* by-products of attaining that goal. Then, and only then, will the moral importance of the end impart moral importance to the by-products of attaining the end. Hence, the welfare state will be justified by communitarian values, where the arrow leads from the sense of community to the welfare state, only insofar as the welfare state *inevitably* follows from people's having a sense of community (or, alternatively, only insofar as removing the welfare state would *necessarily* weaken that sense of community).

The second distinction, as already intimated, is between a causal and a logical interpretation of the arrow linking the welfare state and community attachments. On the strong thesis, the relationship is a logical one: welfare rights logically imply or are constitutive of membership in the community, or vice versa. On the weaker thesis, the relationship is a purely empirical one: welfare entitlements are causally conducive to feelings (either on the part of beneficiaries or benefactors or both) of community attachment, or vice versa.

Establishing a logical link between welfare states and community membership would (subject to the above caveat) provide a strong communitarian justification for the welfare state. Establishing a merely contingent, empirical link would provide a substantially weaker one. How much weaker depends on the strength of the relationship, but there will always be a world of difference between even a very strong empirical link and a purely analytic one.

These two distinctions cut across one another to yield the four cells of Table 4.1. Model A represents the case in which welfare entitlements logically imply community membership: having welfare rights is just what it is to be a member of the community. Thus, in model A,

welfare rights → community membership (proposition A1)

or, equivalently,

~ (community membership) → ~ (welfare rights) (proposition A2).

Model B represents the converse case to that of model A. In model B, community membership is taken to imply welfare rights: having welfare rights is entailed by, but does not entail, your membership in the community. Symbolically, in model B,

community membership → welfare rights (proposition B1)

or, equivalently,

~ (welfare rights) → ~ (community membership) (proposition B2).

Model C represents the case in which welfare entitlements are empirically conducive to feelings of community attachment: the

TABLE 4.1   Variations on the Communitarian Theme

	Priority (logical or causal)	
Relationship	Welfare Entitlements	Community Membership or Attachments
logical	model A	model B
empirical	model C	model D

81

existence of welfare rights makes those who lodge claims under those rights or those who must honor them or both feel part of a community. Model D represents the converse case, in which community attachments are empirically conducive to welfare entitlements: where people feel themselves part of a community, they are likely to vest themselves and others in that community with welfare rights.

These possibilities are logically exhaustive, but they may not be mutually exclusive. It is perfectly possible—indeed, altogether likely—that there will be reciprocal interaction between models C and D, with welfare entitlements enhancing feelings of community attachment which in turn give rise to still further welfare rights. Similarly, there is the possibility that welfare rights may be both a necessary and sufficient condition of community membership, making the claims of both models B and A simultaneously true.

Likewise, there is no reason to suppose that the relationship between welfare provision and community attachments must be either neatly analytic or merely causal. It may well be some mixture of the two. Perhaps there is some "natural" pairing between models A and C (both of which give priority to welfare entitlements) and models B and D (both of which give priority to community attachments). But here again, there may be some room for mixing and matching between the logical model and the sociological one. It may, for example, turn out that welfare rights enjoy logical priority over community attachments (model A), but that, empirically, people have to feel themselves part of a community before they vest anyone with the welfare rights (model D).[6] Or it may happen that, logically, community comes before welfare entitlements (model B), but, sociologically, people have to feel themselves possessed of welfare rights before feeling themselves part of the community (model C).[7]

---

[6] Note Reiman's (1986: 195) analogous observation that, "There is no contradiction in the fact that the sense of justice might arise in community, while the latter already had to correspond to the requirements of justice in order really to be a community. That awareness of grammar . . . develops only among language-speakers does not contradict the fact that language presupposes that people's words are uttered according to some grammatical structure."

[7] Presumably what is really going on in these "unnatural" pairings is just that *both* models C and D are true. In that way, sociological priorities can both respect logical priorities and also throw up these surprising results as well. It should be emphasized, however, that the logical priorities do not strictly *entail* any sociological ones, so it is perfectly possible (though, presumably, empirically uncommon) for the two to diverge systematically.

In the discussion that follows, I discuss each of these models separately. I shall always do so, however, in a way that is sensitive to the possibility that two or more of them might be simultaneously true.

A

In assessing communitarian justifications for the welfare state, let us first consider the ostensibly logical relationships, models A and B. The strong thesis toward which model A points claims that welfare entitlements are somehow constitutive of community membership. That gives the former priority over the latter, not merely empirically but logically. If welfare rights are part of what constitutes a community—part of what it is for a group to *be* a group, and for an individual to be a member of it—then the relationship between welfare entitlements and communities is a strictly analytical one.

The strong thesis represented by model A seems so strong that it is scarcely credible that anyone should ever have embraced it. So far as I know, no one ever has—not explicitly, and with a full view to its complete implications, at least. As applied to other cognate areas of social life, however, some such model seems perfectly plausible; and the analogy to those other areas in which the model is plausible enough seems to have misled many commentators into adopting a similar model of the connection between welfare entitlements and community attachments.

The canonical text here is, of course, T. H. Marshall's 1949 lecture on "Citizenship and Social Class." There, Marshall (1949: 92) maintains that, "Citizenship is a status bestowed on those who are full members of a community. All who possess the status are equal with respect to the rights and duties with which that status is endowed."[8] He goes on to point out, however, that "there is no universal principle that determines what those rights and duties shall be." The history of the development of citizenship is for Marshall, then, the history of expansions of civil, political, and social welfare rights in the eighteenth, nineteenth, and twentieth centuries, respectively.

Whether Marshall means that citizenship implies rights or that rights imply citizenship is unclear. In some of his examples, Mar-

---

[8] That analysis of the notion of citizenship is in itself relatively uncontentious, though what follows from it is, of course, a subject of some considerable controversy. See Karst 1977.

shall seems to suggest that a society is giving a group of people new rights because it firmly believes that they are (and should be) full members of the community already, and it has only just now come to realize that those further rights are due to those who are fully members.[9] (This certainly seems to be what is going on in Marshall's discussion of eighteenth-century expansions of civil rights, for example.) That sort of connection would point to a model like B—or, if the link is thought to be empirical rather than logical, perhaps model D.

Sometimes, however, the connection Marshall sees seems to work in the other direction. By giving people the rights in question, we *make* them full members, on our understanding of what "full membership" consists in. This is clearly what is going on in the case of voting rights. The defining feature of membership in the political community, at least in a community that is governed by rulers whom it itself elects, is having the right to vote. By extending the suffrage in the nineteenth century, therefore, we did not give new rights to people who were antecedently members of the community in question. Rather, we made them members by giving them the rights in question. There, model A really is at work.

Having failed to distinguish these two possibilities sufficiently clearly in his discussion of the earlier stages of expanding rights of citizenship, it is only natural that Marshall should unwittingly be ambiguous as to which version of the thesis he wanted to run when it came to social welfare rights. Yet Marshall is deeply impressed with nineteenth-century extensions of political rights, and he often does try to force both the earlier and later cases into that mold. So, too, does Tawney (1932/1971: 217), in his gloss on Marshall. And so, too, does Parsons (1965), in applying Marshall's model to the problem of "full citizenship for the negro American."[10]

[9] The turn-of-the-century liberal communitarian argument for old-age pensions was that they constitute "a new and wider recognition of the membership of all in the community"—pension entitlements are "a right conferred by citizenship" (Freeden 1978: 201, 224).

[10] Parsons (1965: 720–21) writes, "With reference to the Negro in the United States, I state broadly that although the institutionalization of both legal rights and political participation constitutes the *necessary* conditions of much further progress toward full inclusion in the societal community, that it is not in itself *sufficient*. It also requires the implementation of the social component . . ." (Emphasis added). The language of necessary and sufficient conditions is, of course, indicative of a logical and not merely a sociological connection. It must be said, however, that Parsons himself seems not to see the distinction between the two sorts of connec-

In the universality/selectivity debate, referred to earlier, there are also often intimations of model A. "Means-testing" of social welfare benefits is said to "stigmatize" beneficiaries, symbolically branding them with a separate status. Granting universal benefits to everyone regardless of need is said, conversely, to symbolize the common status of one and all in the community (Deacon and Bradshaw 1983; Spicker 1984). Status, however, is a social creation, constituted out of symbols of one sort or another. While it is not always clear what exactly universalists want to be claiming, it usually seems that they mean to say that the symbols under discussion here do not merely reflect status and stigma constituted out of some *other* set of symbols; rather, they mean to be saying that the symbols contained in the means-test themselves constitute the status and stigma in question.

There is, of course, a perfectly good historical precedent and a perfectly honorable intellectual pedigree for the view that citizenship should be defined in terms of receiving certain sorts of benefits from the state. Walzer (1968: 205) traces to imperial Rome the view that "the citizen can be regarded first and most simply as the recipient of certain benefits that the state, and no other social or political organization, provides." This analysis re-emerges in Bodin's analysis of "a citizen" as "one who enjoys the common liberty and protection of authority." Later still, this analysis gets picked up, in other forms and for other purposes, by a variety of more liberal writers until, on Walzer's account, at least, it becomes *the* liberal theory of citizenship.[11]

What, then, are those state-provided benefits that constitute the defining features of citizenship? Naturally the answer varies with time and place. In Bodin's view, they amounted to the enjoyment of the King's peace and little more. This is "citizenship in the limited sense of a negative liberty to enjoy one's life and goods in immunity from arbitrary action by servants of the prince" (Pocock 1985: 44).

Suppose, however, we were living in another sort of community, where all four of the Four Freedoms are seen to be among those citizen-defining benefits that are (or should be) provided by the state. Then state provision of social welfare benefits to any given individual would, by that community's definition of itself,

---

tions at all clearly; and, if pressed, he would probably opt for the sociological interpretation, as his full title implies.

[11] Walzer's (1983: 79) own clear preference is for the converse argument, model B (i.e., that community membership entails welfare rights).

make that person a citizen. Welfare entitlements, on this analysis, would indeed be constitutive of membership in the community.

Having done my best to make model A look plausible, now let me set out what I regard as some devastating criticisms of its central claims. Model A maintains, positively, that if a person has welfare rights, then he is, by reason of that fact alone, a member of the community (proposition A1); and, negatively, if a person is not a member of the community, then he will have no welfare rights within that community (proposition A2). Model A furthermore maintains those propositions as logical truths. As such, they are meant to be universally and timelessly true. A single counterexample will count as decisive evidence against those logical claims.

Certainly it is (usually and broadly speaking) true that community membership is a necessary precondition of welfare entitlements. Poor though they may be, lifelong residents of Lusaka do not have legal claims to AFDC payments in New York. Examples such as that lend a fair bit of surface plausibility to model A's claims.

But "usually" and "broadly speaking" are just not enough to sustain claims of logical necessity. To say that if a person has welfare rights then he is a member of the community is to say that *every* person with welfare rights is a member of the community; to say that if a person is not a member of the community then he does not have welfare rights is to say that *no* nonmember has welfare rights.

That is clearly untrue. Even defining "community membership" as narrowly as possible—as "legal citizenship"—it is perfectly possible for noncitizens to be given welfare rights. For example, "in most European countries the first Factory Acts seek to protect women and children" by what can be described as giving them proto-welfare rights even though they were "at the time not considered citizens in the sense of legal equality" (Bendix and Rokkan 1964: 78). Or, for another example, the U.S. Supreme Court has recently ruled that resident aliens in the U.S. cannot be excluded, by reason of their noncitizenship alone, from any social welfare benefits to which they would otherwise be entitled under state law (Blackmun 1971: 371). Or, for a final example, until recently travelers in Britain were, if taken ill, treated free of charge in National Health Service Hospitals—even if they were neither citizens nor residents nor even citizens of British Commonwealth nations (Benn 1982: 52).

Defining "community membership" more broadly, the claim is

still untrue. In the anomic "national communities" of post-industrial societies, it certainly is not the case that everyone feels a "sense of solidarity" with everyone who has welfare rights under the law of the land. That it is possible, logically, for welfare rights to be vested in noncitizens or in members of a despised underclass proves that model A is wrong. It does not follow automatically from the fact that you have welfare rights that you are a member of the community; some who are not members of the community, narrowly or broadly defined, do have such rights. Such counterexamples may, of course, be atypical. But when the claim is one of analytic necessity, then a single counterexample, however atypical, is sufficient to disprove the claim.

More casually, and less formally, what model A asserts is this: there is some material possession or set of possessions (or, more precisely, some entitlement or set of entitlements thereto) that constitutes a defining feature of membership in the community.[12] But that implies an image of the community as being something far too monolithic and unitary to represent the typical (much less the universal) case. Somewhere, sometime, there may have been an example of such a community. But in the experience of advanced industrial societies, there are none.[13] The welfare state as we know it—which pragmatically, is the sort of welfare state which we are here trying to justify—is not characteristically found to be associated with that sort of community.

The analogy between social welfare rights and voting rights sys-

[12] The casualness of the informal arguments offered along these lines sometimes leaves it unclear what is being asserted is a variant of model A (i.e., proposition A1: if welfare rights, then community membership) or a variant of model B (i.e., proposition B2: if no welfare rights, then no community membership). What I say here would apply to either variant of the communitarian thesis with equal force.

These are supposed to be arguments to justify the welfare *state*, remember. So the community in question must be coterminous with the boundaries of the political unit. Talking in quasi-Aristotelian terms of the state as a community of communities will not help here (cf. Dewey 1927: chap. 5; Unger 1975: 281–89). Suppose membership in the wider community is derivative from membership in one of the narrower ones; and suppose further that each narrower community has material requisites for membership. Still, there will not necessarily be any common set of material requisites stipulated by the constituent communities which the welfare state that embraces them all can provide to make people members of the smaller (and hence the larger) community.

[13] There is some reason to doubt that even traditional village societies in Africa constituted such a unified community; see Sprinzak 1973. Despite their superficial homogeneity, the Scandinavian countries (which are often taken as the paradigm cases of the welfare state) clearly do not; see Eckstein (1966, chap. 3) and Allardt (1976; 1977) for evidence of this.

tematically misleads. Voting rights are constitutive of citizenship; without them, it is logically impossible to be a citizen (of a democracy, at least). But there are no such logical perquisites of a material sort for citizenship. Certainly there are none for citizenship, narrowly construed as full membership in the *political* community—and there have not been since the property qualification for voting was lifted with the Great Reforms of the nineteenth century. Neither are there any such logical perquisites of a material sort for citizenship, construed more broadly as full membership in the social community. Certainly there may be perquisites of a more empirical sociological sort. In a society where daily conversation revolves almost exclusively around the happenings on last night's television programs, it may be difficult to participate fully in the life of the community if you do not have access to a television set (Townsend 1954; 1962; 1979). But that difficulty is of a practical rather than logical sort. The connection toward which it points is of the form of model C or D, not model A.

Nor is it at all surprising that there should be no such logical perquisites to membership in the sorts of broadly pluralistic societies in which welfare states are standardly set. Even if there are no gaping ethnic divisions, there nonetheless is typically some substantial variation across the national community in people's goals, aspirations, tastes, and lifestyles. In consequence of this diversity, there is and can be no nationwide consensus as to what constitutes material perquisites for full membership in the social community, in quite the same way that voting rights can be universally agreed to constitute full membership in a democratic political community.

To use just one example from Townsend's (1979) masterly attempt at finding some such standard: it may well be true, statistically, that most Britons eat meat on at least four days a week; but those who do not (either by reason of their own dietary preferences, or by reason of their budgetary constraints) hardly count as "social outcasts" in any literal sense of the term (Piachaud 1981).[14] They may not be participating fully in the life of the community.

---

[14] Ironically, in his initial paper, Townsend (1954: 133) himself had made much of the similar point that "things which are treated as necessaries by one group may not be so regarded by another. A few drinks in a pub on a Saturday night after watching the local football match may be as necessary, in the conventional sense, to membership of the poorest stratum of society as a Savile Row suit and business meetings over lunch at the Savoy [are] to membership of a wealthier stratum of society."

But they have not thereby been stripped of membership in it, either. Membership is simply not predicated upon such things.

The error here is analogous to one committed by Lord Devlin (1965) in his plea for the legal enforcement of social morality. At root, his argument comes down to the proposition that social cohesion depends upon a sense of shared morality, and that social cohesion would be lost if the law were to allow violations of that shared moral code to go unpunished. Hart's (1967) devastating challenge was simply to demand that Devlin show him a single tenet of the shared morality such that, were the law to fail to enforce it, society would be rent asunder. The implication of the long silence since that challenge was laid is that there is none.

Here I would enter an analogous challenge to advocates of the community membership model of welfare rights. Produce a single example of a good (or set of goods) that is (or could plausibly be) dispensed by the welfare state without which people could not claim still to be members in good standing of their society. Perhaps there is some such community, or some such commodity, in some society that is unknown to me. I can think of none for any society with which I am familiar.

A second criticism of model A would be that, even if all those objections were waived, it would still fail to provide a welfarist rationale for welfare services. Saying, as model A does, that welfare entitlements are a necessary precondition for community membership is to say that they are a necessary means to that end. But to say that is to say that welfare services are justified (if at all) not because they promote welfare, but rather because they promote community membership. Any contribution that social welfare services might actually make to people's actual welfare is, on this account, purely incidental to their true purpose and real function. And that is an utterly inadequate account of what is really going on in the welfare state.

Just for the sake of argument, let us imagine that we can find some country whose national boundaries truly do encapsulate a single, unified social community. Imagine, for a concrete example, Norway before the influx of "guest workers" and without the Lapps (Eckstein 1966). Suppose, even more implausibly, that there really were some resource that the state can dispense that is truly required for a person to be a "full member" of that society. Let us imagine that this good is health care: a Norwegian incapable of skiing or sailing would be deemed to be just not a Norwegian at all. I have every confidence that this sort of characterization would be regarded as pure caricature by any serious student of Norwegian society; but just for the sake of argument, let us suppose it is accurate. Finally, let us suppose that the state assumes responsibility for doing whatever it can to make sure everyone within its jurisdiction has whatever is required to be a "full member" of the larger community. A Norwegian state, guided by the above vision of Norwegian society, would thus be led to dispense health care generously to all those in need of it.

In that example, a state engaged in dispensing resources which people require in order to be full members of the community would also be dispensing resources which people require to promote their welfare, i.e., health care. But that is only because what people are supposed to require to be "full members" of their society happens also to be something that they require to promote their welfare.

Any connection between the two is purely contingent, and often imperfect. Consider the case of ancient Athens. Promoting full membership in the community, as ancient Athenians conceptualized their community, required little more of the state than that it provide public baths and gymnasiums (Walzer 1983: 70–71); to promote full membership of people in the Athenian community, the state did not need to provide them with a general guarantee even of subsistence itself.[15] Thus, a state acting on a communitarian rationale will not necessarily pursue welfarist policies. Certainly it may stop well short of promoting people's full range of welfare interests.[16]

Finally, recall that saying that welfare rights are somehow constitutive of valuable community attachments would provide a strong justification for instituting such welfare rights only if they provided the *only* way of constituting such attachments. If they were merely one among many ways, then some further argument would be required to show that welfare rights are superior to all the alternative mechanisms that might be available.

Here it seems that no easy generalizations are available. Every-

[15] The Athenian state did intervene to guarantee corn for all in times of general shortage, did provide pensions to the disabled, and did provide a small per diem to those discharging public duties (like attending the Assembly or serving on juries) that served as the functional equivalent of an old-age pension (Walzer 1983: 70–71). The point remains that full membership in the Athenian community did not, in and of itself, guarantee subsistence: in times of nonshortage, able-bodied citizens who declined to attend the Assembly were still allowed to starve.

[16] The Athenian example may seem far-fetched and atypical. But remember, the claim here is a logical one, and one counterexample disproves it.

thing depends upon the "rules of membership" in each community, as that community defines them and itself; there may, or may not, be alternatives to constituting membership out of welfare entitlements just depending upon what the rules of any given community actually stipulate. A few limited generalizations do seem possible, however. Note, first, that membership is essentially a matter of status, and that status is essentially a matter of symbols. From this it follows that, even if that community's rules of membership do stipulate material preconditions of the sort that welfare rights may help people to meet, what matters is not the material possessions per se but rather the symbolic importance that the rules attach to them. This, in turn, suggests that, if a community were so inclined, it could always transfer those symbols of community attachment to anything else. (This is what happened when the property qualification was written out of electoral laws in the nineteenth century, for example.) The upshot of this argument is that, even if a community's rules of membership at present required the granting of welfare rights, it could always rewrite those rules so that would no longer be a precondition of people's membership in the community. Whether granting the rights or rewriting the rules is the easier, or morally preferable, strategy it is hard to say in perfectly general terms. But in any particular instance it might be. So even if model A successfully comes through all the obstacles mentioned above, it may still falter at this last hurdle.

Model A, then, threatens to fail on three counts. First, there seem to be no material goods or entitlements (of a sort that could be secured by the welfare state, anyway) that constitute necessary preconditions for membership in the community, in any communities as we now know them. Second, even if there were, model A would not provide a welfarist rationale for the welfare state; and for that reason it would stop short of justifying necessarily the full range of functions that we think even a minimal welfare state ought to perform. Third, even if welfare rights were one way of constituting community attachments, there may be others having nothing to do with welfare entitlements; and if community is our goal, those other mechanisms might in any given instance be able to substitute for welfare entitlements.

B

Model B argues the converse case. The connection between welfare entitlements and community membership is still seen to be a purely logical, analytic one. But whereas on model A welfare entitlements are seen as implying community membership, on model B that relationship is reversed. On model B, community membership implies welfare rights: if a person is a member of the community, then that person has welfare rights within that community (proposition B1); and if a person does not have welfare rights within a community, then he is not a member of that community (proposition B2).

This is perhaps the most popular variation on the communitarian justification of the welfare state. On the alternative reading of Marshall's lecture (1949) sketched above, the notion that certain groups of people are indisputably citizens comes first; and social welfare rights come afterwards, as a derivation from that fact. Politically, that is precisely the sort of ratchet argument that the poor would find most effective against those who would concede "cheap" symbolic issues of formal status but then strive to withhold the material benefits that might be required to give substance to that status.[17] But philosophically, too, there seems to be much that can be said on behalf of model B's central propositions. Once questions of membership are settled, certain things (welfare entitlements among them) just naturally seem to follow. Rather against the grain of his own broader conventionalist account of justice, Walzer (1983: 79) observes, "No community can allow its members to starve to death when there is food available to feed them; no government can stand passively by at such a time—not if it claims to be a government of or by or for the community." And the example seems compelling: "The indifference of Britain's rulers during the Irish potato famine in the 1840s is a sure sign that Ireland was a colony, a conquered land, no real part of Great Britain." There, it really does seem to be true that "no welfare rights" implies "no community membership" just as one of model B's central propositions (proposition B2) maintains.

In assessing the claim that "certain things, welfare entitlements among them, just naturally seem to follow from community membership," it is crucial what interpretation we place on the words "naturally" and "follow." Perhaps there is a strong empirical, so-

---

[17] As Walzer (1980: 26) has the oppressed challenging the liberal hypocrisy, "Do the middle classes claim to increase the general prosperity? Let them increase *our* prosperity [then]. Do the police claim to defend public security? Let them defend *our* security [then]. Do the rulers of the welfare state claim to maximize the happiness of the greatest number? Let them maximize *our* happiness [then]." See further Goodin 1980: chap. 5.

ciological tendency for the one to follow hard on the heels of the other. But sociological links are the province of models C and D. With model B, what we are looking for is a logical link of some sort.

Model B, again, has two central components. It asserts, positively, that if a person is a member of a community, then he has welfare rights within that community (proposition B1). Negatively, model B asserts that if a person does not have welfare rights within a community, he is not a member of that community (proposition B2). And here, as before, those are claims of analytic necessity. A single counterexample will suffice to disprove them.

For one such counterexample, consider the case of ancient Athens, discussed above. There, people who were indisputably full members of the Athenian community did not thereby acquire anything recognizable as "welfare rights"—they did not enjoy a general guarantee even of bare subsistence. It may of course be true that Athens was atypical in this regard. But where the claim is one of analytic necessity, a single counterexample—however atypical—will suffice to disprove the claim.

Some might try to save this claim by reformulating it. Instead of being a claim about community in general, the reformulated claim would pertain only to our own community. The Athenian counterexample, such commentators may concede, shows that there is nothing in the general notion of community that implies welfare rights. But, they would go on to say, there is something in our notion of *our own* community that makes membership in it entail certain sorts of welfare rights (to subsistence, a decent standard of housing with minimal amenities, etc.).

That rejoinder will not do. The communitarian ideal is merely to produce *a* sense of community—of solidarity and significance— among a group of people. *Which* sense of community is evoked is, from the bare communitarian perspective, a matter of utter indifference. The goal is to produce a community, not a community organized around any particular principle rather than any other.

From the bare communitarian perspective, then, there is nothing holy about whatever may be entailed by our own notion of our own community. Even if our own idea of our own community means that membership entails welfare rights, the crucial point is this: logically, we could equally well organize a community around principles that did not have any such entailments. (Empirically, of course, it may be easier to organize a community around a sense of community that is already extant among us; but that would be an empirical, contingent fact that would be insufficient to sustain the strong claim of analytic necessity contained in model B.)

As I argued at the outset of this section, corollaries of a morally important goal like community can derive moral importance themselves from that of the goal of which they are by-products only if they are *unavoidable* by-products of attaining that goal. The force of the Athenian counterexample is to show that that is not true. There are ways of attaining communitarian goals that do not entail vesting anyone with welfare rights.[18]

There is one last objection to model B that also parallels an argument I made against model A. As applied to model A, the objection was that where community membership was the end in view (and welfare rights merely a means), there was no welfarist rationale for welfare programs; and that being so, many aspects of people's welfare needs might go unmet by a "welfare state" built on those foundations. Here, the converse state of affairs obtains. Where welfare entitlements are the end in view (and community membership merely a means), there is not necessarily any communitarian rationale for welfare programs; and that being so, many aspects of people's community needs may go unmet by a welfare state built on those foundations. That is the parallel problem with model B.

Saying that community membership entails welfare entitlements may be interpreted as saying that expanding our sense of community is a necessary means to the end of promoting people's welfare. But if welfare is the end, then there are lots of other noncommunitarian ways of providing for it. And, perhaps more importantly, there are lots of noncommunitarian reasons for providing for it. The communitarian rationale of promoting a "sense of solidarity" is only one among many. Others include guaranteeing social peace or as insurance (Goodin 1976: 111–12; Dryzek and Goodin 1986).

Less cynically, the reason may be to do our moral duty by the poor. While certainly more high-minded, even that does not count as properly communitarian. "Communitarian ideals call for *sympathetic* concern, a caring for the other 'as if it were oneself,' for

---

[18] People's welfare is sometimes defined (by themselves, or others) as consisting at least in part in membership in some larger social community. Insofar as that is true, then to that extent it is analytically true that any steps taken to further their membership in a community will also contribute to that aspect of their welfare. Still, we do not ordinarily regard the Immigration and Naturalization Service as part and parcel of the welfare state.

some measure of identification with the fate of the other"; and that in turn implies that "communitarian ideals require more than a concern for welfare" of people, because that can be too "impersonal" (Benn 1982: 52–53).[19] Thus, even if motivated by high moral principles of this abstract form, welfare states would lack the solidaristic foundations required for them to have a properly communitarian rationale.

Just as in my criticism of model A it is true that welfare states lacking a properly welfarist rationale may not attend properly to the full range of people's welfare needs, so too in this criticism of model B it is true that welfare states lacking a properly communitarian rationale may not fully or generally serve the cause of promoting a sense of community. Even if model B is right that welfare rights are entailed by community membership, there is more to community than welfare rights and them alone. Minimally, community feeling requires that the welfare rights be vested for the right reasons. But various other public symbols and rituals of membership would surely also be required. Even insofar as the welfare state could discharge such functions, there would be no reason to expect a welfare state built on a welfarist rather than communitarian rationale to do so.

Thus, both attempts at finding logical foundations for the link between welfare entitlements and community membership fail, and they fail for analogous reasons. Model B claims that welfare rights constitute a necessary condition, model A a sufficient one, for realization of the communitarian ideal. But neither claim is true. Contrary to the claims of model B, there are many other ways of constituting community membership, and welfare rights are not even necessarily one. Contrary to the claims of model A, there are many other ways of grounding welfare rights, and community membership is not even necessarily one. From this follows the further criticism that, where welfare rights are seen as a means to community (as in model A), the lack of a properly welfarist rationale for welfare rights means that many aspects of people's welfare might go unprotected; and where community membership is seen as a means to welfare entitlements (as in model B), the lack of a properly communitarian rationale for the welfare state means that many aspects of the welfare state might be derived from other

[19] Hobsbawm (1975: 473) comments similarly on Robespierre's draft Declaration of the Rights of Man: "His view (article XII) was that 'the assistance required by poverty is a debt owed by the rich to the poor'; but a society in which the rich pay for poor relief is far from a fraternal one."

sources and serve other ends. Taken together, such criticisms of the first two models suggests that welfare entitlements neither imply nor are implied by communitarianism—not, at least, in any properly logical sense.

At root, models A and B fail because the meanings and implications of community membership are not fixed in the nature of things, as such models would tend to imply (Dewey 1927: chap. 5; Walzer 1983: 79). Some communities might define themselves in such a way that welfare entitlements necessarily follow from—or are followed by—community membership. But there is no necessary reason that they must, and many (including virtually all welfare states in the modern world) do not. That being so, models tracing any analytically necessary, logical link between welfare entitlements and community membership must be rejected.

C

That is the conclusion that emerges from considering models A and B separately. As remarked at the outset of this section, however, it is perfectly possible for the models to be true when combined in various ways, even if they are not true in isolation from one another.

The first and most obvious possibility is that both model A and model B are simultaneously true. That is to say, welfare entitlements might be both a necessary *and* a sufficient condition of community membership. To assess that claim, we must consider to what extent these two models in conjunction might be able to evade the criticisms levelled at each of them in isolation.

The conjunction of model A and model B succeeds in meeting some of the criticisms lodged in sections II.A and II.B above. That is particularly true of the complaint that welfare states justified by model A lack a welfarist rationale, and that ones justified by model B lack a communitarian one. In the conjunction, model A will provide the communitarian rationale for welfare services that model B alone lacks, and model B will provide the welfarist rationale that model A alone lacks.[20]

The other, more serious criticisms remain as applicable as before, however. In the conjunction of models A and B, the claims of both models A and B are supposed to be true: welfare entitlements are therefore supposed to be both necessary and sufficient conditions of community attachment. Thus, counterexamples

[20] I am grateful to Katrin Flikschuh for this observation.

where there are welfare entitlements without community attachments will continue to undermine the claim that they are necessary—and of community attachments without welfare entitlements that they are sufficient—to produce that result. Having
established that welfare entitlements are neither necessary nor sufficient for community attachment, it necessarily follows that they
cannot be both.

Alternatively, we may try combining models A and B disjunc-
tively, rather than conjunctively. That would amount to a claim
that welfare entitlements are always and everywhere either necessary *or* sufficient conditions of community membership.

That claim has a certain amount of surface plausibility to it. It
would seem that model B can account for all the counterexamples
lodged against model A, and vice versa. The visitor, taken ill,
being allowed to use U.K. National Health Service facilities embarrasses model A: there, clearly, welfare rights do not imply community membership; you do not become a British citizen by being
given a right to an NHS bandage. But that result is perfectly consistent with model B's claim that community membership implies
welfare rights: to say that all members must have such rights is
not necessarily to say that only members should have them. Conversely, the Athenian citizen, though clearly a member of the
polis, being denied any welfare rights embarrasses model B but is
perfectly consistent with model A: to say that all those with welfare rights are members is not necessarily to say that only those
with welfare rights are members.

Notice what is happening in these examples, though. If, in any
given instance, welfare rights do not imply community membership, then that is ascribed to the influence of model B; if they do,
it is ascribed to model A. If community membership does not imply welfare rights, that is ascribed to the influence of model A; if
it does, that is put down to model B. Every possible outcome is
covered by one or the other elements of this disjunctive combination of the two models. It is like saying, "Every animal in the
world is either a ferret or it is not a ferret": true, but utterly unin-
formative.

The same sorts of objections, notice, could be lodged against attempts to rescue these models by weakening the form of logical
necessity at work in them. Suppose we were searching for some
way in which welfare entitlements might be conceptually tied to
community attachments, without being either a necessary or sufficient condition of them. Here is an analogy that might tempt us:

it is not a necessary truth that friends will come to each other's aid, but neither is it merely a contingent causal claim that they usually will do so. What that thought points to is, presumably, something along these lines: "It is a necessary truth that friends will *sometimes* come to each other's aid."

Both model A and model B can be rewritten along these lines. The former would claim, now, that it is necessarily true that welfare entitlements sometimes imply community attachment. The latter, rewritten, would now claim that it is necessarily true that community membership sometimes implies welfare entitlements.

But how are we to refute such claims? To deny revised models, we would have to find some welfare entitlements that are never associated with community membership. I am prepared to believe that somewhere, sometime, everything has been associated with anything else in the mind of man. Human history is sufficiently rich in diverse cultures, and social symbolisms sufficiently flexible, that it would certainly be reckless to claim that anything along these lines is ever impossible. But, just as those who would resist my arguments would complain that a single counterexample is insufficient to disprove anything, so too would I claim that a single example is insufficient to prove anything very interesting, either.

If a single example or counterexample is deemed insufficient to establish anything conclusive either way, then we have passed into the world of empirical rather than purely logical relations.[21] It is to those I now turn.

D

The empirical sociological links remain yet to be explored. Model C is the sociological analogue of model A, treating welfare entitlements as the cause of community attachment. Model D is the sociological analogue of model B, treating community feelings as the cause of welfare entitlements. Sociologically, the influence between fellow-feeling and welfare provision is so obviously reciprocal that it hardly pays to try to keep the analysis of these two models separate; and in my later discussion I shall make no effort

[21] Some may insist that the connection between community attachments and welfare entitlements is neither neatly analytic (such that they are refutable by a single counterexample) nor merely causal, but something in between. Here, however, we pass into the murky waters of "synthetic a priori" statements, from which few return.

to do so.[22] Yet, analytically, these truly are two distinct paths of influence. So at least at the outset, there might be some merit in trying to describe them separately, at least.

The distinction between models C and D might be linked to the early and late writings of Richard Titmuss. In his distinguished volume in the Official Civil History of the Second World War, Titmuss (1950: 506, 508) seems to endorse model D's suggestion that feelings of a shared fate and a community of interest come first, and that the sharing of social resources follows from that:

> That all were engaged in war whereas only some were afflicted with poverty and disease had much to do with the less constraining, less discriminating scope and quality of the wartime social services. . . . The reality of military disaster and the threat of invasion in the summer of 1940 urged on these tendencies in social policy. The mood of the people changed and, in sympathetic response, values changed as well. If dangers were to be shared, then resources should also be shared. Dunkirk, and all that the name evokes, was an important event in the war-time history of the social services.[23]

In his later writings on *The Gift Relationship*, however, Titmuss (1971) seems to place more emphasis upon model C's argument that giving and being given to engenders a sense of community (which, on model D's logic, will then go on to encourage still more giving). These themes are variously echoed: in Tawney's hope that "expansion of collective provision" will produce a "qualitative change in the character of society," moving it "towards the conversion of a class-ridden society into a community in fact" (1932/1971: 221–22); in the British Labour Party's claim that "as we develop our social services we can encourage a growing understanding of our common needs and reduce the pressure of the narrow personal acquisitive instincts of a capitalist society" (1952/1986:

[22] As Walzer (1983: 65) puts it, "Mutual provision breeds mutuality. So the common life is simultaneously the prerequisite of provision and one of its products."

[23] Of course, that phenomenon admits of noncommunitarian explanations as well as communitarian ones. If fates really are shared, and each person's interests inextricably bound up with each other's then the only way one can promote his own interests is to promote everyone's; and therefore actions serving the interests of all might be motivated, not by any genuine concern for others' interests, but merely out of concern for one's own (see chapter 3 for a similar argument). Or, again, where risks are genuinely shared by all alike, social welfare services might be motivated by the individualistic logic of risk-pooling and mutual insurance (Dryzek and Goodin 1986).

169); and in Myrdal's discussion of the way in which the welfare state "creates" social harmony (1960: 56–60).[24]

There are basically two ways of running an argument such as this. One points to a *direct* link, running in either direction, between community attachments and communal provision for people's welfare needs. The root idea here is that "altruism fosters altruism" (Singer 1973: 319). The link being seen as a direct one, it is the very fact of the state's providing welfare benefits (rather than any further facts about what happens as a result of such provision) that generates fellow-feeling and community attachments.

The trouble with all sociological models tracing a direct link, in whichever direction, between welfare services and community attachments is this. The link in view derives from certain contingent features in the design or administration of welfare policies, rather than from any essential feature of the notion of welfare benefits per se. That being so, welfare programs might not—and often do not—serve the purposes that communitarians set for them. At the very least, it must be said that welfare programs are sometimes not the best, and certainly not the only, ways of serving those goals.[25]

All the empirical evidence suggests that what is crucial in building up a sense of community attachment is interpersonal communication and the fostering of interpersonal networks of that sort. The more people see and interact—socially, economically, and especially politically (Barber 1984: chap. 9)—with one another within a group, the stronger a sense of community they will have to that group.[26] Insofar as social welfare programs are designed and administered in such a way that they promote face-to-face interactions between people, they can serve to promote such a sense of community. But a good many welfare programs are not designed in that way; and a good many of the things that are even more responsible for such interpersonal interactions (even limiting our

[24] All this, of course, just echoes the claims of the founders of French sociology—Comte (1848/1953: 101–3) and Durkheim (1925/1961)—that shared social experiences will evoke the "collective conscience" and the morality nascent within it.

[25] It is particularly telling, in this connection, that in his 300-page celebration of the sources of cohesion within the Norwegian community, Eckstein (1966: 85–87) sees fit to devote only three to the role of the welfare state.

[26] See, e.g.: Deutsch et al. 1957; Jacob and Toscano 1964; Hauser 1965; Kasarda and Janowitz 1974; Laumann 1973. Communitarian defenders of the welfare state, such as Walzer (1980) and Dworkin (1985: 211), regularly emphasize the connection between community attachment and participation in the economic, social, and political life of the community, and defend welfare entitlements as a way of fostering that participation.

attention here to things done by the *state*) have little to do with the welfare state.

Social services that are designed in such a way that they promote community-building social interactions might be described, generically, as services characterized by "collective consumption" or "common enjoyment." The crucial feature of those cases is that "*A* enjoys something *with B*," rather than *A* and *B* just enjoying the same things separately (Barry 1965: 231). Examples of cases where the "publicness" of public goods seems to have been engineered in, as a matter of policy in order to promote social integration, might be state schools, mass transport, and the public wards of state hospitals (Margolis 1955).[27]

In other cases, the manner of *administration* of a social service is what does most to promote community-building interpersonal interactions between claimants. The benefits that families derive from transfer payments might themselves be enjoyed completely in isolation from other families; but administrative regulations that require claimants for Supplementary Benefits to attend local social security offices for interviews, or that claimants for old-age pensions or family allowances claim those benefits in person at the village post office, promotes social contact and interaction among those who regularly find themselves sharing the same waiting room or standing in the same queue.[28]

Many social welfare programs are neither designed nor administered in such a way as to promote social interaction, and hence community feelings, however. In the U.S., social security payments are made by checks that are posted to recipients; and, given the popularity of drive-in banking among the elderly who find walking difficult, it is likely that many will rarely stand in queues even to cash those checks, much less to collect them. Medicare and Medicaid will at least partially reimburse people for private or semi-private rooms in the hospital. And so on.

What that goes to show is simply that welfare programs do not

[27] For a poignant description of British National Health Service hospitals in these terms, see Titmuss (1974: 145–51).

[28] Note that Charles Booth's original intention was the opposite when he proposed the rule that "pensions should be payable weekly, at a certain time, at the Post Office and should normally be payable to the pensioner only"; viz., his hope was that "not only would this help to prevent fraud by making it impossible to apply through more than one Post Office but, more importantly, the better-off would so dislike queuing up with the hoi polloi that they would be effectively discouraged" from claiming pension benefits that they do not really need (Collins 1965: 251).

have to be administered or designed in community-enhancing ways. Provision for social welfare needs can be, and often is, made in such a way that people can consume the services privately rather than collectively. Even in the U.K., old-age pensioners have the option of having their pension sent to them in the form of a check or deposited directly into their bank accounts. If they opt instead for wandering down to the local post office to collect the cash, then that is likely to be because they enjoy the social contact with those whom they have already come to regard as "mates." Far from causing (or even importantly reinforcing) community attachments, this form of welfare administration merely acknowledges attachments that already exist.

Furthermore, if interpersonal interactions and networks are what give rise to community attachment, then anything that the state does will make only a very limited contribution toward that end. Let us suppose that it is true, as this hypothesis maintains it is, that simply standing in queue together breeds a sense of community. If it is the conversations that one strikes up as one stands in queue that make one feel part of a community, then it does not matter what one is queuing *for*. Queuing for bread, or concert tickets, or entry to the after-Christmas sales would be expected to have the same effect as queuing for Supplementary Benefits or an old-age pension. Or, again, if it is riding a bus together with others that makes one feel part of a community, then it does not matter one bit whether the bus is owned by the city and run as a community service or whether it is owned by a private, profit-making corporation. In short, many of the things that give rise to social interaction, and hence community attachment, have little to do with the state.

Focus next on those things that the state *can* do to promote social interaction, and hence a sense of community. Even among these, social welfare services play a very minor role. To revert to one of the examples offered above, if standing in the same queue at the local post office is what makes one feel part of a community, then the state does as much or more to promote a sense of community by selling stamps as by providing Supplementary Benefits or Family Allowances or old-age pensions that are to be collected at the same teller's window.

One of the most important influences on social interaction is, presumably, the pattern and stability of residential accommodation. Low-density or high-turnover or socially segregated neighborhoods reduce interaction between people. Medium to high-density or low-turnover or socially integrated neighborhoods increase it. There might be a fair bit that governments can do to shape residential patterns and stability—and to shape in turn the social interactions that follow from them—through laws and regulations governing land-use planning and prohibiting discrimination on the basis of race, ethnicity, or social class (Hauser 1965: 96; Schorr 1986: 44–48). But those have really rather little to do with the state's welfare function per se. The contribution that can be made through welfare-state interventions in the housing market (i.e., public-housing programs) is strictly limited in comparison. It is largely confined to things like locating state-subsidized housing amidst privately owned housing (as with government housing in Australia, or private homes bought with the assistance of Veterans Administration or Federal Housing Administration loans in the U.S.)[29] rather than on council estates (as in the U.K.). How big a contribution public-housing policy might, in this way, make to community building depends naturally upon how large the public program is relative to private market provision. Perhaps it is significant that, in the cases just mentioned, it is the countries with the relatively smaller public-housing programs that attempt to integrate public housing into private neighborhoods.[30]

Another locus of community attachment is the workplace. An impressive array of social psychological findings confirms that "work roots a person in society" (Schorr 1986: 37); unemployment, conversely, not only deprives people of contact in the workplace itself but also leads people to withdraw from various other social activities, too (Eisenberg and Lazarsfeld 1938; Jahoda 1979; 1982; Jahoda, Lazarsfeld, and Zeisel 1933; Marsden 1982). So the first thing that the state can do, to promote community attachments in this connection, is to strive for full employment. Another important influence on social interaction and the sense of community, for those who are in work, has to do with the organization of

[29] Though these U.S. institutions have always had a good record of integrating public housing into private neighborhoods, they historically had a bad record of intentionally perpetuating racially segregated neighborhoods (Grier and Grier 1965: 530).

[30] Where, as in Scandinavia, we find a large program of public housing integrated into private neighborhoods and private apartment complexes, that seems to be more a matter of model D than of model C. There, people already feel part of one and the same community, so private owners do not object to having lots of public housing clients living around them (Gulbrandsen and Torgersen 1974). Whether such policies of integrating large-scale public housing into private neighborhoods would work to build a sense of community where it is antecedently lacking is another question altogether.

work. Decentralized, fragmented mechanistic production tech-
niques reduce interaction between fellow workers; patterns of
work organization that bring people together, creatively collabo-
rating on some shared project, engender a sense of community
(among workmates, anyway—whether or not it spills over to any
larger groups is unclear). Again, there are things that governments
can do, through industrial policy or labor law, to encourage these
sorts of work patterns. The only question, both with regard to
these policies and with regard to full-employment policy more
generally, is whether these are, strictly speaking, part of the state's
welfare function. Both macro-economic management and mandatory industrial democracy seem to go well beyond the minimalist
tasks taken, in chapter 1, to define the welfare state.

Perhaps as important, ultimately, as any of these other policies
in creating an integrated national community is cultural policy.
This is the particular emphasis of writers in the new nations,
trying to meld a single national community out of diverse tribal
loyalties (Mazrui 1972). But notice similarly that Anthony Crosland
(1956: 528), having despaired of traditional socialist instruments
for realizing the "cooperative ideal," concludes that it is "in the
cultural field" where "such an ideal . . . is practicable as well as
relevant." His shopping list of required reforms is a curiously
mixed bag:

> We need not only higher exports and old-age pensions, but
> more open-air cafes, brighter and gayer streets at night, later
> closing-hours for public houses, more local repertory thea-
> tres, better and more hospitable hoteliers and restaurateurs,
> brighter and cleaner eating-houses, more riverside cafes, more
> pleasure-gardens, on the Battersea model, more murals and
> pictures in public places, . . . and so on ad infinitum.[31] (Cros-
> land 1956: 521–22)

[31] August Heckscher (1963: 240–41, 220), President Kennedy's adviser on culture
and the arts, writes similarly: "The welfare state might be defined as that which
seeks by concerted action to increase the private comforts and satisfactions of its
citizens. The state as we have been interpreting it has an essentially different objective. It seeks through concerted action to lift men above private comforts and to
give them some vision of a public happiness. Life does not end with house-keep-
ing. Beyond the menial, uniform, generalized tasks of assuring work and subsistence to all lies the whole wide field where circumstances create opportunities, and
opportunities lead into all spheres of life. No one has said that government must
be concerned only with collecting garbage and building sewers. It also builds
schools. And if it educates the citizens may it not also inspire them? Might it not
also entertain and delight them? The state must see its task in this broad light, for
of all the institutions of the modern world it provides the only hope for lifting men

Some of these proposals, it must be said, seem to have little to do with "culture," high or low. But what may be said of all of them is that they promote opportunities for doing things *in public*. It is joint action and shared experience, Crosland rightly perceives, that is the sine qua non for common culture. Here again, however, the role of the welfare state is strictly limited. Of Crosland's many examples of measures that governments might take to promote public interaction and the common culture that grows out of it, none has anything at all to do with the state's welfare functions.[32]

One aspect of cultural policy that arguably does connect up with the state's welfare function is educational policy. By requiring the attendance of all school-aged children at state-run schools, the state can do much to force social interaction and hence to build a spirit of community. It can do more still by requiring all schools to teach to a common curriculum (Vincent and Plant 1984: chap. 8).

But, first, it is disputable whether compulsory state schooling should be seen as an aspect of social welfare policy at all. Certainly it is meant to make people better off. But so too is national road-building. Schooling, like public-health programs, can equally plausibly be seen as national investments in social infrastructure—as investments in human capital. What lends particular credence to that alternative interpretation is the fact that participation in programs like schooling and public health is compulsory rather than optional (Bendix and Rokkan 1964: 88). That rather suggests that

---

out of the [narrowly] social sphere, and letting them breathe again in the clear air of the public scene." Heckscher is particularly concerned with cultivation of the arts and with "public works projects," on the grounds that a community "can be fully functioning as a community only when it is producing some things that survive the day and come to have a spirit and existence of their own" (1963: 235). Again, none of this has much to do with the welfare state per se.

[32] The same might be said of Walzer's (1982: 12) similar remark that "the idea of the welfare state isn't exhausted by a modest effort, and it wouldn't be exhausted by a major effort, at income distribution, risk control, relief for the poor, and health and unemployment insurance. The word 'welfare' means 'the state or condition of well-being,' and well-being is a moral as well as a material condition. Communal provision is required for the whole range of social goods that make up what we think of as our way of life. Not my way of life or yours, but ours, the life we couldn't have if we didn't plan for it and pay for it together. Not subsistence only, but science, culture, schooling, communication, travel, natural beauty: all this is the public business. State officials with state money sponsor scientific research, underwrite the arts, support educational institutions, provide scholarships to talented students, contribute to public television and radio, build highways, run railroads, maintain national parks and wildlife reserves. These activities are vital to the quality of our lives and to the heritage we hope to leave to our children." So they are; I simply would query whether they can be credibly presented as part and parcel of the state's *welfare* functions.

the programs are not really aimed (not exclusively, anyway) at promoting the welfare (not the self-defined welfare, anyway) of the recipients themselves.

Even if we regard compulsory state schooling as a welfare state activity, however, it is unclear whether it will necessarily have the community-building consequences claimed for it. Social interaction is the key, as I have argued above. And, as advocates of a more thoroughgoing method of day-release, community-based instruction are anxious to emphasize, isolating students in special-purpose educational establishments for the bulk of the day prevents them from interacting in any meaningful way with the rest of the community at all (Newman and Oliver 1967).

Furthermore, even within the school, there might not be much social interaction between different types of students. In a system of neighborhood schools, there will be no more social mixing in the school than outside it: one's classmates will not be importantly different from one's playmates. Even if school catchment areas cut across sociological divisions, streaming within the school, although perfectly defensible on academic grounds, may lead to sociologically homogeneous classes within sociologically heterogeneous schools. And even if one does mix with different sorts of people in school, it remains an open question to what extent attitudes (much less friendships) growing out of those early experiences will survive into later life. Thus, the contribution of state schooling to community-building, though perhaps greater than that of any other program, may end up being rather small.

Finally, as mention of integrating public schools should remind us, there is always the danger of backlash. The aim of forcing people to associate with one another in obtaining or utilizing various publicly provided benefits is to engender a sense of fellow-feeling and community spirit. But the effect may be precisely the opposite. We have to ask why these people were not associating with one another in the absence of those public programs; and if the answer is, in part, that there was some antipathy between them, then the effect of forced interaction may well be (in the short term, at least) only to exacerbate that antipathy. The classic case in point here is the attempt at racial integration of U.S. public schools, and the backlash among whites that it produced (Coleman, Kelly, and Moore 1975; Ravitch 1978). It may, of course, be true that that policy would have proven more successful and less divisive had it been implemented more expeditiously (Hochschild 1984). It may, of course, be true that class antagonisms run less deeply than racial ones. It may, of course, be true that while short-run effects are counterproductive of fellow-feeling, long-term effects may be just the opposite. But the risk that the strategy embodied in model C might backfire can never be wholly ignored.

To this point, I have been principally concerned to deny model C's claim that the welfare state is an important cause of a sense of community. Little attention has been paid to model D's opposite contention, that a sense of community leads to a welfare state. That is for the very good reason that there are few national communities that are true communities, i.e., that have a strong sense of social solidarity running throughout the community. With so few cases to go on, any empirical generalizations must be highly tentative at best. Yet it seems plausible that full-blooded communities should adopt welfare state institutions; and judging from such examples as we have, it seems that they do. Consider Eckstein's comments (1966: 85, 87) on the way in which the welfare state in Norway embodies "the Norwegian sentiment of community in realms of social life. . . . Welfare institutions seem to blend naturally into the general tenor of institutional life, if anything to be particularly friendly, cheerful and warm."

Simply showing that the welfare state follows naturally from a sense of community is not, however, enough to justify the welfare state in communitarian terms. As I emphasized at the outset of this section, even if a sense of community is morally important, and even if the welfare state results from having such a sense of community, the moral worth of the cause does not necessarily transfer to the consequence. That will occur, if at all, only where that consequence is the unavoidable by-product of attaining that morally worthy state of affairs.

Thus, what advocates of model D will have to show, if that model is to justify (and not merely explain) the welfare state, is that if the welfare state institutions were removed from a well-integrated community, then that community would break down. This, again, is an empirical question—and one on which evidence is, inevitably, even more scarce. But, for what it is worth, it might be observed that such modest cutbacks as have happened in Scandinavian welfare programs over the recent years seem not to have done any noticeable damage to the sense of community in those nations (Cerny 1977; Roos 1978).

Arguments justifying welfare programs in terms of any direct link (in either direction) between them and a sense of community therefore look awfully weak. The empirical evidence is thin; and insofar as it allows us to judge at all, the connections seem rather tenuous at best.

E

A second and more plausible type of causal model points to empirical links of an *indirect* sort between the welfare state and the sense of community. It is not the very act of making welfare payments or other transfers that knits the community together. Instead, it is what happens as a consequence of such transfers that does so.

The most standard version of this argument runs the causal chain through notions of equality.[33] In model C's version of the argument, social welfare programs reduce levels of social inequality, which in turn enhance a sense of community. In model D's version, a sense of community leads us to strive to create and maintain rough social equality, and we adopt social welfare programs in order to accomplish that task.

One version of this argument, which should be set aside straightaway, would run the indirect connection through formalistic notions of "status equality." If the only sense in which people are equal is the sense in which they are equally members of the community, then this argument reduces back to that of model A or B above. The only way that this can constitute a distinct line would be for the equality in view to be a rough equality of objective, material conditions. That is the version of the argument on which I shall here be concentrating my attention.

The basic components out of which this general proposition linking welfare services, equality and fellow-feeling is constituted are familiar enough. The welfare state is standardly associated with equality, either as its cause or its consequence. And equality is standardly associated with social solidarity, either as its cause (Mill 1869: chap. 2) or as its consequence (Rawls 1971: 105–6). Writers like Tawney (1932/1971: 43) put this latter proposition particularly forcefully:

> What a community requires . . . is a common culture. . . . But a common culture cannot be created merely by desiring it. It

[33] Describing the ideal of "fraternity" and the mutual aid institutions to which it gives rise, Hobsbawm (1975: 471) writes, "Such institutions or informal practices imply a relationship between a group of equals for the utmost mutual help and aid, given both voluntarily and as of right, but not measured in terms of money or mechanical equality or reciprocal exchange."

must rest upon practical foundations of social organization. It is incompatible with the existence of sharp contrasts between the economic standards and educational opportunities of different classes, for such contrasts have as their result, not a common culture, but servility or resentment, on the one hand, and patronage or arrogance, on the other. It involves, in short, a large measure of economic equality—not necessarily in the sense of an identical level of pecuniary incomes, but of equality of environment, of access to education and the means of civilization, of security and independence, and of social consideration which equality in these matters usually carries with it. (See further Wright 1984)

The welfare state might at least go some way toward creating the sort of rough equality presupposed by the sort of community and common culture that Tawney has in mind.

Similar arguments loom large in the latter-day debates over the nature and extent of poverty in our own societies. Advocates of models of "relative poverty," striving to break free of models of absolute physical necessities of life, emphasize in their studies what is required for people to "participate fully in the life of their community." Following Adam Smith's definition of "basic necessities" (1776: bk. 5, chap. 2, sec. 2), they point to things that "the custom of the country renders it indecent for creditable people, even of the lowest order, to be without." Those who fall below such standards are truly "impoverished"—in a relative, but nonetheless important, sense (Townsend 1954; 1962; 1979).[34] Some of the most standard arguments for state welfare services point to their role in relieving that sort of poverty and thereby facilitating

[34] Miller (1982: 84) offers two reasons why this should matter. "In the first place, it is plain that not merely the extent but also the pattern of a person's consumption changes as his income rises: in particular, certain leisure activities (ocean racing, for instance) are only realistically available to those with high incomes, others (skiing, theater-going) to those with middle-range incomes, still others to more or less everyone." If the communitarian goal is for everyone to participate in the same activities, and participation is a function of income, then everyone must have roughly the same income. Miller's (1982: 84) second argument builds on Douglas and Isherwood's (1979) discussion of the "role of consumption in social life": "social life depends a great deal on the exchange of services, particularly those special services (parties, meals, gifts, etc.) used to mark important occasions (calendar events, weddings, and so forth). People with markedly different incomes find it hard to maintain an equal exchange of services without embarrassment or strain. Of course it would be absurd to claim that no personal friendships ever surmount these difficulties. But again we should not find it surprising that the norm is for people to form social ties with others of roughly equivalent economic standing."

people's participation in the life of the community. In the words of one recent U.S. Supreme Court decision, "Welfare, by meeting the basic demands of subsistence, can help bring within the reach of the poor the same opportunities that are available to others to participate meaningfully in the life of the community" (Brennan 1970: 265).[35] Even those who bemoan co-option of the poor through welfare buy-outs perceive the same phenomenon, though evaluating it differently (Cloward and Piven 1971).

In this "full participation" argument for the welfare state, it is slightly unclear what is the cause and what is the consequence. Usually the emphasis seems to fall upon the way in which welfare entitlements cause (or enable) people to be part—to *really* be part— of the community. But sometimes, especially in the more politicized and rhetorical versions of this argument, the opposite connection is made: these people are part of the community (the "Other America" in Harrington's 1962 title), and it is because they are that we must give them welfare entitlements.

The first thing to note, in assessing these arguments, is that there is no *necessary* link between egalitarianism and communitarianism. The utopian socialist ideal of the egalitarian community is one form of the communitarian vision, to be sure. But there is also the conservative vision of a "hierarchical community established by the principle of estates" (Unger 1975: 188, 249–53).[36] It is this latter idea to which Woodrow Wilson (1887: 222) clearly appeals in describing his vision of a community of nations, a vision "of governments joined with governments for the pursuit of common purposes, in honorary equality and honorable subordination." Historically, that hierarchical form of community is more common than the egalitarian form. Of course, the past may not be a good

[35] In the formulation of John Passmore (1979: 37): "Welfare schemes, national health schemes, pension schemes can be justified in [these] terms: they are necessary if the disadvantaged are to live any but a very restricted kind of life. . . . There is a broad connection between economic security, a degree of health, and the capacity to participate, a connection sufficient to justify the general presumption that such schemes will facilitate, even if they are by no means sufficient to ensure, wider opportunities to participate. . . ."

[36] As Cole (1975: 103) says, "There can exist . . . an attitude of social solidarity permeating a whole people, or at any rate cutting right across class differences . . . only in societies which are either very static, so that habit suffices to hold them together, or very mobile, so that the classes they contain are continually shifting both in their nature and in respect of the individuals composing them. In the former type of society everyone has his station and knows it: in the latter, even if class is still a prominent category, status is no longer definite or unchangeable, and does not mark men off into sharply separated groups." See similarly Crick (1984: 25) and Vincent and Plant (1984: 25ff.).

guide to the present or future in that respect. Perhaps a hatred of domination, "once awakened, can no longer be completely stifled" (Unger 1975: 250)—making the egalitarian community the only form of that ideal that is now available to us. If that is true, however, it must be true as a fundamentally empirical proposition. My point is just that there is no necessary link between egalitarianism and communitarianism. Logically, there are other possibilities we might imagine.

The second thing to note, in assessing arguments indirectly linking welfare programs and social solidarity through their joint connections with equality, is that the connections must be *real* and not merely perceived. If our task were merely to explain what motivates people to adopt welfare programs, then all that would matter is that they perceive (and act on the perception) that there is a link between welfare programs and equality, and between equality and fellow-feeling. For purposes of analyzing motivations and explaining behavior, it would not matter whether or not those links were really there; all that would matter would be that people perceived (rightly or wrongly) that they were.[37] The task here, however, is to provide a communitarian *justification* for the welfare state, not just a communitarian explanation of it. For that, the truth of those large macrosociological propositions is crucial: there must be a genuine causal link between welfare programs and equality, and between equality and social solidarity. Then and only then will communitarian goals truly provide the sort of indirect justification here in view for the welfare state. The weaker either of those causal links might be, the weaker the justification they provide for the welfare state will be.

There is some reason for doubting the strength of both these linkages. Consider first the connection between equality and social solidarity. Not only is there the danger, here as in section II.C above, of backlash among the rich, whose property is being redistributed to the poor. Here there is also the particular danger that even among the poor, egalitarian social reforms may lead to more rather than less social unrest. A substantial body of empirical evidence (Gurr 1970; Hibbs 1972) points to the dangers of a "revolution of rising expectations": the promise of "equal citizenship," especially when conjoined with real improvements in people's objective circumstances, leads them to form subjective expecta-

---

[37] For evidence of systematic misperception of the extent of such things in, e.g., Iceland, see Broddason and Webb 1975.

tions of even more dramatic improvements in the future; at some point, those ever-increasing expectations are bound to be disappointed, and social protest is the inevitable consequence.[38] There is nothing new or surprising in this phenomenon, even in its application to the communitarian case for the welfare state. Indeed, a long-suppressed theme in Marshall's original essay (1949), only recently resurrected, was that citizenship rights have "the potential for exacerbating as well as diminishing the conflict of classes" (Lockwood 1974: 365; Goldthorpe 1978: 201–4).

Those who are concerned to improve people's objective circumstances may, of course, regard modest levels of protest as a small price to pay. But those concerned with equality and the improvement in people's objective circumstances merely as a means to social cohesion cannot. Assuming social protest is the converse of social solidarity (or, anyway, of solidarity with society as a whole, rather than just your little protesting subset of it), then that counts as weighty evidence against the first plank in the indirect communitarian case for the welfare state.[39]

There are, furthermore, good theoretical reasons for supposing that those findings are not just flukes. The most interesting, in my view, has to do with the logic of relative power considerations. In a society of equals, anyone might reasonably hope to win in a power struggle; in a highly stratified society, the winner would be foreordained (Goodin and Dryzek 1980). Resignation to one's fate is a far cry from the sort of social solidarity that communitarians would relish, of course. But so too is the cutthroat competition that might reasonably be expected to arise among a society of equals.

All that communitarians could point to at this stage of the argument, as a mechanism for damping such conflicts, would be some *direct* influence of the welfare state on social solidarity. They may say, for example, that it is because of the *way* in which equality has been achieved (i.e., through the intervention of a "caring welfarist society") that people will behave cooperatively rather than conflictually. Or they may say that people will behave more

---

[38] Notice that it is not equality per se that is counterproductive of community sentiments here; instead it is movement in the direction of equality that has that effect.

[39] It might not be quite conclusive evidence. We may still be willing to trade off a little short-term loss in community spirit for substantial long-term gains in it—if that is indeed the choice we are offered. But there must be substantial evidence for thinking that the long term is going to be so very different than the short term, and we must weigh the future relatively heavily as compared to the present, for this justification to look appealing.

cooperatively because they now enjoy formally equal status with everyone else in their community. But those are precisely the sorts of direct links between social solidarity and the welfare state that have already been discounted.

A spate of recent empirical research also casts some doubt on the further connection, made in this argument about an indirect link, between welfare states and equality. Transfer payments have been notably successful at reducing (though not eliminating) poverty, i.e., bringing people above certain minimal standards (Danziger, Haveman, and Plotnick 1981). But promoting anything like strict income equality is quite another matter. Of course, Tawney's argument might require only a *rough* equality, not a perfect Gini coefficient. Nonetheless, the cross-national evidence suggests that the link is really quite weak. Jackman (1976: 196), for example, reports a partial correlation between "civilian government expenditures per capita" (his measure of the level of welfare state spending) and the Schutz coefficient of income equality that comes to only 0.266. That is rather a weak link in the chain of causation being proposed by the model of an indirect connection, running through equality, between the welfare state and social solidarity.

For a final bit of empirical evidence on the weakness of the overall link between welfare programs, equality, and social solidarity, consider the cross-national social-psychological evidence as to which "distribution rule" people prefer to be used. In one survey drawing together results from the U.S., Sweden, and Germany, a striking result emerges: either "equality" or "need" was ranked as the first-choice principle for distributing goods and services by undergraduates in *all three* countries (Törnblom and Foa 1983). The extent to which redistributive welfare policies are actually pursued in these three countries varies enormously, of course. But assuming these responses represent fellow-feeling or social solidarity, such variations do not seem to make any great difference in the extent to which a sense of community has been established in those countries.

I I I

Stepping back from particular variants of the communitarian thesis, let us now examine the broader "altruism" thesis with which it is linked. As was shown in section I, the communitarian case for the welfare state trades on an analogy between mutual-aid institutions in village society and welfare state institutions in national society. In various respects, and to varying degrees, that analogy is a strained one.

One source of strain lies in nationalizing the notion of community. The welfare state, Walzer argues (1980: 43–44, 48), brings only "the illusion of a common life" because it has not been "concerned with the problem of social scale." He continues:

> If human emotional and intellectual needs are to be fulfilled (partially) within political society, . . . then that society cannot be of any size or shape. It must be built on a human scale, accessible to our minds and feelings, responsive to our decisions. . . . Now all such pursuits . . . lie outside the competence of the state; they belong to a different sphere of activity; they require a smaller scale of organization.

Walzer's particular concern is with the capacity to participate meaningfully in the decisions that shape one's life. But much the same can be said of other aspects of the communitarian ideal, too. Crick (1984: 25) rightly concludes, "The experience of fraternity is learned in small groups; and learned best in small groups which fulfill a variety of roles—working, governing themselves and providing as many of their own services as they can: the image of the commune and of industrial democracy." These are far from idle philosophical speculations. There is a fair bit of evidence that the recent retreat from the welfare state in the U.S., for example, might best be explained as a retreat from a sense of national community back to a sense of local community (Schambra 1985).

These points emerge particularly forcefully in relation to the sort of mutual aid that has here been taken to constitute the core of the communitarian ideal. Mutual aid works among small groups, where everyone knows everyone else. Empathy in the strict sense is only possible where you can know who the others are and how they will be suffering: only then will you be able to conjure up a sufficiently rich image of their circumstances to put yourself mentally in their place. Occasionally, perhaps, newspaper or television reports of particularly sad stories might allow us to conjure up almost as rich an image of some particular welfare recipients whom we have never met. But by the very nature of things, that can happen only occasionally and for only a small subset of welfare claimants in any reasonably large society.

Communitarians express the wish that "fraternity must be extended in such a way that the large scale does not obliterate the small. We do indeed need both" (Crick 1984: 25). And perhaps it is true that it is not absolutely impossible for the welfare state to work on, and through, people's altruistic sentiments. But what does seem inevitably to follow from this argument is this: either the altruism will have to be of a different and far more impersonal form, or else the welfare state will have to work in a highly decentralized fashion through existing community institutions.

No doubt there is some substantial scope for the latter strategy. Social workers are deeply divided on the merits of relocating teams of ordinary social work professionals in community centers and making them more responsive to the community through some combination of formal neighborhood meetings and informal social pressure. (Hadley and Hatch 1981; Barclay 1982: chap. 13; cf. Kahn 1976; Pinker 1982; 1983). Rather more promising is the strategy of using "indigenous non-professionals" in the roles of "case aides, homework helpers and the like. . . . The task is to create valued status positions for those who were formerly passive recipients of assistance" so that they can "become active partners in a joint undertaking of mutual aid" (Coser 1965: 148). But presumably there are fairly strict limits to the extent to which that can be done, too: sometimes specialized skills really are necessary, and unavailable in the community at large. Furthermore, insofar as these schemes are meant to operate alongside and not in place of ordinary, professional social services, experience suggests there will be enormous practical difficulties in blending the two modes of service provision.

> In California, supporters of reduced taxation fantasised about a wave of good-neighbourliness that would sweep the state in a collective volunteer effort to restore services lost as a result of budget cuts. But experience has shown that, as a cheap form of labour, volunteers can exacerbate tensions among staff and between non-governmental organisations and trade unions. They are no substitute for necessary services best delivered by professionals and other types of paid staff. (Kramer 1985: 138)

Hence I conclude that we must, to some really very large extent, end up relying instead upon a more impersonal form of altruism.

Therein lies the second source of strain. By institutionalizing altruism—and thus rendering it both impersonal and compulsory—the welfare state fundamentally changes the nature of the altruism from that which motivates mutual aid in village societies. Titmuss (1971) celebrates the impersonality, and indeed anonymity, of the "gift relationship" embodied in blood donations: British National Blood Transfusion Service donors do not know who is to receive their blood; recipients do not know who gave it. Yet, curiously, such impersonality is the very antithesis of gift-giving as it is ordinarily understood. Gift relationships, and the duties of gratitude to which they give rise, are highly personalized relationships, linking particular benefactors and particular beneficiaries. Morally, we owe (and sociologically, we feel we owe) some return kindness to those who have sacrificed that we might benefit, over and above whatever we might owe to people in general (Goodin 1985b: 99–107). Those obligations, which are the very foundation of mutual aid in village society, are anything but impersonal. Yet when altruism is institutionalized and mediated by the welfare state, relationships cannot be other than impersonal.[40]

Furthermore, the compulsory nature of the relationship between benefactor and beneficiary in the welfare state belies any claim that it reflects a genuine sense of altruism or community. "A forced relationship is no more communal than forced laughter is happy or forced religious observance is faithful" (Reiman 1986: 194). A gift is truly a gift only if given freely, as a token of affection. Among participants in village mutual-aid arrangements, it is at least arguable that people are doing each other favors freely; there is no outside agency compelling them to contribute in each and every instance, anyway. In the welfare state, "gifts" are extracted instead through the coercive agency of the tax collector. Such forced "donations" are not donations at all. Any duty of gratitude that the welfare beneficiary might have would be to the tax collector, not to the people from whom the resources have been extracted.

Correlatively, under mutual-aid arrangements, a beneficiary has no strong rights against his benefactor. He has a right to ask a neighbor for assistance, to be sure; and if the neighbor hesitates to offer it, he may of course perfectly properly point out all the assistance that he has rendered to others (perhaps including the neighbor himself) in similar circumstances in the past. But he has no right to *demand* assistance, and the neighbor is under no strict duty to render it. The duties of benefactors, under mutual-aid arrangements, are more like Kant's "imperfect duties"; and the claims of beneficiaries are correspondingly insecure.

[40] As Canon Barnett (1912/1986: 70) puts it in his plea for charity, "The best form of giving must always . . . be that from person to person. . . . 'The gift without the giver is bare,' and when the giver's thought makes itself felt, the gift is enriched."

From the perspective of communitarians, it is important that this should be so. If the goal is to produce a strong sense of community, with each subordinating his own interests (and perhaps even his own identity) to that of the group, then the individualistic business of demanding one's rights and pressing one's claims seems wholly out of place.[41] Yet it is the hallmark of a welfare state that benefactors are under a strong, perfect duty, and that beneficiaries have correspondingly strong claims against them. For my part, I wholly approve of this feature of the welfare state; many of the most important advantages of the welfare state, revealed in chapters 5 through 7, flow from precisely this source. From the communitarian perspective, however, this aspect of the welfare state is wholly an embarrassment. It is utterly without warrant on communitarian principles.

The true analogue, at the national level, to village mutual aid would seem to be voluntary charity, rather than state welfare services.[42] Mutual aid, after all, is the anarchist's answer—not the statist's. The peculiar challenge before anyone who wants to depict social welfare services as manifestations of generalized altruism is, then, to explain why the coercive intervention of the state should be required at all.[43]

Answers that turn upon peculiarly calculative features of altruists' reasoning seem highly unsatisfactory. True, if people want others to be better off, but positively prefer that that happen by someone else's hand rather than their own, then relief of those in distress would indeed be a public good requiring the coercive intervention of the state in order for it to be secured (Friedman 1962: 190–91; Buchanan 1984: 70–71; Miller 1986). But then they would not be all that altruistic, either. Preferring that the needy be helped by someone else—not because that other person can do a better job, in any sense, of helping them but merely because you yourself

[41] For arguments to this effect, see Marx (1843) and Ignatieff (1984); cf; Campbell (1983) and Reiman (1986: 194).

[42] Liberal communitarians, arguing for turn-of-the-century welfare state innovations in Britain, were particularly insistent on "the need for combining the organized power of the collective" through state action "and personal voluntary mutual aid between men" through private charity (Freeden 1978: 226).

[43] Similarly, it is the vision of New Right writers such as Charles Murray (1985b: 32) that if we eliminate the welfare state as we know it, any remaining social problems would be met by "relatives helping relatives, friends helping friends, and communities protecting communities." If that is indeed what would happen in the absence of the welfare state, then communitarians seeking those outcomes should be arguing against the welfare state rather than in favor of it.

will then not have to bear the cost—is hardly the sort of virtue that communitarians keen on altruism would wish to recommend.

Other answers might turn on the role of the state in coordinating various altruists' actions, assuring everyone that everyone else is in fact an altruist, and channeling the assistance where it is most needed and into the form in which it is most useful (Buchanan 1984: 71–72; Miller 1986; see more generally Goodin 1976: chaps. 4 and 5). No doubt genuine altruists would find all those services highly useful. But taken together, they do not seem to add up to the welfare state—or anything half as extensive.

That is just to say that if people were altruists already, they would not need the welfare state. But perhaps the problem is that they are not (yet) altruists—or not fully, completely, and consistently so. Then the welfare state might be justified in communitarian terms as a device for making them into altruists or for firming up their altruistic inclinations. The welfare state would, on this account, be a character-building institution inculcating values that people ought always to have had anyway, but which they sadly lacked or partly lacked.

It is an open question to what extent the welfare state can accomplish that goal, however. Recent evidence of a "welfare backlash" in states where community sentiment was not already strong (Britain, the U.S.) surely suggests that, beyond some point anyway, the strategy might become counterproductive. In any event, the arguments of section II above suggest that there is little chance that the strategy will work.

I V

In this chapter, I have taken the communitarian ideal as an unquestioned good, and asked only to what extent the existence of welfare state institutions can be justified as a contribution toward the realization of that ideal. On the basis of section II above, I am led to conclude that the welfare state is neither necessary nor sufficient nor empirically particularly crucial to the realization of the communitarian ideal. Communitarian values do not justify the welfare state uniquely; they may not justify the welfare state at all. On the basis of section III above, I am led to conclude that the sort of generalized altruism that communitarians seek may be an impossible dream built on an untenable analogy to village society.

Part II

TOWARD A NEW THEORY

The true moral foundations of the welfare state are not to be found in any of the traditional left-wing arguments about needs, equality or community. Instead, I argue in the three chapters that follow, they are to be found in an older and less fashionable cluster of concepts. These deal principally in terms of nonexploitation and of duties toward dependent others. The welfare state thus construed is not so much a grand plan for social reorganization writ small as it is a modest principle of interpersonal ethics writ large.

In essence, my argument will be that those who depend upon particular others for satisfaction of their basic needs are rendered, by that dependency, susceptible to exploitation by those upon whom they depend. It is the risk of exploitation of such dependencies that justifies public provision—and public provision of a distinctively welfare state form—for those basic needs.

That argument is admittedly circuitous. A less roundabout defense of the welfare state might move directly from the proposition that basic needs are not being met to the proposition that we (individually and collectively—and the state, as the proper repository of our collective duties) should see to it that they are met. The problem to which the welfare state is an answer is, on this view, not that starving people can be exploited; rather, it is that they are starving.

Posed that way, however, the problem is one arising wholly outside the market—outside its operative laws and its underlying justificatory logic. The welfare state, on that more straightforward defense of it, derives its justification from a wholly distinct set of principles standing over or alongside—but entirely outside—the principles at work in the market itself.

It is, of course, the central theme of this book that there are indeed some such moral principles at work justifying welfare state interventions in the market economy. But much of the justificatory weight can be borne by market principles themselves. Much of chapter 6 is devoted to showing advocates of the market that their own principles go a long way toward committing them to at least a minimal welfare state. Not quite all the way, to be sure: some further independent moral principle will always be required to make the last move. Market logic pares down the options dramatically, however. Anyone who wants to embrace the market must either embrace the welfare state as well, or else face morally very unpalatable options at every other turn.

Showing in this way that the welfare state is *almost* implicit in market principles themselves helps to solve a central mystery about the welfare state. If it is conceived as an instrument for making limited interventions in the market economy, then how can we justify both going that far in supplanting the market and also stopping at that point? Most of the arguments for going that far would also be arguments for going a lot further; most of the arguments for not going further would also be arguments for not going that far. Explaining why we should go that far and no further is best done, I suggest, by predicating the justification of welfare state interventions largely upon the justificatory principles underlying the market itself.

F I V E

EXPLOITATION

One of the things that the welfare state is clearly doing, when it supplants ordinary economic markets in distributing needed resources, is preventing the exploitation of those who would otherwise find themselves in desperate straits. On the face of it, that is a minimal task and a modest accomplishment. Further analysis of the notion of "exploitation" and the moral importance attaching to its prevention, however, opens the way for a fuller analysis in chapter 6 of the deeper moral principle upon which, I shall argue, the welfare state truly depends for its most fundamental justification.

Of course, it has long been one of the most sweeping and powerful critiques of the market—since before Marx, running through today's post-Marxists—that the market is systematically exploitative. That is a familiar Old Leftist argument against the market. It is not, however, in and of itself an argument in favor of the welfare state. The reason is that that argument, if true, would justify far more than merely a welfare state. If the market is systematically exploitative, then to eliminate that exploitation the market itself must be systematically replaced. The welfare state does nothing of the kind. It merely supplants the market for the purposes of distributing a certain, limited range of goods and services.

Here I shall maintain that that Old Leftist argument is too sweeping in its condemnation of the market, paradoxically, because it is too narrow in its analysis of exploitation. To get a proper understanding of the concept of "exploitation," we must broaden the notion beyond its very narrowly economic applications.[1] Cer-

Material in this chapter is reprinted from Robert E. Goodin, "Exploiting a Situation and Exploiting a Person," *Modern Theories of Exploitation*, ed. Andrew Reeve (London: Sage, 1987), pp. 160–200, by permission of the editor and Sage Publications Ltd.

[1] Contemporary philosophical discussions of exploitation often tend to adopt this economistic focus, at least as the starting point for their analyses. See, e.g.: Arneson 1981; Buchanan 1979; 1985: 87–95; Cohen 1979; Crocker 1972; Elster 1983; Holmstrom 1977; Panichas 1981; Reeve 1987; Roemer 1982a, b, c; 1985; Steiner 1984;

tainly much exploitation can occur in the process of the production and consumption of commodities. But focusing upon that sort of exploitation alone would, for example, mean that it is impossible to exploit precisely those people whom the welfare state most strives to protect—those who, for one reason or another (age, illness, disability, etc.), can play no part in ordinary labor markets (Tulloch 1983). There is a real risk, then, of mistaking what is peculiar about the exploitation of producers and consumers for what is characteristic of the phenomenon of exploitation in general.[2]

Here my strategy will be to triangulate upon a general theory of exploitation from as many distinct, independent points as possible. As a result of pursuing that strategy, I am led to an analysis of exploitation very different in its implications from the standard, economics-based one. On this analysis, the welfare state, far from being an inadequate instrument for preventing exploitation, turns out actually to be an ideal one.

The general notion of "exploitation," as I analyze it in section I, always consists in a certain sort of behavior in a certain sort of situation. The nub of the matter is invariably "taking advantage," in one way or another. Exploiting a situation amounts essentially to taking advantage of some peculiar features of that situation. Exploiting a person similarly involves taking advantage of some peculiar features of that person and his situation.[3]

While exploiting a person is a special case of exploiting a situation, it is, as I show in section II, a very special case. The former practice is inherently wrong, in a way that the latter is not. Built into the concept of exploiting a person is a notion of "unfairness"

1987; Wood 1972; and Wright 1984. Many of these authors make some effort to transcend that economistic starting point, but invariably it continues to exert a considerable influence over the whole analysis.

[2] In analyses of economic exploitation, for example, the emphasis naturally falls on the production and consumption of commodities carrying value: that tends to suggest that a theory of exploitation should be parasitic upon a theory about the creation and distribution of valued commodities; and it further tends to suggest that only certain sorts of things (i.e., factors of production) are eligible candidates for exploitation. Surely that is too narrow an understanding of exploitation, however. Lovers can exploit one another just as surely as can economic classes. Yet neither party in an affectionate relationship is functioning in any standard sense as a "factor of production"; nor, since neither party is creating valuable objects in any ordinary respect, does it in that context make much sense to define exploitation in the standard economistic terms of receiving commodities that are less valuable than those one has created.

[3] Less elliptically, it amounts to taking advantage of some peculiar features of the situation in which exploiters and the exploited find themselves, where the "situation" is defined so as to include a description of both personal characteristics and impersonal circumstances.

(of "taking unfair advantage") that is out of place in talking of our treatment of mere situations.

Exploring that sense of unfairness further, I am led in section III to conclude that the morally charged form of interpersonal exploitation consists in delicts of a very particular moral duty. Occasions for interpersonal exploitation arise when one person is in an especially strong position vis-à-vis another. The same circumstances that give the stronger party a bargaining advantage over the weaker also impose upon the stronger party a heavy moral responsibility not to take advantage of that bargaining advantage in dealings with the weaker. It is the flagrant violation of this duty—playing for advantage, when morally you are bound not to do so—that we call exploitation. Just as the analysis of the notion of "adultery" is parasitic upon an analysis of the duty of marital fidelity, so too is the analysis of exploitation parasitic upon an analysis of this duty to protect the vulnerable.

Protecting the vulnerable is essentially a matter of preventing them from coming to harm. This has two aspects, as shown in section IV. The first, and stronger, form of the duty to protect the vulnerable is not to inflict harm upon them yourself. That is what happens when you yourself exploit people: you yourself take unfair advantage of others' peculiar vulnerabilities to your actions and choices. The second, weaker form of the duty to protect the vulnerable is to prevent others from inflicting harm upon those who are vulnerable to them. That is what we do through programs like the welfare state. By guaranteeing that everyone's basic needs will be met through the impersonal and nondiscretionary agency of the state, we render otherwise dependent people substantially less dependent upon (and hence less vulnerable to) the actions and choices of particular others, who might otherwise have taken unfair advantage of those dependencies and vulnerabilities to exploit them.

I

First, let us consider the notion of "exploitation" in general. Only persons (or agents more generally, if our concept of agency stretches beyond persons) can exploit anything. As Feinberg (1983: 202) says, "Diseases, landslides and tropical storms have never exploited anything" (see similarly Tormey 1973 and Panichas 1981). But there are a great many things that such agents might exploit. Among them are other people, their foibles, phobias, and physical attributes. Also among them are inanimate objects, such as tools and natural resources; abstract entities, such as ideas, beliefs, and arguments; and various sorts of situations, such as crop failures, natural disasters, miners' strikes, and so on.

Across all these diverse cases, the core notion seems to remain constant: to exploit something is, most fundamentally, to *take advantage* of it (Feinberg 1983: 201). We must, however, be wary of an ambiguity built into the notion of "advantage." In one sense of the word, advantage$_1$ refers to a "superior position: favouring circumstance." In another sense, advantage$_2$ refers to "The result of a superior . . . position. Benefit; . . . increased well-being"; thus the *Oxford English Dictionary* defines "advantage (II,6)." The advantage taken by exploiters is of the former (advantage$_1$) sort.[4]

Certainly it is true that an act of exploitation ordinarily redounds to the benefit (advantage$_2$) of the person who performs it. Otherwise, such acts would not be performed at all. But the connection between exploitation and benefit is a contingent rather than an analytic one. Taking an advantage is not the same thing as taking a good itself. When an armored division exploits a gap in enemy defenses to push through to seize control of a major city, it takes advantage of one thing (the gap) in order to seize yet another (the city) (Kemeny 1983: 223). What is seized in an act of exploitation is thus of merely instrumental value. "Take advantage" might therefore be better understood as "turn to advantage" or "make use of" (Elster 1983: 278). The value of the act of exploitation to the exploiter is not contained within the act itself, but rather in the further advantage$_2$ (i.e., benefits) that follow from seizing the (strategic) advantage$_1$.

Exploitation is an act which, if successful, confers certain perceived benefits upon the exploiter.[5] But to succeed, such acts must succeed on two levels: exploiters must not only successfully seize advantages$_1$ but also successfully transform them into real

---

[4] There might be an objection here to the effect that, if the advantage taken by exploiters is advantage$_1$, then we should be able to say, "To exploit something is to take a superior position over it." But that seems awkward. Surely it is easier to say, "To exploit something is to take benefit of it"; and that, in turn, suggests that exploitation is the taking of advantage$_2$ instead of advantage$_1$. Upon further reflection, however, that objection melts away. What we *take* when we exploit something is, in the first instance at least, *control* (i.e., superior position) over something. "Benefit" refers to the subjective evaluation of states of the world produced by thus manipulating objects in the external world. *Taking* refers to the seizure of something in the external world; it makes no sense to apply that term to internal states.

[5] "Perceived," because of course people may think they are benefiting when they are not really at all.

advantages$_2$.[6] Attempts at exploitation can thus fail in either of two respects. People might fail in their attempts to make use (i.e., seize control) of things they are trying to exploit. Or they may succeed in seizing control of those things, but fail in their further attempt to manipulate them in ways conducive to their larger goals.[7]

Exploitation consists in taking advantage of someone or something, but not every act of taking advantage constitutes exploitation. Retirees who take advantage of their newly found spare time to learn woodworking would hardly be said to be *exploiting* the opportunity to learn a craft. Nor does the Norwegian, taking advantage of January's perfectly seasonal snowfall to ski daily, do anything that we would be altogether comfortable describing in terms of exploitation.

One reason we hesitate to apply the term to such situations might be that we see nothing *wrong* with those activities, and exploitation we deeply suspect must always be wrong. That is true where it is people that are being exploited—of which more later. But that is not necessarily true where things other than persons are being exploited. No one blames philosophers (or perhaps even politicians) for exploiting good arguments. No one blames Javanese peasants for exploiting their exceptionally good climate to grow three rice crops annually, or Wilt Chamberlin for exploiting his remarkable talent for playing basketball to earn a living.

What the woodworking retiree and the skiing Norwegian ex-

[6] Exploitation on this analysis amounts to "seizing an opportunity." But it is the act of *seizing* that opportunity—it is not the act of seeking it, or creating it, or discovering it. Foreign aid donors are often setting up a situation which they can later exploit, making the recipient country's economy dependent in various respects on the donor's (Hayter 1971). So too are American defense contractors setting up a situation they can later exploit when selling the Pentagon cut-rate airplanes under contracts that will allow them subsequently to charge exorbitant prices for spare parts. And so too are miners setting up a situation which they can later exploit when sinking a shaft down to an ore deposit. But people setting up a situation so that it can later be turned to advantage are not exploiting anyone or anything—not yet, anyway. Exploitation occurs only when they cash in on the opportunity, and not a moment before.

[7] Most commentators, being committed to the proposition that successful acts of exploitation must necessarily benefit the exploiter, would call an attempt at exploitation a failure if it failed in either respect. This is not always correct, however. Surely miners who have successfully extracted ore from the ground have successfully exploited the seam, whether or not the ore is subsequently sold for a profit. In cases like those, it seems that the crucial standard of success for acts of exploitation is the first standard (successfully seizing control of and manipulating something), and that alone. Where it is *people* that are being exploited, however, it seems that both conditions must be met. However successfully you manipulate or control others, you will not be said to have exploited them successfully unless you also got some benefit from so doing.

amples suggest instead is that exploitation refers to the taking advantage of an *unusual* situation. Perhaps strictly speaking any aspect of a thing or situation that can be manipulated to your advantage should be said to be exploitable, just as every opportunity should be said to be equally an opportunity. But in practice we tend to save those bigger words for what are thought to be more unusual circumstances. A *"real* opportunity" is something out of the ordinary. So, too, is the opportunity really to *exploit* something.

The connection between the exploitable and the unusual is revealed more clearly in the noun than in the verb. When talking of someone's "exploits," we are referring to brilliant feats and rare adventures. It would be simply inappropriate (or deeply ironic) to describe commonplace, humdrum doings as "exploits." Something more unusual is required to warrant that description.

The adjectival use, too, retains something of this sense of the unusual. We have no hesitation in describing as "exploitative" extractive industries like mining; and we would have little hesitation in describing overly intensive cultivation of farmland in similar terms. Consider in contrast, however, a group of farmers or fishermen who practice a form of scrupulously responsible husbandry, culling no more than the maximum sustainable yield each year. It seems inappropriate to describe their activities as exploitative, although they certainly are taking advantage of the resources of the land or sea. The reason the term does not seem to fit is that they are doing nothing that is necessarily unusual. They can repeat their practices endlessly, in a way that miners or exploitative farmers or fishermen inherently cannot.

Exploitation, then, is a matter of taking unusual advantage. That can occur in either (or both) of two distinct ways. One is by taking advantage of unusual situations. Another is by making unusual use of perfectly ordinary circumstances. There is, for example, nothing in the least unusual about provisions in tax laws allowing farmers to set losses off against earnings in calculating their taxable income. There is, however, something unusual about people buying up failing farms just to make "tax losses" to offset other earnings; and it is by virtue of that unusual use of perfectly usual provisions that we say that "weekend farmers" exploit rather than merely take advantage of the tax code in these ways. Or, again, there is nothing unusual about attractive people flirting. But when this is done in order to persuade a police officer to tear up a speeding ticket, the attractive speeder would be said to have exploited rather than merely to have taken advantage of his/her charms—and that because fixing a ticket is such an unusual use to which to put those charms.

Now, saying that those are "unusual" uses is not to say that they are necessarily infrequent ones. Quite the contrary, I presume that businessmen and blonds do just these sorts of things all the time. What warrants the term "exploitation" being applied to such activities is not necessarily that people are making rare or uncommon uses of certain advantages. It may instead be that they are making *nonstandard* or *nonparadigmatic* uses of them.[8] The standard, paradigmatic use of tax breaks for farmers is to help farm families stay on the land. The standard, paradigmatic use of good looks is for mating. When put to their standard, paradigmatic uses there is nothing exploitative about the use of these advantages. When used to fiddle corporate finances or to fix tickets, there is. Similarly, "one does not exploit a concert by attending it in the usual fashion even though one is using it as a means to some end, but one does exploit it by passing out fliers to the audience on their way out advertising one's clothing store down the street" (Sensat 1984: 33).

Construing "unusual" in this way helps to avoid prejudicing the question of the frequency of exploitation. If exploitation were defined as "taking unusual advantage," and "unusual" were defined as "rare, uncommon" alone, then exploitation would by definition have to be a rare or uncommon phenomenon. That may be true; it may not. But whether true or false, that must be as an empirical rather than as an analytical fact. Any analysis of exploitation that makes it rare by definition is fatally flawed. Saying that the notion of the unusual straddles "rare, uncommon" and "nonstandard, nonparadigmatic" alike goes some way toward avoiding that result.[9]

[8] It is hardly surprising that the notion of the "unusual" should straddle these two senses, one frequentist and the other moralized. The cognate notions of "normal" and "expected" outcomes do much the same. When assigning responsibility for some harm that has been done either accidentally or intentionally, we lay the bulk of the blame on those whose conduct has deviated most from the "normal" course of conduct; and "normal" in this context explicitly straddles notions of what people most frequently do and what people morally should do (Mackie 1955; Hart and Honoré 1959). Similarly, when trying to decide whether a proposal constitutes a threat or an offer, we compare it to the "expected" course of events; and once again, "expected" straddles "predicted and morally required" (Nozick 1972: 112). The same is true of the sense of what is "normal" that we use in reckoning people's moral deserts, as will be shown in chapter 10.

[9] Whether this formulation goes all the way toward avoiding that result is, per-

I I

Next let us consider the notion of "exploiting a person." There are various things about people that we might exploit. We might exploit their strong backs or weak minds. We might exploit their fears, ignorance, superstitions, gullibility, or naiveté. We might exploit their generosity, loyalty, or trust. We might exploit their bad luck, their joblessness, homelessness or illness.

All those things, however, are merely *attributes* of people and their circumstances. Exploiting a person's attributes is not the same as exploiting a person (Feinberg 1983: 213–14; cf. Kleinig 1982: 110). Each of us can sometimes exploit some of our *own* attributes—a runner her stamina, a boxer his reach, etc. We would not thereby be exploiting ourselves; we would just be exploiting certain *things about* ourselves. Similarly, we can take advantage of a person's trustworthiness to secure an otherwise unenforceable contract, and we can take advantage of a person's blindness to conduct taste-tests uncontaminated by visual cues. In both cases, we exploit a person's attributes without necessarily exploiting the person as a whole.

We infer whole-person exploitation from the fact that certain of the person's attributes are being used if they are being used *unfairly*. Thus, taking advantage of other people's honesty or blindness to steal from them constitutes exploiting those people tout court, whereas taking advantage of those attributes for the earlier purposes does not. Exploiting a person is, then, essentially a matter of "taking unfair advantage" of that person.[10]

---

haps, contentious. Consider a society that systematically strip-mines its mineral resources, or systematically enslaves its blacks, as a matter of course. The advantage that the strip-miner takes of the minerals, or the slaveowner of the slave, is then "unusual" in neither of these senses—it is neither infrequent in that society, nor is it nonstandard/nonparadigmatic use in that society. Yet surely, some would say, they still exploit those things. I would resist that suggestion, however. There are many ways of misusing things that are not properly describable as "exploitation." The practices here in view seem to me better described as "squandering" our mineral reserves and "despoiling" the land that used to lay above them, in the one case, and "oppressing" blacks, in the other.

[10] This general formula is widely embraced, but typically only in passing, by commentators keen to investigate some more particular aspect of the general phenomenon. See, e.g.: Cohen 1982: 494; Elster 1982b: 364–65; 1983: 278; Feinberg 1983; van der Veen 1978: 438; and Walt 1984: 242. It may of course be argued that if we use each other for low sexual purposes only, then we exploit each other, but we do not take unfair advantage of each other. But if no "unfair advantage" is taken by either party, then no whole-person exploitation is occurring in this relationship: those individuals are exploiting *things about* each other or *attributes of* each other

Here, as in the more general case, what is taken is strictly speaking an advantage$_1$, i.e., an advantage of a merely strategic sort. But here, even more certainly than in the general case, some further benefit (advantage$_2$) must necessarily accrue to the exploiter if the act of exploitation is to be said to have been a successful one (Feinberg 1983: 215). If the putative exploiter fails to realize some perceived benefits from the act, then either it was not a *successful* act of exploitation or else it was not an act of *exploitation* at all.

Conversely, the exploited characteristically suffers some loss as a result of having been exploited. The status of this proposition is slightly unclear. Most commentators would claim that the exploited must, as a matter of logical necessity, have suffered a loss (some would go so far as to say a loss "equivalent" to the exploiter's gains) to have been exploited at all (Panichas 1981: 231; Roemer 1982a, b; Tormey 1973: 207–8; Wright 1984: 385); but there are worrying counterexamples to the claim of logical necessity here.[11] Similarly, the form that the losses must take is somewhat unclear. Some commentators would talk in terms of real material losses; but others prefer a broader notion of "opportunity costs," i.e., gains that the exploited could themselves have realized if their exploiters had not acted as "parasites" creaming them off (Buchanan 1985: 90; Panichas 1981: 213–14; Roemer 1982a, b; cf. Elster 1982b: 365–69).[12]

Given all the uncertainties surrounding this issue, the most that can be said with confidence seems to be this. It is at least contingently true that the exploited suffers losses in some form or another as a result of having been exploited. Still, the connection be-

---

(e.g., their lust, or lack of self-control) rather than "exploiting each other" in a whole-person sense of that term.

[11] One such counterexample is this. We would certainly want to say that prostitutes are exploited by their clients and pimps, however well paid the prostitutes might be. But that would be a case in which the exploited party suffers no (real, material) losses. You can, of course, argue that their "objective" interests were being violated, even while their subjective interests were being well served. But whatever those objective interests might be, they must clearly be different from the "opposing material interests" that Wright (1984: 385), e.g., equates with exploitation—it is precisely those sorts of material interests that are being well-served in the case of the well-paid prostitute. See further Feinberg 1983: 213.

[12] Against the otherwise attractive "opportunity cost" analysis, consider this counterexample. Suppose that, absent pimps, prostitutes made no money at all. Social attitudes in our society, say, are such that prostitutes plying for trade on their own so offended potential customers' sensitivities that no one would hire them. Are we then to say that the pimps were not exploiting the prostitutes at all, even though they made a fortune from the trade? Surely not: the pimps did exploit the prostitutes, even though there may have been no alternative state of the world in which the prostitutes could have done any better for themselves.

tween being exploited and suffering losses—even if it is only a contingent one—seems sufficiently strong that it makes very little material difference whether the connection is analytic or otherwise.

Exploitation in general is morally ambivalent. There is nothing wrong (nothing necessarily wrong, anyway) with exploiting waves or rocks or sunlight. It is only as applied to our treatment of people that "exploitation" acquires inevitably pejorative connotations. Why that should be so—what is morally objectionable about exploiting people—is something that requires the careful attention of the next several pages. But of this much there can be no doubt: an act of exploiting a person always constitutes a wrong.[13]

The wrongfulness of exploiting people is presumably connected, somehow, to its unfairness. After all, only one thing has changed in shifting from the exploitation of things to the exploitation of persons: the qualifier "unfair" has been added to the general formula of "exploitation = taking advantage." It is in this notion of unfairness that the source of our moral objections to the practice of exploitation is most naturally sought. There are, however, many ways of cashing out this notion. As I shall spend the balance of section II demonstrating, none of the standard substantive notions of unfairness seems quite to capture the wrongfulness of exploitation.

A

Perhaps the most obvious reading of "unfairness," especially in the context of exploitation (and more especially still in the context of economic exploitation), is in terms of force and coercion. On this reading, we say that slaves are exploited by masters who force (or coercively threaten to force) them to work on their behalf; feudal serfs are exploited by lords who extract part of their produce by force or the threat of force; freed slaves in the American South were exploited by white employers using (or threatening to use)

---

[13] To say that such an act necessarily constitutes *a* wrong is not, of course, to say that it is necessarily wrong *on balance* to perform that act. There might be all sorts of other countervailing considerations which, when taken into account, would make an act of exploitation morally permissible (or even desirable) on balance (Feinberg 1983: 220ff.). But those countervailing considerations do not cancel or erase the unfairness of the act, nor therefore do they cancel or erase our moral objections to that unfairness. (Indeed, as Tormey (1973: 212) points out, reciprocal exploitation of two people by one another does not cancel our objections to the practice, but rather doubles them.) The countervailing considerations merely override our objections to the unfairness.

the force of the criminal law to prevent them from accepting more remunerative work elsewhere by breaking their current contracts with their present employers (Roback 1984); and, on Marxian analyses, the wage laborer is exploited because he "is *forced*, by his propertylessness, to work for the capitalist" (Cohen 1979: 343; see also Cohen 1983; 1978: 333; and van der Veen 1978: 449). This is, on one analysis, precisely the sort of exploitation that the welfare state strives to prevent. By giving to people who would otherwise be in fairly desperate circumstances the wherewithal of an independent existence, the welfare state protects them against the allures of fundamentally coercive offers that the market might throw up.

That analysis assimilates the notion of exploitation to that of theft, with which (at least in certain contexts) it obviously has much in common. Such an interpretation is borne out by the way we characteristically speak of exploiters "extracting" benefits from the exploited: to "extract" is, by the *Oxford English Dictionary*'s definition, to "take out by force," or to "draw forth against a person's will." Viewing exploitation in this light would, furthermore, make it abundantly clear what is morally wrong with the practice.

Further reflection reveals serious flaws in this analysis of exploitation-as-coercion, however.[14] Strong though the link between them might be in cases of economic exploitation, it seems peculiarly weak in other contexts. When exploiting friends or lovers, we are not *forcing* them to do anything whatsoever. They do what they do happily, willingly, voluntarily (Wilson 1978). If there is any force involved at all, it is purely self-generated.[15] Perhaps our friends or lovers do what they do under mental duress, in the sense that they do not want to believe that we—whom they regard as friends or lovers—do not reciprocate their feelings. In that way, they may be forcing *themselves* to do or believe something, in some sense. But *we* are not forcing them in any sense whatsoever.

Moreover, if a transfer were effected through sheer brute force, we would ordinarily not describe it (not primarily, anyway) as an act of exploitation at all (Elster 1983: 278–79). The thief who simply seizes his victims' property does not just exploit them—he *robs*

---

[14] For a different argument to similar effect, see Steiner 1984: 227 and Steiner 1987.

[15] Perhaps the same can be said of a society that "exploits" the unpaid labor power of "community carers" (predominantly, unemployed women—see Sundstrom 1982) to take care of the young and the elderly, and in that way keep down the costs of social security.

them. Exploitation implies some measure of cooperation, unwilling or involuntary though it may be, on the part of the exploited. Extortionists, blackmailers, and con artists all enlist the reluctant or unintentional support of their victims in this way. That is the reason we are more comfortable in saying that they exploit their victims than we would be in saying the same about clever cat burglars or muggers.[16]

B

A second way of construing the unfairness that lies at the core of interpersonal exploitation might be as "a certain kind of lack of reciprocity" (Cohen 1979: 343).[17] In a long tradition running from Broad (1916: 390) through Hart (1955: 185) to Rawls (1958: 178), unfairness is standardly analyzed in just those terms (Goodin 1976: chap. 7). And it is true that many central cases of exploitation—again, economic exploitation most especially—display precisely that property. Crucial to claims of international economic exploitation, for example, is the notion of "unequal exchange" between the First World and the Third; crucial to Marxian claims about the exploitation of the proletariat is the notion that (at the very least) capitalists take more than they give in the relationship[18]; and so on.

Again, however, this analysis does not offer a wholly adequate account.[19] It may not be altogether adequate even for the analysis

[16] It may of course be said that extortionists and blackmailers characteristically force their victims reluctantly to cooperate with them, and that that is precisely what the capitalist does to the propertyless worker. On that analysis, exploitation-as-force would be consistent with *some* cooperation of the exploited parties. But the problem with the analysis of exploitation-as-force is the converse: if exploitation is essentially a matter of force, then why in the limiting case of "all force, no cooperation" (i.e., the case of the mugger) would we not describe the situation as one of "mere exploitation"? To say that the model of exploitation-as-force is consistent with less than total force (i.e., some cooperation) is one thing. To say that it is consistent with a finding of no exploitation where there is nothing but force, quite another.

[17] Similarly, Thompson (1968: 222) says that "the classic exploitative relationship of the Industrial Revolution is depersonalized, in the sense that no lingering obligations of mutuality . . . are admitted." Feinberg (1983: 223–34) and Buchanan (1985: 87) also sound similar themes.

[18] Roemer (1982c: 269; see further 1982b) generalizes the classical Marxian definition as follows: "An exploited producer is one who cannot possibly command as much labor value, through the purchases of goods with his revenues, as the labor he contributed in production, and an exploiter is one who unambiguously commands more labor time through goods purchased no matter how he dispenses his revenues."

[19] Steve Walt (personal communication, 1985) has suggested to me yet another way in which the model of exploitation as nonreciprocity might fail. Notice that

of economic exploitation. We would not, I think, want to say that absolutely everyone who has driven a bad bargain is thereby necessarily exploited. Some people just cannot be bothered to shop around for the very best price available, and therefore end up paying more than strictly necessary for their goods and services. But surely we would not want to say, by virtue of that fact alone, that they have been exploited.[20] And, conversely, the sort of exploitation of the disadvantaged that the welfare state strives to prevent is not plausibly analyzable as a breach of reciprocity in any sense. When we worry about the disadvantaged being exploited, our worry is not at all of the form that the disadvantaged have given something to the advantaged for which they will not be repaid.

The shortcomings of this analysis of exploitation as nonreciprocity become all too glaring, once we move only a little beyond the bounds of economic relationships. There is, for example, nothing in the least reciprocal implicit in the notion of a gift. I give it to you free and simple, with neither hope nor expectation of return. Yet people can hardly be said to have been exploited every time they have given someone a gift.[21] Indeed, it is crucial to any affectionate relationship that we should not keep too keen an eye on the balance of benefits and burdens. Someone who repays a favor too promptly, or gives back to friends exactly the same gifts that they

exploitation, construed as nonreciprocity, can occur only where an exchange of some sort (albeit an unequal exchange) has occurred. "But surely," Walt says, "agents can be exploited in two ways: either by entering into [unequal] exchanges or by being excluded from exchanges." Thinking along these lines, we might say, e.g., that the exploitation of slaves consists in their being excluded from ordinary labor markets. Thus it seems that people can be exploited by being prevented from entering into exchange relationships just as surely as they can be exploited within exchange relationships; yet it is only the latter class of cases that the nonreciprocity analysis captures. Upon reflection, however, I am inclined to say that being kept out of exchange relationships is not in and of itself exploitative. What it does do is lay the basis for one's subsequent exploitation in those exchange relationships one is permitted to enter (between slaves and their masters, e.g.). But, as section I above has emphasized, creating the opportunity for exploiting people is importantly different from exploiting them, as such.

[20] The shopkeeper selling the goods at a high price might exploit such a shopper's attributes (his laziness, e.g.), but that does not in the circumstances specified seem to amount to exploiting the whole person. Perhaps the reason it does not has to do with the hypothetical cast of Roemer's (1982c: 269) formulation, quoted above (fn. 18): the shopper *could* have commanded full reciprocity, even if in fact he did not do so. But suppose the shopper is constitutionally lazy—he could not be anything but lazy, in this respect at least, and still remain the same person. I think we would still hesitate to say that a shopkeeper who set a higher price for an object, when the neighboring shop set a lower one, actually exploited this lazy shopper.

[21] Cohen (1978: 332) acknowledges this point when saying, "My neighbour does not exploit me if in friendship I dig his garden for him"; but he seizes the opportunity to reiterate the reciprocity analysis as well by going on to say, "particularly if he stands ready to defend mine against marauders."

have previously given him, is abiding by the rules governing the repayment of commercial loans rather than by the rules governing friendly gestures. Striving for strict reciprocity is inimical to the spirit of affectionate relationships (Goodin 1982: 104–5). Yet on the analysis here in view, doing otherwise constitutes exploitation. An analysis that makes affectionate relationships inherently exploitative is absurd.

Perhaps the answer is that in affectionate relationships it is something other than benefits that we expect to be reciprocated. It is only decent for people to try to reciprocate the feelings of those who care about them. But since feelings are not (or not completely) under our conscious control, we can hardly be blamed for failing to succeed in that task. It is unfortunate, no doubt, but certainly not unfair that you should fail to reciprocate the feelings of someone who cares about you. Whether or not you have exploited the other's affection depends on whether or not you have taken unfair advantage of it. But that is not a matter of how close you came to matching the other, gift for gift, or of how close you came to reciprocating the other's feelings, even. It is instead a matter of how well you adhered to the standard canons of decent treatment of others who are vulnerable to you (Wilson 1978; Goodin 1985b: chap. 5).

What the examples of lazy shoppers and nonreciprocal gift-giving among friends serve to show is that not every case of nonreciprocity is a case of exploitation. That is to say, nonreciprocity is not a sufficient condition of exploitation, in and of itself.

The most that might be claimed is that nonreciprocity is a necessary, but not sufficient, condition of exploitation. Reading carefully, it seems that that may be all that Cohen (1979: 343) is claiming in the passage quoted at the opening of this section when writing that exploitation is "*a certain kind* of lack of reciprocity" (emphasis added).

Saying that nonreciprocity is a necessary but not sufficient condition of exploitation would set us on a quest for some further feature that is also a necessary condition of exploitation and that, when added to nonreciprocity, constitutes a jointly sufficient set of conditions for exploitation. That further feature is likely to prove elusive, given the arguments presented elsewhere in section II about the inadequacy of all the other standard analyses of exploitation as well.[22]

[22] Steve Walt (personal correspondence, 1985) suggests that exploitation might

136

Happily, however, that quest for some further feature is rendered superfluous by the fact that nonreciprocity can be shown not even to be a necessary condition of exploitation. That demonstration turns on the simple fact that we can have such a thing as "reciprocal exploitation" (1973: 212). For an economic example, reflect upon the relations between a monopolist and a monopsonist. For a more personal example, reflect upon the relations between the dowager and the gigolo. Such relationships are undeniably exploitative although arguably reciprocal.

C

When writing that "a skilled exploiter plays on the other's character in a way a pianist 'plays on' the piano," Feinberg (1983: 202–3, 222) suggests a third set of interpretations of exploitation. These center loosely around the notion of "manipulation." In the parlance of games, fair play requires everything to be aboveboard. Manipulation is akin to cheating. And perhaps that is precisely what people are doing when exploiting one another.

This interpretation is not entirely out of place in the context of economic exploitation. Multinational corporations exploit Third World suppliers of raw materials by manipulating prices; OPEC exploits petroleum users by manipulating supply; and so on. But this analysis of exploitation-as-manipulation is obviously most at home in noneconomic contexts. Affectionate relationships are one obvious application. The welfare state is another. The welfare state, after all, is fundamentally designed to prevent the manipulation of otherwise desperate people by those who have resources that they need but that they cannot (absent the welfare state) obtain anywhere else.

Manipulation has three salient features (Goodin 1980, chap. 1). One is that it is an active rather than passive concept. When you manipulate something, you *do* something rather than just sitting around and letting something happen. A second feature is that manipulation is deceptive and, characteristically, hidden from view. A third feature is that manipulation is contrary to the putative will of the persons who are being manipulated.

If exploitation does not characteriatically display all these fea-

---

require the conjunction of nonreciprocity and involuntariness, for example. On this analysis, the reason gift-giving among friends is nonexploitative is that the giving is voluntary. Yet in one of the examples offered in section III.A, friends and lovers could be said to exploit one another even where force was absent, suggesting that "involuntariness" is not a necessary condition of exploitation.

tures as well, then it will not properly be analyzed in terms of manipulation at all. The third feature presents few problems. It seems likely (although not, strictly speaking, analytically necessary) that people suffer from being exploited and therefore would prefer it not to happen to them. The other two features are more problematic, however. Many very standard cases of exploitation fail to display one or the other (or both) of these other two defining characteristics of manipulation.

Take first the matter of deception. It is true that much exploitation is indeed surreptitious. And many otherwise puzzling reports of perceived exploitation can be traced to this feature alone. (Consider, for example, Humphrey Spender's (1982: 17) report that "I felt I was exploiting the people I was photographing . . . without their knowing it . . . even when the aim was explicitly to help them.") It is also true, in purely pragmatic terms, that exploitation may often be necessarily surreptitious. Often it simply would not succeed if the exploitees saw what was happening to them (Cohen 1978: 330). Be all that as it may, however, it is also true that exploitation can sometimes occur right out in the open. No one can deny that OPEC, throughout the 1970s, exploited its near-monopoly on oil to extract high prices from users. Yet no one could deny that they did so in full view, in their regularly scheduled meetings, with the world's television news cameras in attendance.

Consider next the active nature of manipulation. Some say that that is a characteristic of exploitation as well; and it seems that they have linguistic warrant for this judgment. Exploitation, after all, is a matter of *taking* advantage, and "taking" is a distinctly active verb (Feinberg 1983: 204–5; Coleman 1983: 112). Some might further try—in my view, unsuccessfully—to trace the wrongfulness of exploitation to this active aspect of the notion, through appeals to the familiar act/omission doctrine.[23]

The basic premise of such arguments seems incorrect, however. While exploitation might often be active, it is not always or perhaps even usually so (Wilson 1978: 300).[24] Most economic exploi-

---

[23] The act/omission distinction itself carries less moral weight than is commonly supposed (Goodin 1982c: chap. 1; Bennett 1983). But in any case, that would not explain why exploiting a person is so much worse than merely exploiting a situation. Both would be necessarily active, if either were.

[24] It may be said that you have to *do* something to exploit, or else you are just a mere beneficiary of exploitation—like the rich capitalist's child might be. Certainly we want to distinguish the exploiter from the mere beneficiary of exploitation. But "doing something" is not the best way of marking that distinction. Consider the "law of anticipated reactions" as it figures in the community power debate: the

tation, for example, takes place without anyone manipulating—in the sense of actively altering—anything at all. On standard Marxian accounts, capitalists exploit wage laborers even (indeed, especially) in a perfectly competitive market, where none of them could, through their own independent actions, alter prices or wages one iota; and this is a feature that the Marxian analysis of exploitation shares with various other non-Marxian accounts as well (Bloom 1941; Pigou 1932: 556–71; von Weizsäcker 1973).[25] An alternative way of putting the same basic point would be this. Whatever it is that makes us say that capitalists exploit workers, we would say the same whether the capitalists had sought out the workers or whether the workers had come, caps in hand, to the capitalists begging for employment. Where the balance of the initiative lies is irrelevant to our judgments of exploitation. The passive sweatshop owner is not, by reason of passivity alone, any the less exploitative.[26]

D

Another interpretation—a weakened version of the last—assimilates the notion of "exploitation" to that of "using." There is a clear linguistic rationale for that. Exploitation is a matter of "taking advantage of," and (as section 1 above suggests) that is equivalent to "making *use* of." This interpretation also offers a ready—although, as I shall subsequently argue, wrong—answer to the question of why exploiting people is necessarily bad while exploiting things is not. The answer here in view would be that it is necessarily wrong to use people, but not to use mere things (Tormey 1973: 221 fn. 1).

This interpretation escapes more or less successfully the objec-

---

weak do what they think the strong want them to do, sometimes without the strong's even asking, in anticipation of what would clearly happen if they tried to buck the powerful. The passive lord, sitting idly on his cushions while his vassals pile his "share" of their produce at his feet without so much as a summons from him, is clearly the exploiter of them even though he has not lifted a finger.

[25] Of course it is true that even if they cannot do anything to change prices, no one had to go into the market as a capitalist in the first place: they *did that*, at least. But that merely demonstrates active intervention, not manipulation. The latter is impossible without the former, but not vice versa.

[26] Even if people come caps in hand, of course you *do* something in accepting their offers to work for peanuts. But (as in fn. 25) you do not manipulate them in that case. And, besides, waiting for them to come to you is *less* active than seeking them out, but *no less* exploitative; and the failure of changes in the one variable to track changes in the other suggests the absence of any tight linkage between the two.

tions lodged against the last.[27] In other respects, however, the analysis of exploiting people as merely using people is less than satisfactory. To say that we "use people" is merely to say that they play a necessary part in the attainment of our ends.[28] We "use" people, in that sense, in all sorts of ways that do not amount to exploiting them, assuming that to exploit them is necessarily to do them a wrong. Butchers use bakers to get their bread, and bakers butchers to get their meat. Although each undeniably uses the other in these ways, there is nothing (necessarily) wrong or exploitative about such use. Or, again, in affectionate relationships friends or lovers undeniably "use" one another in the sense described above: each plays a necessary part in the other's plans. But there is not necessarily anything wrong or exploitative about that. On the contrary, there would be something deeply wrong with a relationship in which it were not true that one friend figures centrally in the plans of the other.

Some of those counterexamples may be met by saying that using people is necessarily wrong (and hence exploitative) only in cases of "merely instrumental utilization" (Buchanan 1985: 87). Insofar as people are treating others as ends in themselves, and not merely as means, then to that extent the utilization is not wrongful; and, given that exploitation is always necessarily wrong, neither is it therefore an instance of exploitation. That may well be true of the counterexamples of friends and lovers using one another. But it is unlikely to be true of relations among butchers and bakers. That counterexample remains.

The analysis of exploitation as "merely instrumental utilization" of people is sometimes phrased in terms of consent qualifying the

[27] Certainly we can use people without necessarily deceiving them: they can know that they are being used, and still be used (Blum 1973). Blum's article also shows that you can "use" people without necessarily "harming" them: for those who insist upon an analytic connection between exploitation and harm, this would drive a wedge between the notions of exploitation and being used; but if the connection between exploitation and harm is merely the strong empirical connection sketched in section II above, Blum's improbable counterexamples would not necessarily tell against the analysis of exploitation as using people.

As for the other criticism of models of exploitation as manipulation, "using" may be an active verb, but it is less insistently so than "manipulating." Small manufacturers "using" wholesalers to offload their merchandise may be active, perhaps. But they are minimally so—and certainly no more so than in the paradigm cases of relatively inactive exploitation described above.

[28] "Necessary," in the sense of Mackie's (1965) INUS conditions. I do not mean to suggest that there is not another path to the same ends, but only that the "used" person constitutes a necessary part of that particular path that is being taken to them.

wrongness of using people. If people consent to being used by other people (and if, furthermore, their consent figures centrally in the others' reasons for treating them as they do), then people are being treated as ends in themselves and not just means. Exploitation—the wrongful use of people—consists not just in using people, but in using them without their own consent (Feinberg 1983; Kleinig 1982; cf. Buchanan 1985: 88–89). That clearly is not the whole story, though. There are some uses to which people should not be put even with their consent, even if it is full, informed, genuine consent. Someone willing to sell a cornea or rent a womb is (or soon will be) legally prohibited from doing so. Presumably it would be wrong—exploitative—to use a person in such ways, even with that person's complete consent. The equation between consent and permissible use breaks down in the converse case, too. We can use people without their consent, and still not exploit them. I do not wrong, nor hence exploit, an enormously large spectator at a horse race when standing in his shadow to block the blinding sun.

Perhaps all that counterexample proves is that exploitation necessarily consists in the *harmful* use of other people (Buchanan 1985: 87). Where other people have been "merely" used—callously, perhaps, but not particularly to their detriment—then no exploitation has occurred. That analysis can arguably accomodate all the counterexamples offered above. The fat spectator suffered no harm. The butchers, bakers, friends, and lovers all at least *thought* they were benefiting from their relationships.

One disadvantage of that line of analysis is that it requires us to take firm stands on issues that seem better left open. It would, for example, require that we commit ourselves firmly to the proposition that the "merely instrumental utilization" of people is not necessarily to wrong (or hence harm, or hence exploit) them—firm Kantian principles to the contrary.

There is a further problem with that analysis, however. Perhaps the butchers, bakers, friends, and lovers in the above examples all thought they were benefiting from (or at least not being harmed by) those relationships; but, of course, they may have been wrong in those beliefs. Trivially, with the first pair, the butchers and bakers may have been trading in contaminated foodstuffs. More interestingly, with friends and lovers, it sometimes happens that a relationship that is objectively indisputably exploitative is subjectively valued even by the exploited party.

If we want to continue calling those relationships exploitative, and yet to hold onto the "harmful use" test of exploitation, then we must appeal to the objective rather than subjective standard of harm in such cases. Yet that too has its costs. It would, for example, make cases of "self-exploitation" far more common than we ordinarily suppose them to be—for people regularly take advantage of various of their attributes in ways that are objectively harmful but subjectively desirable.

Using people is, I believe, a necessary condition of exploiting them. But it is not a sufficient condition. What more is required in order to make it sufficient is not the presence of harm, or the absence of consent, or the presence of coercion, or the absence of reciprocity, or the presence of manipulation. What is needed is instead some specification of the *ways* in which people are being used. This is partly a matter of what is being used—of "the particular traits or circumstances [of the exploited person] that are utilized" (Feinberg 1983: 217). And it is partly a matter of the uses to which those things are being put. The analysis of exploitation thus reduces to an analysis of why, and in what respect, it is wrong (unfair, exploitative) to use certain attributes of people and their situations in certain ways. It is to this analysis that I now turn.

I I I

Exploiting persons is taking unfair advantage of them, but none of the standard substantive understandings of unfairness surveyed above satisfactorily accounts for the sense of unfairness at work here. Let us begin again, this time taking a more formalistic tack.

Here, as is so often the case, the notion of "unfairness" might best be explicated by reference to the game analogy. "Fair play" is play according to the formal rules and informal ethos of the game. "Unfair play" is play at variance with those standards. "Taking unfair advantage," seen in this light, would consist in availing oneself of strategic opportunities that are denied to one under the rules and ethos of the game at hand.

In philosophical discussions of the "duty of fair play," the emphasis ordinarily falls on the formal rules of the game (Broad 1916: 390; Hart 1955: 185; Rawls 1958: 178). But in the end, it always turns out that what is most crucial in grounding judgments of unfair play is some consideration of the underlying ethos, principles, intentions, or purposes of the game (D'Agostino 1981; Dworkin 1977, chaps. 2 and 3; Feinberg 1980: 289; Rawls 1958: 180). Steiner (1984: 227) offers the compelling example of someone who pigs out at a charity banquet: "It seems unlikely that we should be inclined to judge this . . . 'only fair . . .'; we should want to say, rather, that [the person] was not acting within the spirit of the occasion, that he was not truly a benefactor."[29]

What is fair or unfair, exploitative or nonexploitative, will thus depend heavily on the nature of the game. A forward pass is fair play in the game of American football, but not in the game of English rugby, and so on.

That seems to me exactly right. What is to count as exploitative should indeed depend on context. An act that would be exploitative in one context would not in another: sharp practice would be deeply exploitative in affectionate relationships (between friends or lovers), but not in commercial contexts. There is nothing about acts that make them intrinsically exploitative. It all depends on the context in which they are performed—on the nature of the game that people think they are playing.[30]

This analysis builds an element of subjectivism, and indeed of relativism, into the notion of exploitation.[31] That notwithstanding,

[29] Focusing in this way on the ethos of games seems to me a preferable way of fleshing out the notions of "nature" and "ends" that figure so centrally in Sensat's (1984) analysis of exploitation as the inappropriate use of a thing contrary to its nature.

[30] Therein lies the possibility of exploiting people by deceiving them as regards the nature of the game you are playing and of the rules you are abiding by. As Cohen (1978: 322) says, there would be "no serious unfairness"—no *real* exploitation—in the relations between feudal lord and serf if that were really the true *Gemeinschaft* it pretended to be. Serious unfairness (real exploitation) arose in that relationship because *gemeinschaftliche* games were being played according to *gesellschaftliche* rules.

[31] In my view, however, it does so in about the right place, and in about the right proportions. Certainly we want to say (with Marx, among many others) that people can be exploited without realizing it. Con artists exploit their gullible victims, even if the victims never come to realize that they have been had. So exploitation is not *just* a matter of subjective perceptions. Yet it is that, at least in part. Exploitation is not like starvation, something that can be said to happen objectively and quite independently of one's choice of baselines (Roemer 1982a, b) or customs and standards (Scott 1975; 1976: chap. 6). Exploitation is defined as a violation of the norms governing certain social interactions. Like other violations of social norms (against theft, etc.), people might not in any particular instance discover that a violation has occurred; but that does not mean that a violation has not occurred. Once the norms are set, whether or not they have been violated is an objective fact. The subjectivistic, relativistic element in notions of exploitation comes in the setting of the norms in the first place, not in determining whether or not they have been violated. None of that should be taken to imply a completely relativistic or subjectivist theory of morals, necessarily. There may well be certain norms that are right regardless of local attitudes. But if so, violation of those norms that are objectively right but subjectively shunned in some particular culture (e.g., norms against slavery in the ancient world) would be better described as *oppression* than as exploitation.

we can nevertheless isolate one generic flaw in the sort of unfair play that is associated with interpersonal exploitation. To exploit people is to take unfair advantage of them. Heretofore I have been emphasizing the word "unfair" in this general formula. Now, however, I want to turn my attention instead to the notion of "taking advantage." The generic unfairness associated with interpersonal exploitation lies, I suggest, in *playing for advantage* in situations where it is *inappropriate* to do so. Exploitation, thus construed, consists essentially in an abuse of power (Wilson 1978).

To say that people are exploiting others when inappropriately playing for advantage is not just to say that they are taking advantages$_2$, in the sense of securing goods that should not go to them. Rather, as seen in section 1, they are doing so by inappropriately seizing *strategic* advantages$_1$. Exploitation thus consists in playing games of strategy in circumstances that render them somehow inappropriate.

That, in turn, reveals something about the nature of what is really wrong with interpersonal exploitation. It is not, as Feinberg (1983: 215–19, 224) supposes, just a matter of the "unjust enrichment" of the exploiter. The central immorality is instead more akin to what is called in tort law "abuse of process" (Prosser 1971: 856–58). If I have injured you, then you may sue me; but you may not threaten to sue me merely with a view to obtaining money from me to induce you to drop the threat. To do so would be to abuse the legal process, to use the law empowering injured parties to sue for recovery of damages in an inappropriate way contrary to its intentions and true purposes. Much the same can be said of "blackmail" (Williams 1954). And so, too, with exploitation. It consists in abuse of the process of bargaining, using it in ways that are similarly inappropriate.

What conditions will be deemed to make it inappropriate to play for advantage naturally vary. In modern societies, however, they seem to be principally of four kinds.[32]

[32] These moral constraints on the operation of markets find ready parallels in the peasant societies of eighteenth-century England (Thompson 1971) and contemporary Southeast Asia (Scott 1975; 1976). It is by now clear—from Hirsch's (1976) discussion of the role of the pre-capitalist "moral legacy" in capitalist societies, or from various discussions of the need for Lockean provisos in theories of property acquisition (Bogart 1985), or from the legal unenforceability of "unconscionable contracts" (Devlin 1965: chap. 3; Kronman 1980)—that markets presuppose some such constraints, sociologically, morally, and perhaps even logically. The latter is the strongest version of the claim: markets presuppose legally enforceable property rights, which would be undercut if everything (including judges and constables) were up for grabs in the market.

First, it is thought wrong to play for advantage against other players who have renounced playing for advantage themselves. Paradigmatically, it is deemed inappropriate (unfair, exploitative) to strive for narrow, egoistic advantage over friends and lovers, who have renounced any such pursuit of advantage over you (Blau 1964: 78; Wilson 1978). Allied to that is the notion that you will be exploiting people whenever you betray their trust in you. While those who trust you may not renounce the quest for narrow egoistic advantage altogether, they nonetheless "let down their guard" to some extent with those whom they trust; and it is this very fact that you take advantage of when betraying their trust for your own gain (Feinberg, 1980: 289; 1983: 207–8; Wilson 1978: 302–3; Williams and Hepple 1984: 21). Also in an analogous position are those who are engaged in practices of reciprocal forbearances for mutual benefits. Those who take the benefits without paying the price (in terms of forbearing themselves) exploit those who are doing their bit; and the sense of exploitation here again can be traced to the fact that exploiters are playing for advantage in situations where others have (at least partly) renounced playing for advantage (Broad 1916: 390; Hart 1955: 185; Rawls 1958: 178; Feinberg 1983: 223).

Second, it is thought wrong to play for advantage against other players who are unfit or otherwise unable to play in games of advantage at all. This, I think, is what leads Benn (1967: 71) to say that it is *unfair*, and not just ordinarily dishonest, to cheat a blind person or an idiot (see similarly Feinberg 1980: 289). Something very much like this might explain why we think that dieters are being exploited by purveyors of chocolates who set up displays at supermarket checkout counters to play on their weakness of will. This might also be at least part of the explanation of why we think that drug pushers exploit addicts, and snake-oil salesmen cancer patients: those people are "in no position to bargain" (Feinberg 1983: 208–11, 223–24). More generally, those who are in rapidly declining positions and who in effect have "no choice" but to accede to whatever demands the other might make are, for reasons much like this one, exploited when the other plays for advantage and strikes a hard bargain with them (Feinberg 1983: 208–9; Frankfurt 1984: 6–7).[33]

---

[33] Whether or not you are *coercing* the drowning millionaire into agreeing to pay you a large fortune to throw him the life preserver (cf. Nozick 1972), you are undoubtedly *exploiting* him by so doing. That exploitation does not necessarily entail

Third, it is thought wrong to play for advantage against other players who are no match for you in games of advantage. Even in games of sport, you play only those who are a fair match for you in size or skill. This, perhaps, is the central objection to all forms of economic exploitation. In cases involving vastly disproportionate bargaining power, we think it inappropriate (unfair, exploitative) for the strong to press their advantage against a hopelessly outmatched opponent (Feinberg 1983: 203; Coleman 1983; Kronman 1980; see similarly Sen 1970: 121–22 and Rawls 1971: 134–35 fn. 2 on "threat advantage"). The paradigm case of this might be the monopoly supplier of some commodity that others need desperately, or the monopsony buyer of some commodity that others must sell in order to survive (Robinson 1933: chaps. 25 and 26; Levine 1981, chap. 9; Steiner 1984; 1987; Miller 1983: 83). This is the sense in which the United Fruit Company exploits the so-called banana republics of Latin America, for example; and it is the sense in which operators of the local general store exploited freed slaves in the American South (Ransom and Stuch 1977: chaps. 7 and 8). Similar exploitation of vastly superior strategic advantages occurs in various other contexts as well. This is the sense in which landlords exploit landless peasants (Shapley and Shubik 1967), capitalists exploit wage laborers (Elster 1978a: 88ff.; 1982a: 474ff.; see similarly Arneson 1981; Miller 1983: 84–85; and Pigou 1932: 556–71), and concentrated interests exploit diffuse ones in respect of public goods provision (Olson 1965: 29ff.). This argument will also take up any slack left by the previous one in accounting for the exploitation of drug addicts and cancer patients: they are quite certainly exploited by virtue of their grossly unequal bargaining power, even if they are not quite unable to bargain at all.

Fourth, it is thought wrong to play for advantage when your relative advantage derives from others' grave misfortunes. This is a distinct wrong from the second and third. Exploitation of this form is involved when, for example, "a television news producer photographs at length and close up the hysterical grief of a woman whose children have been killed, down to the last moan, shriek or howl, for the effects on the television audience" and the profits that can be derived from a larger audience share (Feinberg 1983: 223, cf. 208). Responsible members of the Fourth Estate themselves have no hesitation in dubbing this unacceptable "exploita-

---

coercion is established, in rather different ways, by Feinberg (1983) and in section II above.

tion of human sentiment" (Graham 1986: 25). That judgment of exploitation—of unfair, inappropriate use—would remain firm, even if there were several news crews bidding for the rights to photograph the grieving woman, who was therefore offered a good price for the rights. Similarly, operators of circus sideshows exploit the grossly deformed victim of an unusual disease, even if Elephant Man were one of a kind, much in demand, and enjoyed a strong bargaining position and a handsome salary.[34] This is the sense, too, in which undertakers (and, in nineteenth-century America at least, life insurers—see Zelizer 1978) are sometimes said to engage in exploitative practices. The same principle underlies even more clearly the sentiment sometimes expressed that, in dealing with the victims of natural disasters, morality requires that needed materials be supplied either free of charge or at most at cost. Making any profit at all—even the ordinary rate of profit—out of the distress of disaster victims is thought to constitute exploitation.

Exploitation has been characterized as playing for advantage in situations in which it is inappropriate to do so. The catalog of such situations offered above makes no pretense of being exhaustive. But for present purposes it need not be. What is important is not the differences in the various ways it might be inappropriate to play for advantage, but rather what they have in common. They are all, I shall argue, manifestations of one particular kind of wrong.

Exploitation of persons consists in wrongful behavior, but not just *any* wrongful behavior will merit that description. You do not (necessarily) *exploit* people whenever you lie to them, mug them, or break a contract with them, even if those acts redound to your advantage. Exploitation does not consist of wrongful behavior *simpliciter*. It consists instead of wrongful behavior of a particular sort, the violation of some particular moral norm in some particular way.

The moral norm in question is, I suggest, that of *protecting the vulnerable*. This is a generalized version of what lawyers call a "duty of care." It lays upon us a strong moral responsibility to

[34] I take it that it really is "playing for advantage" (i.e., trying to make money) and not merely "inappropriate use" in some more general sense that makes us phrase our objections in terms of "exploitation." If Elephant Man were being displayed, not for profit, but instead to warn pregnant women of the dangers of taking the drug that led to his own congenital deformity, then we may well still want to object to this display as an "inappropriate use" of another human being, but I doubt that we would phrase the objections in terms of "exploitation."

protect the interests of those who are particularly vulnerable to (i.e., whose interests are strongly affected) by our own actions and choices; and it does so regardless of the source of their vulnerability.[35]

I have given reasons for believing that we have some such moral duty elsewhere (Goodin 1985b), and I shall give some more, specifically related to welfare state applications, in chapter 6. My aim in this chapter is merely to build upon the former set of results, and anticipate the latter, so as to show how some such notion as that of a duty to "protect the vulnerable" would help us make sense of otherwise puzzling aspects of the notion of "exploitation."

It is my contention that notions of "exploitation" and of a duty to "protect the vulnerable" are analytically inseparable. Just as the notion of "adultery" is parasitic upon the notion of a duty of "marital fidelity" (it is defined as, and our moral objections to it are traced wholly to, the violation of that duty), so too with the notion of exploitation and the duty to protect the vulnerable. Violation of that particular duty, in a particular way to be detailed below, constitutes the defining feature of interpersonal exploitation. And our moral objections to interpersonal exploitation can be wholly traced to our moral objections to those violations of that duty.[36]

I V

All the cases described in section III above as cases of "exploitation" involve circumstances in which some such moral norm would come into play. In all those cases, the parties described as "exploited" are particularly vulnerable, in some way or another, to the actions and choices of those described as their "exploiters."[37]

---

[35] Much needs to be said to fill out the details of this duty. In the present context, however, perhaps what most needs to be emphasized is that the extent of people's vulnerability varies. Some people are vulnerable to other people quite generally a large proportion of the time and with respect to a broad range of threats to their well-being. Other people are vulnerable only to particular other people, or only in certain passing circumstances, or only with respect to a narrow range of threats. The more vulnerable people are to you, and you alone, in any given situation, the stronger your duty to protect them in that circumstance. But anyone who is vulnerable to you has, to the extent of that vulnerability and by reason of that vulnerability, a claim to your protection under this principle.

[36] Thus, I concur with Roemer (1985b) in supposing that our interest in exploitation is purely derivative, although we differ over what it derives from.

[37] Earlier commentators on exploitation have noted this connection, but only in

Not all delicts of the duty to protect the vulnerable involve exploitation, however. Exploitation consists in violation of that norm, but in some particular *way*. The duty to protect the vulnerable is a two-part duty: (1) firstly, it involves a general duty to suspend ordinary rules of behavior in dealing with those who are particularly vulnerable to you, and, specifically, to refrain from pressing your advantage against them in the way that would have been perfectly permissible in ordinary, everyday relationships; (2) secondly, it involves a duty to take positive measures to assist those who are particularly vulnerable to you.

Corresponding to those two parts of the duty to protect the vulnerable are two distinct ways of failing to meet its demands. One is a weaker form of delict, a "mere failure to discharge" that duty. That is what happens when someone violates the second injunction only. In such circumstances, the person has certainly defaulted on the obligation to protect the vulnerable. Still, the defaulter has not done anything remotely describable as exploiting the vulnerable.

The other is a stronger form of delict, a "flagrant violation" of the duty to protect the vulnerable. That is what happens when someone violates the first injunction as well as the second. Then and only then would we say that a person is guilty of actually exploiting the vulnerable. For that stronger judgment to hold, we would require not merely that the strong neglect their duties toward the weak, but that they actually negate their duties toward the weak. That is what they do when they positively play for advantage against those they are duty-bound not only not to press advantages against but actually to protect.[38]

---

passing; see, e.g., Tormey (1973: 215) and Kleinig (1982: 110). Notice that reciprocal vulnerabilities give rise to reciprocal duties which, if both are violated, would constitute reciprocal exploitation.

[38] Thus, if you let a blind man walk into traffic, you violate your duty to protect that vulnerable person but you do not exploit him, whereas if you say to him, "Give me $5 or I will not tell you where the traffic is," you exploit him. The first case involves what I have here been calling a "mere failure to discharge" the duty to protect the vulnerable. No judgment of exploitation follows from that. The second case involves "playing for advantage" (demanding $5), in what I have here called "flagrant violation" of your duty not only not to play for advantage but actually to help; judgments of exploitation do follow from behavior such as that. Similarly, when you damage your friend's interests wantonly, without gaining (or even seeking) any advantage for yourself from so doing, you have failed to protect your vulnerable friend's interests but you have not, strictly speaking, exploited your friend. The reason, again, is that this involves "mere failure to discharge" the duty. Had you damaged your friend's interests as a means of pursuing your own, it

Protecting the vulnerable is, in its positive aspect, primarily an *end-state* notion. As with all responsibilities, people here are simply assigned responsibility for seeing to it that certain sorts of outcomes are produced; it is left broadly to their discretion how that goal is to be accomplished. All that matters, insofar as discharge of this responsibility is concerned, is that the interests of vulnerable others have somehow been protected (Goodin 1985b: chap 5; 1986c).

Breaches of this moral norm come in the two forms just identified. The weaker form of delict is the mere "failure to discharge" one's positive responsibility—a breach of duty 2 above. That, too, is primarily a matter of end-states. Someone will be said to have failed to protect vulnerable others whenever and why ever their interests have suffered. How that happened is irrelevant to the judgment that it has happened. The judgment of failure is predicated on end-states alone, although, of course, the process by which the failure occurred may well mitigate a person's blame for that failure.

No one would say that we have *exploited* people whenever we have merely failed to protect their interests, however—even if we had strong responsibilities to do so. Sleeping sentries are guilty of all sorts of moral delicts, but exploitation is not one of them. It is the second, stronger sort of breach of the norm of protecting vulnerable others upon which charges of exploitation are grounded.

The second sort of delict is a "flagrant violation" of one's negative duty not to take unfair advantage of the vulnerable—a breach of duty 1 above. This is a fundamentally *process-based* notion. Whereas one's positive responsibilities toward the vulnerable are essentially end-state in their orientation, dictating no particular processes or acts that one must engage in to produce those end-states, one's negative duty toward the vulnerable does indeed specifically prohibit certain patterns of behavior. One must not do any of the several things that would constitute *abusing* those who are particularly vulnerable to one's actions and choices. Committing any of those prohibited acts would constitute abuse (and hence exploitation), even if the vulnerable person's interests happened not to suffer in the particular instance from the act that has been prohibited on grounds of its characteristically harmful consequences. Playing for advantage against others who are vulnerable

---

would have been the sort of "flagrant violation" of the duty that would warrant the description "exploitation."

in any of the ways detailed above would constitute just such abuse. That is the procees we know as "exploitation."

Thus the duty to protect the vulnerable is, first and foremost, a duty laid upon each and every one of us not to do anything that would constitute taking unfair advantage of those who are peculiarly sensitive to our own actions and choices. That is to say, it may well be that the duty to protect the vulnerable gives rise, first and foremost, to a duty not yourself to exploit those who are vulnerable. In its first implication, then, the duty to protect (and not to exploit) the vulnerable is essentially a "clean hands" principle.

But the duty to protect the vulnerable does not stop at that. It is not just a duty to protect the vulnerable against the effects of your own actions and choices. It is also a duty to protect the vulnerable against anyone's actions and choices that would take unfair advantage of their peculiar vulnerabilities.

What is morally objectionable about exploitation of the vulnerable is not that the exploiter commits a wrong, but rather that the exploited are wronged. Pragmatically, of course, the two are inseparable: there can be no exploited without an exploiter, no wronged party without a wronging party. But, morally, it is important to get the emphasis right. What worries us, morally, is the plight of the wronged, not that of the committer of the wrong. Hence, we ought to be as worried about wrongs committed by others as we are about wrongs committed by ourselves.

Thus, for the same reasons we think it morally important to *refrain* from exploiting the vulnerable ourselves we also think it morally important to *prevent* the vulnerable from being exploited, whether by ourselves or by others. In this way, the duty to protect the vulnerable also gives rise, second and secondarily, to a duty laid upon all of us to do whatever we can to prevent anyone from taking unfair advantage of people's vulnerabilities.[39] Just as the negative right not to be attacked entails both negative duties (not to attack others) and positive ones (to pay for police forces to prevent attacks), so too does the negative duty not to exploit others give rise to a positive duty to do things to prevent others from being exploited (H. Shue 1980: chap. 1).

These duties, like all duties, are hedged by all sorts of caveats

[39] Even if people are not particularly vulnerable to your exploiting them, they may nonetheless be vulnerable to you (along with everyone else in the community) insofar as they depend upon the community as a whole, and everyone in it, to establish institutions to protect them from being exploited by those who *are* peculiarly well placed to do so.

and excusing conditions. You are obliged to discharge them only if you can do so without defaulting on other, stronger or more urgent moral duties. You are excused from discharging them if the cost or risk to yourself from doing so would be exorbitant. And so on. But within these reasonable limits, these duties are compelling.

The welfare state, I shall argue in chapter 6, is one particularly apt way of discharging this second sort of duty toward vulnerable others, preventing their exploitation not just by us but by anyone. There are many people who, absent welfare state assistance, would be dependent upon and peculiarly vulnerable to particular other individuals for satisfaction of their basic needs. Through welfare state programs, such people become less dependent upon those particular other individuals. Being less vulnerable to the actions and choices of those particular other individuals, they are less exploitable by them. The elimination of exploitable dependencies in this way constitutes the clearest rationale for the welfare state.

This rationale for the welfare state obviously presupposes welfare programs of a particular form. Most importantly, as the next two chapters shall show, it presupposes that public relief will be administered in such a way as to preclude the dependence of any particular needy recipient upon the discretion of any particular social welfare caseworker. If dependence upon some particular private individuals was merely replaced, in public-relief programs, by dependence upon the discretion of some particular public official, then the needy person would be equally vulnerable (and hence exploitable) under either system.[40] So the rationale for the welfare state here being developed crucially presupposes systems of nondiscretionary entitlements: colloquially, "welfare rights"; more precisely, systems of transfers allowing minimal discretion at point of provision. This central feature of the welfare state is the subject of chapter 7.

[40] People would be exploited differently by public and private agents, to be sure; but the moral objection to the bare fact of their exploitation would not differ. For discussions of the abuses practiced by caseworkers with discretion, see Handler (1973), Reich (1963), and the further references in chapter 7.

DEPENDENCY

Morally, the fundamental justification of the welfare state is that through it we discharge our duties toward dependent others. Those duties are made particularly poignant by certain other aspects of the sort of market society in which welfare states are characteristically set. As I shall show (in sections I, and again V), the "internal logic" of those other more central institutions of market societies goes far toward committing champions of such societies to at least a minimal welfare state. But such "internal logic" arguments do not go quite all the way toward providing that justification. Time and again, some further moral premise is required to complete the argument. Thus, the justification for the welfare state is shown to be a distinctive—and a distinctively moral—one.

The crucial moral premise that is required to underwrite the case for the welfare state turns on the proposition—broached in chapter 5, and defended at greater length elsewhere (Goodin 1985b)—that we individually and collectively have a strong moral responsibility to protect those whose interests are especially vulnerable to our actions and choices. That proposition dictates making provision outside ordinary economic markets for certain kinds of people and certain kinds of interests (as shown in section II below). It also dictates, at least in broad outline, the institutional form that that extra-market provision must take, thereby providing the fundamental justification for the welfare state (as shown in sections III and IV below).

I

In seeking a definition of "the welfare state," chapter 1 has shown that it is properly characterized as a limited adjunct to the market

Material in this chapter is reprinted from Robert E. Goodin, "Reasons for Welfare," *Responsibility, Rights, and Welfare: Essays on the Welfare State*, ed. J. Donald Moon (Boulder, Colo.: Westview Press, 1988) by permission of the editor and Westview Press.

economy. Given that characterization, it is only natural that its justification should first be sought through an analysis of the various ways in which markets might fail.

Both the market and the welfare state aim at essentially the same end, after all. Both are basically mechanisms for promoting public welfare. Morally as well as economically, the fundamental justification of the market is just that under certain tightly specified conditions, the operations of the market will serve to maximize social welfare. That is the central tenet of modern economics, first formulated by Adam Smith (1776) and formally proved in our own day by Arrow and Hahn (1971).

In cases of so-called market failure, maximizing social welfare is precisely what the market fails to do. Therein lies the neoclassical economist's rationale for state intervention—to remedy the many and varied forms of market failure.[1] The first and most natural hypothesis then, is that the welfare state derives its justification from its role in correcting market failures of some distinctive sort.

Notice that justifying state welfare services in this fashion requires us to do more than merely to show that those services serve some clear economic function. Much that the state does to promote health and education, for example, might be construed as "investing in human capital." That is undeniably useful to the national economy; it undeniably promotes economic growth. But just demonstrating that there are gains to the national economy from such activities is not, in and of itself, enough to justify the state's assuming that role. To do that, we must further show that the market will necessarily fail to provide such goods—or at least that the market is an inferior provider of them, as compared to the state (Wolf 1979). In most of these cases, that is not obviously true. A champion of the market might reply, with a fair bit of surface plausibility, that education, health, and housing can all be (indeed, all long have been) provided as private goods through ordinary market transactions; and, he would go on to say, there seems to be no compelling reason, economically at least, why they should not (continue to) be provided in that fashion. Or, alternatively, he might reply that, whatever the failures of the market in this respect, nonmarket institutions are likely to fail even more badly.[2]

---

[1] For a taxonomy, see Bator (1958); for further discussion of these connections with the welfare state, see section II of chapter 8.

[2] Both rejoinders are discussed more fully in section II of chapter 8. The first is not wholly apt, as section II.A there will show; but even on the basis of those arguments, the "human capital" argument for the welfare state is not sufficiently

Or, again, some commentators see the function of the welfare state being one of coordinating people's charitable impulses. Andrew Shonfield (1965: 93), for example, writes that the welfare state "may be regarded as a means of eliminating those individual acts of charity which are designed to mitigate poverty, by centralizing them in the hands of the state." If each of us wants to give our charitable donations to those most in need, then some coordination of our donations clearly is required: otherwise, we may all end up giving to the same individual (because she appeared on last night's television news broadcast, e.g.). But, again, the need for coordination does not in and of itself argue for state intervention. Assuming that each of us genuinely wants his contribution to go to those most in need (and assuming that we are all operating with sufficiently similar standards of what constitutes an appropriate metric of "most in need"), coordination can easily be accomplished without the aid of the state's coercive sanctions. There being no conflict of interest between donors as regards how their contributions are to be spent, all of them would gladly acquiesce in the decisions of some central coordinating body without any threat of legal sanctions (Goodin 1976: chaps. 3–5). In practice, that is precisely what happens when the purely private United Fund coordinates charitable contributions in every major American city.[3]

In seeking an economic justification for the welfare state, then, we must look not merely for ways in which state welfare services provide economic benefits. We must look for ways in which state welfare services provide benefits that private actors in private markets *cannot*. We must look for ways in which markets would *necessarily* fail.

Perhaps the most notorious case of market failure concerns the supply of "public goods." If, as Friedman (1962: 190–91) suggests,

---

strong to bear any large part of the justificatory weight for the welfare state as a whole. The "nonmarket failure" argument is shown, in section II.D, to be potentially telling as regards the contribution of the welfare state to overall economic efficiency, but it is largely irrelevant to questions of the effectiveness of welfare state programs in performing their assigned tasks.

[3] In an interesting variation on Schonfield's theme, Buchanan (1984a: 71) presents a model of charity as an Assurance Game: "I am willing to contribute . . . , but only if I have assurance that enough others will contribute to achieve the threshold of investment necessary for success." But the same objection may be lodged against Buchanan's analysis as Schonfield's: if charity is just an Assurance Game, why should the coercive intervention of the state be required to provide the requisite assurance? After all, in Assurance Games, people are as keen to give as they are to receive assurances that they will contribute provided others do likewise; and each is as good as his word, just so long as others are likewise. Coercion being superfluous in these cases, as too is the state.

"charity" is a public good, then a substantial amount of welfare state intervention might be justified to provide an optimal supply of that public good. The basic argument would go like this. If people are altruistic, in the sense of internalizing the pains and pleasures of others (but, crucially, not in the sense of wanting to help relieve the distress themselves, necessarily), then their utility will increase whenever poor people's utility increases; and this would be true whether or not they were the ones who made donations to the poor in order to bring about that result. In that case, charity would indeed be a public good. Every altruist will have an incentive to free-ride on every other altruist's charitable donations; none of them will end up donating. All of them regret that outcome. All would welcome coercive public intervention to compel donations, instead of letting them remain voluntary (see similarly Buchanan 1984a: 70–71; Miller 1986).

Friedman's argument is plagued with many problems, however. One is that it is terribly sensitive to considerations of how many altruists there are in the community. Ideally, we would like to tax only those who are truly altruists of this sort—only those who actually benefit from the provision of the public good should have to pay for it. In practice, of course, this is impossible, because we cannot discover who they are.[4] As a rough-and-ready second-best measure, we are therefore inclined to tax everyone. But that is justifiable only if we suppose that most of them really are "closet altruists" of this sort.[5] That may or may not be a plausible assumption, depending on the country and the period in question. Yet, morally, we are not inclined to believe that the rightness or the wrongness of the welfare state depends upon just how generously inclined people in some place or some period happen to be.

Besides, this model fundamentally misrepresents what it truly is

[4] We cannot just ask them to identify themselves on their tax returns. For the same reason altruists of this sort would free-ride on charitable donations of other altruists in the absence of government intervention, so too would they deny their altruistic preferences on their tax returns. That is just a way of free-riding on the public transfer payment funded by taxes collected from those who admit they are altruists on their tax return, after all. With all altruists in hiding, however, no taxes will actually be collected for this purpose.

[5] Furthermore, in order to explain the "specific egalitarianism" of the welfare state, we have to suppose that most people are altruistic with respect to some goods and services (i.e., those relating to "basic needs") but not others. Furthermore, in order for those preferences best to be satisfied through in-kind transfers or nonfungible vouchers of the sort that the welfare state ordinarily employs, rather than through cash transfers, we must also make certain additional assumptions about the distribution of income and the variability of tastes across the population (Browning 1975; Weitzman 1977).

to *care* about other people. Charity constitutes a public good susceptible to free-riding (and hence market failure) only if people's
charitable inclinations focus totally on outcomes (i.e., that the poor
be made better off) and ignore altogether questions of agency (i.e.,
that it does not matter who makes them better off). Most of us,
perhaps, would agree that if more good can be done by someone
else, then we should ourselves stand aside and let him do it rather
than insisting upon our own agency. But the model in view goes
well beyond any so sensible a proposition. It depicts as charitable
paradigmatically someone who not only would *let* others help instead but, on balance, would *prefer* that others help instead. But
that is just not what it is to *care* about someone else. That is just
not the way that genuinely *charitable* impulses work.

Here our ordinary intuitions seem well supported by empirical
evidence. On the model of charity here in view, the altruist would
be expected to give less to the poor the more other people are giving. Empirically, the opposite seems to be true (Sugden 1982b).
That being so, however, charity does not seem to be a public good
of the sort susceptible to free-riding, or hence requiring public intervention for its provision.

A more persuasive case for expecting market failures with respect to public welfare provision might be made in a somewhat
more complicated fashion. The private analogue to the social insurance programs which constitute the bulk (if not the whole[6]) of
welfare state activities would be private insurance programs.
There are various ways in which private insurance markets might
fail in these contexts, however.

One of the more important ways has to do with the problem of
"adverse selection."[7] If participation in the insurance scheme were
voluntary, and if individuals had better information concerning
their own true risks than did underwriters, then better-than-aver-
age risks would opt out of the scheme (preferring to self-insure)
and only bad risks would be left in it. Premiums would have to
rise to cover the above-average level of claims from those now left
in the pool. As they did, more and more people would find it to

---

[6] What is left out is noncontributory social assistance benefits, such as those paid
to the congenitally handicapped and those who have never been in employment. I
return to this omission at the end of this section.

[7] The other widely discussed market failure in the insurance realm relates to
"moral hazard"—the tendency of people, once insured, to run far worse risks than
before, because they have less incentive to try to avoid the insured-against contingencies now that they will be compensated should they occur. Moral hazard, however, is a problem that confronts both public and private insurance schemes alike.

their advantage to opt out. Eventually, only the very worst risks would remain in the pool, and the whole scheme would collapse.[8]

To remedy the problem of adverse selection, insurance must be made compulsory. Another problem with private insurance markets would still remain, however. The financial integrity of mutual insurance schemes in the private market presupposes that each person's risks are, to a very large extent, statistically independent of everyone else's. Then and only then will the law of large numbers guarantee that the actuarially expected pattern of outcomes will actually occur, and that premiums collected from "winners" (i.e., those who do not suffer the insured-against contingency) will suffice to meet claims from "losers."

Where risks are interdependent, no such guarantee can be given. Consider the example of unemployment insurance. The probability of any given individual's being unemployed is not just a function of trends within his own firm or industry. It is also a function of the state of the national economy in general. Under such circumstances, it would be impossible to guarantee the financial integrity of any mutual insurance scheme. The problem is not just that actuaries are unable to set the right rate for premiums.[9] What is worse, with interdependent risks there can be no guarantee (as there can, through the law of large numbers, with independent risks) that premiums from "winners" (e.g., those still in work) will suffice to cover claims from "losers" (those out of work) *whatever* rate that is set.[10]

[8] In defending the original 1911 National Insurance Bill in Britain, both President of the Board of Trade Sydney Buxton and Home Secretary Winston Churchill referred explicitly to this problem of adverse selection to justify a compulsory rather than a voluntary scheme. See *Hansard's Parliamentary Debates (Commons)*, 5th series, 26 (1911), cols. 277, 495, respectively.

[9] That, too, poses problems. Some have to do with prediction of the insured-against contingencies, e.g., death or disability, which may be relatively easy for familiar classes of workers but not for new groups (e.g., women) of whom we have no previous experience on which to base actuarial estimates (Brilmayer et al. 1980). Others have to do with predicting the rate of return on investment (Hannah 1986: 96). Government actuaries are no better able than private ones to predict these things, of course; but, again, with general fund revenue standing behind them to remedy any errors they might make, it is less important for them to get it right.

[10] Epstein (1985: 649–50) offers a parallel example: "A life insurance program that covers all the workers in a firm may find that all are subject to a common risk of death. . . . So long as the insured risks may be interdependent, the insurance company is no longer in the enviable position of a bookie who stands to win no matter what state of the world emerges. Instead, if the common risk materializes, the insurance company stands to suffer very heavy losses. If all other factors were held constant, insurance companies would drop out of a market" where risks were interdependent in this way. See similarly Creedy and Disney (1985: 15).

That market failure is perhaps the most important argument for collective intervention in certain insurance markets. The government must act as underwriter of last resort, providing re-insurance out of general-fund revenues as necessary. Social insurance must, in that way at least, supplant purely private insurance.[11]

Much welfare state activity can thus be justified as social insurance designed to remedy the failures of private insurance markets. Much of it cannot, however. (That is especially true of welfare-state activity traveling under the heading of "social" or "public assistance.") The reason is that insurance is not fundamentally redistributive at all.

Superficially, of course, a fair amount of redistribution does go on within insurance schemes. There is redistribution between different periods of a person's life—from working to nonworking years in "child benefit" and "retirement insurance" schemes, for example. There is redistribution between different people—from those who do not suffer certain contingencies to those who do, for example. And so on.

At root, however, insurance is "expectation-preserving," and nonredistributive for that reason. The function of insurance is merely to remove uncertainty. It works by transforming a statistical expectation into an equivalent certainty. People are charged premiums proportional to their risks. Those in desperate circumstances, whose every expectation is of probable disaster, can derive no comfort from such a solution.

---

[11] Indeed, the need for '"National Insurance" was initially traced precisely to the frequent insolvency and actuarial unsoundness of voluntary Friendly Society mutual insurance schemes. Canon Blackley (1878: 835), in his pioneering plea for national insurance, estimated that "nine friendly societies out of ten in the kingdom" were "insolvent"—a fact broadly confirmed by the report of the 1895 Royal Commission on the Poor Law (Collins 1965: 253). There was, of course, every hope among its advocates that a national insurance scheme could be actuarially sound and financially solvent in a way that voluntary mutual insurance schemes could not, and therefore that the state need not be "brought in to make up a deficiency" in the National Insurance Fund owing to its insolvency, as the President of the Board of Trade, Sydney Buxton, was at pains to reassure the Commons in debates on the 1911 National Insurance Bill; see *Hansard's Parliamentary Debates (Commons)*, 5th series, 26 (1911), col. 275. Although the National Insurance Fund is self-financing when all goes according to plan, it is the obligation of the state to "provide absolute security"' when things do not go according to plan (Collins 1965: 253–54), acting as underwriter-of-last-resort. The state has indeed taken upon itself precisely this role in the operation of state-sponsored social security schemes. Note, for example, that "where there has been a funded pension scheme in the public sector, specifically accumulated funds have often proved inadequate to meet the pension promises made, but the taxpayers have usually bailed out the staff and rescued their pension entitlements," most recently in the case of U.K. postal workers (Hannah 1986: 93).

Imagine someone with a 50 percent chance of getting either 5000 calories or none. Actuarially fair insurance would (at best, ignoring administrative costs, profits, etc.) guarantee to provide that person 2500 calories in bad times, in exchange for a premium of 2500 in good times. The upshot is that that person enjoys 2500 calories, no matter what happens. But if minimum subsistence requirements were 4000 calories, insurance would have merely transformed a probable disaster into a certain one for that individual.

The most basic criticism of the insurance model of social welfare, then, is a moral one. Insurance norms simply cannot justify the welfare state's most characteristic function, which is to guarantee to meet the basic needs of those persons who are antecedently most likely not to meet them without assistance.[12]

There are various other ways in which welfare services might be regarded as necessary adjuncts to the market economy, correcting recognized market failures of one form or another. Those arguments are important for the purposes, in chapter 8, of countering the New Right's allegations that the welfare state is an unmitigated drain on economic efficiency; and, given that chapter 8 also shows the negative effects of the welfare state on economic efficiency to be quite weak, those arguments are quite strong enough for those limited purposes. Suffice it to say for now, however, that none of them is sufficiently strong to form any important part of the positive case for the welfare state as a whole. For that, we should be looking elsewhere.

I I

The true justification of the welfare state is not, I submit, to be found in the rigidly economistic logic of correcting market failures, narrowly conceived. Instead, it is to be found in the role of the welfare state in safeguarding the preconditions of the market.[13] There are three such preconditions that merit special attention here.

---

[12] For a discussion of how "social insurance" differs from "true" (i.e., private) insurance, see Hayek (1960: chap. 19) and Titmuss (1968: 173–87). On the nonredistributive nature of insurance, see Goodin (1982c: chap. 8) and Dryzek and Goodin (1986).

[13] There are also, of course, various macrosociological arguments that welfare state redistributions are politically necessary to "legitimate" market society and quiet social unrest. The focus of those arguments, however, is upon why legitimation is needed and how, social-psychologically, it is accomplished: an explanatory task. The focus of this book is upon how legitimation is achieved morally: a justificatory task.

First, markets presuppose secure property rights. Indeed, strictly speaking, it is the rights rather than the goods themselves that are bought and sold in market transactions. A variety of arguments (political, sociological, and ultimately moral) converge on the conclusion that the only way to secure the rights that are transferred in market exchanges is with some extra-market guarantee that everyone's basic needs will be met regardless of the outcomes of market transactions.

Second, allocating some things through the market presupposes that not everything will be so marketed. A variety of arguments (political, sociological, economic, and ultimately moral) converge on the conclusion that there are certain things which must not be marketed, if other things are to be. In order for there to be one sector that is governed by the laws of the market, there must be some other sector that is not.

Third, it is crucially presupposed that participants within the market sector are essentially independent agents. A variety of arguments (political, sociological, economic, and ultimately moral) converge on the conclusion that dependent agents ought to be beyond the play of market forces. In order for people to participate in the market as independent agents, there must be some non-market sector to meet the sorts of needs that would otherwise render those people dependent, and hence unqualified for market relations.

The welfare state underwrites all these crucial presuppositions of market society. It provides certain sorts of things for certain sorts of people outside the market. And in providing for dependent agents outside the market, it does so on terms that render them substantially independent in their market transactions.

A

Notice, first, that markets presuppose secure property rights. The quintessential market activities of buying and selling presupposes that buyers cannot just *take* what they want, without giving anything in return. Buyers will be willing to buy—and sellers will be able to sell—if and only if those presently in possession of the goods have some secure, enforceable title to retain possession of those goods, unless they voluntarily transfer that title to another.

More will be said of the "enforceability" of those property rights in section II.B. Let us focus here upon the "security" of those rights. It has long been said, by cynics of both the Left and Right alike, that the welfare state was no more than an organized scheme for bribing the potentially restive underclasses into quiescence. The real sociopolitical aim of the welfare state is, according to these commentators, to buy off the poor and thus to dispel any threat of revolution. Bismarck, being particularly blunt on this score, is their prime exhibit. But, arguably, the same intentions might have guided everyone from Roosevelt to the guardians of the old English poor law to rural landlords in Southeast Asia (Cloward and Piven 1971; Higgins 1978; 1980; Scott 1976).

Of course, intentions are one thing, effects are another. It may well be that, whatever their founders' intentions, the real effects of social welfare policies have been to stoke up rather than dampen down threats to private property. The evidence of the "revolution of rising expectations" literature (Gurr 1970; Hibbs 1973) might be called upon in support of this hypothesis: the more people get, the more they come to expect in future; and when a sufficiently large gap opens up between expectations and attainments, as inevitably it must, they engage in violent protests in consequence.

But the "social control" theorists of welfare policy and the "revolution of rising expectations" theorists of social protest might both be right. The latter warn that violent threats to private property will ensue from making people better off than they are at present; the former maintain that violent threats to private property can be forestalled, in times of economic crisis, by ensuring that people's existing standard of living not decline. Psychologically, at least, forestalling a decline is importantly different from promising an increase. Social welfare policies instituted at a time of economic crisis, with a view to maintaining the status quo for those whose standard of living would otherwise take a precipitous fall, might thus prevent them from striking out against private property in a way that similar policies instituted in a time of economic prosperity would not.

Still, this sociopolitical logic can take us only part of the way toward a case for the welfare state. The crucial point here is just this. Those who are most in need of the welfare state's assistance are people who, for one reason or another, have little power to secure adequate rewards in ordinary markets. But for the selfsame reasons that they command little power in the market, they also command little power outside it. Those who gain least in markets are also least able to mount any serious extra-market threats to private property. Thus, if the logic of the welfare state is to buy off potential troublemakers, then nothing need be given to, e.g., the very old, the very young, the blind, or the disabled.[14] Yet those are precisely the people that the welfare state rightly strives to protect, first and foremost.

For an adequate analysis of the welfare state phenomenon, then, we must look beyond the internal sociological and political logic of the welfare state and to its underlying moral logic. The property rights that are presupposed by market transactions might be perfectly secure, in an ordinary physical sense, if the very weak were denied the welfare state's protection. Being so very weak, they could mount no serious threat to them, anyway. But—speaking now morally rather than merely physically—there is another sense in which their property rights would not be at all secure.

The first step in this argument is to notice that morally we may have rights that we are physically incapable of enforcing. A standard case in point is that of the quadriplegic watching a thief's hand closing on his watch: no one could doubt the man's right, both legally and morally, to retain his watch; yet no one could doubt the man's physical inability to stave off the theft.

The next step in the argument is to recall that everyone has, morally, the right (which, physically, they may or may not be able to act upon) to do whatever is necessary to preserve themselves. Included in this is the right to take other people's private property, if necessary for self-preservation (Grotius 1625: bk. 2, chap. 2, secs. 6–9; Hobbes 1651: chap 14; Urmson 1958).

But notice, finally, that to say that the destitute have, morally, the right to take my property is equivalent to saying that my title to that property, morally, is less than completely secure. I may, morally, defend my possessions against some—but not all—comers.[15] There are, of course, many things I can do to make my prop-

---

[14] Waldron (1986: 481), seemingly wedded to a narrow contractarian reading of this tale that would indeed put the emphasis upon the physical security of property, concedes that "the very weak and the elderly" fall outside the protection of his welfare state, since they can make no "credible" threats to anyone else's property. He suggests that "a couple of epicycles" might be added to accommodate these cases, one having to do with the sympathy that the powerful might feel for the weak (his example being a mother for her child) and the other having to do with insuring oneself against someday being weak by promoting strong social welfare programs for all now, when one is still strong. Those sorts of moves mop up some of the counterexamples—but not all of them, and indeed not the worst of them. The spectre of the uncared-for orphan remains in the first epicycle, and of the congenitally handicapped in the second.

[15] Notice that this argument would work equally well whether we regard "doing whatever is necessary to preserve oneself" as a "right" or merely as a "liberty." It would be just as wrong for a property-owner to infringe another's liberty to take

erty physically more secure against their attacks. But to make it morally secure, I must protect it against such claims of necessity; and the only way to do that is to ensure that those claims will never arise. The only way to do that is to make sure that others' necessities are satisfied otherwise. That the market clearly cannot ensure. That is precisely what the welfare state strives to do. (Waldron 1986: 475ff.) Thus, the welfare state might be regarded as an essential means of securing—morally, more importantly than physically—the property rights upon which markets are built.

B

There are various other respects in which it is a condition of certain things being marketed that other things not be. To some extent, this is dictated even by narrowly economic considerations. As argued in section II.A above, the market presupposes a system of enforceable property rights, guaranteeing that transfers occur only voluntarily. But if all things, including enforcement mechanisms (police, judges, etc.) were up for auction to the highest bidder in the market, the system of property rights upon which the market depends would itself be undermined (Arrow 1972: 357). Another economistic argument has to do with the need for "trust" in certain sorts of transactions. Where buyers cannot monitor directly the quality of the good or service being purchased, they have to trust the seller if they are to enter into the transaction at all; and where the seller is thus trying to show himself trustworthy, he "cannot act, or at least appear to act, as if he is maximizing his income at every moment of time" (Arrow 1963: 965).

Those narrowly economistic considerations relate to the internal—and almost strictly logical—presuppositions of the market. Something in the very nature of markets makes it impossible for them to operate unless those preconditions are met.

Focusing exclusively on such internal, logical presuppositions of the market would badly understate the limits on the reach of the market, however. In addition to the logical preconditions of the market, there are also sociological ones of a similar form. Sociologically, too, it seems to be a precondition of buying and selling some things that not everything go onto the auction block. Sociologically, it seems to be a precondition of some things being mar-

---

what he needs (the property-owner has, in Hohfeldian terms, "no-power" to do so) as it would be for him to infringe the other's right to do so.

keted that some other things—some goods and some relationships—should be beyond the reach of the market.

Details vary from society to society. But in virtually every society, there is thought to be a broad class of people with whom it would be wrong to deal on a purely market basis. And there is thought to be a broad class of goods and services which it would be wrong to buy and sell in ordinary economic markets.

In purely market terms, for example, someone in a very strong position would be able to drive a very hard bargain indeed with someone in a very weak position. Reflect for a moment on Nozick's example (1972: 115) of someone "negotiating" with a drowning millionaire to supply him with a life preserver. The very factors that make it possible, in purely market terms, to drive a hard bargain with the millionaire make it utterly outrageous to do so. That would, as I have argued in chapter 5, constitute the height of exploitation; it would amount to taking grossly unfair advantage.

What makes the taking of advantage (i.e., market behavior) unfair varies from situation to situation. It might be that you are playing for advantage where those playing "against" you have renounced playing for advantage themselves, as when you exploit friends or lovers. It might be that you are playing for advantage against people who are unfit for games of advantage (like stealing from the blind) or who are not a fair match for you in games of advantage (owing, e.g., to differential information [Arrow 1963: 965] or power). Or it might be that your advantage is unfair because it derives from the other's grave misfortune. Each of those cases has been discussed in greater detail in chapter 5. What unites all these cases of exploitation, as shown there, is that by behaving according to ordinary market precepts in such cases you would in fact be violating your strong duty to protect those who are particularly vulnerable (for one reason or another, in one way or another) to your actions and choices.[16]

To some extent, these sociological limits on the reach of the market may derive again from the "internal logic" (here, the internal *sociological* logic) of market society. Some such neofeudal principle of protecting the vulnerable would surely have been required, in

---

[16] Notice that causal histories—how they ended up in their weak position or you in your strong position—are irrelevant to the strength of this moral duty. The fact that they got into the situation through their own improvidence does not relieve you of your duty (Goodin 1985b: chap. 5). Neither does your duty depend upon you being responsible for putting people in their present predicament, e.g., by depriving them of opportunities that they had and would have preferred to pursue absent your intervention (cf. Zimmerman 1981).

the transition from feudalism to capitalism, as a kind of "hold harmless" clause guaranteeing that no one would be made worse off by the switchover.[17] And perhaps some such guarantee to "protect the vulnerable" even today serves an important role in reassuring those who intermittently threaten to disrupt social order in a big way.

But here again, "internal logic" arguments will take us only part of the way toward an adequate analysis of the phenomenon. The crucial point, here as in section II.A before, is that those most in need of protection will characteristically be those least able to make trouble for society if they are denied it. Assuming it is they whom we most especially want the principle of protecting the vulnerable to protect, that principle must be understood as being primarily a moral appeal rather than as a political or sociological imperative alone.

Just as there are certain interpersonal relationships which should stay outside the market, so too are there certain goods and services which should be supplied outside the market. To some extent, this proposition derives from the last. In some cases, the reason that certain goods and services should be supplied outside the market is just that those are things that vulnerable others, with whom we should deal on nonmarket terms, require from us.

Beyond that, however, there is a further need to protect those things which we "take particularly seriously" from contamination by the "commercialization effect." As Hirsch (1976: chap. 6) wryly observes, "bought sex is not the same." The market has a "corrosive effect" on values, debasing what was formerly precious and apart from the mundane world, by allowing everything to be exchanged for everything else. In the end, we are left with nothing but a "vending machine society" (Okun 1975: chap. 1), where everything is available for a price (Goodin 1982c: chap. 6).

What sorts of goods and services we decide to take especially seriously, and toward which we therefore adopt this special sort of attitude, naturally varies from society to society. But conspicuously among them, in an individualistic market society at least, must be those things that are intimately connected to people's self-respect and dignity. Morally, that must be so: the only reason to respect people's choices (as the market ethos commands) is that

---

[17] Indeed, according to Macpherson (1985: 1), "The idea of economic justice arose only when market-determined systems of production and distribution encroached on politically determined ones. . . . It arose then as a defensive action against the encroachment of the market on traditional political society."

we more fundamentally respect people, their dignity and their self-images (Goodin 1982c: chap. 5). That, for example, is why we give people nonfungible rights of various sorts. As Okun (1975: 19) says, "If someone can buy your vote, or your favorable draft number, or a contract for your indentured service, he can buy part of your dignity."

Conspicuous among those things which are intimately connected with people's dignity, in turn, are those things which are required to meet material necessities. There are few things less dignified than rooting around someone else's garbage pail for your evening's supper.

C

Notice, next, the various ways in which participants in markets are presumed to be essentially independent agents. Let us start, once again, with economic theory. There, the case for the optimality of market allocations presupposes perfect competition. Operationally, that is standardly taken to mean that there are so many buyers and sellers that none can independently alter the price of goods bought or sold.

Where buyers are dependent upon a single supplier, or sellers upon a single buyer, for some good or service (and where furthermore it is not a viable option for them to abstain from buying or selling the good or service in question), competition is far from perfect. In the classic case, a profit-maximizing monopolist can produce less than optimal and charge more for it. In the analogous case nearer our present concerns, those who enjoy a privileged position vis-à-vis some particular other agents who are dependent upon them for supplies of needed resources can practice "price discrimination" against their dependents, charging them more than they should (i.e., would, if there had been a perfect market) for the needed goods and services.[18]

Much welfare state provision of needed resources is aimed at avoiding dependencies of just this kind. In the absence of state provision, people would be dependent upon a small set of particular others—family, friends, and neighbors—to provide needed

---

[18] On price discrimination in general, see Pigou (1932: pt. 2, chap. 17) and Robinson (1933: bk. 5). Sraffa (1926: 549), although explaining the attachment between particular consumers and particular suppliers differently, similarly shows that even with "a very slight degree" of attachment there is a tendency for "the general price of the product . . . to reach the same level as that which would be fixed by a single monopolistic association in accordance with the ordinary principles of monopoly."

resources. Those being purely voluntary transfers, the superordinates in the relationships would be at liberty to impose whatever conditions (demand whatever "price") they liked for the needed assistance (Goodin 1985d, e). In light of such potential for the imposition of restrictions equivalent to "price discrimination" in markets, there is no reason to suppose that the results of "free" exchanges of this sort would be in any way pareto-optimal.

Allied with this is the problem of "desperation bidding." It is a familiar phenomenon for someone dying of a disease that is curable, but only through a very expensive treatment, to be "willing to throw in all he owns" in exchange for such treatment (Calabresi and Bobbitt 1978: 121).

Those who are "desperate" in this way might best be conceptualized as people who will not be able to go on to the next round of a game unless they secure some needed resource (medical care, food, shelter,etc.) in the present round.[19] They are therefore willing to bid everything they own in this round, even if that leaves them with nothing for the next, because unless they win this round of bidding they will not survive into the next. Simply by virtue of this temporal lumpiness, anyone in a position to practice "price discrimination" against them could extract an exorbitant "price" from desperate dependents.

Even from a narrowly economic point of view, there might be certain things wrong—inefficient—with such temporal lumpiness as this. These inefficiencies would have to do with the failure of proper futures markets to emerge. For at least one of the reasons that people often find themselves engaged in desperation bidding is that they have been denied full present access to resources that they could expect to enjoy over the course of their lives as a whole. And desperation bidding often consists essentially in an attempt to secure just such access to expected future resources now, when they are needed—access that would be provided automatically if there were a proper futures market in operation.[20]

[19] This connects up with the arguments in chapter 2, section V about the temporal priority of need-satisfaction.

[20] Thus, Atkinson and Stiglitz (1980: 349) write, "A second illustration of the consequences of market failure is provided by the case of an intertemporal economy where only spot markets exist—no future contracts can be entered into. (One important reason for the non-existence of futures markets is that the agents potentially involved may not be alive.) In this situation it is possible that the competitive economy may follow a path that is Pareto-inferior." Fleming (1978) calculated that, on certain plausible assumptions about the other values in the equation, the optimal ratio of unemployment benefits to gross wage is less than fifty percent when

The source of the blockages to such markets are multiple, and their particular effects varied. As regards the causes of such market failures, most seem to have to do with something akin to the economist's "moral hazard" notion. Whether or not expected future resources do in fact materialize is largely a function of the future behavior of the person presently raising monies on the strength of those future expectations. The more successful he is in that effort, the more heavily his future will have been mortgaged; and hence he has less incentive to invest the needed effort in realizing those expectations, which, in any case, will now redound principally to the benefit of his creditors.[21]

Whatever the source of such market failures, and however varied their particular effects, the misallocation of resources consequent upon them is nonetheless clear. People end up buying less now, or paying more for it, or both, than they would have done had such markets been in operation.[22] And what would have happened had markets been functioning effectively in all respects is, of course, the proper benchmark by which to judge the efficiency of allocations in market societies.

Talking in this way of the *inefficiency* of desperation bidding captures only half of our objection to it, however. The economic argument just sketched traces the inefficiency of desperation bidding to the failure of the market to allow people access to their expected future resources. That is all well and good for those who are suffering some temporary embarrassment, and whose future expectations are rosy. But what about those who can only expect a future as bleak as their present? Even with perfectly functioning futures markets, they would get no relief. We have no grounds, then, for saying that it is inefficient to leave them to suffer. Yet

---

capital markets are perfect, but is over seventy percent when they are nonexistent (i.e., when savings and borrowing are disallowed within the model).

[21] Similar risks of self-induced defaulting are presumably what led to the prohibition of "post-obits," i.e., the practice of borrowing money against an expected future bequest. The more money an heir-presumptive raised in this way, the greater the incentive for the benefactor to write him out of his will (Trollope 1883).

[22] Often it is said that, on the contrary, desperation bidding leads people to end up buying too much of the good in question and paying too much for it (Zeckhauser 1973: 162; Calabresi and Bobbitt 1978: 115–22). That is true, however, only if we take people's ex ante judgments (as reflected in insurance decisions they have made) as authoritative over their ex post judgments (of how much they now want to spend to cure this disease, e.g.). There is no reason to do so. We know that people systematically underinsure, for all sorts of perfectly understandable (if utterly irrational) psychological reasons. See Goodin 1982c: chaps. 3 and 8; Kahneman, Slovic, and Tversky 1982; and Sugden 1982a: 213–14.

surely our objections to desperation bidding increase, rather than diminish, if it is to be desperation bidding in perpetuity.

A large part of our objection to desperation bidding must, therefore, be moralistic rather than economistic. The fundamental objection must be to the *unfairness*, and not to the mere inefficiency, of such exchanges. Even economists can appreciate that "trades that are made as a last resort . . . could not be fair trades . . . [They] would be distorted by vast differences in the bargaining power of the participants and by the desperation that spawns them" (Okun 1975: 19–20). Neither American nor English law is now prepared to enforce such "unconscionable contracts" (Devlin 1965: chap. 3; Kronman 1983).

Just as dependency undercuts the presumption of formal economic markets, so too does it undercut the presumptions of other sectors of society organized along quasi-market lines. Among these, in the sort of liberal democracy standardly associated with market societies, is the political arena. There, politics is conceptualized as just another kind of market, where the competitive struggle is for people's votes rather than for their money.

In the quasi-market of politics, just as in the formal market of economics, it is crucially presupposed that those in whom sovereignty is vested (consumers in the one case, electors in the other) are fundamentally independent agents. Those who are so dependent upon others that they might be obliged to bend their wills to those of their masters are deemed unfit subjects upon whom to confer sovereignty of either sort.[23] In economics, their dependency potentially skews their decisions as to how to allocate their economic resources; in politics, their dependency potentially skews their decisions as to how to allocate their votes.[24]

---

[23] As Schumpeter (1950: 254) says, "Volitions and inferences that are imposed upon the electorate obviously do not qualify for ultimate data of the democratic process." Just as those who are dependent upon others are at risk of having their wills *bent* by them, so too might those under the influence of others sometimes be at risk of having their wills *subverted* by them. It is the latter sort of interference—via the effects of propaganda, advertising, and pressure-group activity in particular—that most worried Shumpeter. It was that which led him to recommend that the competitive struggle for people's votes be confined to the choice of leaders, rather than to the choice of policies themselves.

[24] This is a central theme in the civic humanist tradition traced by Pocock (1975: e.g., 210 and 386; 1985: e.g., 48, 107, 66–70). It runs, variously, through the Putney debates (Woodhouse 1961: 82–83), Jefferson's *Notes on Virginia* (1785: query 19), and Blackstone's *Commentaries on the Laws of England* (1783: bk. 1, chap. 2, sec. 2). As Blackstone there writes, "If it were probable that every man would give his vote freely and without influence of any kind, then every member of the community, however poor, should have a vote in electing . . . delegates. . . . But, since that can

The "independence" qualification has, over the years, been used to justify disenfranchisement of diverse groups of potential electors.[25] Servants and apprentices were excluded, on grounds of their presumed dependence on their masters. Women were excluded, on grounds of their presumed dependence on their menfolk. And so on.[26]

A similar presumed lack of "independence" was traditionally used to justify the disenfranchisement of recipients of alms. The reason given—there, as in the cases of servants, apprentices, and women—was simply that "they depend upon the will of other men and should be afraid to displease" them (Petty, in Woodhouse 1951: 82). Or, as others have put it, "Whose bread I eat, his song I sing" (ten Broek and Wilson 1954: 265).[27]

---

hardly be expected in persons of indigent fortunes, or such as are under the immediate dominion of others, all popular states have been obliged to establish certain qualifications, whereby some who are suspected to have no will of their own are excluded from voting, in order to set other individuals, whose wills may be supposed independent, more thoroughly upon a level with each other" (Cf. Macpherson 1962: chap. 3; 1973: chap. 12; 1985: 102). Similar themes are sounded in Norwegian and German suffrage debates (Bendix and Rokkan 1964: 97). This theme tends to get submerged in later liberal discussions (Miller 1978), but arguably remains always central to the deeper logic of the liberal theory of citizenship (van Gunsteren 1978).

[25] At least it served as the excuse: Kousser (1983) argues that the real reasons were often otherwise.

[26] The other members of this conventional catalog—Catholics and Jews—were presumably excluded less on grounds of dependence upon anyone else than on grounds of voluntary subservience to someone (their submission to a higher spiritual authority counting as the functional equivalent of allegiance to a foreign crown).

Interestingly, ways were found to argue for extending the suffrage to wage-earners even within this larger logic: "Wage earners outside the immediate household of the employer" were, in some sense, perhaps, "dependent" upon their employers; "but it was not evident that they would inevitably follow their employers politically" in the way that servants in their own households would have ordinarily done (Bendix and Rokkan 1964: 98). Notice, in this connection, Tocqueville's (1840: vol. 2, chap. 5) reports: "In democracies, . . . the servant always thinks of himself as a temporary inmate in his master's house. [The master] has not known his ancestors and will not see his descendants [as masters would have done in aristocracies]; he has nothing lasting to expect from them. Why, then, should [the servant] identify his life with his master's, and what reason could there be for such a strange sacrifice of himself [merging his sense of his own self and interests with those of his master]?"

[27] "Dependence begets subservience and venality, suffocates the germ of virtue, and prepares fit tools for the designs of ambition," inveighs Jefferson in his *Notes on Virginia* (1785: query 19). Jefferson's own advice to his fellow Virginians was that, "While we have land to labor . . . , let us never wish to see our citizens occupied at a workbench, or twirling a distaff"; he admonished them to engage in husbandry rather than manufacture or commerce. Others writing at about the same time, however, saw commerce as an alternative solution to the same problem of

That concern was quite a valid one, given the way in which poor-law relief was traditionally administered. At best, it was regarded as a form of "gratuity."[28] As such, its dispensation was wholly under the discretionary control of poor-law guardians. Recipients of such gratuities were, indeed, dependent upon the favor of the guardians for their continued support. So too were welfare recipients dependent upon the favor of state officials who, in the early years of this century, assumed responsibility for the administration of still largely discretionary programs of social assistance. So too, indeed, were employees dependent upon the discretion of their employers to grant them retirement pensions, which were purely *ex gratia* in most firms well into the early years of the twentieth century (Hannah 1986: chap. 1).

In the welfare state, in contrast, assistance is placed as far beyond the discretionary control of those charged with its dispensation as it is possible to place it. To be sure, needy citizens will still have to depend upon such assistance for satisfaction of their needs. Critics of public relief programs make much of that fact, and of the presumed psychological damage that such dependence inflicts.[29] What those writers overlook, however, are the important differences between different kinds of dependency.

In a welfare state, needy citizens no longer depend—as historically they did (and, if the New Right gets its way, as once again they would) under a regime of public or private charity—upon the arbitrary will of those dispensing the benefits. In a welfare state, the decisions of social service administrators are not left to their own arbitrary will. Instead, those decisions are tightly circumscribed by rules from above.[30] Recipients of welfare state relief are

---

personal dependence, pointing to "the mobility of the individual in an increasingly commercial society" (Pocock 1985: 107).

[28] Worse, when many U.S. state courts held that public assistance constituted a "payment of gratuities to individuals from the public treasury" of the sort standardly prohibited by state constitutions, it was justified instead by appeal to the state's "police power" (Smith 1949: 269). Looking upon public assistance payments as a mode of social control, in this way, not only allows but encourages administrators of the programs to set terms and conditions upon payment of benefits, in ways that compromise the independence of recipients.

[29] See, e.g., Hegel (Moon 1987), Tocqueville (1835/1983), Anderson (1978: 56, 153) and Murray (1982: 9; 1984: 64–65). Writers of the New Right, in particular, emphasize that "throughout American history, the economic independence of the individual and the family has been the chief distinguishing characteristic of good citizenship"; and that "to measure progress along these lines we must calculate . . . how many people would be poor if it were not for government help," which they scorn as "the dependent population" (Murray 1982: 9).

[30] This is true formally, at least; in practice, bureaucrats may still exercise consid-

thereby freed to vote as they please, without having to fear that alms-givers might withdraw their assistance in a fit of pique.

The sort of dependency for which the welfare state constitutes a cure is that which is akin to peonage. And the welfare state, characterized as it is by nondiscretionary benefits, addresses that particular problem quite successfully. It renders the poor politically independent of those who are directly responsible for providing them with needed resources.[31]

I I I

The problem that the welfare state is designed to answer, then, is the problem of dependency.[32] And the problem of dependency is the problem of exploitation. Under the law of the market, those who are dependent could and would be mercilessly exploited. Economically, you can drive a very hard bargain indeed with someone who is desperately in need and dependent upon you for satisfaction of that need. Morally, however, you must not do so.

The point of extra-market provision for basic needs, on this argument, is to prevent the exploitation of dependencies. Not all extra-market institutions necessarily attempt (much less succeed in) that task. Precursors to the welfare state conspicuously failed in it, treating public assistance as a gratuity to which any number of strings might be attached, thereby putting those dependent upon such assistance at the mercy of the largely arbitrary will of those

---

erable discretionary power, some of it within the rules but much of it outside them (van Gunsteren 1978: 29–32; Chapter 7 below). Recipients are still dependent upon legislators to enact and to fund social welfare programs, of course. But the greatest risk of exploitation of dependencies arises where discretion is exercised at the point of provision of the good or service, not much further up the line as with the legislator's discretion.

[31] Some would suggest that we disenfranchise those with an interest in the outcome, preventing welfare recipients from voting up welfare payments just as we prevent U.S. congressmen from voting up their own salaries during a session of congress. Then, however, every owner of private property would have to be disenfranchised, since they too clearly benefit from certain of the state's activities (e.g., the exercise of its police power). See Kousser 1983: fn. 30. This will be taken up again at the end of section III below.

[32] Notice the emphasis upon "dependency" in the early and influential opinion of Justice Daniel Brewer (1875: 74–75). "Something more than poverty . . . is essential to charge the state with the duty of support [of indigents]. It is, strictly speaking, the pauper, and not the poor man, who has claims on public charity. It is not one who is in want merely, but one who, being in want, is unable to prevent or remove such want. There is the idea of helplessness as well as destitution. We speak of those whom society must aid, as the dependent classes, not simply because they do depend on society, but because they cannot do otherwise than thus depend."

administering such assistance. Everything from their morals to their family budgets were subject to administrative scrutiny.[33] In saying that extra-market provision for basic needs *can* render people independent in the ways that morally matter, then, I do not mean to imply that it necessarily *must*.

Let us assume, however, that that *is* our goal. There are various strategies available to us for pursuing it. One way to prevent the exploitation of dependencies is to eliminate dependencies. There is much that the state can do along these lines. While much of that lies outside the ambit of the welfare state proper (being the business of macroeconomic policy or social policy more generally), there is nonetheless much that the welfare state, even narrowly construed, can do along these lines. It can, for example, often prevent the infirm aged from having to enter nursing homes, simply by providing home help and meals-on-wheels (Kane and Kane 1979; Gibson 1985).

Some would argue that that strategy, especially as it is practiced by the welfare state, amounts merely to shifting dependencies, not to eliminating them at all. People who would otherwise be dependent upon a nursing home are dependent instead upon state-provided assistance to keep them out of a nursing home. The elderly are no less dependent than before. They are just dependent upon different people.

The general thesis underlying this challenge seems to be that there is always some constant quantity of dependency which can be shifted around but never eliminated. I am skeptical of that thesis. But since I am unsure how to individuate (and hence to enumerate, much less to weight) different distinct dependencies, I am unsure how such a position could ever be proven or disproven.

The better defense of the welfare state, in my view, ducks that question altogether. It rests instead on the second broad strategy for avoiding the exploitation of dependencies.[34] Whereas the first

[33] For examples, see: ten Broek and Wilson 1954: 264–65; Reich 1965: 1247–51; and UK SBC 1977: para. 1.43.

[34] And, as chapter 5 has shown, all exploitation is the exploitation of dependencies or vulnerabilities (terms which I here use interchangeably). Not all forms of unfair dealing necessarily involve the exploitation of such vulnerabilities or dependencies, of course. Being tricked into paying vastly over the market price for an item through fraudulent misrepresentation of the goods is David Miller's (personal correspondence, 1986) example. But neither do all forms of unfair dealing necessarily involve exploitation. It would, to persist with Miller's example, be odd to say that everyone who has been disadvantaged by a breach of the Trades Description Act has been *exploited*, as opposed to having been cheated, tricked, or duped. (Certain things about them e.g., their ignorance or gullibility, have been exploited, to

strategy aimed at the elimination of dependencies, the second aims merely at preventing their exploitation. While this may be a less flamboyant solution to the problem of dependency, it is a more precisely focused one. The objections discussed above, recall, were not to the existence of dependency but merely to its exploitation. Eliminating dependencies, although more flashy, is a more roundabout strategy for solving that problem. Eliminating dependencies is helpful insofar as that which does not exist cannot be exploited. But it is the exploitation of the dependency rather than its existence per se that, on the arguments developed above, really matters.

There are four conditions, all of which must be present if dependencies are to be exploitable.[35] First, the relationship must be *asymmetrical*. In any reasonably complex society, most people are dependent upon a great many other people for a great many things. Interdependence is the essence of all mutually profitable trades, of all political alliances, and of all friendships and loving relations (Baldwin 1980; Wilson 1978). No one thinks that there is anything wrong with such relationships merely by virtue of the fact that people within them depend upon one another. The reason is precisely that, being relationships of *inter*dependence, neither party can exploit the other through a credible threat to withdraw from the relationship. Each depends on the other in turn, and that mutual dependence guarantees the relationship against exploitation.

Second, even in an asymmetrical relationship, to be truly exploited the subordinate party must *need* the resource that the superordinate supplies.[36] There happens to be a single supplier of

---

be sure—but then, that is merely to say that the buyer was vulnerable to and dependent upon the seller for an honest description of the goods.) Insofar as a form of unfair dealing does not involve the exploitation of vulnerabilities or dependencies, it seems better to describe it not as a case of exploitation but rather as a case of one of those other sorts of abuse.

[35] These are discussed in more detail in Goodin 1985b: chap. 7.

[36] I say "truly exploited," because the monopoly supplier of desirable but not strictly necessary luxury goods can indeed take advantage of his market power to charge marginally more for figs in our village than the market price in the nearest big city, where there are many suppliers. That might, at first blush, appear exploitative. But my inclination is to say that it is not "truly" so—there is nothing particularly unfair about seizing such advantages, and it is "taking unfair advantage" that constitutes exploitation, as analyzed in chapter 5.

Arguably, this condition should be phrased: "The subordinate party must *believe* he needs the resource." The logic underlying that suggestion is that people will be as desperate to satisfy perceived needs as genuine ones, even if those perceptions are in error. I prefer the present formulation on the grounds that, although any

figs in our village. I depend upon him for my supply; he does not depend upon me for my custom (there being many fig-lovers in our village, who will buy his figs if I do not). Still, unilateral though my dependence upon him is, he cannot exploit me because if push comes to shove I can always protect myself by withdrawing from the relationship. Fond though I am of figs, I do not strictly need them. If the price becomes exploitative, I will simply do without them.[37]

Third, to be truly exploited, the subordinate party must depend upon some *particular* superordinate for the supply of needed resources. If there is a multitude of providers I can choose between, then no one of them (nor, absent some extraordinary feat of collective action on their part in forming a cartel, all of them taken together) can exploit me. Much though I depend on farmers as a group for my food, I am not exploited by them because there are so many I can choose between to satisfy my needs.

Fourth, the superordinate can truly exploit the subordinate only if he enjoys *discretionary* control over the resources that the subordinate needs from him. Consider my relationship with my bank manager. The relationship is clearly asymmetrical: he has something I need (my savings, deposited in his bank), while I have nothing he especially needs in return. Let us suppose that I need my savings desperately for some particular purpose—an operation, say—and that I have no other source of funds. Hence the situation meets all the criteria for a morally worrying dependency relationship so far laid down. Still, we need not be worried. The point is that my bank manager has, in the final analysis, no discretionary control over my savings. When I present him with a properly completed withdrawal form, he has no choice (legally) but to present me with my money. Hence, the dependency is simply not exploitable.[38]

---

given individual's perceptions may be in error, all people's perceptions are unlikely to be (or remain, even if they all briefly are) in error; and so far as the public policy question of what resources should be publicly provided is concerned, it is the "standard" perception rather than anyone's idiosyncratic perception of need that matters.

[37] See, e.g., Sraffa 1926: 545–46; Hayek 1960: chap. 9; and Plant 1985: 305.

[38] As Rousseau (1762a: bk. 2) points out, "If there is any cure for this social evil [of dependence of men on men], it is to be found in the substitution of law for the individual, in arming the general will with a real strength beyond the power of any individual will. If the laws of nations, like the laws of nature, could never be broken by any human power, dependence on men would become dependence on things; all the advantages of a state of nature would be combined with all the advantages of social life in the commonwealth."

Preventing the exploitation of dependencies by making assistance to needy, dependent people largely nondiscretionary is the hallmark of the welfare state. There, benefits are bestowed "as of right." While I regard "welfare rights" as not quite right for the purpose (for reasons I shall explain in section IV briefly and in chapter 7 more fully), that phrase does effectively emphasize what is crucial in the welfare-state approach to dependency. That is that the supply of certain resources to those in need of them should, insofar as humanly possible, be put outside of the discretion of the officials responsible for dispensing them. By curtailing discretion, we will have curtailed the risk of people being exploited, however much they may still need the resources being dispensed or however few other sources of supply they may have.[39]

Thus, the state *can*, through nondiscretionary transfers of resources, prevent the exploitation of dependencies. To say that it can is not, however, the same as saying that it necessarily will. Before advocating that strategy unequivocally, then, we must first consider the risks that that policy's aims will be systematically subverted by external forces in the course of its implementation (Wildavsky 1979; Wolf 1979).

For that strategy to succeed, it is necessary both (a) that adequate resources be transferred to guarantee that people's basic needs will be met and (b) that that transfer occur in ways that are substantially independent of any discretionary power on the part of those responsible for effecting the transfer. The latter seems particularly impervious to subversion as the implementation phase. Of course there are limits to the extent to which discretion can be

[39] See, e.g.: Smith 1946; 1949; 1955; Marshall 1949; Keith-Lucas 1953; Reich 1964; 1965; Goodin 1985b: chap. 7; chapter 12 below. It is of course possible that people's "welfare rights" might conflict with one another. My argument here does not deny this fact, but merely implies: (a) that that should be avoided insofar as possible— through, e.g., generous funding and proper structuring of the assistance programs designed to meet people's basic needs; and (b) that where such conflicts are unavoidable, there should insofar as possible be some central, legislative determination of which right wins out over which other, so as to avoid a conflict of laws or of rights giving rise to discretion in those administrators who are directly responsible for dispensing the benefits. Neither does my argument here deny the fact that the political behavior of would-be welfare beneficiaries might be skewed by the availability (or possibility) of social welfare programs. But saying that people are dependent upon programs, and that their dependence upon those programs skews their votes, is importantly different from saying that people are dependent upon particular other individuals who can thereby control their votes. In the welfare state, the poor are not dependent upon the arbitrary will of any other person. They are no less free to vote independently than is the oil tycoon, who depends upon the government's policy of oil depletion tax allowances for his profits.

eliminated, as chapter 7 will show; but insofar as policies laying down strictly defined legal rights and duties are possible at all, administrators refusing to abide by those prescriptions can and standardly will be prosecuted for administrative misconduct in the ordinary way. Implementation failures, there, are not greatly to be feared.

The greater threat is that not enough resources will be devoted to the task actually to relieve dependencies in the population, thereby forcing people to fall back upon discretionary family, friend, and charitable relief to supplement nondiscretionary state assistance. The evidence suggests that even the minimal U.S. welfare state has made major strides toward reducing the incidence of income poverty, and the dependencies that that creates (Danziger, Haveman, and Plotnik 1981). Still, it has not eliminated all of it, and it can hardly be expected ever to do so.

Failure to implement the policy completely, in this respect, does not compromise the whole project, however. What matters morally is not how much aid is siphoned off, but rather how much gets through (Goodin and Le Grand 1987: chap. 10). If exploitable dependencies are bad, then their partial elimination is preferable to their not being eliminated at all. Hence, implementation failures in the form of insufficient funding merely make the programs less successful than they might have been, here. They cause the programs to be only partially successful, but not to fail completely.

I V

Viewed from this angle, conventional understandings of the welfare state can be shown to be morally near the mark, but also slightly off the mark. Ordinarily, for example, it is said that the welfare state provides needed resources "as of right," and the notion of a welfare "right" is ordinarily meant to be taken quite literally.

The notion of a "right" is not quite what is needed for the purposes which the welfare state serves, however. As I shall argue at greater length in chapter 7, the notion of a "right," strictly speaking, implies a restrictive notion of who has "standing," legally, to claim and to complain. In the context of the welfare state, and given what we know about the propensity (not to mention capacity) of poor people to pursue legal claims for themselves, that restriction is wholly inappropriate.

It *is* essential that we should think in terms of firm legal rules

which bind, insofar as possible, officials to provide welfare benefits to all those who are qualified to receive them. But what is crucial about those rules is that they should allow minimal scope for
official discretion, rather than that they should take the particular
form of rules embodying welfare rights. We should instead be
thinking in terms of imposing obligations, duties and responsibilities upon officials dispensing welfare benefits. It is important—
for their self-respect, if nothing else—that recipients should be
given standing to claim such benefits, and to complain if they are
not given them when they are due them. But it is also important
that such standing to complain about nonfeasance or misfeasance
of official duties not be limited merely to would-be beneficiaries,
who would be understandably reluctant to antagonize officials
with whom they must continue to deal.

Or, again, we standardly talk in terms of the welfare state's
meeting people's "basic needs." To this point, I have in this chapter conformed with that standard usage. But the upshot of chapter
2 was of course that no neat account of "needs" can be given that
would effectively distinguish them from "mere wants" in a way
that would justify the priority we ordinarily think should be accorded to needs over mere wants. Certainly needs do correlate, in
a rough-and-ready way, with factors that *do* deserve such priority.
As shown in chapter 2, however, the correlation is only an imperfect one, and does not translate into a blanket priority for needs
over wants as such.

My discussion of preventing exploitation of dependencies once
again helps to cast this old problem in a slightly new light. Needs
give rise to exploitable dependencies because people in need have
"no reasonable choice" but to pay any price, comply with any conditions that those upon whom they are dependent for satisfaction
of their needs might care to lay down. It is simply "not reasonable" to expect them to do without the needed resources instead of
complying.

The "no reasonable choice" standard is much weaker than the
"no choice" standard that is ordinarily—and rightly—taken to define "needs." Those things which we need are standardly said to
be those things that physically (or, perhaps, psychologically) we
simply cannot do without. There are certain purposes for which
that stronger standard is clearly more appropriate. Central among
them is the matter of removing moral responsibilities for actions
done under duress of one sort or another. Exculpation clearly does

179

require that it was impossible, and not just awfully costly, to do the right thing (Frankfurt 1973: 77; Waldron 1986: 480–81).

For purposes of identifying which dependencies might prove exploitable, however, the weaker standard is quite sufficient. Very strong desires can be exploitable in much the same way as physical requirements or psychological compulsions. You can drive a very hard bargain with someone who is dependent upon you for something he desires very badly, and who sees himself as having "no reasonable choice" but to accede to whatever demands you might make. In practice, it may (and often will) be every bit as hard a bargain as you would be able to drive with someone who is dependent upon you for something that he strictly needs, and who objectively has "no choice" but to accede to your demands. If preventing the *exploitation* of dependencies is our aim, then we should be equally concerned with the protection of those who have "no choice" and of those who have "no reasonable choice." Each is potentially as exploitable as the other.

Thus, it is the business of the welfare state to prevent the exploitation of dependencies, and that is a matter of providing support to people who would otherwise be left with "no reasonable choices." That, in turn, might explain why the "needs" to which the welfare state responds are defined by relative and shifting standards, rather than being absolute and invariable across all societies.

There are some things which it would be inconceivable to do without (and unreasonable to expect anyone to do without) in American society, but which are standardly done without in Sudanese society. An upshot of this is that Americans would ordinarily be willing to engage in something very much like "desperation bidding" to avoid doing without things that a Sudanese would not think twice about doing without. To avoid the exploitation that that willingness to engage in desperation bidding makes possible, the American welfare state must provide things that a Sudanese welfare state need not.

The standard of what constitutes having "no reasonable choice" varies not only across societies but also across time. Assuming constantly increasing standards of living, what it would have been perfectly reasonable to do without seventy-five years ago it is simply not reasonable to do without today. An upshot of this is that we are willing to engage in something very much like desperation bidding to avoid doing without things which our own grandparents did not think twice about doing without. To avoid the exploitation that that willingness to engage in desperation bidding makes possible, the modern welfare state must therefore provide many things that the welfare state of earlier eras did not need to provide.[40] This can help to explain the escalating claims of the welfare state over time, both in terms of the range and the level of services it takes upon itself to provide and in terms of the cost to the public treasury of its doing so.

V

The welfare state thus succeeds in removing certain things from the market, and distributing them through another mechanism altogether in such a way that people's basic needs are met. In that way, it helps satisfy the first two preconditions of market societies. Furthermore, that extra-market allocation is done in such a way as to guarantee that there cannot be any exploitation of the dependencies for which it caters. In that way, the welfare state also underwrites the independence of people, which is the third precondition of a market society.

The latter, however, goes well beyond what the logic of the market strictly requires. All that that logic demands is that dependents not be allowed to participate in markets. That is consistent with either of two possible approaches to the problem of dependency. One is to make extra-market provision for dependents' needs in such a way as to leave them still exploitably dependent, and for that reason precluded from participating in markets and quasi-market politics. The other is to make extra-market provision for dependents' needs in such a way as to render them independent, and hence qualified to participate in markets and quasi-market politics. If the latter solution is preferable to the former, it must be so for *moral* reasons. So far as the "internal logic" of arguments for markets are concerned, it is a matter of indifference which solution we select.

[40] The point is not that people's tastes change, but rather that their circumstances do. Suppose people have a tendency to get desperate (and hence exploitable) whenever there is a threat of their present standard of living being reduced by, say, fifty percent or more. Then the higher the present standard of living, the higher their "desperation point," and hence the higher the "social minimum" that the welfare state in their society will have to guarantee. While this explanation of the relativity of the "needs" to which the welfare state responds is not predicated on changes in people's tastes, it *is* predicated on other facts about people's tastes, and in that way provides an essentially subjectivist account of the phenomenon. There may also be objective grounds for taking account of relativities, as shown in Sen (1983).

Historically, the former was the option standardly pursued. Those in need of extra-market assistance were branded "paupers," stripped of their rights of citizenship, and confined to the workhouse to earn their keep. The dependent poor were thus kept from contaminating market society in its many forms. Politically, recipients of poor-law relief were formally disenfranchised. Economically, they were effectively precluded from participation in the market economy by rules governing the conditions, forms, and levels of relief granted.[41] Having thus guaranteed that recipients of poor-law relief would not be participating in the market or quasi-market institutions of society, their extreme and continuing dependence upon the largely arbitrary will of poor-law officials posed no threat to those other institutions.

Within the narrow "logic of the market," there can be no objection to such arrangements. All that that requires is that participants in markets be independent agents. There is no objection, internal to that logic, to the existence of dependent agents elsewhere in society, just so long as those agents are kept out of the market. By all accounts, the poor law was remarkably successful in accomplishing that task.

While such arrangements violate none of the narrow tenets of the logic of markets, there is still much to object to in them. The first objection is narrowly pragmatic: too many people would have to be excluded, on these principles, for the market or the polity to function effectively. Duncan (1984: 4), reporting the results of a University of Michigan panel study spanning ten years in the late 1960s and 1970s, observes that "nearly one quarter of the population [of the US] received income from welfare sources at least once in the decade." Barring a quarter of the population from the market or the poll booth would, just speaking in narrowly pragmatic terms, wreak untold economic and political havoc on the country.

Beyond narrow pragmatism, however, we would find that sort of caste society morally repugnant. Communitarians are right in this respect, at least: we think our society truly ought to be a single-status moral community. And here, at last, we have found the argument (which proved so elusive in chapter 4) to explain why

---

[41] Perhaps the most dramatic examples are the late-nineteenth-century American "seed and feed" cases, holding that farmers fallen on hard times could, under the poor law, be given grain to eat but not grain to plant or to feed to their livestock. The result was to guarantee that the farmers would be dependent upon poor-law relief in perpetuity, rather than re-establishing an independent economic existence for themselves after a bad harvest in one year (Brewer 1875).

this communitarian goal should imply a welfare state. If full participation in our societies is conditional upon a person's being a minimally independent agent, then morally we must not only serve the needs of those who are dependent upon us but also do what we can to render those persons independent.[42]

This distinctively moral goal, so badly flouted by the caste society of the old poor law, is successfully accomplished by the modern welfare state. Providing as it does needed assistance in a substantially nondiscretionary manner, the welfare state safeguards those dependent upon its services from several forms of exploitation. It thereby secures for them the sort of minimal independence that is required for them to participate in the other market and quasi-market sectors of their society.[43]

[42] At least so far as they want to be. There are, of course, various arguments against holding people in an unnecessarily dependent status against their will, couched in terms of self-respect, autonomy, etc. (Goodin 1982: chap. 5; 1985b: chaps. 7 and 8; 1985e; see also Postow 1978–1979 and Weale 1982: chap. 3). The point about these arguments, however, is that they move outside the narrow bounds of the argument for the market itself. They do not have to do with what is required to make market societies work, either pragmatically or morally. The "imperatives" that they represent are thus distinctively moral, and morally distinctive.

[43] In van Gunsteren's (1978: 29) phrasing, "Effective citizenship does not only require a political say and a legally protected status, but also a certain level of socio-economic security. Older theories of citizenship did not ignore this requirement. They solved the problem it posed by denying citizenship to those who did not have independent and secure socio-economic positions already. The welfare state accepts all its subjects as citizens and aims to guarantee to all and each of them the minimal socio-economic security that the free exercise of citizenship requires."

S E V E N

DISCRETION

It has long been said that a—perhaps the—defining feature of the welfare state is its commitment to providing a certain range of goods and services to its citizens "as of right." From T. H. Marshall's lecture on "Citizenship and Social Class" forward, we have grown accustomed to tracing the history of the welfare state in terms of the expanding "rights of citizenship" (Marshall 1949; 1965; 1981). From the welfare rights movement of the 1960s onward, we have grown accustomed to thinking of welfare rights as the clear alternatives to more odious forms of official discretion (Piven and Cloward 1971: chap. 10; Titmuss 1971b; Jowell 1973). From the preceding two chapters of this book, it is clear that something very much like welfare rights is central to the ethical justification of the welfare state.

The concept of a "welfare right" is only a first approximation to what is needed for those purposes, however. It is a reasonably close approximation; and, for a great many purposes, it can serve as a perfectly adequate place-holder in arguments about the welfare state.[1] But, strictly speaking, what those arguments require is not the notion of "welfare rights" at all.

Straightaway I should say that I shall be raising none of the once-standard philosophical objections to the very notion of a "welfare right" as such. Early critics of the U.N. Declaration of Human Rights, for example, used to protest that the notion of positive rights is nonsense, insisting that we can properly talk only of negative rights against interference from others (Raphael 1967). But that claim has now been effectively withdrawn (Waldron 1984: 11). It is now well established that certain rights of both a negative ("security") and a positive ("subsistence") kind are not only com-

Material in this chapter is reprinted from Robert E. Goodin, "Welfare, Rights and Discretion," *Oxford Journal of Legal Studies*, 6 (May 1986), 232–61, by permission of the editor and Oxford University Press.
    [1] I took this shortcut myself in Goodin (1985c: 784).

patible with but are actually presupposed by all rights claims (H. Shue 1980).

My worry with welfare rights is less foundational and more pragmatic. I am concerned, not with any incoherence in the concept itself, but rather with the question of whether such rights are what people really need in order to secure their welfare interests. Threats to those interests arise from nature on the one side and from petty officials on the other. It is the latter sort of threat—arising from abuse of official discretion—that provides the principal focus for this chapter.

My conclusions are largely discouraging. Some kinds of discretion are ineliminable, and some problems with discretion are apparently insurmountable. After having mapped the dimensions of the concept (Section I) and shown why some forms of discretion are logically ineliminable from any system of rules (section II), I proceed to survey four major moral objections to discretionary powers (section III). These problems all seem to be inherent in discretion, in the sense that there is no way to curtail the problems without curtailing the discretions themselves (section IV). But in three out of the four cases, rules designed to overcome these problems with discretion could—and probably would—reproduce the very same problems themselves (section V). Thus, of the many things wrong with discretion, there seems to be only one—its tendency to manipulation and exploitation—that a regime of strict rules could hope to remedy. Even then, that is best accomplished through rules different in form from the standard "welfare rights," and by focusing instead on notions of officials' duties and responsibilities (section VI). As for those problems with discretion that rules cannot hope to remedy, the best strategy would probably be to try to circumvent them through more generous funding of the social services (section VII).

I

"Discretion" admits of two types of characterization, one positive and one negative. On the positive characterization, an official can be said to have discretion if and only if he is empowered to pursue some social goal(s) in the context of individual cases in such a way as he judges to be best calculated, in the circumstances, to promote those goals.[2]

[2] I am indebted to Jeremy Waldron (personal correspondence, 1985) for this formulation.

The negative characterization of discretion is well represented by Dworkin's remark that "discretion" is "like the hole in the doughnut," which "does not exist except as an area left open by a surrounding belt of restriction" (Dworkin 1977: 31). On that negative analysis, "discretion" is a residual notion, defined in terms of its opposite: viz., official outcomes (typically, officials' decisions) being strictly determined by rules, and rules alone. The sheer absence of rules is not enough to qualify the situation as "discretionary," however. There is, for example, no rule governing the color I as a homeowner paint my bathroom; yet it seems distinctly odd to prattle on about my "discretion" in the matter. Where freedom is taken for granted, the situation seems ill described in terms of discretion at all. Only when there is some prima facie expectation that the decision will be subject to constraints of a particular, rule-like form is the absence of such constraints a matter for comment. And, more to the present point, only then is it describable as an occasion for the exercise of "discretion" at all. Were I a public-housing tenant, subject to various other rules about repainting, then I might be said to have discretion if those rules left open the question of bathroom colors in a way that as a homeowner (not ordinarily subject to any such rules) I am not. Thus, discretion refers to an area of conduct which is generally governed by rules but where the dictates of the rules are indeterminate. In short, discretion refers, negatively, to a lacuna in a system of rules.

These two characterizations, one positive and the other negative, give a different flavor to discussions of discretion, perhaps. Formally, however, I take them to be extensionally equivalent. Since my focus here is upon ways of limiting discretion rather than of extending it, the negative characterization—emphasizing the role of rules in restricting discretion—will prove the more useful.

Various different *types* of discretion can be identified by reference to rules of the general form:

> *Rule R*: If some individual I, who satisfies certain background conditions B, displays characteristics K in circumstances C, then an individual O, who occupies official position P, should do thing T to or for that individual I.

In the context of social welfare policy, I will typically be a claimant, O a caseworker (and P the position of "caseworker"). K will refer to the claimant's personal characteristics (e.g., old age, blindness), and C to various other impersonal features of the claimant's circumstances (e.g., homelessness, joblessness). *B* will refer to background conditions required for the claimant even to have legal standing to file a claim (e.g., citizenship, residency, paid-up national insurance contributions). The treatment *T* will characteristically refer to the providing or the withholding of some particular benefits or services stipulated in social security legislation.

With this general characterization of a rule in hand, we can now distinguish several varieties of discretion.

> 1. *Strong discretion.* To say that an official *O* enjoys "strong discretion" in respect to some treatment *T* is to say that: (a) there is some rule *R* allowing the official *O* to provide treatment *T* to or for individuals; but (b) the rule imposes no constraints on what treatment the official gives to any particular individual *I* (i.e., the rule contains no reference to factors *B*, *K*, or *C*).

Strong discretion is sometimes defined, more simply but less precisely, as the *absence* of any rule *R*.[3] Although this may be a useful shorthand, it is, strictly speaking, incorrect. Discretionary power is power exercised *under* some rule. Those exercising it have broad latitude under that rule in deciding how to exercise that power. But unless the power derives from some rule in the first place, it would not constitute a case of discretionary power at all. Hence the necessity of clause 1(a) in the above definition.

The opposite of strong discretion is, obviously, weak discretion. This can be defined as follows:

> 2. *Weak discretion.* An official *O* can be said to enjoy "weak discretion" if: (a) there is some rule *R* directing official *O* to provide treatment *T* to or for individuals *I* under certain conditions *B*, *K*, and *C*; but (b) that rule leaves the official with some latitude in deciding either *who* (i.e., which *I*) is to benefit or what (i.e., which *T*) beneficiaries are to receive.[4]

Official rules are sometimes explicitly permissive in these respects. Rules sometimes say, for example, that anyone displaying certain attributes *may* be given certain benefits (e.g., job training), without requiring that everyone displaying those attributes *must* be given

---

[3] Dworkin's (1977: 32) comment that, in cases of strong discretion, the official "is simply not bound by standards set by the authority in question" admits of such a reading—although possibly not the one Dworkin intended.

[4] These two types of weak discretion, combined with strong discretion defined above, correspond to Campbell's (1978) three kinds of discretion.

such benefits. Or sometimes rules say that anyone meeting certain descriptions should receive treatment within some specified range (e.g., for convicted thieves, one to five years' imprisonment), while leaving the choice of the precise treatment within that range to the official's discretion.

This suggests another pair of contrasts:

3. *Formal discretion.* If options as regards beneficiaries *I* or treatments *T* are explicitly written into rule *R*, officials *O* will be said to have "formal discretion."

4. *Informal discretion.* Officials *O* will be said to enjoy "informal discretion" if they enjoy options as regards beneficiaries *I* or treatments *T* that are merely implicit in the statement of rule *R*.

Typically, informal discretion derives from vagueness in the formulation of the rule-statement. Vagueness in specifying who is to receive benefits (i.e., in specifying *C*) or under what circumstances they are to be received (i.e., in specifying *K* or *B*) might leave officials with substantial effective discretion in applying a rule. Formulae like "exceptional needs"or "exceptional circumstances," built into the U.K. Supplementary Benefits scheme by the Social Security Act of 1966, were very permissive indeed. So too were provisions built into the U.S. statutes providing Aid for Families with Dependent Children (AFDC) stipulating that eligibility is predicated upon the home being "suitable," the mother or adult caretaker being a "fit and proper" person to care for the dependent children, and so on (Handler 1973: 11). Vagueness in specifying treatment *T* can also leave officials with considerable latitude. Familiar fudges of this sort trade on notions of "suitable" or "appropriate" treatment, "treatment in the best interests of the child," and so on (Freund 1921; Gummer 1979: 216–18; Handler 1979: 8–9).[5]

These two distinctions cut across one another, yielding four composite categories. Officials can enjoy *weak formal* discretion, where their options are explicit in the rule; or they can enjoy *weak informal* discretion, where they are not. They can enjoy *strong formal* discretion, where the rule granting them power pointedly re-

---

[5] In such cases, it seems that the law was left vague because lawmakers thought the social goals would be better pursued if officials had broader discretion. In other cases, laws are left vague (and, therefore, officials are left with discretion) because the lawmakers could not agree on any single purpose or goal, and they adopted a vague formula to patch over cracks in the enacting coalition (Prosser 1981).

frains from setting conditions for the exercise of that power. They can also enjoy *strong informal* discretion. This is perhaps a less obvious category, but it is nonetheless real and nonetheless important. It is often unclear whether rule R (or any rule R) applies, either because it is unclear whether official O satisfies all the conditions laid down by the job description P or else because it is unclear whether claimant I satisfies background conditions B. By virtue of these ambiguities, the official would then be said to enjoy strong informal discretion in applying rule R.

There is yet another set of distinctions that cuts across all those others:

5. *Provisional discretion.* An official O is said to have "provisional" discretionary power if: (a) rule R gives that official some discretion, either strong or weak, formal or informal, in deciding what treatment T to provide to or for individual I; and (b) official O's decision in that regard is subject to review, and possible overturning, by some other official OO.

Clause 5(b) makes the lower-level official's discretion "provisional" in the sense of being "temporary," i.e., pending higher-level review.[6]

6. *Ultimate discretion.* An official O is said to have "ultimate" discretionary power if: (a) rule R gives that official O some discretion, either strong or weak, formal or informal, in deciding what treatment T to provide to individual I; and (b) official O's decision in that regard is not subject to review or possible overturning by any other official OO.

Obviously, strong and weak discretionary powers can come in either of these two forms, provisional or ultimate. Similarly, provisional or ultimate discretionary powers can be either formal or informal, i.e., either explicit or implicit in the statement of the rules. The case of formal, explicit grants of either form of discretion is utterly straightforward. The fact that such powers are sometimes granted informally and implicitly is equally undeniable.[7] But

---

[6] Dworkin (1977: 32) runs together "weak" and "provisional" discretion. Both forms are indeed weak, in some sense or another; they display different forms of weakness, however, and deserve to be distinguished.

[7] A striking case in point is early Victorian emigration officers. The discharge of their duties was characterized by "the absence of a real superintendence. No person or department within the colonial office was directly and specifically responsible for the officers. Hay acknowledged and filed their correspondence; but other-

it is a phenomenon that is slightly more complicated to analyze. Essentially, the informal, implicit granting of ultimate discretionary power amounts to a failure of the rules to empower any other official *OO* to review the judgments of official *O*; then, by implication if not by formal edict, official *O*'s discretion in the matter is ultimate. The informal granting of provisional discretionary powers amounts to the explicit granting of rights of review to some other official *OO*, conjoined with an implicit pledge on the part of that official *OO* that such power will not in fact be used to override official *O*'s decisions.

For the sake of brevity, I shall in the balance of this chapter refer to the situation in which an official has formal, strong, ultimate discretion as being a situation in which he has "complete" discretion in the matter.

I I

It is widely agreed that a certain amount of discretion will inevitably prove necessary. Those concerned with social assistance typically give examples such as the need to allow officials discretionary powers to make extraordinary payments to people in truly exceptional circumstances, such as fire or flood (UK SBC 1977: para. 7.54; UK DHSS 1978: para. 9.47; Donnison 1977: 534; Handler and Sosin 1983).

Now, it may well be a bad idea—for all sorts of reasons—to curtail such discretion, either by prohibiting such payments altogether or by codifying them in the ordinary rules of social service departments. But all of those reasons, whatever they are, are of a practical character. The "necessity" in view there is pragmatic rather than logical necessity. Eliminating such discretions may be inadvisable, but it is not logically impossible.

That weaker sense of inevitability does not here concern me. I shall instead be discussing two ways in which discretion is inevitable in the stronger sense. These are discretions that are inevitable in the sense that they are logically necessary to the operation of any system of rules. Such discretions are truly ineliminable: they cannot be eliminated except by eliminating the system of rules itself.[8]

The first such aspect of discretion concerns the fundamental

---

wise, unless a scandal arose or an expenditure was proposed, they were left entirely to their own devices" (MacDonagh 1961: 108).

[8] And since "no rules" is itself a rule, they cannot be eliminated in that way, either.

choice of which rules to adopt in the first place. Such discretion is ineliminable, in that it cannot be removed from the system altogether. Of course, it can be removed from any particular official or level of officials.[9] Indeed, such discretion can be moved all around the system: it can be shifted from lower-level officials to higher ones, or onto judges, or onto Parliament, or whatever. There may be meta-rules telling us when to apply particular first-order rules; there may be meta-meta-rules telling us when to apply particular meta-rules, and so forth. But at some point the regress must stop.

In a straightforward analogy to Gödel's theorem (Nagel and Newman 1959), a system of social rules simply *must* appeal to something outside itself at some point or another. To what it appeals is an open question. For John Austin it is a "general habit of obedience" to Sovereign; for H. L. A. Hart it is some combination of "serious social pressure" externally applied and a "critical reflective attitude" internalized by those subject to the rules (Hart 1961). But wherever and however you stop the regress, it is clear that there must be something standing outside and underlying the system of rules. Insofar as it does, then someone, somewhere must enjoy discretionary power in adopting one set of rules rather than another. The question is not whether someone somewhere in the system will have discretion of this sort, but merely who.[10]

A second respect in which discretion is ineliminable is in the act of bringing particular cases under the ambit of general rules. Acts imply agency; and rules, whatever might be said about them, cannot plausibly qualify as agents in their own right. As Hart (1961: 123) wryly remarks, "Particular fact-situations do not await us already marked off from each other, and labelled as instances of the general rule, the application of which is in question; nor can the rule itself step forward to claim its own instances." Here, too, there is necessarily scope for independent judgment.[11]

[9] That said, it must also be observed that much rule-making and rule-changing discretion will probably inevitably remain with the administrator; indeed, this is the essence of "administrative discretion" as presented by Warwick (1981), for example.

[10] Dworkin 1963; van Gunsteren 1976: chap. 4. Notice that questions about the derivation of rules are different from questions about the enforcement of rules. Problems of infinite regress in the latter realm can be solved by "self-referring laws," as shown by Hart (1983: 170–78); but this solution cannot be plausibly employed in the former realm as well. Notice, too, that there can sometimes be self-contained systems of social rules (like, e.g., etiquette) that emerge from social practice without any lawgiver laying them down. That is best treated as a case of *everyone* having rule-making discretion.

[11] Some prefer to call this "judgment" rather than "discretion"; see Titmuss (1971b: 119), Donnison (1977: 534) and UK SBC (1977: para. 1.39).

Even where fairly precise decision criteria are laid down (as in the British Social Security Act of 1980, for example) the criteria still admit of substantial scope for interpretation in their application. A rule that says, "Pay an old-age pension of £60 per week to anyone over 65 years of age" would seem to admit of relatively little discretion in its application to any particular case. The presentation of a birth certificate would usually settle the question of the applicability of this rule to the case of any particular claimant.[12] But even in such relatively clearcut cases, there is always still some scope for independent judgment: officials must exercise discretion, for example, in deciding whether or not they believe the document to be genuine (Titmuss 1970: 264).

Again, although the exercise of this second sort of discretion is inevitable, the question of *who* is to exercise it remains open. At least in the first instance, it will typically be exercised by the line staff, who are the ones that initially confront clients and render a decision on their pleas by bringing their cases under the ambit of various general rules. Caseworkers' discretion in classifying claimants may, of course, be merely provisional and subject to higher-level review. When such review is undertaken, discretion passes from the caseworkers to their superiors. And if superiors' decisions are themselves subject to appeal and review by still higher-level officials, the discretion migrates still further up the hierarchy. Here again, however, the buck must stop *somewhere*. This form of discretion, like the last, must be exercised in an ultimate way by someone somewhere in the system. The only question is, *by whom*?

Saying that it is "just" a question of who exercises these discretions is not to say that we are indifferent as between the various possibilities. On the contrary, we seem to have strong views on these matters (Baldwin and Houghton 1986). We much prefer rule-making discretions to be exercised by legislators, and rule-applying ones (of an ultimate sort, anyway) by judges. We worry much less than we might otherwise do (and perhaps should still do) when these discretions are left to such agents as those (Atiyah 1978); and why we do so is in itself an interesting question. Part of

---

[12] Handler (1973: 10), for example, writes of the analogous U.S. program: "The Social Security system (OASDI) is an example of a social welfare program where legal protections seem to be adequate. Eligibility conditions and level of benefits are clear and readily susceptible to proof in the event of a dispute. A claimant shows his age or other eligibility status (for example, survivor), past employment that is covered by the Social Security Act, and earnings records. Benefits are paid according to fixed schedules." And so on.

the reason may have to do with the relatively greater capacities of these agents to make substantively correct decisions: legislators can take a broader view than can a caseworker who is immersed in the details of some particular case, and judges can reach a more considered opinion on a particular case than can a harried caseworker who is preoccupied with the details of many complicated claims all at once. Another important part of the reason may have to do with their greater accountability: legislators and judges, even, are more powerfully and directly accountable to the sovereign (construed as the electorate or the Crown) than lowly caseworkers. But whatever reasons we may have for thinking that some allocations of these ineliminable discretions are superior to others, they cannot change the fact that those discretions are indeed ineliminable.

I I I

Here I shall trace four distinct strands to the opposition to discretionary powers. For these purposes, I shall focus upon the limiting case of "complete" (strong, formal, ultimate) discretion. The objections which I here canvass pertain to discretion quite generally, as the breadth of my examples will show. But I shall also try to show through the use of actual examples or "stylized facts" that these general problems are of particular relevance to the social services.

A

The first problem with discretion can be couched in terms of *manipulation and exploitation*. Indeed, it is in one sense the classic objection to one person's having discretionary control over the disposition of resources which another person needs that that person thereby acquires *power* over the other. Such a person can lay down all sorts of demands and back them up with threats to withhold the needed resources from the other unless that person complies with those demands. If the threatener really does have complete discretion in the disposition of those resources, there would seem to be nothing to prevent the making or carrying out of those threats. And if the other person really does need the resources in question, there would seem to be little that that person could do but to comply with the demands (Goodin 1985b: chap. 7).

Possibly the most dramatic example of such manipulation via discretionary powers comes in connection with the penal sanction in eighteenth-century England. The gentry enjoyed substantial discretionary powers, firstly, in deciding whether or not to prosecute, since the vast majority of prosecutions were then private prosecutions. Secondly, there was considerable scope for judges to exercise discretionary power in recommending "mercy" for convicted criminals. (Fully half of those convicted of hanging offenses in this period were not, in fact, hanged.) Parasitic upon that discretion was the further discretionary power of local gentlemen and peers either to lobby or not to lobby for a pardon for the convicted criminal. From all that discretionary control over the criminal sanction, the gentry derived substantial power to control the population at large in a variety of ways not formally covered by the law. Since poor people could never know when or in what ways they might need to appeal to the gentry's mercy, and since that mercy was wholly discretionary, they dared not do anything to offend them. "Discretion allowed a prosecutor to terrorize the petty thief and then command his gratitude. . . . In the countryside the power of gentlemen and peers to punish or forgive worked in the same way to maintain the fabric of obedience, gratitude and deference" (Hay 1975: 49).

That is a particularly dramatic example of discretion serving as a source of illicit power. It is widely remarked, however, that social welfare programs serve the same social-control functions, and that they do so in much the same ways. "The law of social welfare grew up on the theory that welfare is a 'gratuity' furnished by the state, and thus may be made subject to whatever conditions the state sees fit to impose" (Reich 1965: 1245).[13] Legislatures, exercising their undoubted discretionary powers, sometimes impose social-control riders on welfare legislation. Some of the conditions they lay down bear some obvious, direct relationship to the purposes of the programs. Others do not. Notable among these is the requirement in the U.S. Economic Opportunity Act of 1964 that participants in Lyndon Johnson's Great Society must swear allegiance to the U.S. Constitution (Reich 1965: 1250).

Administrators of welfare programs, too, often exercise their discretionary powers "to impose standards of morality [on welfare recipients that are] not imposed on the rest of the community" (Reich 1963: 1359; see also Reich 1965: 1247; Smith 1949: 275–80; Campbell 1978: 66–67). Some of the more striking examples of

[13] See further Smith (1949), Reich (1963; 1964), O'Neil (1970: esp. chaps. 2 and 9) and Handler (1979: 3–8). There is surprisingly strong adherence to this view even among claimants, to judge from Briar (1966).

such abuse of official discretion grow out of the discretionary powers of administrators of public housing projects to evict, or to deny admission to, those who are in some ill-defined way "undesirable" tenants (Davis 1969: 78 ; see also O'Neil 1970: chap. 8).

Another more systematic source of this tendency for social workers to employ discretionary powers to manipulate client behavior has to do with the theory of poverty that is today prevalent among social-work professionals. Poverty is there traced to "individual character defects or family pathology" or to a more general "culture of poverty" (Handler 1973: 5). The "logical conclusions" of this theory are that there should be "an enormous centralization of official discretionary power over clients": there should be "a comprehensive, integrated family service" with a "government monopoly of social services"; and there should be a single caseworker, or team of caseworkers, responsible for the treatment of any given family according to some integrated case plan tailored to the needs of that particular family. "Because most clients will be poor and very dependent, they will be forced to submit to these official decisions as the price of receiving the goods and services. . . . This is the administrative reality beneath the rehabilitation rhetoric" (Handler 1973: 143).

The upshot is "a manipulative, moralistic attempt at changing behavior" of clients through use of caseworkers' discretionary powers (Handler 1973: xii; see also Handler and Hollingsworth 1971: 129). The standard cases come from AFDC workers in the U.S. But consider the parallel practices of Children's Officers in Britain:

> Child care officers have let electricity remain off for considerable periods (but only in the summer) in order to induce more cooperative efforts. There are cases where departments have let families get evicted and rehoused in welfare accommodation to induce them to view their situations more "realistically"; all part of a therapy plan. (Handler 1968: 486; see similarly van Krieken 1986)

All of this is done through the exercise of the caseworker's discretionary powers; all of it is done with a view to changing client behavior.

That such abuses of discretionary powers have occurred has by now been officially conceded. In its review of the U.K. Supplementary Benefits system, the Department of Health and Social Security itself acknowledged that the discretionary elements for-

195

merly contained in that scheme were "an element of the scheme
. . . [that was] open to exploitation and pressure" (UK DHSS 1978:
para. 9.10; see also Donnison 1976: 348).

Note that the objection is not to the laying down of conditions
per se. There is nothing that is always and ever wrong, either conclusively or even presumptively, with laying down conditions that
others must meet before you do something good (or refrain from
doing something bad) to or for them. My greengrocer offers me
beans on condition I pay for them; whether he provides me with
beans is entirely within his discretion, and no one would regard it
as an unacceptable exercise of that discretionary power for him to
make delivery of the beans conditions upon receipt of my money.

What is presumably objectionable is instead the *circumstances*
surrounding the laying down of conditions. That is, what is objectionable is laying down conditions in circumstances wherein the
other party has "no reasonable choice" but to comply. The same
thing that makes the other person have "no other choice"—his
vulnerability to and dependence upon us for the needed resource—gives rise to a strong obligation on our part to provide
him with that needed resource. To say that we are morally bound
to provide it is also to say that it would be morally wrong of us *not*
to provide it unless conditions are met. The setting of conditions
in these circumstances amounts to the threat to do something immoral; and it is, therefore, itself immoral (Haksar 1976). That, in
essence, is why setting conditions in such circumstances is "exploitative"—that is why it amounts to taking unfair advantage of
people.

Such an analysis can straightforwardly explain our objections to
forcing needy people to rely upon family, friends, or voluntary
organizations for assistance (see chapter 12). Those agents can,
and altogether too often do, take advantage of such dependencies
to force recipients of their largesses to do what they want them to
do in all sorts of ways. (Praying in the Salvation Army soup
kitchen is the standard example, but the most wickedly exploitative practices probably come at home, when aged relatives are
forced to lodge with grown children's families; see Townsend
1957.)

But what, some may say, if the conditions were—as they would
say is typically the case with the social services—merely for the
recipient's own good? The model of poverty as pathology sees social workers as the functional equivalent of medics, curing and re-
habilitating people through the reforms that they force upon them

196

through the manipulation of social welfare benefits. Exploitation, as analyzed in chapter 5, requires that the exploiter gain and that the exploited usually lose. If the conditions laid down for receipt of welfare benefits were truly for the recipient's own good, then that would not be true: the recipient would actually have gained, and the caseworker has gotten nothing out of it except satisfaction with a job well done.

A good case can be made for the exploitativeness of even that relationship, however. Social workers may not gain anything personally, but their employer (the state, society) does, in the form of social control. Through the conditions attaching to the receipt of benefits, welfare recipients are forced to reform their behavior, and lead less deviant and more socially approved forms of lives. Whether societies "really" benefit from enforcing conformism and reducing variation in lifestyles is, of course, an open question. But they (or their rulers) certainly *think* that they do, and subjective accounts are what really matter here. Similarly, whether or not the reformed welfare recipients "really" benefit from having been forced to forsake their old ways is an open question. But it is their subjective assessments that matter here, again. Some of them may have welcomed the changes. A vast majority of them probably did not.

The upshot is that a higher standard of conduct is imposed upon welfare recipients than upon the public at large. It is not wrong (anyway, not illegal) to drink; it is not wrong (anyway, not illegal) to smoke expensive cigarettes. It is only wrong (anyway, legally discouraged) to do so if you are poor. The conditions that caseworkers characteristically impose upon welfare recipients discourage such behavior. If society wants to discourage drinking or smoking, however, it should do so across the board. It should not take advantage of needy people's plights to enforce standards upon them that are not enforced upon the rest of society.

As analyzed above, the legitimate purpose of social welfare programs—and of grants of discretionary powers within such programs—is to meet our collective obligations to provide needed resources to people who would otherwise lack them. Using that discretion to impose conditions unconnected to that purpose is simply "inappropriate."[14] It amounts to taking advantage of the

---

[14] Defenders of such conditions will, of course, claim that they are highly appropriate, because they are indeed connected to the purpose of relieving distress (at least in the long run) and are not (or not just) a matter of social control. Some of

situation in which discretion has given one power over others to realize benefits (or pursue projects, more generally) in some other sphere altogether. Taking advantage in such ways amounts to exploitation, pure and simple.

The form of unfairness embodied in such exploitative practices is akin to the notion, alluded to in chapter 5, of "abuse of process" in the law of torts (Prosser 1971: 856–58). If I have injured you, then you may prosecute me for it. But you may not threaten to prosecute me, merely with a view to obtaining money from me to induce you to drop the threat. To do so would be to abuse the legal process—to use the law allowing prosecution of those who have caused injuries in a way that is wholly inappropriate, contrary to its intentions and true purposes (Williams 1954: 79). So, too, does social workers' setting of certain sorts of preconditions that must be met before they will exercise their discretionary powers to their clients' advantage constitute an exploitative abuse of the purposes for which the discretion was (or should have been) granted in the first place.[15]

B

A second objection to discretionary powers is couched in terms of *arbitrariness*. Insofar as someone enjoys complete (strong, formal, ultimate) discretionary control over some matter, then it follows from the definitions offered in Section I that that person is not obliged to have, much less to give, any reasons whatsoever for deciding one way rather than another. That is to say, someone with complete discretion is at liberty to act "arbitrarily" not only in the weak sense of "acting without reasons that are known to and can be relied on in advance by those affected by his actions," but also in the strong sense of "acting without reasons" altogether. That follows simply from the definition of "complete discretion." (Whether or not anyone ever actually enjoys such complete discretion is, perhaps, another matter.)

Whereas with rule-governed decisions one is obliged to demonstrate that one has made the right decision, with completely dis-

---

the conditions probably could be defended in these terms. Most almost certainly could not.

[15] Courts similarly construe the notion of "abuse of discretion": "discretion must be exercised in the manner intended by the empowering Act," or else it will be held ultra vires (Wade 1982: 352, 355, 361). Invalidating administrative acts in this way, however, constitutes solving the problems with discretion by eliminating discretion, as section IV below will argue.

cretionary decisions one need merely demonstrate that one was within one's right in making the decision as one has done (Mashaw 1983: 9–10). There will typically be review bodies charged with the task of determining whether or not officials have kept within their powers. Such reviews designed to preclude officials from acting outside their proper spheres do not, in and of themselves, necessarily diminish the discretionary powers of officials to act within their proper spheres. In practice, however, this power of review tends to be used in such a way as to render officials' discretion substantially less complete than it might at first appear to be. From Coke's day forward, English courts have imposed substantive tests as well as formal ones in determining whether officials have acted within their proper powers. Discretionary power, it is said, is granted to officials in order for them to make "reasonable" decisions; unreasonable decisions thus exceed their powers and are to be held ultra vires (Wade 1982: 353 and chaps. 2, 12).[16] That is merely to say that the official's discretion is not "complete" (because it is not "ultimate"). The problems with discretion (here, arbitrariness) are solved merely by reducing discretion.

Insofar as some matter truly is within the *complete* discretion of some official, there is very little for others (be they that official's notional superiors, or other agencies or branches of government) to consider on appeal. In such cases, appeals panels will have to confine themselves to a very narrow range of questions. They may ask whether the case was indeed one over which the official in question truly enjoyed discretionary power, and whether the decision rendered actually fell within the limits of that official's discretion. They may even go so far as to enquire whether there was at least *some* reason for front-line officials to decide the case as they did (Wade 1982: 289–90; Handler 1979: 51). But insofar as complete discretionary power is truly lodged with those lower-level officials themselves, a "higher-level" appeals tribunal cannot properly substitute its judgment for theirs.[17]

[16] Ruling on a complaint against arbitrary evictions from public housing, a U.S. court of appeals has held similarly, "The government as a landlord is still the government. It must not act arbitrarily, for, unlike private landlords, it is subject to the requirements of due process of law. Arbitrary action is not due process" (quoted in Davis 1969: 80).

[17] Wade 1982: 34–36; see similarly Marshall (1984: 82) on the powers of the U.K. Parliamentary Commissioner (the "ombudsman"). Insofar as appeals tribunals *do* substitute their judgment for that of lower-level officials (in effect, rehearing the case), then the ultimate discretionary power rests with the appeals tribunal and the lower-level official only enjoys "provisional" discretion; that was the case with U.K. Supplementary Benefits Appeals Tribunal prior to the 1980 reforms, for ex-

Avoiding appeals is sometimes precisely the intention underlying the grant of discretion. One early and particularly dramatic case in point comes in Oliver MacDonagh's (1958a) study of early Victorian policies concerning the powers of emigration officers at U.K. ports to set and enforce standards governing the stowage of iron cargoes on passenger ships. When one such officer came under threat of suit for abusing that authority, the powers-that-be responded by giving such officers absolute and complete discretionary powers in such matters, explicitly with a view to preventing any further such second-guessing of officers' judgments.

Opposition to the arbitrariness of discretionary powers has a long and glorious history. It figures centrally in Dicey's plea (1908: 108) for a "rule of law, not men". On his analysis, the "rule of law . . . means . . . the absolute supremacy or predominance of regular law as opposed to the influence of arbitrary power, and excludes the existence of arbitrariness, of prerogative, or even of wide discretionary authority on the part of the government."[18]

That case has been made so often and so persuasively over so many years that there are relatively few offenders left. Nowadays the argument is principally leveled against parole boards, which insistently (and, in the U.S., in defiance of the clear provisions of the Administrative Procedure Act) refuse to give reasons for their decisions on the parole petitions which come before them (Davis 1969: 126–33).

Until recently, however, the failure to give reasons for action (at least to give them as a matter of course) characterized the administration of social welfare policies as well. Supplementary Benefit claimants in the U.K. were not routinely given an explanation of how the officer in charge of their case arrived at the figure representing how much they would receive in benefits; they had to ask for an A124 form is if they wanted such an explanation (Briggs and Rees 1980). And the same was, until recently, true even on appeal. Since the decision of the Appeal Tribunal was to be final, it was

---

ample (UK DHSS 1978: para. 3.6). Jeremy Waldron is right to point out, in personal correspondence, that there is often a good reason for insulating the grant of discretion from appellate review: viz., if discretion is given to officials so that decisions can reflect the full facts of particular circumstances, then it would be counterproductive to allow a superior body which is less well-acquainted with the particular circumstances to substitute its judgment for theirs.

[18] Administrative lawyers now seem satisfied that discretions can coexist with the rule of law. The review mechanisms they trust to guarantee the absence of arbitrariness, however, do so only by reducing discretionary powers, thus confirming the thesis of section IV below. See Wade (1982: 22–26 and chap. 12) and Davis (1969: 27–44).

long held that "there was 'absolutely no reason at all' why reasons should be given if there was no further right of appeal."[19] Later it was decided that appellants should be supplied with written reasons for the tribunal's decision, but only upon specific request; such requests were received from only two percent of appellants (Herman 1972: 56). Now, at last, written statements of tribunals' reasons are compulsory. But still it is the case that claimants are unclear in their own minds "about the extent to which they are eligible for discretionary payments, and are critical of what appear to be arbitrary and discriminatory benefits which some receive but others do not" (UK DHSS 1978: para. 9.5).

C

A third objection to discretionary powers is that from their arbitrariness there necessarily flows *uncertainty, unpredictability, and insecurity*. Insofar as some matter is completely discretionary, and depends wholly upon some official's own arbitrary will, those who are subject to the decision will have no good way of predicting what the outcome will be (Hayek 1944: 12; Franks 1957: 6). At most, they might try to make some inferences based on the official's past practices. But since there was never any compelling reason for the official to behave in one way rather than another in the past (or at least since no such reason was enunciated in the past), there is no particularly good reason to expect similar decisions in the future, even from the same official. Still less is there any reason to expect that other officials will fit the pattern of the first.

All those points are familiar from the arguments of legal philosophers of the Realist school. To those arguments must be added another, this one owing to rule utilitarians. Many worthwhile projects can be realized only insofar as we can confidently predict what others will do, and frame our own action plans accordingly. Hence, discretion-mad act utilitarians, choosing to do exactly the right thing in each and every circumstance, may, by reason of the unpredictability of their behavior, end up doing more (indirect) harm than (direct) good (Hodgson 1967; Kydland and Prescott 1977; Atiyah 1978: 20–23).

Throughout history, this unpredictability objection has been central to arguments against discretionary powers. Coke picturesquely contrasts "the golden and straight metwand" of law with

[19] Testimony of Sir Harold Fieldhouse, secretary of the National Assistance Board, to the Franks (1957) committee; quoted in Bradley (1975: 40).

"the uncertain and crooked cord of discretion."[20] Hayek (1944: 78) inveighs against social planning on account of its "progressive introduction of . . . vague formulas into legislation . . . and of the increasing arbitrariness and uncertainty of, and the consequent disrespect for, the law. . . . " Merchants and manufacturers whose activities are subject to state regulation constantly complain that, when those regulations are enforced by officials with broad discretionary powers, uncertainty and unpredictability is thereby engendered (MacDonagh 1958a: 39). Even those who would have little sympathy with the cause of business in general nonetheless see an important connection between procedural due process and fixed, predictable rules (Fuller 1964; Kearns 1977).

The poor are, and rationally should be, particularly sensitive to any such uncertainties. The poorer one is, the more urgent one's need to be able to budget in advance. Even subsistence farmers in Southeast Asia clearly prefer a lower average payoff with less variation from year to year to a higher average payoff with more variation, as is evidenced by their continuing to plant traditional strains of rice in preference to the new strains of "wonder rice" (Scott 1976). In Tawney's analogy, the poor are like people up to their necks in water. Any slight wave will drown them.

Many see the modern welfare state as an instrument for providing the poor of our own societies with a certain level of "security" akin to that offered by traditional rice cultivation in peasant societies. That is undoubtedly what Charles Reich (1964; 1965: 1255–56) thinks the "new property" is—or could and should be.

On this account, what is wrong with the charity-based approach to welfare is that charitable contributions are discretionary, and being discretionary they are (from the point of view of the recipient) utterly unreliable. There is no particular reason for any particular individual to be favored by such benefices in the first place. Neither is there any particular reason to expect that such benefices will continue, once they have started. Such is the way of discretion.

Parallel complaints are, not surprisingly, lodged against discretionary elements in modern social welfare programs. "Discretion means uncertainty," some bluntly say (Briggs and Rees 1980: 4; see similarly Jowell 1973: 189–90 and Campbell 1978: 64–65). Various examples lend credence to that claim. In the U.S., for example,

[20] Coke, 4 Inst. 41, quoted in Wade 1982: 22. See similarly Hart (1961: chap. 7) and Atiyah (1978: 32).

public housing authorities have broad discretionary powers to evict "undesirable" tenants, and they exercise that power by instituting a regime of "month-to-month leases [that] maintain tenants in a state of insecurity" constantly (Reich 1965: 1250).

Again, however, the broad point is by now pretty well accepted. Even the U.K. Department of Health and Social Security, in its review of Supplementary Benefits, describes as the prime failing of the discretionary components of that scheme the fact that "they make it more difficult for claimants to understand the extent of their entitlement to benefit"; and the DHSS report elsewhere says, "It is essential that the detailed rules and practices of the scheme should be set out publicly in a sufficiently authoritative form for them to be followed consistently by both the officials administering them and the appeal tribunals" (UK DHSS 1978: paras. 9.10, 3.13; UK SBC 1976: para. 2.17; Donnison 1976: 348).

D

A fourth broad class of objections to discretionary powers is couched in terms of *privacy and intrusiveness*. The ethos of discretionary judgments is that they are to be made on the basis of the "full facts" of the particular case: such decisions are to be made with reference to "the case in the round," rather than with reference to some selective aspects of it artificially isolated by some narrow rules, and so on. Now, if this advantage is to accrue, officials guided by discretion must necessarily base their decisions on more information about individual claimants than would officials guided by rules alone. Such an argument may not justify officials in gathering any and all information that they might like about claimants; it only justifies them in gathering information arguably relevant to the decision at hand. But it remains inevitable nevertheless that in order to get the positive benefits we desire from discretion (treatment better fitting the particular case), there must necessarily be a more intrusive administrative apparatus prying more deeply into the private affairs of claimants.

Charges of "snooping" are leveled with some regularity—and often with considerable justification—against officials enjoying discretionary power in the administration of social welfare programs. One interwar example from Britain concerns the investigations of officials responsible for payment of unemployment benefits only to those "available for work" but unable to find it. The Divisional Controller for the South-East reportedly advised investigators, "It has proved more fruitful to call, ostensibly in error, at a neighbour's house instead of the correct address and to allow the line of inquiry to develop in accordance with the reception given by the neighbour. . . ." (quoted in Deacon 1976: 59–60).

Similarly in our own day, British Supplementary Benefits officers administering discretionary clothing allowances under provision for payment for "exceptional needs" often ask claimants to present their old shoes or overcoats to demonstrate that they are indeed in need of replacement. Supplementary Benefits officers sometimes impose a scheme of "voluntary" savings for claimants who have demonstrated themselves incapable of handling their own money by making regular deductions from their entitlements (UK SBC 1977: para. 1.43); and U.S. welfare workers engage in similar practices (ten Broek and Wilson 1954: 264–65). The discretionary means that were chosen to enforce anticohabitation ("man under the bed") provisions in welfare laws involved, in the U.S. at least, "midnight searches" of the most intrusive kinds (Reich 1963: 1347). While those particular practices have now ended, similar ones continue. Still we find in the U.S. that "merchants may be asked for information" about applicants for public welfare, "financial data is checked, the whereabouts of relations is sought, . . ." and so on (Reich 1965: 1247–48). There is simply no settled judgment as to how much personal information administrators should, or legally could, collect about applicants for public relief (Handler 1979: 110–16).

I V

Next I shall pose essentially the "reformist" question. Is there any way to overcome the problems with discretion, described above, that does not entail depriving officials of discretion? I shall argue that the answer is no. The problems are inherent in the practice of discretion and can be overcome (if at all) only by removing discretion from officials.

The clearest example of such an inherent problem is "arbitrariness." Insofar as an official has complete discretion, then to that extent the official is not *bound* by anything (rules, reasons, or what have you) to decide one way rather than another. The official may, and usually will, have various reasons for deciding a case as he or she did; the official might volunteer (or might even be legally obliged to enunciate) the reasons. But the point about completely discretionary decisions is that, being completely discretionary, those reasons were not (and are not, in the future) binding. The official was (and is) free to act on those reasons. Equally, the official was (and is) free to act on any of several others.[21] Completely discretionary judgments are, to that extent, always and necessarily "arbitrary" decisions in that sense.

Of course, it may well be true that few decisions are ever completely discretionary. Discretions are often hedged—more or less successfully—with guidelines, standards, principles, parameters, and so on (Derthick 1976; Brown and Frieden 1976). Court-imposed standards of "reasonableness," already referred to, are one important example. Kenneth Culp Davis's (1969: chap. 4) various proposals for further "structuring discretion" would all hedge discretion in this way.[22] Likewise, discretions are often hedged with review and appeals procedures. Davis's (1969: chap. 5) various proposals for "checking discretion" would all thus further hedge discretion. But insofar as guidelines, etc., are binding rather than merely advisory, or insofar as higher tribunals substitute their judgment for the official's own on the particulars of the case, then to that extent the official is thereby deprived of discretion. Our objection to the arbitrariness of that official's discretionary power may have been overcome, but only by removing discretionary power from that official.[23]

Much the same is true—and for much the same reasons—of the "insecurity" objection. Insofar as completely discretionary decisions are necessarily arbitrary, they are to that extent necessarily unpredictable. Those who must rely upon them for needed resources suffer a certain amount of insecurity in consequence.

Again, there are various ways to ameliorate this insecurity. Probably the best proposal is for everyone to be guaranteed a certain baseline—a "security level"—with deviations from that being

[21] There may be some reasons upon which he cannot act—his discretion may be narrowed in that way, while remaining complete over the narrower range of reasons for which he may still act or refrain from acting. But proscribing some reasons as bad ones is not the same as prescribing others as mandatory.

[22] Notice, however, that insofar as officials who have formally been granted discretion by the legislature exercise that discretion by blindly following some rule, courts will strike their decisions down as "unreasonable" (Wade 1982: 330).

[23] The same is true of "due process" constraints on discretion. Insofar as that is a purely procedural test, demanding merely that proper procedures (fair hearing, adequate notice, etc.) be followed, then there is no guarantee that the decision was reached for the "right" reasons, or indeed for any nonarbitrary reasons. Insofar as "due process" contains some substantive test (such as that the decision be "reasonable"), then to that extent it limits the arbitrariness of discretionary judgments—but only by limiting the discretionariness of discretionary judgments.

permitted only in the upward direction. Much of the social security system is now like that. Everyone is guaranteed a basic pension or grant, and deviations from that (e.g., Supplementary Benefits) only make people better off than they would have been at that baseline (Marshall 1949: 111–13; Briggs and Rees 1980: 46). Notice, however, that this guarantee of a "security level" works only by depriving officials of some of their discretionary powers. Specifically, it deprives them of discretion to vary the payment below the baseline: they enjoy only unidirectional discretion, to raise but not to lower the award. Thus, the "insecurity" objection too can be solved only by depriving officials of some (although not necessarily all) discretion.

Broadly speaking, the same is true of the objection that discretion opens the way to exploitation. This, too, seems to be an inherent feature of any system of discretionary powers. There is, of course, one easy way to eliminate the risk of exploitation. The root of the problem, as shown above, is that the official might lay down illicit conditions upon the exercise of his discretion; and if that is the problem, the remedy is simply to prohibit the laying down of such conditions. That (or, more precisely, its converse) is what we already do through laws prohibiting the bribery or corruption of public officials. Once again, however, this amounts to overcoming the problems with discretion by curtailing discretion itself. Officials can be prevented from exploiting the power their discretion gives them over claimants only by curtailing their power to exercise that discretion conditionally.[24]

With the "intrusiveness" objection, the story is only slightly different. I must concede that I find nothing in the notion of "discretion" itself that makes this an inherent consequence of its exercise. It is perfectly possible for officials to exercise discretionary power without knowing anything at all about the people and their problems. Under such circumstances, of course, the arbitrariness objection would begin to bite all that much harder. But, more to the point, discretion would defeat its own purpose. The whole ration-

---

[24] Some may deny this, saying that although officials' power to exercise discretion conditionally is restricted, the *scope* of discretionary powers (i.e., the *range of options* they may exercise unconditionally) remains as broad as ever. But surely the proper way to define the extent of an official's discretion is in terms of the *number* of options rather than merely the range of options available to him. Someone who can choose to give a claimant £1 or £5 or £10 or £20 surely has more discretion than someone who can choose to give a claimant either £1 or £20 but nothing in between, even though the "range" of options (defined in terms of endpoints) is the same in both cases.

ale for giving officials discretionary power rather than obliging them to follow slavishly some rule is to allow (indeed, to require) them to tailor their treatment of individuals to the peculiar circumstances of those particular individuals. If they are to do this, it seems that a good deal of "intrusiveness" *is* a necessary concomitant.

How much intrusiveness is strictly necessary may, of course, be debatable. It may well be that caseworkers characteristically collect far more information than they really need. But I am inclined to suppose that this matter admits of no more general a resolution than the other. How much information it is necessary to collect should, I suspect, best be left to the caseworker's discretion for the selfsame reason as we left the broader decision of how to handle the case to the caseworker's discretion in the first place. In this way, I think we can reasonably say that "intrusiveness"—or at least the risk thereof—is inherent in the *rationale* for discretion, if not in the notion of "discretion" itself.

V

Logically, the opposite of enjoying discretion is being bound by a rule. So, logically, the natural response to finding that there are certain problems inherent in discretion is to impose rules in the place of those discretions. The assumption that that will automatically solve the problems of discretion, however, entails an unwarranted presumption that every problem necessarily has a solution. Saying that the problems identified above are inherent in discretion means that those problems can be resolved, if at all, only by curtailing that discretion through rules. But it is perfectly possible that those problems cannot be solved in that way, either.

The problems discussed above may be inherent, not merely in discretion but also in the purpose which those discretions were supposed to serve. If so, then any system (rules, or anything else) that also serves those purposes will also necessarily display those same faults. Here I shall argue that this is true of three out of the four objections to discretion canvassed above. Specifically, I shall show that, for those three problems: (1) the objectionable features which are inevitable in discretionary powers are nonetheless possible in a system of rules; and (2) the same considerations that drove us toward discretion in the first place would drive us to use rules in such a way as to reproduce the same problems there as well. Only the "manipulation/exploitation" objection escapes that trap.

Consider first the "arbitrariness" objection. The problem there was that officials with complete discretion did not have to give any reasons for their actions. With rules, *almost* the same is true. Admittedly, officials do, after a fashion, have to offer a "reason" for their decisions: they have to point to some rule or another. But rules typically serve as shields, permitting "unreasoned legalistic official behavior with no apparent rational relation between fidelity to the rule and [the] original ends" for which the rule was promulgated (Jowell 1973: 193; cf. Titmuss 1971b: 128–29).

A rule is not a reason. There may or may not be any logic behind the rule—either in general, or in its application to this particular case or to cases of this kind. But even if there were some compelling logic underlying the rule, a rule-following official would not be obliged to communicate that underlying logic to claimants when rendering a rule-based decision on their cases. Insofar as he is officially obliged to "give reasons" for his decisions, the giving of reasons need consist in no more than citing the rules.

There are, moreover, powerful pragmatic reasons for officials not going beyond the mere "citing of rules" to explain the underlying logic and principles of the rules to claimants. If officials were to do so, then claimants whose petitions fell outside the strict letter of the law would begin arguing with officials, trying to show that their cases really did come within the spirit of the rule nonetheless. Insofar as the officials are bound by a strict set of rules (as would seem to be required to curtail arbitrary discretion), however, officials would have no scope for deciding cases according to the spirit rather than the letter of the law. Since they do not, explaining rules' underlying logic to claimants would be powerfully counterproductive.[25]

The same sort of conclusion holds, for different reasons, as regards the "insecurity" objection. The problem there is that claimants never know what they are going to receive when officials have complete discretion over their grants. But the unpredictability of discretionary official decisions derived, at least in part, from

[25] Indeed, there may be an underlying logic, principle, or reason that would dictate the *opposite* conclusion to that which follows from a strict application of the rule to the present case; yet it is in the latter direction that nondiscretionary, rule-bound officials must move. This fact is what gives rise to complaints of penalizing "technical violators" (Jowell 1973: 192), and to complaints of "regulatory unreasonableness" (Bardach and Kagan 1982).

the variety of considerations which should legitimately be taken into account in deciding the proper award. Insofar as the rules that replace discretion attempt to capture the same range of considerations, their operation may (at least from the clients' point of view) be as unpredictable as the discretionary caseworker's.[26]

We can, of course, reduce the unpredictability of the verdicts rendered by rule-abiding officials by restricting the range of considerations that the rules direct them to take into account. But if those considerations were ones that really needed to be taken into account in rendering the "right" decision, then predictability of this sort is gained at the cost of rendering objectively "worse" decisions.[27]

Much the same tradeoff reappears with respect to the "intrusiveness" objection. Officials following rules might be just as intrusive as officials following their own discretion. It all depends on what sorts of factors (e.g., "cohabitation" the rules direct (or allow) them to take into account, and what sorts of powers (e.g., midnight searches) the rules give them to acquire those facts. We can, of course, reduce the intrusiveness of rule-governed officials by restricting the range of things the rule instructs (or allows) officials to do or to consider. And in the particular case just mentioned (midnight searches for men under the bed) I suppose we are probably all inclined to opt for that solution. But more gener-

[26] When pre-1980 Supplementary Benefits claimants were supplied with a Form A124 detailing the basis of the officer's decision on their claims, 22 percent reported not understanding the calculations, 16 percent the language, and 19 percent the whole thing (Briggs and Rees 1980: chap. 6). The 1980 reform of Supplementary Benefits moved away "from a scheme with relatively loose legislative framework and many discretionary provisions . . . to one governed by regulations covering all aspects of entitlement" (Beltram 1984: 3). But "by November 1981 there were not only 13 sets of incredibly complex supplementary benefits regulations plus seven sets of amendments, but also a very extensive internal code of instructions for benefit officers" (Foster 1983: 125). Not surprisingly, Beltram (1984: 4) reports that caseworkers administering the reformed scheme say that claimants still do not "understand how the scheme works." As the UK SBC (1976: para. 2.20) had anticipated, complexity proves as baffling to claimants whether codified in formal rules or embodied in informal practices.

[27] Hart (1961: 126) says, "We may fasten on certain features present in the plain case and insist that these are both necessary and sufficient to bring anything which has them within the scope of the rule, whatever. . . . To do this is to secure a measure of certainty or predictability at the cost of blindly prejudging what is to be done in a range of future cases, about whose composition we are ignorant. We shall thus indeed succeed in settling in advance, but also in the dark, issues which can only reasonably be settled when they arise and are identified." D'Amato (1983) shows how relatively precise rules become increasingly uncertain over the course of time and applications, for just such reasons. For various welfare-based examples, see Simon (1983).

209

ally, a certain amount of intrusiveness is inherent in tailoring the treatment to the claimant's peculiar circumstances; and rules can eliminate that intrusiveness only by forsaking that goal.

Thus, I am left with the conclusion that the problem to which stricter rules governing official behavior is the solution is *not* the problem of arbitrariness or insecurity or intrusiveness. There is nothing in the nature of rules to guarantee that they will necessarily, automatically solve those problems; and there is much in the background circumstances to suggest that whenever we are tempted by discretionary solutions, the same things that tempt us in them are likely to make any rules we adopt as bad as discretionary powers in all three ways. With respect to the third problem (intrusiveness) in particular, rules are in exactly the same position as discretionary powers: the evil in view is a necessary concomitant to a valued end, and the same considerations that led discretion-based regimes to countenance intrusiveness would exert the same sort of pressure on rule-based regimes as well.

Ultimately, the only problem with discretion to which rules are the solution is the problem of "manipulation/exploitation." If an official's treatment of some particular individual is strictly dictated by some rule, then that official cannot (legally, at least) threaten or offer to vary the treatment depending on the claimant's conforming to some other illicit conditions the official might care to lay down (Smith 1946; 1949; 1955; Goodin 1985b: chap. 7). Of course, rules may be more or less precise; and insofar as they allow officials some leeway for choices in how to treat claimants, then to that extent the officials can still attempt to exploit that position of power over claimants. But that is just to say that rules may still allow officials some (weak) discretion. If we fear exploitation of such discretion, then the solution is merely to eliminate it: i.e., to write rules that dictate officials' decisions strictly, tightly, and unambiguously in each case, insofar as possible.

V I

A regime of rights is one alternative to a regime of discretionary powers. But contrary to what is sometimes implied (especially by writers in social administration), it is not the only alternative. Here I shall first set out, in fairly formal fashion, the three distinct rule-based alternatives to a regime of discretionary powers.[28] Then I

---

[28] Yet another option is to remove all decision power in applying rules from peo-

shall discuss the appropriateness of each alternative remedy for the problems with discretion discussed above.

A

All alternatives to discretionary powers are, generically, strategies for using a formal set of *legally-binding rules* to exercise *control* over *lower-level agents* of state authority. That far, all the strategies here to be discussed are alike. They are all essentially variations on that one theme.

The distinctive feature of *rights* is that they constitute *control from below*. Specifically, rights allow citizens to exercise control over agents of authority by stipulating certain things that those agents must do to or for the rights-holders, or certain things that those agents must not do to rights-holders. Rights thus constitute one clear way of diminishing the discretionary power of state officials, by giving those subject to their authority a certain measure of legal control over them.

Broadly speaking, the alternative to rights-based controls on official discretion is a system of controls based on notions of officials' *obligations*. This strategy, in its various forms, constitutes *control from above*.[29] A regime of official obligations provides a mechanism for higher officials to control lower ones, and (assuming no slippage) ultimately for the highest—in a democracy, the sovereign electorate—to control the lowest minion. That is the other logically possible way of limiting the discretion of intermediate state officials.

This second, obligations-based strategy admits of two basic variants. Obligations can come in the form of either duties or responsibilities. *Duties* stipulate particular *actions* which state agents must take or refrain from taking. *Responsibilities*, in contrast, stipulate particular *outcomes* which state officials must produce or avoid producing. In the former case, lower-level officials are answerable to

_____

ple in the bureaucracy, vesting it instead in preprogrammed computers which calculate benefits on the basis of information punched into them by claimants and which dispense benefits rather like automatic bank tellers do money. That way, while some discretion would remain with the computer programmer (the rule-writer, as it were), none would remain at the point of service/benefit provision. Much progress has been made in the development of "expert systems" for assisting administrators of social welfare programs in applying the rules (Lamb 1986; Rose 1986: 30–35). Still, it is clear that anything remotely approaching the "automatic teller" fantasy sketched above is some way distant.

[29] Handler (1979: 101–2) similarly distinguishes top-down approaches to the control of official behavior from the bottom-up approach of the welfare-rights movement.

higher-level ones for what they did or did not do. So long as they did what they were duty-bound to do, they will be deemed to have discharged their duties, no matter what happened in consequence. In the latter case, the lower-level officials are answerable to higher-level ones for what happened. So long as the right consequences have been produced (and no duties violated in the process), the officials' responsibilities will be deemed to have been discharged, regardless of how in particular those results were brought about (Goodin 1986c).

B

Turning now to explore the comparative merits of each of these strategies, let us first consider the choice between "rights" and other forms of rule-based controls on official discretion. There are, of course, various rival theories of rights (Waldron 1984: 9–12). This is hardly the place to enter into that controversy. For present purposes, it is enough to note that the only theory of rights which makes them importantly different from other forms of rule (obligation, duty, responsibility) in constraining official behavior construes rights as "powers" (Hart 1955; Feinberg 1980: chaps. 6 and 7).

The chief rival to the Power Theory of rights is the Benefit (or Interest) Theory. On that account, to be a right-holder is merely to be the direct, intended beneficiary of another's duty-bound performance. But if that is all there is to rights-based controls on official behavior, then rights-based controls just reduce without residue to duty-based controls. Talk of rights might serve some rhetorical function in persuading legislators to impose certain duties on officials. Once imposed, however, it is the duty that does all the work in constraining official behavior. Rights serve no further purpose.

The Power Theory envisages a larger and more distinctive role for rights in constraining official behavior. On that account, rights are "protected choices." To have a right is to have a legally protected power to choose between demanding or waiving your right to the other person's duty-bound performance. That makes rights and duties correlative, once again: if what it means to have a right is to have the legal power to manipulate another's duty in the ways just described, then it is logically impossible to have a right without someone else's having such a duty in the first place. But whereas on the Benefit Theory rights-based controls on official behavior are just duty-based controls and no more, on the Power Theory rights-based controls are duty-based controls plus something more. What "more" is added is the right-holder's power of choice in claiming or waiving his entitlement.

Thus, even at their most distinctive, rights-based controls on official behavior are just duty-based controls plus something more. I submit that the strength of rights-based control strategies in solving that one problem which rules in general can solve at all (i.e., manipulation/exploitation) derives from what rights-based and duty-based control strategies share in common. The weakness of the rights-based control strategy derives from what is peculiar to it alone.

The strength of the strategy is this. Where welfare recipients have a right to welfare payments, officials have a correlative duty to supply them. (At least they have such a duty if the claimants do in fact apply for such benefits.) That being so, officials cannot exploit claimants by threatening to withhold benefits unless certain preconditions are met. The crucial thing in that argument, however, is the official's duty—not the claimant's right.

The weakness of the rights-based strategy is that, insofar as it is a distinctive control strategy at all, it depends upon rights-holders actually claiming or demanding their rights. In a purely rights-based system, the right-holders alone have legal standing to complain if officials fail to do their correlative duties. It seems to be sheer folly, however, to make their getting their due contingent upon their demanding it, since we know so well that (for one reason or another) a substantial number of them will in fact not do so.

This argument contains two strands, one conceptual and the other empirical. The conceptual claim is that, in a purely rights-based system, right-holders alone have legal standing to complain if their rights are not respected. Some would resist this claim by pointing out this would make nonsense of the "right to life," understood as a right not to be murdered: logically, it would be impossible for the bearer of that right to seek redress if it were violated; but we would be most reluctant to deny, for that reason alone, that one could ever have a right to life. Yet insofar as anyone is entitled to seek redress for murder or attempted murder as a *private* (i.e., tort) wrong, it is precisely the victim or the victim's successors, in whom his legal personality is vested upon his demise.

Others might resist this conceptual claim by saying that it is not only the right-holder who can demand that his right be respected or who can complain if it is not. It is the duty of the police to prevent rights violations, and of the public prosecutor to bring legal action against those who have violated the rights of others. But in so doing, it is the *public* rather than the private wrong that concerns those public officials. The wrong there in view is not violation of the victim's "right to life" but is, instead, "breach of the King's peace," or some such. That is a different right: a right owed to all of us not to have people murdered around us, if you will. Insofar as the *private* wrong—the wrong involved in violation of the victim's right to life—is to be redressed, it is up to the victim or his successors to bring action. The public prosecutor is constitutionally incapable of bringing civil, tort actions.

The second claim involved in this argument is the baldly empirical one that substantial numbers of people will not, in fact, lodge such a protest.[30] The empirical evidence on this score is pretty well incontestable. Even businesses subject to state regulation prove reluctant to press their "rights" against administrators guilty of abusing them: "the costs or risks involved are too high," more often than not (Handler 1966). The poor are more reluctant still to press a claim. This is true even of straightforward legal claims against private individuals, for, e.g., compensation in cases of automobile accidents (Carlin, Howard, and Messinger 1966: 69–84).

---

[30] David Miller (personal correspondence, 1986) suggests that effective control of official discretion depends only on *enough* rights-holders being willing to press their claims that officials will be deterred from withholding anyone's entitlements. But deterrence works only if officials who have been found to be wrongfully withholding benefits will be subject to some *extra* penalties, over and above having to pay the claimant what has always been owed to him. The social services, as presently practiced, are totally lacking in such penalties. There are penalties for wrongfully honoring claims, but there are none for wrongfully denying them (Brodkin and Lipsky 1983). Consequently, when welfare agencies lose a legal case and are forced to honor a claim that they had originally denied, they have no incentive to go back automatically and reverse all their other decisions in similar cases; for that, further litigation is usually required (Lynes 1970: 126; Piven and Cloward 1971: chap. 10). Neither do welfare agencies have any incentive not to make similar "mistakes" in their future dealings with the same claimants; indeed, they sometimes seem to do so intentionally, as a means of punishing him for challenging them last time (Handler 1979).

The social services could, of course, be reformed in this regard. Penalties for wrongful denial could be enforced against erring officials; or tort actions against the state (as suggested in Schuck 1980; 1983) might be allowed. Even then, however, it is still an open, empirical question whether "enough" claimants would come forward to press their rights in order for officials to be sufficiently deterred. The evidence referred to below rather suggests that not enough would, unless the tort damages were very lucrative or unless the penalties were so stiff that only a handful of successful prosecutions would be deterrent enough.

And it is all the more true of other, more complicated claims (UK SBC 1977: paras. 7.43–7.48).

The poor are particularly unlikely to press any legal claims to welfare rights, especially. Just consider all the steps involved in the process, and what, at each step, might prevent a poor claimant from proceeding.

> In order for this system to function, . . . the potential claimant has to be aware of the fact that he has a legal right that has been violated; he has to be aware that a remedy is available; he has to have the resources with which to pursue the remedy; and he has to make a calculation that the expected benefits of pursuing the remedy outweigh the possible costs. Only if all of these conditions are fulfilled will the adversary [i.e., the rights-based] system work. If any of them is not fulfilled, there will not be a complaining client and the alleged deprivation of a legal right will not be challenged. (Handler 1979: 48)

Empirical evidence, however, suggests that each of those conditions is likely not to be fulfilled. Many poor people are simply unaware of their legal rights and of the remedies available in case of breach; and many more, although informed of "fair hearings" provisions and such like when first applying for aid, found the information simply not relevant at the time and forgot all about it (Bond 1975; Handler 1979: 48–49). Resources—of time, psychic energy and expert advice—are all desperately short among the poor. Furthermore, even if they could muster such resources, it is far from clear that it would be wise for the poor to invest them in pursuing a welfare-rights claim that might alienate an agency with which they have to have a continuing relationship, and upon whose continued discretion they will be forced to rely. Empirical evidence on the behavior of welfare claimants suggests that each of these steps individually constitutes a serious obstacle to claiming and that, cumulatively, the obstacles will typically prove insurmountable—and will remain so, for most, however much help they get from poverty lawyers and supportive neighborhood ground in lodging their claims.[31] In light of these sorts of obstacles to claiming, it is

---

[31] Handler (1979: 48–51); see also Briar (1966), Handler and Hollingsworth (1970; 1971), Scheingold (1974) and, more generally, Nelson (1980); cf. Bull (1970), and Piven and Cloward (1971: chap. 10). Given these problems with the rights-based strategy, it might pay to reflect on how we ever got the idea of enforcing social welfare claims in that way. Historically, the answer is tied up with arguments for

pure folly to trust clients pursuing their own claims to exercise anything like comprehensive, effective control over state officials.

Significantly, welfare rights fail for reasons that are intimately linked to the reasons that welfare rights are needed at all:

> welfare recipients . . . are very dependent, fearful, poverty-stricken people who desperately need what the welfare system has to offer. They face a highly discretionary system and are simply in no position to challenge it. *It is dependency on discretionary authority that defeats the exercise of legal rights.* (Handler 1973: 12, emphasis added)

A system of obligations-based controls on official discretion, in contrast, does not depend upon social welfare clients themselves to exercise the controls.[32] Obligations-based systems can give all sorts of different people legal standing to intervene to demand that officials do in fact discharge their obligations.[33] There are good

---

"social insurance," which was to be insurance in just the same sense as private insurance. The political point of this analogy was that insurance schemes cannot be means-tested: anyone who paid insurance premiums is entitled to benefits whenever any of the insured-against contingencies actually occurs (Blackley 1878; Beveridge 1942: para. 402; and Marshall 1949: 265). The reason the problems which are sketched in the text with "welfare rights" were not readily anticipated is, basically, that experience with insurance (especially private insurance, but to some extent even earlier forms of social insurance) had been of a rather different kind, in two respects. A different social strata had participated in traditional insurance schemes, and to some degree continued to predominate in early forms of social insurance (old-age pensions, national insurance) as well. And the understanding of what precisely constituted a relevant "contribution" to the insurance scheme (i.e., National Insurance contributions), and of to what precisely that contribution entitled one was much clearer. When the Social Security Act of 1966 vested an analogous welfare right in every Briton, both those latter points were powerfully ambiguous.

[32] Similar reasoning underlies sec. 38 of the U.K. Power of Criminal Courts Act of 1973, allowing criminal courts to issue a "criminal compensation order" requiring convicted defendants to pay compensation to their victims: in that way, "the victim will not be deprived of compensation simply because he lacks the courage or determination to pursue a civil remedy" (Williams and Hepple 1984: 6).

[33] Petitioners would be seeking not their rights-based entitlements but rather a writ of mandamus to compel officials to do their duties or, in dramatic cases, a criminal prosecution for breach of duty (Williams and Hepple 1984: 8, 62–63; Wade 1982: ch. 19). Under such rules, various people other than the direct, intended beneficiaries *can* be accorded standing. That is not to imply that they necessarily *will* be. A revised and more generous notion of standing is also required. According to the poor law conception of standing, which persisted into the 1940s, paupers themselves lacked standing to complain, having forfeited their rights of citizenship quite generally upon applying for relief (Marshall 1949: 262–63; 1965: 269). Yet according to the prevailing notion of standing, no one else had standing to take public officials to court to demand performance of their duties toward the poor, either: only those with a "legally protected interest" in the administrative action in ques-

reasons for counting would-be beneficiaries among those potential plaintiffs.[34] But there is no good reason to make them the *only* potential plaintiffs, as purely rights-based control strategies would do.[35] Under obligations-based strategies, there would be more and more effective test cases brought because more and more effective people would be allowed to bring them.

C

Next let us consider the choice between duties and responsibilities, the two obligations-based strategies for controlling official behavior. The difference between them, as described above, is between act-oriented and results-oriented modes of control. Sometimes we might have some independent moral concern with the way people are treated (e.g., wanting them to be treated courteously by welfare workers), regardless of the end-results of the administrative process. Deontological moral theories make a fetish of such concerns. However, more often—and especially with regard to welfare policy—we seem principally concerned with consequences. If so, then we should choose between these two control strategies, depending simply upon their relative efficacy in producing the outcomes we desire.

Both duty-based and responsibility-based strategies are, at root, strategies for superiors exercising control over subordinates. In the duty-based approach, what superiors are trying to control is behavior of subordinates. For this sort of control to be effective, superiors need to be able to monitor and control effectively the activities of subordinates—and, through them, of subordinates'

---

tion were traditionally thought to have standing; and the public at large had no such "interest," narrowly construed. From the 1960s onward, however, notions of standing have been broadening to allow a wide variety of people to challenge a wide variety of administrative actions. This has now happened in both British law (Wade 1982: 572–79, 640–43) and American (Jaffe 1961; Davis 1970; Albert 1974; Stewart 1975).

[34] Some have to do with protecting the beneficiary's self-respect and dignity (Feinberg 1980: chap. 7), others with protecting his autonomy (Buchanan 1984b: 79–80). More pragmatically, giving the intended beneficiary a special claim (whether phrased in terms of "rights" or not) will help to ensure that when officials are found to be in delict of their duties compensation or restitution will be made to the direct, intended beneficiary of their duty-bound performance rather than, e.g., a fine being levied that is then deposited to general fund revenue (Buchanan 1984b: 74–75).

[35] In practice, of course, the cooperation of claimants is often pragmatically required—e.g., in testifying against officials who abuse their powers and violate their obligations. Hence, some of the same problems are bound to reappear under an obligations-based system; but not all of them will.

subordinates, and so on down the chain of command. Often this is impossible, by the nature of the task. Michael Lipsky's (1980) "street-level bureaucrats," for example, must by the nature of their jobs (teaching, policing, etc.) do their work well away from their supervisors' prying eyes (Gummer 1979). The more slippage there is in any step in this monitoring and control process, the less effective the duty-based strategy of control will be.

In the responsibility-based strategy, what superiors are trying to control is outputs.[36] For this sort of control to be effective, superiors need to be able to monitor and to control effectively the outputs of their subordinates. This might appear, at first blush, to be the easier of the two approaches, but appearances may well be deceptive. Arguably, it is precisely the inability to monitor outputs that forces governments to provide certain services directly rather than contracting out to private suppliers (Gibson, Goodin and LeGrand 1985; Blau 1963: chaps. 3 and 11). And the difficulties with meaningful statistical reporting of the *real* outputs—the ones that matter—are particularly acute in social welfare policy (Handler 1966: 181–83). Thus, the relative effectiveness of these two control mechanisms comes down to a question of whether officials' superiors are better able to monitor and control the officials' activities or their outputs. This is an empirical question, the answer to which is likely to vary from case to case.

Our particular concern, in the present context, is not with the relative effectiveness of these two control strategies tout court, but rather with their relative effectiveness at remedying abuses of discretion (and, more particularly still, the exploitation and manipulation of that discretion). At first glance, it might seem that responsibility-based controls must always prove inferior in that particular respect. After all, they leave officials with substantial residual discretionary power in deciding how best to accomplish the prescribed results.[37]

Certainly it is true that responsibilities entail formal discretionary powers of a particular kind. Where responsibilities prove to be more effective control strategies than duties, however, the implication must necessarily be that in those circumstances a regime of

---

[36] For arguments in favor of such results-based controls, see Schultze (1977), Ackerman and Hassler (1981) and Goodin (1982: chap. 4).

[37] This follows analytically from the concept of "responsibility" here isolated; see Goodin (1986b) and Feinberg (1980: 137). But it is not just a peculiarity of this analysis. Woodrow Wilson (1887: 213), for example, writes that "large powers and unhampered discretion seem to me the indispensable conditions of responsibility."

strict duties would, in effect, leave subordinates with even broader (albeit informal) discretionary power. (Remember, the reason responsibilities prove superior to duties is that superiors are relatively powerless to monitor or control the behavior of subordinates.) Hence, the question of effective control of subordinates *tout court* and the question of how best to prevent abuses of discretionary powers by subordinates is one and the same question. Where responsibility-based regimes prove superior on the former criterion, they prove superior on the latter one as well.

V I I

The arguments offered above lead to a pair of pretty depressing conclusions. First, as shown in section II, discretionary powers are to a certain extent *ineliminable*. Worse still, some of the more worrisome aspects of discretionary powers seem to be among these.

By their very nature, rules must be interpreted by officials in the process of applying them to particular cases. In the course of interpreting the rules, however, those officials often subtly redefine them. "Bureaucratic disentitlement" is a popular way to cope with cutbacks in agency funding (Lipsky 1984). But this process must be seen for what it is: the administrative arrogation of what is properly a legislative function. There have been several compelling studies illustrating this practice among street-level professionals (Lipsky 1980; 1984; Stone 1984; Schorr 1985). More worrying still, there is a substantial body of evidence that the very lowest-level functionaries, such as clerks and receptionists, are among its most common practitioners.[38]

Second, the problems we find with the exercise of discretionary powers are to a large extent *insurmountable*. Of the many problems posed by officials possessing discretions, a regime of rights is the proper solution to none, and a regime of rules more generally to only one.[39] It is important to see what rules can do: they can pre-

---

[38] See, e.g.: Mechanic (1962); Blau (1963: chaps. 2 and 5); Zimmerman (1971); Hall (1974); Lipsky (1980: 198); and Foster (1983).

[39] Handler (1973: chap. 7) suggests two other strategies. Neither of them is at all satisfactory, however. One of them is to distribute social welfare benefits in cash rather than in kind. While that would certainly make it more difficult for caseworkers to exercise one form of control over client behavior (i.e., to control directly the end uses to which benefits were put), it does little to prevent caseworkers from laying down preconditions for receipt of the cash; and if they are particularly concerned about end uses, they can always make it a precondition of getting money next time that clients produce receipts to show where they spent the money last time. Ironically, Handler (1968) himself, in an earlier study of Children's Officers

vent the manipulation and exploitation of those dependent upon state services by officials responsible for the administration of those services. It is equally important to see what they cannot do. They cannot (necessarily, or without substantial costs in other respects) prevent intrusiveness, arbitrariness or insecurity. For much the same reasons that discretionary decisions *must* display those attributes rule-based decisions *can*, and *probably will*. That, too, is an important finding.

Those latter problems associated with discretion are, in some deep sense, insoluble. Insofar as they trouble us, therefore, the proper way to handle them is not to try resolving them at all. Rather, we should try *circumventing* them. That is to say, we should seek ways to avoid the circumstances that push both discretion-based and rule-based systems in these undesirable directions.

The problems described above all seem to arise, most fundamentally, from the effort to make sure that assistance is granted to everyone who needs/deserves assistance, and *only* to those who need/deserve it. That is why, even within a rule-based system, we are required to take account of a vast array of personal circumstances, thus rendering decisions unpredictable and leaving claimants feeling insecure. That is why, even with a rule-based system, we must collect vast amounts of personal information, with all the intrusiveness that that inevitably entails. That, too, is why even with a rule-based system officials dare not (for fear of inviting still more formally invalid claims) enunciate any principles they might perceive underlying the rules—thus giving rise to arbitrariness, or at least the appearance thereof, from the claimant's point of view. All these things stem from the attempt to make sure that *only* the

---

in Britain, uncovered substantial evidence of manipulation of cash payments in these ways, so it is odd that he should suddenly turn into their champion. Handler's other suggestion is for "a pluralistic approach," breaking the public monopoly on social services through "greater use of private social service agencies" (Handler 1973: 156). But as he goes on to acknowledge, "For reasons of prestige and professionalism these [private] agencies serve the middle class and refer [to the public agencies] the poor who seek their help" (Handler 1973: 156). That problem may be overcome through generous systems of public subsidy to private agencies that take poor clients, as Handler suggests, although one rather suspects that crafty private suppliers will find ways of making their clients seem poorer than they really are to collect the subsidy. The problem that remains—and is the more serious one—is that private agencies are, by their natural inclination, even more moralistic than public ones, and the sheer force of competitive pressure is unlikely to overcome those natural inclinations unless the competition is fierce indeed. More likely, the number of competitors will be small, the competition oligopolistic, and both public and private agencies as morally censorious as ever.

needy/deserving receive the benefits (Donnison 1977: 535; Hill 1969).[40]

The best strategy, in my view, for circumventing those problems turns on that insight. Imagine a world in which officials were guided only by the first half of that twin obsession: suppose officials are anxious to ensure that everyone who needs/deserves benefits gets them, but that they are utterly unconcerned to ensure that only they receive them. By adopting a rule of systematically erring on the side of generosity in this way, officials could obviate the need for any of the mechanisms that give rise to the objections of arbitrariness, insecurity, or intrusiveness, as described above. Of course, it is still perfectly possible that those disagreeable attributes might be displayed (quite needlessly) in a discretion-based system: those possibilities, as I have shown in section IV, are inherent in any such system. But working with a rule-based system, we could guarantee that the rules governing official behavior (operating under a meta-rule of generosity) would display none of those disagreeable attributes.

A rule of generosity would have one further advantage. In section II it was argued that someone, somewhere always has to have some discretionary power in any system of rules. That is inherent in the nature of rules themselves. But it is important, morally, that the *right people*—or at least the *people in the right positions*—be the ones to exercise such discretions. There are various considerations to be taken into account in deciding what is the right place to settle discretionary power. On the one hand, the greater capacity of lower-level officials to produce an answer that takes full account of the particular circumstances of the particular case argues for vesting discretion at a lower level; on the other hand, the greater accountability of higher-level officials to the sovereign (the monarch, Parliament, electorate, etc.) argues for vesting discretion at a higher level.

An underfunded discretionary authority, however, brings us

---

[40] As Handler (1973: 137) says, "The situation facing the caseworker—the line official in the social service department—is an overabundance of clients seeking relatively scarce resources. Discretionary administrative power has been created by scarcity; the system of allocation is the exercise of that discretion." What is worse, in underfunded systems, administrators are forced to choose between many different claimants, each of whom is eligible but not all of whom can be assisted with the resources available. Smith (1949: 280) comments that "broad discretion . . . results from the traditional practice in welfare legislation of enacting general measures which create a large class of eligibles, and then appropriating funds which are insufficient to aid all those who come within the terms of the legislation" (see similarly Friedman 1969: 230–31).

the worst of both worlds. Overworked caseworkers or their immediate superiors are forced to adopt rules of their own devising to batch-process claimants.[41] We thereby lose whatever advantage we might have expected from vesting discretion lower down. But at the same time, we put into operation a system of rules promulgated by those not in authority to make rules. If we were going to have cases being decided by rules rather than individualized discretion, we should have had the rules enacted in the proper way by the proper authorities rather than being made up by beleaguered street-level bureaucrats as they went along.[42] More generous funding would solve these problems, too, allowing street-level bureaucrats to exercise discretion as it was meant to be exercised.[43]

In certain respects, my "rule of generosity" is merely an artful dodge around problems of discretion. It certainly does not meet the problems head-on. But I am inclined to think that it is none the worse for that. If the dodge really is a *successful* dodge—if it really does get around the problems—then that is, for all intents and purposes, just as good as solving the problems.

Some will no doubt find more principled objections,couched in terms of the "inequity" and "injustice" done to the truly needy/deserving by giving benefits to the unneedy/undeserving as well (Handler 1979: 6-7). Sometimes it is true that "supply-side solutions" are unsuccessful evasions of distributional problems; and sometimes it is true that people are made worse off by another person's being made better off (see chapter 9). However, the benefits provided by the social services do not seem to display any of

[41] Lipsky (1980). Donnison (1977: 535) similarly bemoans as "clumsy local improvisations" the sorts of rules the Supplementary Benefits system was forced to adopt in light of rising caseloads conjoined with severe staffing restraints. Ironically, this seems to be just the sort of thing Davis (1969: chaps. 2 and 3) is advocating as "administrative rule-making."

[42] That is to say, if we are to have something like the A-Code guiding the behavior of National Assistance and, later, Supplementary Benefits officers, it should be regularized by approval of Parliament—as has now been done by the Social Security Act of 1980—rather than being merely an in-house invention (Beltram 1984: 23). Alternatively, if we leave discretionary power in the agencies, we should make those agencies more directly politically accountable—e.g., by popular election of agency officials, as one American suggests (Stewart 1975: 1791–93).

[43] P. S. Atiyah (personal correspondence, 1985) has similarly suggested that some of the reasons we are relatively comfortable with judges exercising discretions have to do with the time and money lavished on judicial proceedings, thereby increasing the odds of a "correct" determination. There is no reason to believe most welfare claims require anything like so much attention; but, on a smaller scale, more generous funding might help make us more comfortable with those exercises of discretion, too.

the more specific characteristics that are required for any of that to be true.

The only real objection to my "rule of generosity" is the economic one. Systematically erring on the side of generosity would indeed cost the Treasury, and perhaps cost it dearly. If my other arguments are correct, however, doing otherwise has its costs, too. It might be harder to put a price tag on moral affronts, like arbitrariness, insecurity, and intrusiveness. But the mere fact that we cannot count them quite so readily does not make them any less of a cost.[44]

[44] Elsewhere I have shown that on straightforward welfare-economic calculations we should be *more* inclined (not *less*) to err on the side of kindness in deciding social welfare entitlements in bad times, when claim levels are legitimately high (Goodin 1985a). That is merely to say we should be more willing to commit more social resources to welfare programs when need for them is high. Of course, resources may be genuinely scarce, and not all claims may be able to be met: then we would be in a genuinely "tragic" situation, where distributions might have to be governed by very different principles.

Part III

AGAINST THE NEW RIGHT

Against the welfare state, the New Right launches a large array of different attacks. In one way or another, however, all of them hark back to the moralistic political economy of the nineteenth century and before.

One pair of New Right attacks is plainly economic in character. The argument considered in chapter 8 criticizes the welfare state for its alleged inefficiencies; that considered in chapter 9 proposes to substitute "supply-side" solutions in place of the welfare state's distribution-side ones. Two more of the attacks are plainly moralistic in tone. The argument taken up in Chapter 10 holds that the welfare state wrongly rewards the morally undeserving and penalizes the deserving; that taken up in chapter 11 protests that the welfare state infringes people's freedom in various ways. Yet another attack—considered in chapter 12—is basically social-psychological, but with moralistic overtones and economic ramifications: this holds that the welfare state undermines self-reliance.

In defending the welfare state against such attacks, my rejoinders will of necessity be as varied as the New Right's own arguments. At root, however, I shall be continually arguing that the New Right's moralistic political economy is a conjunction of dubious economics and even more dubious ethics. Sometimes the New Right argument turns on empirical propositions that are doubtful at best (and sometimes plainly untrue). Other times, New Right arguments are flawed in some important theoretical way—either conceptually confused or morally perverse. In any case, my conclusion is that, for a variety of reasons matching the variety of attacks, the New Right's case against the welfare state cannot be sustained.

While I shall do as much as is necessary to call into question the dubious empirical propositions of the New Right, my primary focus in these chapters will continue to be normative. I shall be making two quite distinct sorts of arguments against the New Right's moral principles. Sometimes I shall launch a limited attack upon the moral principles that the New Right is urging. Thus, for example, chapter 8 will show that efficiency is a morally important value, but not nearly as fundamental as New Rightists allege: morally, it is a derivative value, and those deeper values from which it derives its value argue in favor of a welfare state even when efficiency itself may not. Or again, desert is shown in chapter 10 to be a morally important notion in its place, but New Right arguments apply it where it has no place; freedom is an important goal, but the New Right focuses too narrowly upon what chapter

11 shows are probably some of the less important aapects of this highly complex notion; and self-reliance is a morally important goal, but not (as I show in chapter 12) in the perverted form being urged by New Rightists in their attacks on state welfare provision.

Sometimes my attack on the New Right's normative propositions will also take another form. Where they assert that the welfare state is morally objectionable because it undermines some particular value, I argue that (on a proper understanding of the concept, or a proper reading of the empirical evidence) the welfare state can actually be seen to be, on balance, promoting that self-same value. The strategy is thus one of turnabout. In none of these cases is that strategy quite *so* successful that any large part of the positive case for the welfare state should be seen to rest upon those arguments alone. Either the values in question are just not all that important, or else the welfare state's contribution to them, while on balance positive, is just too mixed or ambiguous or non-unique for any very powerful case for the welfare state to be built on those foundations. Ultimately, the positive case for the welfare state must in my view rest on the propositions developed in chapters 5 through 7. Still, while the turnabout arguments in the chapters that follow may not be sufficiently successful to form any major plank in the positive case for the welfare state, they nonetheless seem sufficiently successful to undercut decisively the New Right's attacks on the welfare state couched in those terms.

E I G H T

EFFICIENCY

Perhaps the most familiar and long-standing charge, in the New Right's indictment of the welfare state, is that social welfare measures undermine economic efficiency. The basic function of the welfare state, as analyzed in chapter 1, is to "modify the play of market forces." But the market, just as surely as the welfare state, aims at (and, under certain idealized conditions, arguably succeeds in) maximizing social welfare. When the welfare state sets about "modifying the play of market forces," it upsets incentive structures that are essential if the market is to play this role. Specifically, the welfare state is alleged to introduce disincentives to work, save, and invest. The cumulative effect is said to be the diminution of the social welfare of society as a whole, and of the poor most particularly.[1]

There is nothing new in these allegations. As early as 1787, The Reverend Joseph Townsend was warning that "to promote industry and economy it is necessary that the relief given to the poor be limited and precarious." Such sentiments were powerfully echoed by Thomas Malthus (1826) and the Poor Law Commissioners of 1834 (Blomfield 1834). Indeed, as Blaug (1963: 151) says,

> No matter which authority we consult on the English Poor Laws in the nineteenth century the same conclusions emerge: the Old Poor Law demoralized the working class, promoted population growth, lowered wages, reduced rents, destroyed yeomanry, and compounded the burden on ratepayers; the more the Old Poor Law relieved poverty, the more it encouraged the poverty which it relieved; the problem of devising an efficient public relief system was finally solved with the pas-

---

[1] "The poor most particularly," because it is the conventional wisdom within this camp that most economic gains for them have come not as a result of antipoverty programs but rather as the result of economic growth; so whatever reduces economic growth, on this account, harms first and foremost the poor (Murray 1982; 1984).

229

sage of the "harsh but salutary" Poor Law Amendment Act of 1834.

The latter was harsh indeed: the notorious "principle of less eligibility" meant that the relief recipient's lot was to be made so very unattractive, as compared to that of the "independent labourer of the lowest class," that no one would apply for relief except under conditions of extreme necessity. Such punitive relief policies were long thought necessary to guarantee that poor relief did not constitute a disincentive to labor and hence a barrier to economic efficiency.

Economic historians have long challenged this account of the effects of the old poor law, of course. And it has long been known that the "harsh but salutary" new poor law of 1834 did less good than expected because, as it turned out, "the bulk of relief recipients were . . . not the able-bodied, but rather the helpless and dependent sick, aged, and infirm" (Blaug 1963: 177; see further Booth 1891; 1892).

Still, the New Right has taken up this age-old refrain with gusto. Charles Murray, in his influential book, *Losing Ground*, baldly asserts "three core premises . . . that need to be taken into account" in framing social policy:

> *Premise 1*: People respond to incentives and disincentives. Sticks and carrots work.
>
> *Premise 2*: People are not inherently hard working or moral. In the absence of countervailing influences, people will avoid work and be amoral.
>
> *Premise 3*: People must be held responsible for their actions . . . if society is to function. (Murray 1984: 146)

Such claims are common currency among New Rightists like Martin Anderson (1978) and George Gilder (1981).

In assessing these claims of the New Right, I shall first turn to the empirical evidence. There has, by now, been quite a bit of econometric work done on the effects of transfer payments on labor supply and, to a lesser extent, on their effects on savings and investment. The results of those studies, summarized in section I below, suggest that the New Right badly exaggerates any such effects that social welfare programs might have. Next I turn to demonstrate the various ways in which welfare programs might actually make positive contributions to economic efficiency. Those effects, section II shows, are probably sufficient to more than counterbalance the slight negative effects with which the New Right is so obsessed.

Both of those rejoinders amount essentially to meeting the economists on their own ground. In section III, I move to the higher ground of moral principle and mount a limited challenge to the efficiency principle itself. Social principles, I shall there be arguing, have a logic of their own. When explicitly embracing one principle such as efficiency, we are obliged also to embrace certain other principles which are logically implicit within that principle. In the case of efficiency, those other principles seem to be ones of satisfying people's wants and, deeper still, of respecting persons. Those principles underlie and give meaning to the efficiency principle, which therefore must yield to them in cases of conflict. Thus, even if there is a tradeoff to be made between "efficiency" and "equity" (Okun 1975: chap. 4)—and the empirical arguments of the first two sections suggest that there is not—our commitment to efficiency can in this way still commit us, in certain circumstances, to overriding considerations of efficiency and moving more in the direction of a welfare state.

I

New Right critics of the welfare state's deleterious effects on economic efficiency typically point to three types of effect. The first two are "labor supply" effects: the non-poor have less of an incentive to work the more of their earnings that they have to pay in taxes to finance the welfare state; and the poor have less of an incentive to work the more unearned income they can expect to receive from the welfare state. The third effect concerns saving and investment behavior: the more that people can expect to receive from the state by way of an old-age pension, the less incentive there is for them to save privately or to invest in private retirement pension plans; and, assuming that the state funds its own old-age pension scheme out of current contributions (as, typically, it does), then that means a reduction in total capital formation in the economy as a whole. Such empirical evidence as is available on each of these topics will be considered in turn.

A

The effect of welfare state tax levels upon the labor supply of the non-poor is now and long has been known to be negligible. Okun

(1975: 96–97) reports flatly that "dozens of researchers have plowed into this area: they have uncovered virtually no significant effects of the present tax system on the amount of work effort of the affluent." Or, again, Atkinson and Stiglitz (1980: 49–50), summarizing a large body of survey research, conclude "that for the majority of the workers covered by these studies the effect of income taxation [on labor supply decisions] is of secondary importance. Typically between 65 and 80 per cent report that their decisions are not materially influenced and the remainder are split fairly evenly between incentive and disincentive effects."[2]

The typical economist's explanation of this puzzling phenomenon is that "income effects" and "substitution effects" just about balance each other out. The higher the tax rate, the less remunerative any given hour's labor will be; but, then again, the higher the tax rate the longer you have to work to realize the same level of after-tax earnings. A more sociological explanation seems more plausible, however: "high-income people are more motivated by the 'scores' they make—their pretax income—than by the actual disposable income they receive" (Lindblom 1977: 44; see further Bronfenbrenner 1971: chap. 10). If success in the status game is a function of pretax earnings, then people will continue expending the same effort in that game whatever the rate at which those earnings are taxed.

Whatever the reasons, however, what matters for present purposes is just the "record of unanimity" among a wide variety of studies that there are virtually no work disincentives for the nonpoor arising from the income tax (Bronfenbrenner 1971: 130). As Barlow, Brazer, and Morgan (1966: 2) write, "The picture of the high-income individual emerging from our study is that of a hardworking executive or professional, whose decisions about how much to work are dictated by the demands of his job and by his health, rather than by taxes or other purely pecuniary considerations."

[2] Of course, people may respond one way in interview situations and quite another in the real world, so in principle observed labor market behavior would be a preferable indicator. The evidence there, however, "does not deal directly with taxation but rather draws inferences from the response to net-of-tax wages" on the assumption that "the effect of income tax operates in the same way as any other reduction in net earnings" (Atkinson and Stiglitz 1980: 50). Economically, that assumption *should* be correct; sociologically, it might not be, for reasons given below. Note that Rosen's (1976a, b) study, which does deal directly with taxation, examines the effects on married women, whose behavior is known to differ markedly from that of primary earners.

B

The empirical findings are rather more complex when it comes to the labor-supply effects on income transfer recipients. Fortunately, however, the *Journal of Economic Literature* has now published a masterly synthesis of the findings of over two hundred studies of this matter. Danziger, Haveman, and Plotnick's (1981: 996) best guess, based on all those studies, is that the major U.S. income transfer programs, all taken together, are probably responsible for a total reduction of work hours by recipients amounting to 4.8 percent of total work hours of all workers in the U.S. Fully half of that loss, on their estimates, is accounted for by just two programs: old-age and survivors insurance, and disability insurance. Social insurance programs taken as a whole account for almost four-fifths of the loss. In contrast, all of the means-tested programs of "public assistance"—AFDC, SSI and Veterans' Pensions, Food Stamps and Housing Assistance and Medicaid—together account for just over a fifth of the lost labor supply.

While it certainly is not trivial, economically, to lose 5 percent of labor power, neither is it an economic catastrophe. The economic effect of this loss is further mitigated by the fact, too, that the hours are lost from those who are some of the least productive (or, anyway, some of the least valued) members of the workforce: the old, the ill, the disabled, the unskilled. In light of this, Danziger, Haveman, and Plotnick (1981: 1020) conclude that the real "earnings loss resulting from the 4.8 percent labor supply reduction" probably comes to only "about 3.5 percent because not all of the additional labor supply would find employment and because persons subject to the work disincentives of current transfers tend to have below average wage rates."

C

Findings on the effects of income-transfer (principally, old-age pension) programs on private savings and investment are very much more uncertain. Some studies purport to find that the U.S. Social Security scheme has reduced private savings by anywhere from 30 to 50 percent; other studies, employing marginally more defensible model specifications, find no significant effect. On balance, Danziger, Haveman, and Plotnick (1981: 1003, 1005) conclude that "there is little robust time-series evidence of a significant negative relationship between Social Security and private savings" and that "the cross-section results . . . yield much the same mixed picture. . . . " Their best estimate of the overall effects is couched in the following, cautious language:

Given the wide variation in the estimates of savings impacts, we venture the tentative conclusion that income transfer programs have depressed annual private savings by 0–20% relative to their value without these programs, with the most likely estimates lying near the lower end of this range. (Danziger, Haveman, and Plotnick 1981: 1006)

On that lower estimate, the effects of welfare programs would again appear to be economically somewhat marginal. Reducing savings and hence investments by, say, 5 percent is not trivial, economically; neither is it a major economic catastrophe. Should the true value lie toward the higher end of the range, the economic consequences could be considerable, though. Losing 20 percent of private savings could indeed be something serious, economically.

Even that is not necessarily dire, though. Notice that the problem, economically, with reducing private savings is that that reduces capital formation and funds for investment. If social security programs do depress private savings, however, there are various ways of stimulating investment and capital formation without abandoning (or even substantially altering) those programs.[3] As Arthur Okun (1975: 99) writes,

The nation can have the level of saving and investment it wants with more or less redistribution, so long as it is willing to twist some other dials. For example, any threat that . . . [welfare programs] . . . would make savings inadequate could be offset by more federal saving through budget surpluses or more middle-class saving through special incentives. Similarly, investment demand could be bolstered by easing credit policies or strengthening investment tax incentives.

Thus, although we cannot say with quite such confidence that the effect of social welfare programs on private savings and investment is negligible, we can say with considerable confidence that there is no need to repudiate those programs to overcome those effects.

---

[3] One way of altering the program would be the abandonment of pay-as-you-go principles, partially or totally, in favor of some sort of reserve fund; the latter would act as a kind of publicly enforced savings plan (Musgrave 1983).

D

The upshot of this brief survey of empirical findings is this. The effects of the welfare state on economic efficiency are many and varied. On some of them, the evidence is fairly conclusive; on others, the error bands are still pretty wide. From what we now know, however, it is clear that the effects of social welfare programs along the lines of those in the U.S. have only a marginal impact on economic efficiency. Labor supply of the affluent is virtually unaffected by the taxes required to support welfare services at those levels. Labor supply of welfare recipients is reduced, but only by about 4.8 percent; and the loss, in terms of their earnings, to the GNP is only about three-quarters of that. There may—or may not—be serious disincentives to private savings and investment resulting from old-age pensions. But if there are, there are other and better ways to encourage capital formation than reducing or eliminating state pensions.

I I

According to the conventional economic wisdom, the costs of the welfare state come in terms of economic inefficiency, while its benefits come in terms of social equity (Okun 1975). Whether or not we regard the welfare state as desirable, on balance, depends upon just how much of the one goal we are prepared to trade for just how much of the other—and, of course, upon how big the costs and benefits in view actually turn out to be.

There is considerable evidence that, in the U.S. at least, the benefits are large and the costs low. In exchange for the 4.8 percent reduction in labor supply and of between zero and twenty percent in private savings, we achieve a reduction of 75 percent in poverty and of 19 percent in the Gini coefficient of income inequality (Danziger, Haveman, and Plotnick 1981: 1019). Only one who attaches very low priority, indeed, to the equity side of the equation could easily scoff at such results.

Now, of course, equity is every bit as worthy a goal for our economy as is efficiency. Indeed, on the arguments to be developed in section III, perhaps it is even more so. First, however, I want to try to meet efficiency-oriented critics of the welfare state on their own ground. Having shown that they exaggerate the ways in which the welfare state undermines efficiency, I now want to show that the welfare state can also contribute to economic efficiency.[4] If anything, those effects are likely to be even stronger than the others. Thus, far from undermining economic efficiency, the welfare state, on balance, probably promotes it instead.

The way in which the welfare state contributes to economic efficiency is by remedying various sorts of "market failures" that impede the functioning of ordinary economic markets. Some of those have been discussed in chapter 6. Desperation bidding, for example, results in the inefficient misallocation of economic resources; the welfare state prevents that. Insurance markets inevitably fail when confronted with risks that are not statistically independent of one another; the welfare state corrects that market failure, too. And so on.

In chapter 6, there was no attempt at a systematic survey of the ways in which markets might fail and the welfare state might help to remedy those failures. The aim there was merely to pinpoint those market failures that could serve as a launching pad for my own ethically based defense of the welfare state. Since the end there in view was an ethical rather than an economic defense of the welfare state, there was no need to survey all forms of market failure.

The task now before us, however, is purely economic. It is to defend the welfare state against allegations of economic inefficiency. For that purpose, a more systematic survey of the ways in which the welfare state corrects market failures is in order. Here I shall concentrate on three classic modes of market failure: public goods, economies of scale, and imperfect information. Where any of these three conditions are found, the proof of the inevitable ef-

---

[4] Mann (1985: 19) enters an analogous protest against the rhetorical strategy of the British Labour Party: "During the last election campaign Michael Foot sought to counter Tory ideology with a series of alternatives: 'fairness', not 'profits'; a 'caring society', not one dominated by the pursuit of wealth. . . . Such contrasts are still the stock-in-trade of Labour leaders. But this is to make the Labour Party into a kind of church or charitable organization. Labour is not for caring *rather than* wealth. In fact democratic socialism has a superior theory of how wealth is created in modern society: *through* a fair society based on the cooperation of free citizens. Social citizenship is not a charitable urge—it is the way toward a more productive, more generally creative society." Similar attempts at rhetorical turnabouts were also common among turn-of-the-century New Liberals, who reacted to the efficiency-dominated ethos of their own age by arguing, as one writer put it, that social assistance can be defended "not as an eleemosynary but as a business proposition" (quoted in Freeden 1978: 241). Likewise, in contemporary America, "liberal Democrats have adjusted to the business school lingo of the [age] . . . 'We still want to inoculate children against disease,' says Ann Lewis, director of Americans for Democratic Action. 'But now we call it an investment in human resources ' " (Smith 1986: 108).

ficiency of the market fails and the state is at least potentially a superior provider of the goods or services in question. Here I shall argue that that is true for a great many of the goods and services provided by the welfare state.[5]

A

Much that the welfare state does has undeniably economic aspects to it. One perfectly apt characterization of many of its activities is as an "investment in human capital." The idea here is just that there is, within a nation's population itself, much productive potential; but to bring out that productive potential, people must be healthy, educated, well fed, etc. The welfare state guarantees that such basic needs are met. In so doing, it thereby contributes to ensuring a productive labor force and, hence, to economic productivity itself. Economically, people are just another resource; the welfare state contributes to economic efficiency by guaranteeing the preconditions for making the most effective utilization of that resource.

That the welfare state contributes in this way to economic efficiency is pretty well indisputable. Whether the state's contribution here is strictly necessary may be more disputable. After all, each of us has capital in ourselves (our skills, etc.); and any return on further investments in that capital stock will accrue first and foremost to ourselves, its owners. If we are such hot investment opportunities, why then can we not attract private agents willing to invest whatever it takes to make us maximally productive, in exchange for the promise of some share of our future earnings?

A perfectly reasonable first approximation to an answer would be that the payoff in any particular case would be too long-term and too uncertain to attract private investors. In the short term, there is bound to be some investment opportunity offering a higher rate of return; in the long term, there is bound to be some other investment opportunity offering a more certain return. That those other investment opportunities with those characteristics should exist is inevitable in (indeed, essential to) capitalist market economies. That being so, however, it is fruitless to expect private agents to find it comparatively attractive to invest in human capital. If it is to be done at all, the state must do so by default.

[5] See Bator (1958) and Steiner (1970) for the underlying economic principles, Buchanan (1985: esp. chap. 2) for an ethical critique, and LeGrand and Robinson (1984) for applications to the welfare state.

The deeper question, of course, is why it should be done at all. The reason presumably has to do with the notion of "collective goods," and with the full utilization of economic resources as such a collective good. If someone lacks the requisite human capital (training, stamina, etc.) to make full use of his natural talents, then it is that person himself who is in the first instance the loser when he proves unable to attract a good job. But all those other people who might have entered into exchanges with him, benefiting from his skills, will also lose; and so will those who would have bene- fited from exchanges with them, in turn. Just as in macroeconomic management the general "state of the economy" is a public good which inevitably benefits everyone, so too is the "state of the workforce." Having a fit and skilled workforce benefits so many people in the country in so many ways, directly and indirectly, that it can truly be counted as a public good, available to all and from whose benefits none can be excluded. Being a public *good*, it ought to be provided; and being a *public* good, only the state can provide it.

The argument from human capital provides a rationale for a wide range of welfare state policies. Health, education, housing, and food-stamp policies are all arguably addressed to aspects of human capital. There is another public-goods argument that is ad- dressed more narrowly to policies aimed at promoting the welfare of children and their immediate families (called, variously, Child Benefit, Family Allowance, or Aid to Families with Dependent Children).

The argument here is that, over and above the interest that any of us may have in our own children's future, we all have an inter- est in there being a next generation. Some of our motives in this regard may be noble (e.g., wanting someone to continue "our way of life" after we are gone) and others ignoble (e.g., having enough wage-earners paying social security taxes to fund our own old-age pensions, when it comes time for us to collect them). Whichever our motive, however, either would lead us to desire the existence of a next generation. Now, if a next generation of Americans exists for one of us presently alive, it must exist for all of us. Hence it is a public good. Any incentives we want to provide for people to produce the next generation must, therefore, be provided by the state rather than left to the private market.

Those are the most important public-good aspects of welfare state activities, in my view. There are, however, various other more limited arguments along these lines that ought to be acknowledged, if only in passing. Probably the least convincing is that which depicts charity as a public good; that argument has been described, and debunked, in chapter 6. Another variant on that is more plausible, however. Suppose that people happen to have preferences about what sort of society they want to live in, as well as preferences about what sort of lives they personally want to lead. Then the satisfaction of the publicly oriented aspect of their preferences must, of necessity, be a public good. It is impossible to promote one sort of society (characterized, e.g., by a Gini coefficient of income inequality that is less than 0.10) for one person in the society without producing the same result for everyone else in that society. Insofar as people have publicly oriented preferences of that sort, then their satisfaction is a public good—and necessarily so (Steiner 1970: 31; Miller 1981: 326–67). Still, that argument is contingent upon people's preference functions having a certain content; and, while I do not find this as implausible as I do that ascribed to people by the model of charity-as-a-public-good, it would be wrong to assume that this feature were universal in all people's preferences.

Other arguments linking welfare state activities to public goods provisions are similarly limited in scope, applying to a narrow set of policies or to policies only under a narrow set of circumstances. An example of the former might be public-good aspects of public health policies: inoculation against contagious diseases protects not only the person inoculated but also those who might have caught the disease from him. An example of the latter might be welfare policies designed to promote the collective good of public order, quelling nascent rebellion or stemming thievery during some particularly hard times economically. The public good components of both types of policies are undeniably present and constitute compelling arguments for state- rather than private-market provision of the goods, so far as they go. Neither of those arguments goes far enough often enough to justify any very large part of the welfare state program on that basis, however.

B

Consider next the problem of increasing returns to scale. The classic economic argument for the efficiency of markets presupposes perfect competition, which in turn presupposes a virtual infinity of buyers and sellers none of whom has any market power. Where there are economies of scale, that situation will not last long.

Larger units, being able to produce more economically, undercut and drive out of business smaller units. The resulting concentration within the market affords the decreasingly many (and increasingly large) units to engage in "oligopolistic competition" or, in the limiting case, monopolistic practices. Those are not only "exploitative" and "unjust"—more to the present point, they are technically inefficient, in the neoclassical economist's own sense of the term. Where there is the prospect of increasing returns to scale, then, there is no reason to suppose that ordinary economic markets will yield efficient outcomes; and there is at least a presumptive case for greater efficiency to be realized through state interventions.

Many aspects of the social services are, indeed, characterized by such increasing returns to scale. This is particularly true of programs characterized by the provision of in-kind goods and services. Everything from school textbooks to housing complexes and prescription medicines is cheaper when bought in bulk. It is, perhaps, less obvious that there can be any substantial economies of scale where what is being provided is counselling or cash. Even there, however, the economies may be present.

This is especially true of cash-transfer programs that can be conceptualized as social insurance mechanisms. U.K. evidence suggests that "insurance companies first moved from individual to collective pension sales in the inter-war years because they perceived the possibilities of economies of scale and reductions in transaction costs." Hannah (1986: 142, 36) goes on to say that "nothing has changed in the logic of that strategy," as indeed it has not: there still remain substantial economies to be exploited from "the pooling of risks inherent in group schemes." The more widely risks are spread, the more confident an underwriter can be in his actuarial calculations (and hence the less of a surcharge he will have to levy to protect himself against unexpected eventualities).

Such potential for economies of scale constitute a case for state intervention in markets for social services. But it does not, in and of itself, dictate what form those interventions should take. Direct public provision is one alternative; state regulation of private market providers is another. Which is to be preferred on grounds of efficiency depends just upon whether it is more cost-effective for state officials to monitor and control the behavior of their subordinates or their subcontractors (Gibson, Goodin, and Le Grand 1985). The outcome of such calculations will naturally vary from case to case. Either way, however, the state would be intervening in markets to ensure that people receive certain basic social services. Such interventions, whatever the precise form they take, could always plausibly be regarded as welfare state activities.

C

Imperfect information constitutes a third class of cases in which even neoclassical economists would have to concede the appropriateness of public intervention in ordinary markets. Even perfectly competitive markets can satisfy people's preferences efficiently only on condition that people know what they want and how to get it. Where their information on either of these matters is imperfect, a market is no guarantee of allocative efficiency, understood broadly as getting maximal satisfaction out of any given stock of resources; markets might give people what they demand, but that may or may not turn out to produce the results that they really want. Where state officials possess better information on either of these matters than people themselves do, there is a case to be made for the superior efficiency of non-market, state-directed allocations.

This is arguably true of most of the social services. People may well know what end-results they wish for from housing, health, or educational policies. But all those policies draw, to a greater or lesser extent, on complex bodies of technical information. Those in need of the services are, for a variety of reasons, ordinarily in a substantially worse position to master all that technical detail than would be state officials charged with the day-to-day administration of the services.[6]

That is just to say that state officials are probably better informed as regards questions of what are the best means to people's chosen ends. It may also be true that they are better informed even as regards questions of what peoples ends really are—or will be. We

[6] In some cases (e.g., health care) this might be because the consumer himself is a fitful and often desperate user of the service. When the need arises, there is often simply not time to master the literature for himself. In the case of education, teachers must have more information than their students or else they would have nothing to teach them; so the consumers of that good are inevitably at an informational disadvantage vis-à-vis the suppliers. (Suppose parents chose teachers and schools and curricula in their children's behalf; even there, the parents would have an informational stock to match the teacher's only in the rare case of their being highly educated professionals themselves.) More generally, services provided for the disadvantaged will be going to people who are disadvantaged in, among other areas, educational attainments, so their information stock will inevitably be low and their skills in acquiring and assimilating further information will be undeveloped.

ordinarily assume that people are the best predictors of their own future preferences. But that is not necessarily true, especially where the prediction in question concerns a person's reactions to a rare occurrence of which the person himself has little or no prior experience. Someone who has never been unemployed, for example, may well underestimate just how severe the distress of unemployment would be and say he preferred a higher wage without unemployment insurance to a lower one with it; or someone presently young may underestimate the needs of his old age and state a preference for higher wages without the guarantee of a pension to a lower wage with it. Both of those judgments are predicated, in part, upon predictions about how it would feel to be in certain circumstances (unemployed; old) without the benefit of state support. Both of those predictions are likely to be in error, in the sense that once in those circumstances (once old, or unemployed) the worker himself would almost certainly agree that he had previously underestimated his needs and desires badly. State officials have considerable experience with people in all sorts of different social situations, and they have much more information on which to base judgments about what people really would want in a wide variety of different circumstances. What they lose in not knowing each person's idiosyncrasies as well as that person knows them they more than make up by knowing how most people react to situations that that person has never had to experience and can scarcely imagine (Goodin 1982c: chaps. 3 and 8).

D

All these are ways in which the welfare state might, by remedying well-known market failures, actually promote economic efficiency rather than undermine it. Writers of the New Right would counter claims couched in terms of theories of market failure with their own "theory of non-market failure," consolidated by Wolf (1979) on the basis of various previous contributions in the "economic theory of bureaucracy" owing to Stigler (1975) and Niskanen (1971; 1975).

The fundamental methodological premise underlying this argument is utterly unexceptionable. When evaluating alternative institutional arrangements, we must compare like with like. Specifically, it is wrong for us to compare the market as it is with the state as it might be. Either we must compare the market, warts and all, with the state, warts and all; or, if we insist upon talking about the state in some idealized fashion, we must compare it with the market at its idealized best, too.

From there, New Right theorists of non-market failures go on to show that, for each broad category of potential "market failure," there is a strictly analogous category of potential "non-market failure." Thus, Wolf (1979) matches market "externalities and public goods" problems with non-market problems of " 'internalities' and 'private' goals"; problems of "increasing returns" in the market with those of "redundant and rising costs" in the non-market sector; problems of "market imperfections" with those of "derived externalities" in the non-market sector; distributional inequities arising from the effects of "income and wealth" in the market with those arising from the effects of "influence and power" in the non-market sector.

Some of those analogies are quite close, others (e.g., between "externalities" and "internalities") are more than slightly strained. But no matter. Nothing turns on the claim that, for each and every class of market failure, there is a matching class of non-market failure. All that really matters in this argument is the proposition that there are reasons for supposing that both institutions—both the state and the market—are potentially inefficient in their pursuit of social goals. From that it follows that demonstrations of the inefficiency of the one do not necessarily, in and of themselves, prove the superior efficiency of the other. We must instead consider the *relative* efficiency with which each of these institutions pursues the goal, in each particular instance.

That proposition, too, I take to be utterly unexceptionable. Indeed, it is partly on the basis of it that I hesitate to make the positive case for the welfare state hinge on any arguments about its role in remedying market failures. And it is partly on the basis of it that, even for the negative purposes merely of denying the alleged economic inefficiency of the welfare state, I offer the ethical arguments of section III below to supplement the efficiency claims made in this section.

The relative seriousness of market and non-market failures must, of course, be assessed on the basis of empirical evidence on a case-by-case basis. Still, a few general comments about general tendencies might be in order here.

Underlying all the particular incidents of non-market failure that are detailed in Wolf's (1979) seminal article is a more general theory of the dynamics of public bureaucracy. The fundamental elements of this theory, made explicit by Wolf himself, are familiar currency among "economic" or "public choice" theorists of bu-reaucracy (Niskanen 1971; 1975; Fiorina and Noll 1978). On the de-mand side, it is in the interest of both legislators and executives to promote high levels of public activity; on the supply side, goals are vague, production functions obscure, and output (still less out-come) measures unavailable. Public bureaux are thus not subject to "bottom line" assessments, to competitive pressures, or to cred-ible threats that consumers will withdraw their custom; in short, they are not subject to "market discipline." That being so, they are therefore free to set their own internal standards of success and to pursue their own goals, independently of and perhaps at some considerable cost to the "public interest." In its most crass form, this is taken to imply overexpenditure on the part of budget-max-imizing bureaux (Niskanen 1971; 1975; cf. Dunleavy 1985). In its more subtle form, it implies a skewing of public expenditure, with too much effort being devoted to projects in the interest of concen-trated constituencies with entrenched political or bureaucratic ad-vocates and too little to diffuse interests lacking them (Goodin 1982d; Wolf 1979 remarks similarly in passing).

Now, so far as economic efficiency itself is concerned, a skewing of public expenditures might result in misallocation of social re-sources every bit as serious as systematic overexpenditure on bu-reaucratic goods and services in general. In that narrowly eco-nomic sense, the non-market failure is genuinely a failure, and potentially every bit as serious as market ones.

In another sense, however, non-market failures of this sort are not failures at all. Specifically, they are not necessarily failures by their own internal, program-specific standards of success. There is nothing in the theory of non-market failure to say, for example, that welfare bureaucracies necessarily fail to promote social wel-fare.[7] On the contrary, the non-market failure here in view derives

---

[7] It might be argued that the same lack of "output" measures that potentially give rise to nonmarket failures in Wolf's (1979) model also give rise to the potential for welfare bureaucracies to pursue "internal" goals that depart, to some greater or lesser extent, from their official welfare-provision function. But that argument turns on the proposition that internal goals will depart dramatically from official missions, whereas it is much more plausible to suppose that bureaucrats are to a large extent "mission-committed" (Downs 1967: chap. 19; Margolis 1975; Goodin 1982d). Furthermore, insofar as output measures are unavailable—insofar as prod-uct quality is unascertainable—then to that extent markets of the ordinary sort are impossible, so however well or badly welfare bureaucracies serve their function it is better than markets could do. More generally, wherever we can monitor inputs more effectively than we can monitor outputs, we can exercise quality control over the final product more effectively through internalizing the production process

precisely from the fact that they promote it too well (or, anyway, spend too much trying to do so).

Failing to spend the optimal amount promoting welfare is importantly different from failing to promote welfare. It is the former, and that alone, to which the defensible version of the theory of non-market failure points. Thus, that is an important theory in connection with claims about the impact of welfare states on economic efficiency. It is a largely irrelevant theory in connection with claims about the effectiveness of welfare states in achieving their assigned tasks.

I I I

The upshot of arguments presented so far in this chapter is that the effect of the welfare state on economic efficiency is much more doubtful than writers of the New Right claim. Its impact is mixed, at worst. On balance, its impact may well be positive. True, the welfare state might undermine economic efficiency through its impact on labor supply and upon savings; but, as I have shown in section I, the first effect is marginal and the second uncertain. Set against that are the many, diverse ways in which the welfare state actually contributes to economic efficiency by remedying market failures of perfectly standard sorts. The standard proofs of the superior efficiency of markets notoriously fail where there are public goods, increasing returns to scale, or imperfect information. The social services are characterized by all those things, as shown in section II. Given the possibility of non-market failures, paralleling market ones, we cannot automatically infer from those facts that the non-market institutions of the welfare state necessarily contribute to economic efficiency, on net, when trying to remedy those market failures. But at least it is clear, from that demonstration, that they might. Thus, even if economic efficiency were our paramount social goal, it is far from clear that the welfare state should be shunned.

Next, however, I want to query whether the goal of efficiency should enjoy pride of place at all.[8] In mounting this limited chal-

---

within the organization rather than externally contracting out for the goods or services (Goodin and Le Grand 1987: chap. 6).

[8] The remainder of section III draws upon material reprinted from Robert E. Goodin and Peter Wilenski, "Beyond Efficiency: The Logical Underpinnings of Administrative Principles," *Public Administration Review*, 44 (November/December 1984), 512–517, by permission of the my coauthor, the *Review's* editor and the American Society for Public Administration.

lenge to the moral importance of efficiency norms, the structure of my argument will be as follows. First, I observe that we explicitly commit ourselves to all sorts of principles. Next, I observe that implicit within the social principles to which we explicitly commit ourselves are certain other meta-principles, which underlie and give meaning to those "surface principles." By committing yourself to the one principle, you are also implicitly committing yourself to all the others that that one entails. You may not intend to do so. You may not want to do so. But, logically or morally, you have to do so.

That is not to say that the pursuit of the one principle leads inexorably to the satisfaction of the other. Quite the contrary. There is a real danger that the pursuit of the surface principle may, from time to time, lead to outcomes inimical to the more fundamental principles which it was meant to serve. Surface principles must not be allowed to eat away their own foundations in this way. Meta-principles must necessarily trump surface ones in cases of conflict.

These arguments apply with equal force to anyone and everyone who embraces any of a wide variety of principles. They obviously apply to legislators. But they also extend to every citizen with political preferences. And they also extend to civil servants who believe themselves to have no political preferences, but merely to be committed to certain formal values of "due process," etc. The argument of this section is that all these people have committed themselves to certain socio-political principles, whether substantive or procedural in nature; and all must therefore be bound by the logic of those commitments.

No doubt "efficiency" is akin to "motherhood" for most commentators, functioning as an unanalyzed, unquestioned "good thing." Its meaning is, for most of them, contextually determined. And this contextualism, in turn, allows a variety of potentially conflicting principles to travel together under the name of "efficiency."[9] Still, there is a recognizable common core of meanings, and it is this core which I shall here be attacking. Thus, my attack will not necessarily engage every possible variant of the efficiency

[9] What leads to an efficient organization within the central offices of the Ministry of Public Works might not lead to the most efficient building of bridges, for example—efficiency in pushing paper is not the same as, and may even be inimical to, efficiency in pouring concrete. Evidence from recent attempts at introducing "quality control" procedures in social welfare programs suggests that an analogous principle may hold true there, as well (Brodkin and Lipsky 1983).

norm.[10] Nevertheless, I trust that most can agree that the position under attack is other than a complete caricature.

A

Clearly, what stands most immediately behind the goal of "efficiency" is the more fundamental goal of "want-satisfaction." The only reason we think it is good to use resources efficiently is that the same stock of resources, efficiently used, will satisfy more wants rather than less; or, alternatively, if we can achieve a desired satisfaction of wants with fewer resources then there will be resources left over to satisfy other wants. Either way, more wants will be satisfied, and we think it is better to satisfy more wants rather than less.[11] From each individual's point of view, it is better to conduct one's own affairs efficiently because that frees resources for getting more of what one, as an individual, wants. Analogously, from society's point of view (that of a benevolent despot, perhaps), it is better to conduct our collective affairs efficiently because that frees resources for getting more of what we as a society want.

That want-satisfaction is what underlies the goal of efficiency might seem to be an unexceptionable discovery that has not taken us very far.[12] But it can, as I shall show, have some striking practical ramifications.

Firstly, this brings efficiency down to the status of an instrumental means of achieving want-satisfaction. As such, it is on a par with all other means of satisfying wants. Therefore, *the dictates of efficiency can be overridden by other want-regarding arguments.* It should have no greater legitimacy for administrators of public pol-

[10] In particular, advocates of cost-benefit analysis might try (with varying success) to find a "shadow price" for each of the considerations I shall discuss below, thus incorporating them all into a notion of "efficiency" that is broader than the one I shall be attacking. But then, on that broader notion of "efficiency," the welfare state will turn out to be "efficient" if the rest of my arguments in this chapter prove successful.

[11] Strictly speaking, efficiency norms merely commit us to the proposition that it is better to satisfy more rather than less *of those wants which governments should satisfy.* Some would say that there are certain sorts of wants which should not be satisfied at all; others that there are certain sorts of wants which should be satisfied, but not through government action. None of the examples offered in the text, however, are likely to be caught by these caveats.

[12] Hodgkinson (1978: 183) argues, for example, that the related meta-value of "effectiveness," defined as "the accomplishment of desired ends," is simply tautological. But that argument turns on a logically fallacious slide between "desired" and "desirable"; the parallel fallacy in John Stuart Mill's (1863: chap. 4) "proof of the utility principle" is now widely recognized.

icies than many other considerations which they are inclined to dismiss as extraneous to the policymaking or administrative process. Once administrators commit themselves to efficiency, they implicitly commit themselves to weighing various other aspects of administration which also contribute to the satisfaction or frustration of wants.

The point here is that people have all sorts of wants, and decision-makers are obliged to respect them all if they respect any of them. People may, for example, desire *equity*, even at the cost of efficiency; or they may want to have certain *procedures* employed in making decisions, even if that is not the most efficient way of going about things.[13] Devotees of efficiency might be inclined to shun such goals or procedures, on the grounds that on balance more of people's preferences could be satisfied better through some other less cumbersome procedures or by focusing on some other goals altogether. But if satisfying people's preferences is truly our goal—as talk of efficiency necessarily implies that it is— then we are obliged to take heed of *all* their preferences. Efficiency cannot be used as an excuse for systematically thwarting whole classes of desires that people may harbor.[14]

Thus, it may well be inefficient, in some narrowly economic sense, for the welfare state to pursue goals of equity, equality, fairness, or social justice. But if people happen to harbor those goals, then they have every bit as much claim upon want-regarding policymakers' concerns as those goals that promote economic efficiency. And it may well be inefficient, in some narrow administrative sense, to follow procedures that respect people's rights and

[13] For example, we may want public participation in decision-making regarding public service delivery, or employee participation in corporate or civil service decision-making, or certain procedures to be followed for safeguarding the rights and interests of beneficiaries of public services. Following such procedures might render decision-making less "efficient," in some sense—certainly public participation, employee participation, and appeals procedures introduce delays and eat up other resources. But that very familiar argument misses the point that people have preferences for procedures as well as for outcomes.

Or, for another example, consider the alleged inefficiency of democratic procedures. Third World dictators often maintain that denying people's civil liberties and human rights would lead to more efficient decision-making, faster economic growth, etc. As it happens, these arguments are probably empirically incorrect (Goodin 1979); but even if democracy were less "efficient," in any standard GNP-maximizing sense, we might nonetheless want to run our affairs democratically.

[14] There may, of course, be some independent, ideal-regarding reasons for pursuing those goals or procedures as well. Notice that I am here focusing exclusively upon want-regarding reasons: *if* people want those goals or procedures, then policymakers and administrators should respect their preferences.

give them due process. But, again, if people happen to harbor preferences for such procedures, then they have every bit as much claim upon policymakers' attention as preferences for administrative efficiency.[15]

Secondly, focusing upon want-satisfaction rather than efficiency per se emphasizes that it is *better to satisfy wants inefficiently than not to satisfy them at all*. The alleged inefficiencies of various methods of pursuing social goals typically serve as a ground for vetoing them. But since we can always envisage a more efficient way of doing almost anything, it is entirely conceivable that *all* proposed projects might be vetoed on such grounds. That, however, would undermine the logic of efficiency itself. The only reason we have for worrying about the efficiency of a project is that we want to satisfy people's wants as well as we can. Given that rationale, it would be obviously self-defeating for efficiency arguments to be used to refuse to satisfy any of people's wants.

The characteristic administrative form this fallacy takes is as follows. First some policy P_1 is rejected on the grounds that some other policy P_2 would achieve the same goal more efficiently. But then for one reason or another P_2 is not pursued, either.[16] Governments decline to build high-tech hospitals, for example, on the grounds that "community health programs" are a more efficient response to the needs; but then they fail to fund those, either. Governments fail to build work-based child-care facilities in government office blocks in the central business district because it is

[15] Among the quasi-procedural desires that may be particularly relevant to the social services is a desire for there to be *no procedures*. That is, they may want certain natural, spontaneous public gestures. These by their nature cannot be performed efficiently: a cold, calculating approach would, in these cases, prove self-defeating. In disaster relief programs, spontaneity is of the essence. Such aid is meant by the donors—and desired by the recipients—as a spontaneous gesture of community concern. Such programs tend to be administered very inefficiently indeed. But any attempt to impose rigorous eligibility tests, or to require careful accounting on the part of recipients, would preclude the program from achieving this crucial goal. Similarly, Titmuss would say, with blood banks: even if a commercial blood bank were in some sense more efficient (in generating more blood for the same dollar expenditure, say), it would achieve this greater "efficiency" at a great cost, viz., undercutting community ties that can only be promoted by a spontaneous, gift-based system (Titmuss 1971a; cf. Arrow 1972, and Singer 1973). Indeed, perhaps any seriously held moral principle would preclude the narrow sort of calculating that constitutes efficiency calculations as ordinarily understood (Goodin 1982c: chap. 6).

[16] Wildavsky (1979: chaps. 1, 16, and passim) similarly suggests that when we find one problem too hard we should simply drop it and turn to another we can solve more easily. In his version, however, the argument is not run through the notion of efficiency (as his chapter 5 makes clear).

more efficient to have children cared for in the neighborhoods where they live; but then they fail to fund community-based child care. Or, again, central government leaves all sorts of tasks (curriculum development, etc.) to state or local governments on the grounds that those nearer the people can perform those tasks more efficiently; but then the lower-level governments also fail to take them up. And so on. Now, of course, there comes a point at which the only available method of pursuing a goal might be *so* inefficient that it is better to pursue some other goals entirely. But typically the inefficiency will be far less dramatic. Then it truly would be better to pursue the goal as inefficiently as need be, rather than not to pursue it at all.

Thirdly, focusing upon want-satisfaction rather than efficiency per se reminds us that *not all wants carry the same weight*. Efficiency fetishists often seem to move from the proposition:

1. It is better to pursue goal X efficiently than inefficiently;

to the proposition that:

2. Efficiency is better than inefficiency;

and from there to the practical implication that:

3. It is better to pursue goal Y efficiently than goal X inefficiently, if those are the only choices available to us.

Remember, however, that efficiency per se is not our real aim— our real aim is want-satisfaction. And the strength of our wants not only varies, but varies independently of the relative efficiency or inefficiency of the instruments available to us for pursuing those wants. Even if we have only very inefficient instruments available for pursuing our top-priority goal, we may still prefer to pursue it instead of some lower-priority goal which we might be able to pursue far more efficiently. The classic case is job-training. It may be more cost-effective to train middle-class people, since their background helps them pick up the skills quickly and easily. But we may nonetheless decide that it is (for precisely these reasons) far more important to train truly disadvantaged members of the community, even if doing so is necessarily less efficient in the sense of fewer people overall having successfully completed the training program.

Related to that is the idea that *everyone's wants do not weigh the same*. As in the job-training case for example, members of the community sometimes accord special importance to the satisfaction of the wants of certain segments of the population—the young, the old, the poor, the handicapped, the disadvantaged, etc. Economists have developed simple methodologies enabling us to surmise from the actual choices that are made what "distributional weights" are implicitly assigned to the want-satisfaction of various groups; and applying these methodologies, it becomes clear that different people's want-satisfactions are indeed being weighed very differently (Weisbrod 1968).

The pursuit of efficiency, as ordinarily conceived, does not sit happily with this fact. For, as is well known, efficiency in all its manifestations is sensitive only to the overall quantity of want-satisfaction (Wildavsky 1966). It (like related notions of utilitarianism) is officially indifferent to *whose* wants it is that are being satisfied; and unofficially it often tends actually to be biased against the wants of people who weigh most heavily with us, on the grounds that they are relatively inefficient at translating objective resources into subjective pleasures (Friedman 1947). Now, I am here entering no objection to pursuing distributional goals as efficiently as possible. But I do want to emphasize that the narrow-minded pursuit of "efficiency" will, more likely than not, only succeed in frustrating distributional goals that enjoy the same status as those wants which efficiency itself is supposed to serve.

Of course, there are various ways of refurbishing these standard efficiency calculations so that they can be made to take distributional considerations into account. That, after all, is why economists devised the notion of "distributional weights." But that whole approach fundamentally misses the point. It treats distributional considerations as side-constraints which must be satisfied in an optimizing equation; it treats distributional preferences, preferences for *whose* wants are satisfied, as a separate sort of consideration to be traded off against considerations of efficiency. My argument is that they are not distinct goals at all, but rather that both are manifestations of one and the same meta-goal of want-satisfaction. To feign concern for the wants served by efficiency but indifference to the wants served by distributional constraints amounts to simple inconsistency. Whatever reasons we have for worrying about one sort of wants, those reasons apply with equal force to the others as well.

B

All that I have said so far in this section just amounts to variations on one basic theme. Efficiency, I have been arguing, is only one way of promoting want-satisfaction; it cannot, therefore, be allowed systematically to frustrate people's wants without simultaneously denying its own raison d'être. Although that provides grounds for many important critiques of the efficiency principle as it ordinarily operates in practice, it is still not the most fundamental possible level of critique.

So far I have been talking mostly in terms of contradictions between goals of efficiency and those wants which people might *happen* to have. If people happen to want certain processes to be employed, or for certain people to benefit, then the ordinary operation of efficiency standards will have to be modified accordingly. Now, it is hard to envisage a society in which people did not have *any* preferences of this form. Still, it is logically possible; and in that (barely) possible world, the meta-principle of want-satisfaction discussed above would act as no constraint on efficiency calculations more narrowly conceived.

Over and above that meta-principle of want-satisfaction, which may conceivably lack force in any particular case, there is a logically prior meta-principle (a meta-meta-principle, if you will) that applies in any possible world. One strategy for arriving at this more fundamental meta-principle is to ask: "What *should* people want, and why?" To answer that question, however, I would have to provide a full-fledged philosophical theory of the good. That would be an ambitious task, and there would be little hope of providing any solution that would not be highly contentious.

Here I shall instead pursue a different tack. There is another way of getting at the really fundamental meta-principle, still tied to want-satisfaction and yet at the same time free of any contingencies of taste. This would be to ask: "Why satisfy wants?" Of course, there is one way of answering that question which would throw us back on a theory of the good, i.e., "We should satisfy people's wants because they want what is good." But that cannot be the whole story, or probably even the most important part of it. For surely we think it is good to satisfy people's wants even if, at least at the margins, what they want is not good according to any broader standards. There is, in other words, some independent value in satisfying people's wants that is not traceable to anything about the *content* of those wants. This is where I shall search for our most fundamental meta-principle—in this quasi-formal rather than substantive aspect of the desirability of satisfying people's wants.

252

Our most basic proposition is that it is our *respect for persons* which underlies the desire to satisfy people's wants. We respect wants because we respect people, not vice versa. In a sense, it could hardly be otherwise. People make choices, choices do not make people. Wants, choices, etc., inherently attach to wanters or choosers. A disembodied want or choice is simply inconceivable.

But beyond all that, there is a further and more important point to be made. Our *reasons* for respecting wants and choices is that that is how we show our respect for the people whose wants or choices they are. So even if there could somehow be wants or choices that were disembodied (or embodied in digital computers) there would be nothing about those wants or choices that is morally compelling in the same way people's wants or choices are (Goodin 1982c: chap. 5).

What constitutes showing people respect is, perhaps, contentious. What constitutes showing them disrespect is much less so. That category includes, paradigmatically, whatever deprives them of their basis for *self-respect*. Whatever it is to respect people, it cannot entail depriving them of respect for themselves (Hill 1973). Social psychological studies reveal various impediments to self-respect. Primary among them are things like poverty, joblessness, and the denial of basic human rights (Goodin 1982c: 89–94; see further Eisenberg and Lazarsfeld 1938; Jahoda 1982; Kahn 1972; Lane 1982; Scholzman 1976).

Those, clearly, are conditions which it is within the government's power, through social welfare policies, to alter. Policies designed to do so might not always be efficient, in any standard sense. (Say what we will about the economic value of human capital, it is in practice often most "efficient" to allow at least some people to remain poor, or perhaps altogether unemployed, at least for substantial periods.) But if respect for persons is the value that most deeply underlies our attachment to efficiency norms, then we are further obliged to do whatever that requires, regardless of any superficial inefficiencies that that might involve. Otherwise "efficiency" quickly undermines its own moral foundations, denying the very principle (respect for persons) that morally legitimates it in the first place.

C

My limited critique of the efficiency principle, in section III of this chapter, has thus dealt with connected phenomena on three levels. Ordinary discourse—among politicians, bureaucrats, and citizens—deals in terms of one level of principles. Goals of efficiency, like those of democracy, equity, efficiency, and due process, all operate on this level. Call those P-level principles. The operation of those P-level principles leads to certain outcomes (O, for short). All that is familiar enough. The distinctive feature of my argument is the third level, the meta-principles, MP, that logically underlie those surface principles.[17] So, schematically, we have Figure 8.1.

My argument has been this. If the outcomes are to be justified, these links must be tight. But in practice there is altogether too much slippage in all too many cases between meta-principles MP and outcomes O. To tighten up the overall link (numbered 3, in Figure 8.1), we need to revise the surface principles P so as to tighten up the link (numbered 1, in Figure 8.1) between them and the meta-principles that give them their meaning and their moral force.

This pattern of analysis is importantly different from the two more standard patterns of analysis in these realms, concentrating as they do on quite different ones of those linkages. One is the argument in terms of unintended consequences (Merton 1936; Hall 1980). The idea there is that policymakers adopt some principle with the intention of producing some sort of outcome; but they end up producing a different (perhaps a diametrically opposed) sort of outcome instead. Whereas I have been critiquing outcomes

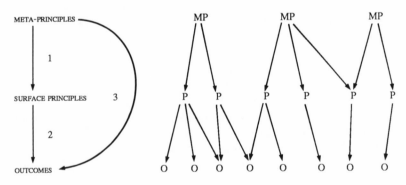

FIGURE 8.1   A Hierarchy of Moral Principles

[17] Furthermore, as I argued in section III.B, there might be a hierarchical structure among meta-principles themselves; there may be meta-meta-principles like "respect for persons," which, in turn, legitimate meta-principles like "satisfy people's wants."

in terms of meta-principles (finding in link 3 in Figure 8.1 the symptom, and in link 1 the cure), the unintended consequence argument points to link 2 (between principles and outcome). That makes it a far less powerful argument than my own. It may afford a certain amount of leverage for critiquing principles which prove to be systematically counterproductive of their *own* ends. But that style of argument offers no scope for critiquing the principles themselves (i.e., the ends that those principles aim to pursue). Some notion like mine of "meta-principles" is needed to provide that sort of leverage.

My approach contrasts, secondly, with that which is couched in terms of simple *tradeoffs* (Okun 1975; Wilenski 1980–1981). There are a great many values we would like our policies to serve. But, alas, all good things do not go together, and often it will be necessary to sacrifice some increment of one goal to provide some increment of satisfaction of another goal. This argument is different again from that which I have been offering, however. Whereas I have been discussing the relations between meta-principles and surface principles, the tradeoff argument concerns itself exclusively with relations among various surface principles.

The disadvantage with that is that, when considering principles which all stand on the same level, there are virtually no grounds for arguing that one should be accorded a higher priority than any other. Thus, for example, the pursuit of efficiency and the desire to pursue certain procedures are often seen as conflicting principles. Such procedures may embody goals such as fairness or equity. Which path we take is, within the tradeoff model, seen to be dependent upon how much weight we happen to place on efficiency, as against fairness or equity. Each is regarded as a goal in itself; the weight to be given to each is seen to be an arbitrary decision dependent upon our values. As economists are fond of saying, "It's all a matter of taste." Thus, the tradeoff model is radically underpowered compared to my own. The advantage of focusing as I have here done on the relations between principles and meta-principles is that, since meta-principles clearly stand above the principles, they clearly override them in cases of conflict.[18] That is

---

[18] One variant, standing halfway between the tradeoff model and mine, would be this. Some particular meta-principle gives rise to several seemingly independent surface principles. Although they appear to be independent principles which we are free to trade off just as we please, this is only an illusion. All can be traced back to one and the same meta-principle, and the same meta-principle that gives rise to all of them also tells us how to trade them off for one another. If in fact it does, this is a powerful form of argument. But often it seems that a meta-principle can give

an argument that can be made, once again, only within the sort of framework that I have here been advocating.

IV

The conclusions of this chapter are fairly straightforward. The New Right is simply wrong in thinking that the welfare state is a major hindrance to economic efficiency, and it is simply wrong in thinking that economic efficiency is itself of any ultimate moral importance. The same deeper moral considerations that make us value economic efficiency would also make us value various social welfare policies, even if they were economically inefficient. But, as it happens, the empirical evidence suggests that they are not. Of the three negative effects that the New Right claims the welfare state has on economic efficiency, the evidence suggests that one is nonexistent, another is slight, and the third is highly uncertain; in addition to those negative effects, there are also positive contributions that the welfare state might make to economic efficiency that the New Right studiously ignores. Far from constituting a hindrance to economic efficiency, then, the welfare state might actually promote it. It does not do so strongly enough that its contribution to economic efficiency could constitute any important part of the positive case for the welfare state, I quite concede. But the welfare state's positive contributions to economic efficiency certainly are more than strong enough to counterbalance the slight negative effects that are so central to the New Right's critique of it.

---

rise to several subsidiary principles without dictating the proper tradeoffs between them. So this trick will not always work.

N I N E

SUPPLY-SIDE POLICIES

There is a second strand to the New Right's economistic critique of the welfare state. The first holds that the welfare state, by inducing economic inefficiencies, is destructive of other important social goals such as economic growth. The second strand goes on to say that, in so doing, the welfare state is being indirectly self-defeating, undermining its *own* goals. Logically and historically, the New Right maintains, the best way of relieving poverty is through economic growth. Reflecting upon the considerable progress made against poverty in the U.S. during the postwar economic boom, compared with the comparatively slight progress made since the mid-1960s, Charles Murray (1982: 16) quips, "If the War on Poverty is construed as having begun in 1950 instead of 1964, it may fairly be said that we were winning the war until Lyndon Johnson decided to wage it."[1]

What advocates of the welfare state offer is a frankly distribution-side solution to what they see as a distributional problem. The problem, in their view, is that some people have less than they need. Others have more than enough. The welfare state solution to the perceived problem is therefore a perfectly direct one: redistribute resources from those with more than enough to those with less than enough.

As an alternative, writers on the New Right propose a supply-side solution to those distributional problems. They say that the welfare state, being a frankly distributional solution to a distributional problem, at best redistributes goods between people work-

Material in this chapter is reprinted from Robert E. Goodin, "Supply-Side Politics: Circumventing the Claims of Justice," *Politics*, 18 (November 1983), 57–67, by permission of the editor.
[1] Charles Murray (1982: 11) expands: "The answer—perhaps surprisingly to those who have ridiculed 'trickle-down' as a way to help the poor—is that changes in GNP have a very strong inverse relation to changes in poverty. As GNP increases, poverty decreases. The simple correlation coefficient for the period 1950–1980 is -0.69," where the "variables are the first difference in real GNP per household and the first difference in percentage of population under the poverty line using the official measure of poverty."

ing within a fixed stock of goods; they further fear, for reasons discussed in chapter 8, that the welfare state will probably also induce economic inefficiencies that will actually reduce that total stock. Market-led growth, in contrast, increases the total stock of goods available, thus making it possible to improve the position of the worst off without reducing that of the better off. In that way, New Right advocates of markets over welfare states attempt to offer supply-side solutions to distributional problems (Gilder 1981; Murray 1982; 1985).

There is nothing particularly new in these proposals. In a way, they just take off from Hume's (1777: 145) insight that questions of distributive justice only arise under conditions of moderate scarcity. The implication of that is that increasing the supply of goods (or proposing or promising or pretending to increase it) can be an effective way of circumventing the claims of justice. The demands of distributive justice can thus be evaded by transforming issues of distribution into issues of supply.

Attempts at such evasions are really quite common, as I shall show in section I below. The bulk of this chapter is, however, given over to a survey in section II of what is wrong with this trick. There is no simple objection to the maneuver in all its manifestations; instead, it reveals various different flaws in various different circumstances. Putting together all those partial objections, I conclude in section III that, while increasing supply might sometimes work to solve distributional problems, that will not often happen. By and large, we really will require distribution-side solutions like the welfare state to cope with distributional problems.

I

Perhaps the most compelling example of supply-side solutions being offered for distributional problems in the social welfare field is provided by Amartya Sen's enormously important work on *Poverty and Famines* (1981b; see also Sen 1977; 1981a). Our naive expectation—embodied in the principal *Oxford English Dictionary* definition of the word, no less—is that a "famine" is caused by an "extreme and general scarcity of food." Sen, however, examines the five greatest famines of modern times, and he finds this "food availability" hypothesis systematically contradicted in all of them. Take the example of the Great Bengal famine of 1943:

While 1943 was not a very good year in terms of [rice] crop availability, it was not by any means a disastrous year either. The current supply for 1943 was only about 5 per cent lower than the average of the preceding five years. It was, in fact, 13 per cent *higher* than 1941, and there was, of course, no famine in 1941. (Sen 1981b: 58; see also 1977; 1981a: 422)

In many cases of famine, not only is there food available in the famine-stricken area, but there is actually an outflow of food from the area. The most notorious case is of the Irish famine of the 1840s, when "huge quantities of food were exported from Ireland to England throughout the period when people of Ireland were dying of starvation" (Woodham-Smith 1975: 70). But lest this be thought purely a manifestation of brutal British colonialism, Sen (1981: 461; 1981b: 161) assures us that there were similar outflows of food from the famine-stricken Wollo region of Ethiopia in 1973, and there may have been similar outflows from famine-stricken Bangladesh in 1974 as well.

All this leads Sen to the conjecture that mass starvation during famines is not caused by a shortage of food per se, but rather by a shortage of entitlements to food among certain sectors of the population. The problem of famines is, on this model, a problem of the distribution of rights to food; it is not, or at least not mainly, a problem of a shortfall in the overall supply of food. Sen conducts a careful analysis of who starves and who does not in each famine in order to test this hypothesis. Its success is nothing short of overwhelming.

That may be the most dramatic example of the trick of misspecifying distributional problems as supply problems. It is nonetheless important, however, to recognize similar maneuvers in day-to-day policymaking. Consider in this connection three major areas of social welfare policy, which will be used as running examples in the discussion that follows: education, housing, and health policy. All, I will argue, are plagued by supply-side responses to essentially distributional problems.

In education policy, the standard response to almost all the familiar problems is a distinctively supply-side response. Perhaps the paradigm case is Title I of the U.S. Elementary and Secondary Education Act of 1965, which attempts to address the special needs of disadvantaged students simply by committing more resources to their education (20 USCA 241a et seq.). Whatever the complaint, the solution always seems to be the same. What we need, it is said time and again, are *more* teachers, *more* buildings, *more* books.

If the Coleman Report is to be believed, however, none of that really matters. Or at least none of those factors is correlated with educational achievement in any measurable way. What does matter—indeed, all that seems to matter—is the socioeconomic status of a student's classmates (Coleman et al. 1966). If that is so, then creating equal educational opportunity is inherently a distributional issue. No amount of money spent on schooling would solve the problem. Only a redistribution of students could accomplish that task.

That argument relies on empirical findings which are, admittedly, contentious (Mosteller and Moynihan 1972). But there is another, leading to similar conclusions, that relies on logic alone. Insofar as people take a purely instrumental view of education, regarding it as nothing more than a means of attaining social status or one of a fixed number of good jobs, then merely increasing the supply of education is futile. Suppose, for example, everyone's real goal is to be in the top tenth of the social hierarchy, and that places in that hierarchy are awarded purely according to educational attainment. (Think, for example, of France.) Increasing the supply of education does not necessarily do anything to increase the supply of desirable places—ten percent is ten percent, even in the New Maths. It merely means that better credentials will now be required to win one of those places. Similarly, increasing the supply of education does not necessarily do anything to increase the supply of good jobs (unless teaching itself is included); it merely inflates the educational credentials that will be required to secure any one of them. Insofar as this instrumental view of education prevails—and I daresay an element of it is always present—then to that extent education becomes a pure distribution problem admitting, logically, of no supply-side solution (Boudon 1974; Hirsch 1976, chap. 3; Ng 1978).

Consider next the problem of housing. This, too, is ordinarily conceptualized in terms of "undersupply"; and the standard response here, too, is simply to build more and more units. Notice, for example, the words of the U.S. Housing Act of 1949:

> The Congress hereby declares that the general welfare and security of the Nation and the health and living standards of its people require housing production and related community

development sufficient to remedy the serious housing shortage, the elimination of substandard or other inadequate housing through the clearance of slums and blighted areas, and the
realization as soon as feasible of the goal of a decent home and
suitable living environment for every American family. . . .
(42 USCA 1441)

No doubt house-building is one way of solving some of the
problems of housing. Occasionally it may be the only way of solving them, as was undoubtedly the case in postwar Britain, where
over a third of the housing stock had been damaged or destroyed
by bombs. But ordinarily it is neither the only way nor even necessarily the best. If nothing else, the recent squatter's movement
throughout Western Europe has at least succeeded in demonstrating that there are lots of habitable buildings sitting vacant in all the
major city centers. In American cities, there always used to be a
fair bit of empty accommodation—and even more empty land on
which public housing projects could have been built—in white
neighborhoods, while blacks were crowded into every corner of
the ghetto (Meyerson and Banfield 1955: chap. 2). In Britain, the
1947 planning legislation similarly underwrote the existing pattern of "high density inner cities and low density suburbs"; and
that

> reinforced an unequal status quo, accepting that those living
> at low levels of amenity would be rehoused in a sanitized en-
> vironment at reduced but still comparatively high densities,
> while those living at higher levels of amenity in suburban
> areas would continue to do so. (Dunleavy 1981: 71)

All these examples might, perhaps, be put down to special circumstances: property speculation in the first instance, racism in
the second, "great planning disasters" in the third. But there is
one virtually timeless truth which cannot be dismissed so easily.
The rich have bigger houses, while the poor have bigger families.
Poor people everywhere live in cramped quarters, not because
housing is in short supply but merely because they cannot afford
to buy or rent what is on offer. The problem of housing is, then,
at least partly one of distribution.

Furthermore, some of the problems are not even in part problems of supply. Notice that there is almost never an overall shortage of housing right across the entire nation. Usually there is an
actual oversupply of housing in country areas. The undersupply

occurs in the urban centers. Even within the cities, people refuse to live in certain sorts of housing (e.g., high-rise housing projects). The demand is for a certain standard of housing (most especially, housing of a certain density) within a certain distance (or travel time) from certain places. Once we realize that, we come to see the housing problem in almost any reasonably crowded city as virtually a pure distributional problem.[2] Working within a fixed geographical space, it is logically impossible to house more people without changing the housing density.

Finally, consider one of the most vexing issues in health policy. That concerns provision of expensive life-saving apparatus, archetypically, the kidney dialysis unit. Of course, so long as those machines were scarce relative to the need for them the issue of distribution simply had to be addressed. Someone simply had to decide who got treated and who did not. But responsibility for deciding who lives and who dies does not sit lightly on the shoulders of those charged with it. Doctors did not want it, and when it was shifted onto public advisory panels (the most notorious being the "Seattle God Committee") the public would not wear it.

There was only one thing to do. If the distribution problem has proven insoluble, all that is left is to try to transform it into a problem of supply. Hence the problem of kidney dialysis machines came to be seen as one of a shortage of machines—"We just do not have enough to go around; *that* is the trouble." This perception of the problem prevailed not only among the public at large but also among legislators. The Social Security Amendments of 1972 made it U.S. policy for every victim of end-stage renal disease to have access to a kidney dialysis unit provided at federal expense (42 USCA 1395 rr; see also Rettig 1975).

Once again, a supply-side solution hoped to preempt distributional problems. And in one way clearly it did; there was no longer any problem about deciding who was to get treatment on the kidney dialysis unit and who was to be left to die. In another way, however, it only shifted the distributional problems around. Investing a billion dollars or so every year in kidney dialysis, without simultaneously increasing the overall medical budget by anything like that amount, effectively deprives lots of other sick people of different sorts of treatments they need equally badly (Calabresi and Bobbit 1978: 134–43; Zeckhauser 1973a: 164ff.).

[2] I say "virtually" in recognition of the fact that faster roads or trains can indeed increase the supply of land within the "acceptable" travel time of the city center, and thus provide at least a partial supply-side solution to the problem.

I I

The attempt to offer aggregative, supply-side solutions to what are basically distributional problems can, therefore, be seen to be a very common one, especially in the social welfare field. But what, exactly, is wrong with it? Nothing, necessarily: I can find no single fallacy that is inherent in the logic of all supply-side arguments per se. It therefore follows that, logically, it is perfectly possible that supply-side solutions might be acceptable (indeed, ideal) from time to time. What I can find, however, is a bundle of flaws that are associated contingently but frequently with supply-side solutions. The combination of these (and these in combination—for any given policy can display many of these flaws at once) would seem to suggest that exclusively supply-side solutions to distributional problems are ordinarily unacceptable.

Of course I do not mean to denigrate considerations of supply altogether. After all, it is impossible to distribute or redistribute anything without first having a supply of it on hand to distribute or redistribute. My thesis is not that supply-side considerations are completely irrelevant to public policy. It is instead that policies focusing exclusively on the supply side of the equation ordinarily prove to be unsatisfactory as responses to distributional problems.

Increases in supply are usually unnecessary and are almost always insufficient to solve distributional problems. Recall the case of the Great Bengal famine. There was no need to increase the supply of rice. There was already plenty to keep everyone alive, if only it had been properly distributed. Nor would increasing the supply necessarily guarantee that everyone would be saved from starvation. There are lots of ways of distributing the new surplus (so the relatively rich or their animals could eat better) that would leave as many poor people starving as before. As Sen (1981b: 158) says, "A fall in food availability per head for the world as a whole is neither a necessary nor a sufficient condition for the intensification of hunger in the world . . ."

Even where increasing supply is one possible way of solving distributional problems, it is usually not the best one. Think again about the famine example. Perhaps it is possible through Green Revolution technology to increase the supply of food so dramatically that the rich (and their animals) are all sated, with some surplus left over for the poor to enjoy. But we would have to increase the supply of rice by an absurdly large amount to produce that effect. Furthermore, that strategy might be positively counterproductive. To produce such a rapid and dramatic increase in food production, we would have to work primarily through the larger and more heavily capitalized farmers; that would make them richer still, thereby providing them with still more resources with which to outbid the poorer consumers for foodstuffs (Christensen 1978: 773–74).

At this point, however, perhaps it is best to turn to my catalogue of possible complaints against supply-side policies.

A

One crucial component in the case against supply-side remedies is that they characteristically tend to be partial rather than comprehensive in their scope. They are therefore guilty of "partial optimization." That is the familiar fallacy of optimizing on one dimension while ignoring all the rest, with potentially disastrous consequences.

This might underlie at least some of the problems with "positional goods."[3] Sometimes positional goods are positional because they are in fact "intermediate goods," valued not in themselves but merely as a means of obtaining some other "end-goods" which are valued in their own right. (Think, for example, of money or instrumentally valued education in my earlier example.) Now, it follows from the way that these terms are defined that only an increase in the supply of end-goods can bring increased satisfaction. An increase in the supply of intermediate goods, unaccompanied by any such increase in end-goods, makes us no better off at all. So some of the frustrations associated with positional goods may be traced to a curious kind of partial optimization— increasing the supply of money without increasing the supply of things we want the money to buy, and such like.

Another more straightforward example of this phenomenon is the medical resource policy discussed above. Congress attempted to get itself off an uncomfortable distributional hook by increasing the supply of kidney dialysis units; but in so doing it neglected to increase by the same amount the funding for medical care overall, leaving other programs (e.g., kidney transplants) starved of funds. The obvious way to remedy that over-sight is to make the policy more comprehensive, increasing funds for medical care overall.

[3] I refer, more precisely, to what Harrod (1958) calls "oligarchic wealth." Hirsch (1976: chap. 3), while borrowing this notion, expands his concept of "positional goods" to include more ordinary economic externalities (most especially, physical crowding). See also Ng (1978) and Ellis and Kumar (1983, esp. chap. 1).

But that money, too, has to come from somewhere—education, highways, defense, somewhere. So when it is a question of money, supply-side policies can work in a suitably comprehensive fashion only by increasing the overall wealth of the community. That is why "supply-side economics" is so widely taken to constitute the paradigm of a supply-side remedy, hoping as it fondly does to use tax cuts to stimulate economic productivity and hence overall national income.

The only way a supply-side policy can ordinarily escape the charge of "partial optimization" is, therefore, by simultaneously increasing the national product. That, in turn, explains the strictly limited scope for supply-side policies in a single sector. There might, of course, be some opportunities to re-jig health or education expenditures so as to increase the national product: such expenditures are, after all, investments in "human capital," as shown in chapter 8. But to constitute a completely comprehensive supply-side remedy, any such policy would have to yield enough profits to "pay for itself"; and if that is to be construed as it usually is in terms of "opportunity costs" (i.e., the payoff that would have come from putting those resources to their most productive alternative use), then the investment would have to pay off very handsomely indeed to pass that test. Few social welfare policies can do so. In chapter 8 I argued that social welfare programs probably do more good than harm to the national economy; but that is merely to say that their benefit/cost ratio is positive, not that it is maximal among all the alternative policies that could be pursued with the same limited set of resources. For all those social welfare policies that cannot pass that more stringent test of profitability, supply-side prescriptions must therefore necessarily be a ruse that involves partial optimization of one sort or another.

B

One of the strongest objections to supply-side prescriptions is that they may be (and often are) based on *theories* that are either *fraudulent* or *nonexistent*. Sometimes there is no empirical evidence backing up the theories; sometimes there is no theory backing up the inductive generalizations. Whichever, it would be sheer recklessness to follow their guidance (Goodin 1982c: chaps. 1 and 2); and for those occupying positions of great public trust, being reckless is an even more grievous sin than simply being wrong (Hare 1957: 23).

This is certainly a complaint which is commonly lodged against the most famous modern manifestation of supply-side analysis, the Laffer curve. Laffer's supply-side economics and the Reagan budgets based on them are excoriated by one distinguished economist as a

> victory of ideology over evidence. The supply-sider's economic theory was born on a cocktail napkin. Notwithstanding attempts of well-financed research to bolster these views, it has received no serious statistical validation. Indeed, the bulk of the economic evidence suggests that the personal tax cuts [this theory recommends] are ineffective instruments for promoting savings, investments or productivity. (Nordhaus 1981b; see also 1981a)

Galbraith characterizes supply-side economics as "a relatively sophisticated form of fraud"; Heller likens it to Laetrile, Solow to "snake oil." But it is not just professional economists who take offense at the lack of evidence to back up the theory. Much the same objection is implied in the politicians' and press corps' favorite term of derision, "voodoo economics" (Gardner 1981).

Of course, supply-side policies are not all necessarily guilty of this error, nor are they unique in committing it. The objection is to half-baked theories as such, and that is an objection that can tell equally well against theories of the Left as of the Right.

Supply-side theories are, however, guilty of one particular theoretical failing. They tend to assume that it is possible, at least in principle and probably in practice, to increase the supply of any and all goods that might be in demand. But it is impossible to increase the supply of some goods, such as those that are valued on account of their histories—family heirlooms or Aboriginal sacred sites, for example. With those we have a strictly fixed supply, and the only question is how we are going to distribute them (Goodin 1982b; 1983). Increasing the supply of goods is also logically impossible for the class of "positional" goods. It is logically impossible for two people to be first in any queue. One has to be first and the other second; or we can, if we like, assign them the position of "joint first," relegating them both to the artificial position of 1.5. But, strictly speaking, they cannot both be first. Now, insofar as the goods that people want are positional goods in this sense—or, I should say, insofar as this positionality is what people value in those goods—the problem of the distribution of these goods is a pure distribution problem. Any attempt at a supply-side solution is logically incoherent. But, of course, not all goods are purely positional goods, so this stops short of condemning all supply-side policies.

My conclusion, then, is that our objections to supply-side policies can to some extent be traced to our doubts about their promise actually to solve the distributional problems in view. In some cases, we think that that promise is empirically groundless; in others, that it is theoretically without foundations; and in still others, that it is logically incoherent. This is a powerful critique of supply-side policies, even if it is only a partial one.

C

A third objection is that supply-side politics sometimes pretends to solve conflicts that are in truth *insoluble*. Political science, we have long been taught, is the study of "who gets what, when, and how." Political conflicts are predicated on conflicts of interest. And conflicts of *interest*, if ignored, do *not* go away. Therefore, all the standard devices for smoothing over behavioral conflicts—supply-side politics, corporatism, consociational democracy, or what have you—must necessarily do so by *fudging* conflicts of interest rather than by resolving them. The effect, all too often, is merely to allow one side to win without a fight. Insofar as there truly is a conflict of interest there is to that extent, and by definition, simply no scope for mutually profitable compromise.

Whether or not that critique is valid in any particular case depends, naturally, on the precise extent of the conflict of interest between the parties to the conflict. Only in a strictly constant-sum game is there literally *no* scope for cooperation. While some commentators might characterize ours as a *Zero-Sum Society* quite generally (Thurow 1980), that is surely an exaggeration. Doubtless there are a great many opportunities to profit from coordinating behavior (Goodin 1976). Equally clearly, there are some struggles that are genuinely constant (if not strictly zero) sum. Competition for "positional" goods is one of the more important examples. Insofar as people are competing for places in a ranking, there is no scope for increasing the supply of valued goods (places). You cannot increase the number of places at the top—at least not without lowering the top itself. And in many more struggles, "indivisibilities" among the goods at issue may equally well preclude any effective bargaining or compromise solutions. The color of the flag that flies over Ulster is one classic example (Rose 1971: chap. 14). The fate of Aboriginal sacred sites is, perhaps, another.

D

A further objection, which perhaps comes closer to identifying what is peculiarly wrong with supply-side politics, is that it is *morally arbitrary* in various respects. This sort of criticism has long been directed at the economic theory of "trickle down." That strategy, unkindly but irresistibly described as "feeding the sparrows by feeding the horses" (Safire 1972: 683), asserts that increasing the quantity of goods supplied to the rich will also indirectly increase the quantity of goods available to the poor. But suppose the goal is just to pump more money into the economy, as with ordinary demand-stimulation policies. Then assuming wealth can filter up to the rich just as easily as it can trickle down to the poor (and further assuming that it will not even itself out perfectly in either case), it would be morally arbitrary of us always to inject public funds at the top rather than the bottom of the social pyramid.[4]

Various arguments couched in terms of incentives (to labor, save, or invest) are offered for supposing that this flow can only work in the downward direction. Those arguments are themselves open to some serious challenges, as shown in chapter 8. But even if they were correct, the charge of moral arbitrariness would still stick. The reason is that supply-side strategies take the status quo as the starting point; they guarantee that no one will ever be made worse off by any changes from that (at least in terms of the absolute size of their holdings). Supply-side policies therefore necessarily enshrine the present distribution. And that is morally arbitrary.

Guaranteeing that no one will lose makes good political sense. No doubt it is useful in neutralizing opponents and smoothing the passage of otherwise controversial proposals (Leman 1979). But morally the guarantee makes no sense whatsoever. There is no reason to presume that people positively deserve whatever they

---

[4] In the "Cross of Gold" speech that won him the 1898 Democratic Presidential nomination, William Jennings Bryan effectively sets up this "arbitrariness" objection: "There are two ideas of government. There are those who make believe that, if you will only legislate to make the well-to-do prosperous, their prosperity will leak through on those below. The Democratic idea, however, has been that if you legislate to make the masses prosperous, their prosperity will find its way up through every class which rests upon them" (quoted in Safire 1972: 682).

presently have. Nor, negatively, is there even any reason to suppose that they do not deserve to have it taken away. They may
have stolen it, in which case justice surely demands a redistribution from the thieves (or their heirs) to the legitimate owners (or
their heirs). By taking the status quo as an unexamined starting
point, supply-side politics thus opens itself to objections of moral
arbitrariness (Barry 1980).

Once again, supply-side politics is not alone in committing this
sin. In economics, the criterion of Pareto-efficiency does the same.[5]
In law, "hold harmless" clauses similarly guarantee "that whatever changes are made in existing programs a current recipient
will be protected from loss" (Leman 1979: 104). Political proposals
for "consensual decision-making" are similarly guilty of demanding unanimous consent itself (Barry 1965: 243–44; Rae 1975). All of
these, however, really do look like cognate strategies. It is hardly
surprising, therefore, that all members of the same theoretical
family should share all the same flaws.

E

Objections to supply-side politics might go even further along
these same lines. It is not just that the rich get no poorer under
supply-side policies. Sometimes they actually get richer—and not
just richer, but often disproportionately richer. What really ran-
kles, in other words, is that in consequence of supply-side policies
the rich often not only hold onto the same absolute share of things
but they hold onto (or indeed increase) their *relative* shares.[6]

Why, it might be asked, should relativities matter? Why should
we object to the rich getting very much richer, just so long as the
poor get a little richer in consequence, too? Why object to some
people being made better off if no one is being made worse off?
Psychologically, envy certainly is understandable. Perhaps it is
even inevitable. But moralists widely regard it as disreputable, as

---

[5] That is why the New Political Economists reformulated it in the form of a *hypothetical* compensation test. They did not necessarily want to enshrine the present
distribution, which is what would have happened had they required that compensation actually be paid.

[6] This is an empirical proposition, to be sure. There is no reason that this necessarily had to happen under supply-side policies. But there are all sorts of reasons
to expect that empirically it is extraordinarily likely. Notice that this consequence is
clearer (if not, strictly speaking, more likely) under supply-side policies than it is
under the cognate strategies involving Pareto-efficiency, "hold-harmless clauses,"
and consensual decision making; and that I suggest, explains why we view supply-
side policies with greater disdain than those other more abstract principles.

a sentiment that is unfit to shape our social life (Rawls 1971: secs. 80–81).

There are, however, two perfectly good reasons for worrying about relativities, envy aside. The first builds on the argument against the moral arbitrariness of guaranteeing that no one will be worse off than they are under the status quo. Notice that, in the growing economy envisaged by supply-siders, guaranteeing people the same relative share as before guarantees them *more* than guaranteeing them merely the same absolute amount.[7] Either guarantee is morally arbitrary, to be sure. But presumably it is worse, morally speaking, to guarantee arbitrarily a larger sum than it is to guarantee arbitrarily a smaller sum.[8]

The second reply builds on the proposition that sometimes relativities really do matter objectively, and not just because people feel subjectively "envious." One person's gains sometimes really do make another person objectively worse off in consequence. That is classically the case when the stock of goods remains fixed, but your opponent in an auction gains more money with which to bid; and that is also what happens in the case of "credential inflation" discussed above, and indeed in all cases of inflation in general.[9] One person's gains can also objectively harm another through "crowding" effects due to more ordinary economic externalities: other cars on the highway genuinely do get in your way; other cottages in your isolated mountain valley genuinely do spoil your view; and so on (Hirsch 1976: chap. 3). Some such dynamic also underlies Townsend's (1954; 1962; 1979) notion of "relative poverty," discussed in chapter 4. As your society as a whole gets richer, you objectively "need" more in the way of material goods to participate fully in the shared life of your community. For example, conversations in the bar tend to focus on last night's television programs only if sufficiently many families have access to a set: not having a television did not cut you out of too many con-

---

[7] Notice that the choice between these two sorts of guarantees only arises in a growing economy: it is logically impossible to guarantee everyone the same absolute share in a shrinking economy. In a static economy, the two guarantees amount to one and the same thing.

[8] On some views of ethics, of course, wrong is wrong and arbitrary is arbitrary— moral badness admits of no gradations. But I take it that that simply cannot be right.

[9] Inflation creates the illusion of making people better off by giving them more money. But of course this is merely an illusion, if the increased supply of money is not matched by an increase in the supply of real goods. Critics have long claimed that Keynesianism depended on precisely this illusion, and would cease working once it was shattered (Hayek 1958; Rose and Peters 1978: 185).

versations when only a handful of people had them; it does now that more than 95 percent of households are so equipped.

Once again, this is only a partial objection to supply-side policies as such. Not all of them necessarily attempt to guarantee that everyone will retain the same relative share as is presently enjoyed; and not all concern with relative shares is necessarily morally warranted. But to a large extent, both *are* true. Insofar as they are, this constitutes another good argument against supply-side solutions.

F

Another set of objections might build on the proposition that even if supply-side remedies really would solve distributional problems, they would do so too *slowly*. Economists have traditionally been somewhat insensitive to the passage of time and the effects it might have, not only on their theories but also on people's lives (Robinson 1980; Zeckhauser 1973b). So, too, do "political scientists devote too much effort to finding out *what* happens and why, and not nearly enough to finding out *when* it happens and why," as I argued elsewhere (Goodin 1982a: 57). So, too, perhaps, do liberal philosophers in general.[10]

In the present context the point is just this. What a straightforward redistribution would accomplish in an instant, supply-side policies would accomplish only in due course.[11] That has always been one of our major objections to the economic theory of "trickle down." It is also one of the more obvious objections to "grandfather clauses" in laws, exempting present operators from the requirements of new legislation (Leman 1979). And it has long been among the most important objections to public works projects,

[10] "In the liberal view of rational man, the inescapable fact of the passage of time, or man's mortality, is noted and commented upon, but death is treated as accidental to man's nature as a moral and political being. It terminates life, but does not infiltrate it, as it were. For Kant . . . moral agents *are* literally timeless" (Wolff 1974: 131).

[11] This, I submit, is a necessary feature of these two styles of policy rather than merely a contingent fact about the variants presently pursued. Supply-side policies must by their nature take some time to produce any distributional consequences; there is no equivalent reason why, in theory, a more straightforward redistribution of income or wealth could not be accomplished virtually instantaneously. Of course, there may be all sorts of reasons in practice for delay occurring: bureaucracies move slowly, etc. Political constraints would surely afflict supply-side and distributional-side remedies alike, however. The only systematic difference in timing will therefore presumably favor straightforward redistribution.

such as the American urban renewal program (Anderson 1964: chap. 5).

One of the more compelling examples of this objection at work comes in the course of the 1940 debate over the British War Damage Insurance Act. The government thereby assured property owners that war damage would be fully repaired if possible or compensated if not; but where residential accommodation was concerned, it proposed to ask householders to wait until the end of the war, when labor and materials would once again be plentiful. It was hoped that this long-term supply-side remedy would defuse short-term demands for redistribution of such houses as remained undamaged. The trick worked, by and large. But it did not pass without comment. One MP rose during the debate to protest that,

> to be fair and just to everybody . . . the damage should be [compensated] at the time it takes place. I do not want a man to wait until the war is over, to wait, it may be, for two, three, or more years. I understand the position regarding difficulties of labour and material, but I do not understand why a man, because he owns a house, should be put under any greater hardship [than a factory owner]. (Craven-Ellis 1940: 1291)

Needless to say, however, at the end of the day the Treasury view prevailed.

But why should timing matter? The answer may turn out to be a little more complicated than might be supposed. The easy answer is, of course, that in the long run we are all dead. If the benefit does not appear for a very long time, I might not even be alive to receive it. In any case, the later it is in arriving, the less time I will have left to enjoy it.

In one way, however, it might be justifiable to neglect such considerations. What I have in mind is something akin to the "post obit bond," a device much favored by nineteenth-century novelists, whereby the eldest sons of the landed gentry borrowed against their certain inheritance of an "entailed" estate (Trollope 1883). Suppose it is certain that you will receive exactly $1 million in exactly ten years' time, but that you are presently penniless. It is silly to starve—perhaps to death—for ten years, and then suddenly to become a millionaire. So you go to your moneylender to see what can be done about it. Assuming your future really is as certain as I have described (and that capital markets are functioning properly), it ought to be easy enough to borrow now against your future fortune.

The bottom line is that it should not matter when you receive the money, provided it is sufficiently certain that you *will* receive it. On that analysis, the only thing wrong with delayed benefits is that they are less certain.[12] In the present context, that can only mean that we (or, more precisely, our moneylenders) are doubtful that supply-side policies really will work to deliver the promised benefits to the poor. So this objection collapses back into the second: supply-side policies are bad because we have insufficient reason to believe that they will work their distributional miracles.[13]

That objection works very much within the neoclassical orthodoxy. Various other powerful objections to delay arise once we move outside it. One obvious one is that capital markets might not function nearly so smoothly as we might wish. Hence, even if the poor person's future fortune were absolutely secure, it may still prove impossible to borrow against it.[14]

Another more interesting objection is this. The preceding argument presupposes that what you can borrow from the bank is as good as what you will later receive from the state. If that later award will itself come in the form of cash, this is a safe assumption. But there is no reason to assume universal fungibility. Not every good is tradable for every other, either in markets or even in our own private utility functions (Goodin 1982b:60–62; 1983). Suppose that what the state promises is some valued status (e.g., citizenship) or some service that it alone can provide to facilitate valued personal relationships (new child adoption laws, e.g.). Or suppose that what justice demands is that the state arrange for the return of some irreplaceable asset stolen from you (e.g., sacred sites stolen from Aboriginals). Then it matters very much *when* the

[12] Of course, it is not just as good to receive exactly the same sum now as later. If we got it now we could invest it at compound interest and have substantially more by the time the later date rolls around. So, strictly speaking, what I am saying is that under the stipulated conditions we should be indifferent as to whether we receive a certain sum now or, at some later date, the same sum plus interest. These sums must of course be calculated in real (i.e., inflation-adjusted) terms.

[13] The doubts have several sources. We may doubt the theory underlying the supply-side policy, and hence doubt that it could ever deliver the distributional goods. Or, given that it will take a fair while to work, we may doubt that the government will persist with the policy long enough to produce benefits for everyone—especially those who are at the bottom of the heap and at the end of the queue.

[14] In the debate over the War Damage Insurance Act, for example, one member of Parliament asked, "Does the promise of the Government [to compensate for war damage after the war] in any way create a negotiable security? . . . If it is not, is it anything upon which a man can raise money, a kind of post obit as it were?" The solicitor-general, mindful of the need to control the money supply to forestall wartime inflation, replied no to both questions. See *Hansard's Parliamentary Debates (Commons)*, 5th series, 367 (1940–1941), cols. 1141–42 and 1186.

goods are delivered. Not only would money-lenders be unwilling to loan money against such collateral; the money could not really compensate you, anyway.

Under certain plausible conditions, then, the objection that supply-side policies work slowly can remain a powerful and independent one. This clearly is true either where capital markets fail in the ways described, or where "incommensurable" goods are at stake. Perhaps it even remains true where beneficiaries of belated public largesses are simply lacking in the financial sophistication required to translate future fortunes into present benefits in these ways.

G

Waiting, notice furthermore, is not itself distributively neutral. Perhaps it is always unfair to some extent to ask people to wait for what is due them. But it is particularly unfair to make the disadvantaged wait, for they are being asked to bide their time in an exposed position. The longer they have to remain there, the greater the chances that something will come along to swamp them altogether.

This is true in purely physiological terms. The poor are vastly more likely to die young. It is also true economically. Having less of a cushion to fall back upon, they are more susceptible to financial ruin. Politically, too, their position is particularly precarious. Those whom present distributions disadvantage are unlikely to have the wherewithal to sustain for long any very powerful political movement. In purely political terms, a waiting game plays into the hands of their opponents.

Insofar as supply-side policies promise only a delayed solution to distributional problems, then, they create more distributional problems than they solve. Asking people to wait for benefits, when some can afford to wait and others cannot, is itself a distributive injustice. And that is one to which there is no supply-side solution.

I I I

Politically it is hardly surprising that supply-side solutions are so widely embraced. Guaranteeing that "everyone's a winner"— which is, of course, precisely what such solutions purport to guar-

274

antee—is an obviously attractive coalition-building device (Lehman 1979). The political logic is transparent. It is the ethics of the matter that here concern me. We know why politicians want to offer such guarantees; the question is simply whether they can reasonably expect to honor them.

Sometimes they can. Since so much of this chapter has been devoted to showing what might be wrong with supply-side politics, it is perhaps important to repeat what I said at the outset: increasing supply is occasionally the best and occasionally the only way to solve distributional problems. But I suspect this is likely to be true *just* occasionally.

In my critique, I have shown that supply-side policies might sin in any of seven ways. There is, however, nothing inherent in the logic of such policies to suggest that they must necessarily sin in any of them. What is needed, then, is a more fine-grained analysis of the moral acceptability of supply-side policies on a case-by-case basis than is ordinarily offered, either by the champions or by the opponents of such strategies.

Some supply-side policies are worse than others. Conversely, some are better than others. Which class will predominate—what our on-balance assessment of the strategy should be—can only be ascertained after much case-by-case analysis. But I am myself inclined to doubt that there is much comfort to be had for supply-siders from that exercise. In reflecting upon such policies, it seems to me that our thoughts naturally tend to gravitate toward the less objectionable instances anyway—increasing food stocks during an objective shortage, and the like. That is why the strategy is ordinarily held in little if any disrepute, whereas my arguments here suggest that it can (depending on circumstances) be deserving of the very deepest scorn. So far as the morality of supply-side politics is concerned, then, I suspect that the news can only be worse than we might preanalytically expect.

The most unfortunate concatenation of circumstances for supply-side attempts to remedy distributional problems would be as follows:

A. The supply-side analysis is partial rather than comprehensive in its scope.

B. It is far from certain that the supply-side remedy will work, either to increase the total supply or to give any substantial portion of that larger total to those who are distributively disadvantaged.

C. There is a substantial conflict of interests, approaching a constant-sum struggle.

D. There is no reason to suppose that the advantaged deserve to keep what they have.

E. Supply-side measures will make the rich richer in ways that actually injure the poor.

F. Supply-side measures will be slow in yielding any benefits to the disadvantaged, and there is no way for them to borrow against their expected future benefits.

G. Waiting harms the distributively disadvantaged more than others.

Certainly there is no reason to believe that this combination is impossible. Logically, these conditions unfortunately hang together only too well. The more partial the scope of the solution relative to that of the problem (A), the greater the doubts that the solution will in fact work (B). Uncertainty about the success of the strategy (B) makes borrowing against expected future gains difficult (F). In a constant-sum game (C), the gains of the rich come at the expense of the poor (E). And in a constant-sum game (C), logic alone will suffice to guarantee that there is no scope for evading distributional issues by increasing the supply of goods (A and B). So at least five of these seven conditions are tied up in a neat little package. While I see no reason for supposing that the other two are necessarily tied in as well, neither do I see any reason for supposing that they are necessarily excluded from this package. There is, then, no obvious logical incompatibility between all the conditions that combine to make supply-side remedies a real moral horror. On the contrary, quite the reverse seems to be true.

Particularly as applied to the sort of situation to which the welfare state is a response is this combination of circumstances absolutely commonplace. Typically, there is no good reason for supposing that supply-side remedies would work and many for supposing that they would not; those arguments have been discussed both here and in chapter 8. But even supposing that supply-side remedies in this realm would work, it is clear that it would at the very least take two or three years for them to do so. Recalling the discussion of "desperation bidding" in chapter 6, however, it is equally clear that the needy are operating on a dramatically more truncated time horizon than that. Unlike the rich, they cannot afford to wait. Condition G is so powerfully satisfied that what may, in the long term, be a positive-sum game has for the poor been transformed into a fiercely constant-sum game (condition C). Conditions A, B, E, and F follow from that. The only question that remains, then, is the question of moral deserts, and that is the subject of the next chapter. Thus, the supply-side strategy for supplanting the welfare state stands comprehensively condemned on at least six out of seven criteria.

Where supply-side solutions fail in any or all of those ways to solve distributional problems, we will be forced to face up squarely to the true nature of the problems. It will once again have become clear that distributional problems call for distributional solutions. Of course, the requisite redistributions might not be forthcoming, for all sorts of familiar political reasons. Without minimizing those practical obstacles to redistribution, I would nonetheless insist that flawed supply-side remedies are not somehow second-best alternatives to redistribution. Insofar as they display any of the flaws I have here isolated, to that extent they offer *no solution at all* to distributional problems.

T E N

DESERT

A second major theme in New Right criticism of the welfare state is moralistic, drawing on ethical notions of moral deserts, of freedom or of self-reliance. These moralistic challenges are taken up in turn over the course of the next three chapters.

The first such challenge concerns what people morally deserve. Moral deserts, as they are standardly understood, are predicated upon what people are or what they have done (Feinberg 1970: 58; Kleinig 1971: 73–75). In the market, people do not (characteristically, at least) get something for nothing. Ordinarily, they have to have *done something* to earn whatever they got.[1] Whether or not they have done enough to justify the full amount of their rewards is another matter, perhaps. But at least they have done something. That makes market outcomes at least prima facie deserved, the New Right would say.

Contrast that with the case of welfare state benefits. Many of the most important forms are nowise conditional on any prior performance or character trait of the recipient. Contributory social insurance programs are a slight exception. There, people have done something (i.e., made quasi-insurance premium contributions) to justify their receiving the benefit. But those programs are only slight exceptions, because what beneficiaries have done is usually very transparently not enough to justify (in the market-based terms in which this argument operates) the full benefit they receive: social insurance contributions standardly fail to reflect full actuarial risk (Hayek 1960: chap. 19; Titmuss 1968: 173–87). And the case is even more clearcut with programs of social assistance or noncontributory categorical assistance. There, assistance is con-

Material in this chapter is reprinted from Robert E. Goodin, "Negating Positive Desert Claims," *Political Theory*, 13 (November 1985), 575–98, by permission of the editor and Sage Publications Inc.

[1] Even capitalists have done something, either as investors risking their capital or as entrepreneurs discovering new opportunities (Arnold 1987). For a nice discussion of the ambiguities and dubious assumptions involved in desert-based arguments for the market, see Buchanan (1985: 51–53) and Nell (1987).

ditional merely upon people's falling into certain categories or upon the shortfall between their needs and their resources. Characteristically, recipients will have done nothing (nothing meritorious, anyway) to warrant payment of welfare benefits: they cannot be said to have done anything to "earn" such assistance. Instead, it is given to them regardless of what they have done, and often in spite of what they have done. For such reasons, the New Right maintains that, morally, all welfare benefits are largely (and noncontributory assistance is wholly) undeserved.

In its most extreme form, then, the New Right indictment of the welfare state in terms of moral deserts holds that the tax-transfer system as a whole is just one big, infernal machine for taking from the deserving and giving to the undeserving. What people have properly earned in the market is taken from them in taxes. It is transferred to welfare recipients who, at best, have done virtually nothing to earn those benefits and who, at worst, may have come to their present plight through some misconduct of their own and thus be powerfully undeserving of either sympathy or social assistance.

In a less extreme form, the New Right indictment would accuse the welfare state of ignoring the differential moral deserts among claimants to welfare benefits. Some people have misbehaved egregiously, and come to their present plight through their own misconduct. Others (widows, orphans, and the congenitally handicapped being the examples standardly invoked on such occasions) have fallen into distress through no fault of their own. Universalistic social services treat all alike. Such treatment is "too bad for the good, too good for the bad," to borrow a phrase from the Majority Report of the 1909 Royal Commission on the Poor Law that the modern New Right would wish to echo (quoted in Pope, Pratt, and Hoyle 1986: 26). They, too, would want the "deserving poor" treated one way, and the "undeserving poor" quite another (Handler and Hollingsworth 1971).

Such views are standard and unsurprising coming from Victorian moralists such as Malthus (1826: bk. 3, chaps. 5–7), Sumner (1883: chaps. 1, 9, and 10) and Spencer (1884: chap. 2).[2] What is

---

[2] Herbert Spencer (1884: chap. 2), for example, protests that "sympathy with one in suffering suppresses . . . remembrance of his transgressions. The feeling which vents itself in 'poor fellow!' on seeing one in agony, excludes the thought of 'bad fellow,' which might at another time arise. . . . When . . . the miseries of the poor are depicted, they are thought of as the miseries of the deserving poor, instead of being thought of, as in large measure they should be, as the miseries of the undeserving poor . . . bearing the penalties of their own misdeeds." William Graham

surprising is to see such distinctions reemerging in our own day. In the most influential New Right tract on modern American social policy, *Losing Ground*, Charles Murray (1985: 183, 29) complains,

> The unwillingness to acknowledge moral inequality was a hallmark of Great Society social programs and persisted throughout the 1970s. . . . Poverty was not a consequence of indolence or vice. It was not the just deserts of people who didn't try hard enough. It was produced by conditions that had nothing to do with individual virtue or effort. Poverty was not the fault of the individual but of the system.

Murray maintains that this "fallacy" lay at the root of all the Great Society's failures. In its place, he urges as a fundamental premise of social policy the proposition that "people must be held responsible for their actions." "Whether they *are* responsible in some ultimate philosophical or biochemical sense," Murray (1985: 146) goes on to say, "cannot be the issue if society is to function." Similarly, when President Reagan (1981: 361) says that "those who through no fault of their own must depend on the rest of us . . . can rest assured that the social safety net of programs they depend on are exempt from any [budget] cuts," the unstated implication is clear: viz., there are other people whose poverty *is* their own fault, and who therefore can enjoy no guarantee of generous social assistance from his administration.

Sumner (1883: 22–24) similarly protests that "humanitarians, philanthropists and reformers . . . gloss over all the faults of the classes in question, and . . . exaggerate their misfortunes and their virtues. . . . When I have read certain of these discussions I have thought that it must be quite disreputable to be respectable, quite dishonest to own property, quite unjust to go one's own way and earn one's own living, and that the only really admirable person was the good-for-nothing. . . . The man who has done nothing to raise himself above poverty finds that the social doctors flock about him, bringing the capital which they have collected from the other classes, and promising him the aid of the State to give him what the others had to work for. . . . On the theories of the social philosophers to whom I have referred, we should get a new maxim of judicious living: Poverty is the best policy. If you get wealth, you will have to support other people; if you do not get wealth, it will be the duty of other people to support you." Although writers such as Spencer and Sumner are now regarded rather as cariactures, their views on these matters were not wildly out of step with the "enlightened" opinion of their age. Such views were echoed, in slightly muted form, by J. S. Mill (1848: bk. 5, chap. 11, sec. 13; 1869: chap. 4) and even by the influential early advocate of national insurance, Canon Blackley (1878: 837–38). Such attitudes also continued to shape social policy throughout the period: as late as 1895, the U.K. Royal Commission on the Aged Poor was recommending, for example, that "evidence of an industrious or independent life is presumptive proof of thrift, and entitles the applicant to better treatment than the wastrel or drunkard" (1895/1985: 52).

The aim of this chapter is to defeat this moralistic challenge to the welfare state by undercutting notions of positive desert upon which it depends. Notions of positive desert, I shall argue, have no important role to play in social policymaking. I shall launch three separate attacks. The first is essentially conceptual. I show, in section I, that the negative notion of the "undeserved," rather than the positive notion of the "deserved," constitutes the moralized core of the notion of desert. Arguments against the welfare state tend to appeal to these discredited notions of positive deserts, whereas notions of negative deserts that are here vindicated are consonant with all sorts of welfare state policies.

My other two attacks on the notion of desert as applied to the welfare state's activities are largely practical in nature. One, developed in section II, is that we can make only very limited claims, if any at all, about positive entitlements to probabilistic outcomes; yet those are typically precisely the sorts of outcomes that the welfare state seeks to remedy. Another, developed in section III, is that there are certain circumstances in which considerations of desert should be put into abeyance. Situations in which someone's basic needs are at risk—as they typically are, where welfare state interventions are concerned—are among them.

These three arguments are independent of one another. The success of any one of them is nowise contingent upon the success of any other. But they all converge toward the same basic conclusion, viz., that notions of positive desert ought not play any important role in social policymaking of the sort with which the welfare state is concerned.

I

J. L. Austin's (1956) famous paper on "Ifs and Cans" opens with the immortal question, "Are *cans* constitutionally iffy?" By that, he means to query whether every statement about what someone can do must, analytically, contain implicitly within it certain "if" clauses ("if he wants to," "if he really tries," "if the gods are willing," etc.). If so, then a large part of what we really mean by saying that someone can do something lies in unpacking these suppressed "if" clauses.

Here I want to raise an analogous question about the notion of personal deserts. To embody my thesis in a similarly catchy maxim, I shall be claiming that deserts are constitutionally "wouldy." Or, to unpack that phrase, when we say "x *deserves* y" we are really saying "x *would receive* y in the normal course of events." Or, to unpack it further still, "x *would receive* y, in the absence of certain *untoward* interventions z."

My argument here is that, just as we must excavate the ifs to get at the cans, so too must we focus clearly on the "untoward" intervening factors upsetting the "normal" course of events in order to fix our notion of personal desert. The upshot of my argument will be that that notion is essentially negative in character. The core notion is not that of the "deserved" but rather that of the "undeserved," of those untoward intervening factors upsetting the "normal" course of events.[3] In Austin's phrase, "undeserved" wears the trousers.

To show that this is so, I shall start from the simple proposition that "desert" is an inherently moralized notion. To be a notion of "desert" at all, it must imply that, ceteris paribus, people ought morally to get what they deserve. I shall proceed to argue that the negative notion of "undeserved" is crucially moralized in this way, but that the positive notion of "deserved" is not. I shall show that the notion of positive desert is either a residual notion lacking moral force, or else it is a derivative one borrowing whatever moral force it possesses from other nondesert considerations.

Any notion of what is positively deserved is usually merely residual, what is normally left over after certain confounding features have been factored out. No moral force necessarily attaches to that residual. Removing all that is undeserved leaves us *not* with something that is necessarily deserved, but perhaps merely with something that is neither deserved nor undeserved.

When, as occasionally happens, there are properly moral arguments for ascribing positive deserts (e.g., to prizes or commendations), those arguments look outside the notion of desert for their moral force. It is those nondesert considerations, rather than considerations of desert per se, which give us reasons for believing that people ought—rather than just reasonably (and, in that restricted sense, legitimately) expect—to receive what they would ordinarily receive in the ordinary course of events.

What is at stake in this argument, so far as the welfare state is concerned, should be clear. The notion of positive deserts is crucial to the case of New Right opponents against the welfare state.

---

[3] Feinberg (1980: 265, n.2) notes similarly that "it is much more convenient, when doing moral philosophy, to speak of injustice than to keep to the positive term, justice. That greater convenience is an undeniable fact." Feinberg lets the point drop there, however, saying, "I shall not speculate here whether it has any theoretical significance."

Without some such notion playing an important moral role, they cannot claim that the poor positively deserve their plight, and hence ought not (or need not) be assisted. Nor, without some such notion, can they claim that the rich positively deserve their wealth, and hence ought not have it taken from them by the tax collector. Both of those propositions play on the positive sense of personal desert that I here call into question.[4]

The sense of desert that remains morally important in the wake of this challenge—the negative notion of the undeserved—is the sense that is crucial in arguing for the sort of remedial policies that characterize welfare state activities. The "deserving poor"—with whom the New Right officially sympathizes and whom they would have the state assist—are not deserving in any positive sense. Widows, orphans, and the congenitally handicapped cannot point to anything special in their character or past performances that would mark them out for especially favorable treatment. Instead, their claim to be "deserving" of state assistance is grounded merely in the negative fact that there is nothing there to warrant their present pains, either. They have done nothing to deserve the suffering that fate has bestowed upon them, and *that* is why public action to relieve their distress is said to be justified.[5] They are not positively deserving of the relief; they are merely negatively undeserving of the suffering. This negative notion of the undeserved that is so crucial in underwriting social assistance schemes will remain as the only morally important one in the wake of my conceptual challenge to the notion of positive desert.

A

When describing someone's deserts, we characteristically say things like, "He has it coming," or, "It is due him." But those,

---

[4] When talking of "positive desert claims," I refer primarily to "positive assertions"—claims that something or another *is* deserved. I shall also be talking primarily about "positive desert claims" in the sense in which outcomes in view are positive (i.e., valued from the point of view of the recipient) rather than negative (i.e., disvalued). The latter—deserved punishments—are the focus for most discussions of desert, and are implicitly or explicitly the model for much writing on positive desert claims (Simon 1978–1979). Perhaps there it *is* more legitimate to make positive assertions about deserved outcomes; but if so, then that only goes to show that punishment is a very special case, importantly different from social welfare policy, e.g., and should not be taken to constitute the paradigm case for all applications of the concept of desert. Even where punishment is concerned, however, note that "desert" still seems to be a "wouldy" notion in some important respect, as is shown in Manser's (1962) penetrating analysis.

[5] In the words of Charles Murray (1984: 223), "There is no such thing as an undeserving five-year-old."

notice, are forms of language that we ordinarily employ in making predictions. When saying that the train "is coming" or "is due," we mean merely to say that it *will* soon arrive—or at least that it should soon arrive, absent untoward interventions of terrorists, frozen points, failing signals, etc.

Looking below the form of words to the substance of our ordinary judgments about personal deserts, their essentially predictive "wouldy" nature remains. We typically say that the fastest runner, or the one who has trained the hardest, deserves to win the race. What more is that than the prediction that, ceteris paribus, the fastest or best trained will win the race?[6] Certainly he would ordinarily be expected to do so in the normal course of events, unless he is tripped, tricked, etc. Likewise, we say that the best-qualified applicant deserves the job, or the lowest bidder deserves to win the contract. And what more is that than the mere prediction that, ceteris paribus, the best-qualified applicant and lowest bidder will get the nod? Given the way the market ordinarily works, certainly they would ordinarily be expected to do so in the normal course of events—unless the committee awarding the job or contract were engaging in nepotism, racial or sexual discrimination, etc.

The same is true of the subclass of "institutionalized" or "rule-based" desert statements (Kleinig 1971: 75–76). We say that an elderly person deserves (i.e., is entitled to) a pension, provided he meets all the conditions laid down in the relevant statute and administrative rules. What more is that than merely to say that social security officers would, in the normal course of events, follow the rules and give him one? We say a thief deserves (is negatively entitled to) punishment. What more is that than merely to say that the courts would, in the normal course of affairs, mete out such punishments as are laid down in the law?[7]

---

[6] Similarly, when the analysis is cast in the past tense—"he had it coming" or "it was due him"—the basic reference is to what we should ex ante have predicted. Desert-based claims can be either more or less conclusive. To say that someone deserves something in the less conclusive sense is merely to say that he has *some* desert-based claim to it. But, of course, others might have more or stronger desert-based claims to the same thing, which will therefore override X's. "X deserves y" in the stronger, more conclusive sense, if, and only if: (1) X has a desert-based claim to y; and (2) X's desert-based claim to y is stronger than anyone else's desert-based claim to y. Unless stated otherwise, I shall here use "deserves" in the weaker, less conclusive way.

[7] Suppose there is a rule, but that it is not ordinarily enforced by judges or administrators. Then when they actually do make an exception and enforce the rule, we would surely be inclined to describe the consequent benefit or burden not only

284

Of course, not all predictions entail desert claims.[8] Minimally, we must stipulate that desert claims mark out that subset of predictions predicated on some facts about a person's *character* or *personal history* (Feinberg 1970: 58; Kleinig 1971: 73–75). We may want to go further, saving the term "deserves" for cases where those actions or character traits were *voluntarily* chosen. Or we may want to go further still, saying that P deserves q only if P has voluntarily acted (or voluntarily chosen character traits that lead him to act) with the *intention* of producing q. Whichever way we choose to mark off the subset of desert predictions, it is clear that some way is needed: not every prediction can be an ascription of desert.

It is the converse proposition that interests me here. Are ascriptions of desert anything more than merely predictions, albeit ones of some special sort? And if that is all they are, what is the moral force of those mere predictions? In what sense, if any, are we morally obliged to make mere predictions come true?

B

One ready answer to such questions—and one that is wholly consonant with the more standard analysis of deserts as *positive* claims—is to say that what normally happens does so because that is what people *deserve* to have happen. The implication here is that our world is a fair world, broadly speaking; and what normally happens in it is that people receive a fair return for what they are or what they have done. On this analysis, "normal" would be just another way of saying "is morally entitled to." Were that analysis correct, then my argument that statements of moral deserts characteristically just refer to what would normally happen, far from undercutting old-fashioned positive-style desert claims, would actually have vindicated them.

Certainly there is an element of truth in that analysis. In ordinary moral discourse, terms like "normal" and "expected" standardly "straddle *predicted* and *morally required*" (Nozick 1972: 112; see also Mackie 1955; Hart and Honoré 1959). What is considered

---

as "unfair" or "inequitable" but also as "undeserved" in any but the narrowest legal sense.

[8] That is to say, not all things that we would predict happening in the normal course of events to person P are things we would necessarily say P deserves to have happen to him. We predict, quite confidently, that P will die if his lungs cease to function; but we would hardly say that P deserves to die, unless perhaps his lung failure stems from his cigarette smoking. Conversely, when someone jumps from a ten-story building and lives, we say, "By rights he should be dead"—not exactly a desert statement, perhaps, but surely the first cousin to one.

"normal," for purposes of assessing personal deserts, does likewise. There, too, the "normal course of events" is not *just* the most frequent or most common course which events would ordinarily take. It is that in part, but only in part. To decide what is "normal" in those contexts, we also need to factor out the influence of certain (possibly quite common) "untoward interventions."[9] In this sense, at least, the notion of "normality" that enters into judgments of personal deserts is indeed a moralized notion.

But if factoring out "untoward interventions" is the *only* sense in which it is a moralized notion, then the moralism embodied in the notion of "normality" would underwrite moral judgments only of a *negative* sort. It would allow us to say that some outcomes—those proceeding from "untoward interventions"—were morally improper. It would not allow us to make any positive moral judgments about the moral propriety of the particular outcomes that would otherwise have occurred.

To say that untoward interventions are morally improper is not necessarily to say that the ordinary course of events is morally proper. That is just not the part of the notion of "normality" that carries any moral charge, at least according to everything that has been said so far. The distinctively moral component of the notion of "normality" comes in factoring out immoral untoward interventions. What is left—what would be "normal" in an idealized world absent such interventions—is "normal" just in the straight statistical sense.

A tripartite division is crucially at work here. Alongside the more familiar categories of the deserved and the undeserved is a notion of that which is neither deserved nor undeserved. Cancelling out the effects of untoward interventions merely moves us from the moralized category of the undeserved to that morally neutral intermediate category. Some further argument is required to move us from there to any properly moralized notion of what is positively deserved. Clearly, everything which is not undeserved is not itself deserved.

What the notion of desert essentially does is point the finger at illicit interventions which are *un*deserved and which preclude people from getting what, in the ordinary course of affairs, they would receive. Even some ostensibly positive judgments and injunctions actually carry just such a fundamentally negative mes-

---

[9] That is why the analysis of deserts must be cast in the subjunctive—in terms of what *would* happen, had nothing untoward occurred, rather than in terms of what *will* happen. Notice that the notion of the "untoward" (as a sort of inverse of Nozick's "expected") straddles "unlucky" and "improper," too.

sage. Notice, for example, that a "good conscience" consists primarily in the *absence* of guilt feelings. Or, again, notice that much of what a judge is doing when instructing a jury positively to "decide this case on its merits" is to instruct the jurors to ignore certain things (such as the defendant's color, class, sex, etc.) which should *not* be taken into consideration in their deliberations.[10]

On my analysis, then, when we talk about what people deserve we are merely talking about what they would receive (or would have received) absent the intervention of certain untoward (statistically unusual/morally improper) circumstances. The sharp moral edge of the notion of desert is on the negative side, challenging those illicit interventions which are *un*deserved and which preclude people from getting what, in the ordinary course of affairs, they would receive. The positive edge—what people would ordinarily receive—is morally very blunt indeed. There is a good reason for thinking that the former is negatively undeserved, but not for thinking that the latter is positively deserved. It is clearly wrong for the best-qualified applicant for a job to be passed over because she is a black woman, and the employer is racially prejudiced; that job denial is undeserved, in a way that morally matters. It is not clearly right, in anything like the same way, that the unskilled laborer who resigns one position should be unable to find another. Statistically, of course, that is precisely what he can expect, when the unemployment rate is running at 10 percent or more. But that is not his fault. That is merely a background fact of life that is neither deserved nor undeserved.

C

My "wouldy" account of desert is basically designed to undermine the notion of positive deserts. I maintain that people are usually

[10] Or, yet again, notice how that which is "deserved" is often described as that which is "appropriate," "fitting and proper," "suitable," etc. That form of words seems to point to a positive correspondence of some sort between the characteristics of the person and the characteristics of the things he is said to deserve. But in social contexts just as surely as in sartorial ones, what constitutes a "good fit" is enormously variable, being largely a matter of taste and style. Any number of things might correspond adequately to characteristics of the person or situation to be deemed "fitting" or "appropriate." The primary use of the notion of "appropriateness" is once again negative. When the sign on the door of a restaurant makes "appropriate attire" a condition of entry, it is not really specifying in any positive way what diners should wear. (If the owners wanted jackets and ties, they would have had to say so explicitly.) The basic function is instead to remind customers of what *not* to wear (standardly, in Australia, singlets and bare feet). The negative—the concept of the "inappropriate"—here again seems to form the core of the concept.

said to "deserve" things merely because that is what they would ordinarily or normally be expected to receive. There may or may not be other moral reasons for them receiving what they ordinarily would. But if there are, these are not reasons of desert per se. This, then, is my second conceptual point: positive desert claims are parasitic upon some larger scheme, whether natural or social, that gives rise to such expectations about what the "ordinary" or "normal" outcome would be.

We say that winners deserve to win just so long as no morally groundless intervention interferes with the ordinary scheme of things. If we insist upon running footraces, then truly the lame do not deserve to win; if we insist upon running an apartheid system, then truly blacks do not deserve the same treatment as whites; if we insist upon running a pure market economy, then those with no marketable skills deserve to starve.

What we are really interested in, however, is the external rather than just the internal evaluation of such schemes. If the proposition "P deserves q" is to have any real moral force, then it must surely imply more than merely that "under existing arrangements P would ordinarily get q." It must also imply that the existing arrangements are themselves morally justifiable. Unless some kind of independent argument can be given for the outcomes that the "normal course of events" would ordinarily throw up, it constitutes no kind of claim at all to insist that, "Well, P *normally would* get q" (Wasserstrom 1980: 75–76; see also Campbell 1974: 3).

Insofar as desert-claims are predicted on the normal operations of the natural (i.e., nonsocial) world, no independent argument can be given. Saying that something would normally come your way naturally amounts to nothing more than making a straightforward statistical prediction. You do not *deserve*, in a positive sense that is in any way morally charged, that particular outcome.

(The most that you might enter is a claim couched in terms of your reliance on reasonable expectations about the ordinary course of events. You were counting on that outcome; you incurred costs in so doing; now that those expectations have been upset, you deserve compensation for those costs. But to say that you might deserve compensation for your reliance on reasonable expectations that y is going to happen is not to say that it is in any way morally desirable that y should happen. Suppose that manufacturers of a swine flu vaccine were compensated for reasonably relying on the U.S. government's prediction of an epidemic: that would hardly imply that it would have been desirable, morally or otherwise, for the swine flu to have reached epidemic proportions.)

Insofar as desert-claims are predicted on normal operations of the social world, there may (or may not) be moral as well as statistical reasons for things to happen as they normally would. We have reasons—moral reasons, among others—for setting up our social institutions to operate as they do. And since there might be moral rather than merely statistical grounds for expecting that P would normally receive q from some social institution S, that might seem to suggest that there may be some moral grounds for claiming that P positively deserves q. That, in turn, threatens to reduce at least this part of my analysis back to the standard one once again: people might deserve what they deserve by virtue of their merits or demerits. All I have done, on this analysis, is to add an intervening variable: people deserve what they deserve by virtue of expectations about the ordinary course of events, which in turn are governed by people's merits and demerits.[11]

That, however, would be a mistaken analysis. Although we certainly do have reasons (maybe even moral reasons) for setting up social institutions as we do, these are not reasons of desert or merit. Indeed, to some extent what counts as merits or demerits may depend on the sort of institution we set up.[12] Physical prowess is a merit when we set people the task of running a race; mental agility when designing a bridge; honesty when testifying in court; cunning when conducting a military campaign; marketable skills are a merit when operating in the context of a market economy; socially useful skills a merit when operating in the context of a command economy. Insofar as merit is institution-specific, that notion cannot provide any independent basis for choosing between alternative institutions.[13]

[11] Unlike Rawls (1971: sec. 17), I do not argue that deserts are nonsense because people do not deserve the personal attributes upon which they are predicated. Instead, I argue for that conclusion by saying that they do not "deserve," in any strict sense of the word, the social institutions that reward personal attributes. The notion of "desert," I maintain, makes sense as a way of entering claims within an established system of social rules and practices, but it makes no sense (or, anyway, none if taken literally) when used to enter claims to have alternative systems of rules and practices applied.

[12] This is reminiscent of Urmson's (1950: 163) argument, in his paper "On Grading," that an apple which displays all the attributes of a good cabbage would be a pretty bad apple: standards of "goodness" vary according to what we are talking about.

[13] This is not to deny that we have any independent moral notions of virtues and vices, merits and demerits, that transcend our social institutions. Certainly we do. I merely mean to suggest that, with the possible exception of the criminal law, our

In any case, it is evident that the notion of "desert" itself has no place in morally underwriting the "scheme of things" in terms of whose ordinary operations claims are grounded. We may say that the winner of a footrace deserves the medal, or the winner of market competition deserves his profits. But we would never say that anyone *deserves* to have bits of precious metal allocated according to the outcome of footraces, or of market competitions either. We might be able to give all sorts of reasons for running footraces or market competitions. But saying that people deserved to have a race to run in would never be among them.

There can be positive desert-claims arising *under* a set of social rules, then, but not *to* that set of social rules. Positive desert-claims cannot provide the moral foundations for the rules themselves. Those must instead be derivative from some other moral values. So, too, consequently, must any positive desert-claims derivative from those rules themselves be ultimately derivative from some other moral values unconnected with personal desert.[14] And if the

---

social institutions do not—and probably should not—encapsulate those more basic moral notions of merit and demerit. Even the criminal law, it may be observed, operates with a severely truncated set of such notions.

[14] When—as occasionally we do—we use the language of deserts in connection with claims *to* a set of rules, we do so in an extended sense of one sort or another:

A. Usually, positive desert claims *to* rules are just desert claims *under* meta-rules that are actually operative in the society. When we say, "He deserves to have the rules pertaining to treatment of prisoners of war applied to him," we are merely saying that there is some meta-rule (the Geneva Convention) which dictates that he should receive that treatment. When we say that "anyone who can climb that rock deserves $50" (Barry 1965: 112), that, too, is just a reference to some implicit meta-rule in our society: since we offer similar sums for climbing similar rocks (or for performing feats of similar difficulty), we would ordinarily expect, under that meta-rule, a similar reward to be offered for this one. Insofar as arguments of consistency or comparability underlie positive desert claims, they all seem to be rule-based in similar ways. While desert claims to have certain rules applied might arise in this way under a meta-rule, the point remains that that meta-rule is not itself grounded in considerations of desert.

B. Occasionally, we use an extended sense of "desert" to argue for a genuinely different set of rules to be applied. We say, "There ought to be a mechanism for rewarding behavior or talents like this," or, "There ought to be a mechanism for compensating harm like this," without invoking any analogy to how we treat other cases or in any other way invoking any implicit or explicit meta-rule. Here, we truly are saying that this *should* be the rule, not just that it (in some extended sense) already *is* the rule. When invoking concepts of desert in this way, we are doing something akin to what we do when invoking concepts of "natural rights." To say that "P has a right to x" is to say that P has that right under existing law; to say that "P has a natural right to x" may just mean that that is what the law *should* be. "Desert" might similarly be used in both intra-systemic and extra-systemic senses. In the standard, intra-systemic sense, analysis focuses upon what the rules are; in the extended, extra-systemic sense, it focuses on what the rules should be. But calling them "rights" or "deserts" in this extended sense is not to say that they

moral force of positive desert-claims is derived from other sorts of moral arguments altogether, then here again (just as in chapters 2 and 8) the selfsame arguments that justify the systems in terms of which desert-claims can be lodged might also justify sacrificing claims of desert to some other sorts of claims altogether.

I I

The previous, conceptual challenge to the notion of positive desert-claims (to the notion that taxpayers positively deserve to keep what they have earned, or that the poverty-stricken positively deserve their suffering) has dealt in terms of certainties. That is to say, I have heretofore been talking of outcomes that would, without any doubt, have occurred in the normal course of affairs.

Such certainty itself is far from normal, however. Typically, all we can say is that it is more or less likely that some particular outcome would obtain in the absence of untoward interventions; only very rarely can we say that it is certain that any particular outcome would have occurred. This is especially true of the outcomes at issue in desert-based arguments about the welfare state. Someone who works harder usually, but not always, earns more money. Someone who quits an unskilled job in times of high unemployment usually, but not always, remains unemployed for some considerable time before finding another. Such uncertainties about what would naturally follow from any particular course of action do much to undercut any claims about what people deserve in consequence of those actions, as I shall here show.

In previous sections, we were concerned with the case where "P would get q in the normal course of events." I translated that into a desert-statement by substituting "deserves" for the phrase "would (certainly) get in the normal course of events."[15] Here we

---

already *are* rights or deserts in some extra-systemic way; it is merely to say that the rules should be changed in such a way as to make them rights or deserts in the standard, intra-systemic way. Extra-systemic references to rights or deserts are, I would argue, references to the *form* which expanded entitlements should take, rather than references to the grounds upon which those expansions are to be justified. I am grateful to Philip Pettit for suggestions along these lines.

[15] The familiar expression, "P deserves a break," would seem to belie this ordinary-expectation analysis of desert. For a "break" is, by definition, fortuitous—a matter of chance, luck. It therefore looks like something that we are not ordinarily inclined to say with any confidence at all "would happen," however many untoward events are bracketed off. Yet we still say, occasionally, that "breaks" are deserved. This usage can be assimilated to my "wouldy" analysis of desert in either of two ways. One points to the fact that sometimes "people make their own

are concerned with the case where "P would probably get q in the normal course of events." But that cannot be translated into a desert-statement by substituting "probably deserves" for the phrase "probably would get in the normal course of events." Surely it is wrong to say that someone who has purchased a lottery ticket probably deserves the prize; and more still that someone who has bought ten tickets is ten times more likely to deserve the prize than the person who has bought only one.

When introducing probabilities into the proposition "P deserves q," the probability does not attach to "deserves." It attaches instead to q. The person who has purchased one lottery ticket deserves a chance (i.e., some probability) of winning the prize. The person who has bought ten deserves ten times as many chances, or a probability ten times greater. But we would not (at least until after the drawing) want to say that either of them either absolutely or even probably deserves the prize.[16]

The "probability of getting q," which P deserves, is to be analyzed in terms of the probability which would obtain (or would have obtained) in the absence of "untoward interventions," analyzed here just as before. If P bought one of a thousand lottery tickets, he deserves a probability of $p = 1/1000$ of winning the prize. The reason is simply that that is the probability which

---

breaks." There are various ways in which you can tempt fate or force fortune. Being in the right place at the right time might be a matter of dumb luck or of careful planning. And so on. Insofar as it is this sort of thing to which we refer when saying, "P deserves a break," we are not really talking about "breaks" at all in the ordinary sense. We are instead merely saying that P has planned carefully and well, and that we would ordinarily expect such plans to bear fruit. P deserves a break in the same sense as before, i.e., P would ordinarily get a break in such circumstances, ceteris paribus. Alternatively, we might say "P deserves a break," meaning that term to be understood quite literally, when P has experienced an unprecedented run of bad luck. To say in these circumstances that "P deserves a break" is merely to express faith in the fairness of the processes that collectively travel under the name of Fortune. Someone who has rolled snake eyes five times in succession would not ordinarily roll snake eyes a sixth time. We would say he deserves a break in his luck, and by that mean that we would ordinarily not expect his luck to continue so bad for so long. Implicitly, we are threatening to start checking the dice if he doesn't get a break soon. We stick to our notion of what he deserves, even in the face of mounting evidence that that is not what we should expect him to get. The reason, once again, lies with the definition of what is "normal" and of what interferences with the normal course of events count as illegitimate (e.g., loading the dice).

[16] Of course, P does deserve q contingently—if the probabilities pan out, if his lottery ticket is drawn. And, of course, whether that contingency is realized may indeed be a matter of probabilities. So perhaps in some sense we might truly say that P probabilistically deserves q. But that is different from saying that P probably deserves q. The law has been singularly slow in coming to realize that "the chance itself is an interest worthy of redress" (King 1981: 1381).

would obtain absent untoward interventions, such as the organizers removing his ticket from the box before the drawing.[17]

The proposition that "P deserves the probability p of q" might be boiled down still further using the notion of a statistical expectation. That is to say, what P deserves is the product of p times q. If he bought one out of a thousand tickets for a lottery the only prize in which is $1000, his statistical expectation is a payoff of $1.[18] That is what he deserves—and that is all he deserves. In practice, of course, he will inevitably get either a little less or a lot more, either nothing or the whole $1000. And that in turn suggests that the outcomes of lotteries (and, indeed, of a broad class of analogously lumpy, probabilistic events) are inherently, to some greater or lesser extent, undeserved: the losers always deserve more (sometimes much more) than they get; the winners never deserve as much (sometimes not nearly as much) as they receive.

That my analysis yields this result is, I think, one of the larger points in its favor. It is in this respect clearly superior to many of the more standard analyses of personal deserts. Some analysts tend to assume that you deserve whatever you get, in the absence of contraindications (what I have called "untoward" interventions), just so long as there is something in your character or history to ground the desert-claim. Other analysts tend to assume that you do not deserve anything, in the absence of strong evidence in your character or history that you deserve it fully.[19]

[17] Some people (among them, John Passmore in a 1983 ANU seminar discussing an earlier version of this argument) would reply at this point that they are so strongly opposed to talking about deserts in a probabilistic context that they would not even regard removing a person's lottery ticket from the box as violating his deserts. But surely this is just an overextension of the perfectly proper principle that he does deserve any particular outcome. Surely he does at least deserve a chance, once he bought and paid for it in the form of the lottery ticket. David Miller (personal correspondence, 1986) would prefer to talk in terms of a person's "entitlements" rather than his "deserts" in this case, regarding the purchase of a lottery ticket as being akin to a contract. For that reason, entitlements are involved, too. But I see no reason for denying that deserts are involved as well. Certainly the person has done something (i.e., bought the ticket) to deserve a chance. I see no grounds for denying that that action can constitute the basis for a desert claim—or at least no grounds that would not also rule out other actions (such as training hard for a race) that advocates of desert-based moralities would clearly want to count.

[18] Pointing to the "statistical expectation" as the appropriate measure of deserts in such cases is essentially to invoke once again a notion of what constitutes the ordinary course of events. Calling something the "statistically expected" outcome is saying that that is what would ordinarily happen, in the sense either of it being the thing that is most likely to happen this time or of it being the thing that is most likely to happen in cases like this if they were repeated a great many times. In the ordinary course of events, this is what would happen; and that is what people therefore deserve.

[19] Nozick (1974: 213–27) is an example of the former, Rawls (1971: 73–75) of the

Both presumptions are untenable.[20] The person who buys a $1 lottery ticket surely has done something to deserve the $1000 prize. But surely the little thing he did—buy a $1 ticket—was far too little to ground the claim that he deserves the full $1000 prize. Setting the presumption one way leaves him deserving too much. Setting it the other way, too little. What he really purchased, and what he therefore deserves, is no more and no less than a chance of 1 in 1000 of winning $1000. Or, in statistical terms, what he has bought—and what he deserves—is the expected payoff of $1.

Consider, again, someone who takes risks with his health—driving without fastening his seat belt, for example. He has done something silly, and in some sense he deserves to suffer the consequences of such silliness. But being thrown through the windshield is surely far more punishment than he could be said to deserve.[21] He was, after all, running only a 1 in 10,000 chance of crashing. His deserts, calculated as in the lottery example above, would be only 1/10,000th of the pain he suffers going through the windshield.[22]

---

latter. Opponents of the fault system in accident law confront the same problem in reverse: "To treat fault as a necessary condition of legal liability—'no liability without fault'—means that a person who causes loss without fault should not be required to pay for it. But it also and necessarily means that the person to whom the loss is caused will have to bear the burden himself. We have therefore a different rule for plaintiff and defendant; the plaintiff but not the defendant must bear the burden of loss or injury caused without his fault." Conversely, and equally unjustifiably: "fault is like a magic talisman; once it is established, all shall be given the injured party. It is generally immaterial whether the fault was gross and the consequences trivial, or whether the fault trivial and the consequences catastrophic. . . . Yet we know very well that the consequences of a negligent action are often out of all proportion to the fault that gave rise to it. A piece of momentary thoughtlessness on the road may cost someone's life with incalculable loss to his wife and children. But similar acts of thoughtlessness may be committed by scores of others every day with no such disastrous consequences. . . . Thus it seems that whether an act of negligence ends up in the accident statistics or as a near miss is almost pure chance: it has little correlation with the defendant's culpability" (Atiyah 1970: 415, 417; see similarly Bohlen 1910, and Calabresi and Hirschoff 1972: esp. 1059 and 1085).

[20] As Day (1981: 65–66) terms them, "The 'victims of misfortune' fallacy rests on a failure to grasp the concept of chance. The 'no pure accidents' fallacy rests on a failure to appreciate the large part which chance plays in our lives. . . ." See further Day 1977.

[21] If crashes were truly the "normal" outcomes of such imprudence, then within my model I would have to say that the reckless driver truly would deserve to crash. But that would be true only if the crashes were certain, or at least so common as to be the standard outcome; and in such extraordinary circumstances this conclusion might not be all that counterintuitive after all.

[22] If risks are small and frequent, we may be prepared to let the wins and losses lie where they fall each time, trusting that things will soon balance themselves out. But that rationale works *only* where risks are small and frequent, as pointed out by

Where people are unlucky and risks turn into disasters, they might deserve to suffer somewhat. After all, they have taken the risks. But they do not deserve to suffer *that* much. We should therefore take steps to alleviate their suffering. Maybe not *all* their suffering. After all, they deserve *some* pain; it would be wrong, therefore, to do so much for them that they are left as well off as they would have been had they not taken any risks at all.[23] But more often than not nature takes care of that for us. People will typically have suffered some losses that we can do nothing to set right, so some of their suffering (whether or not it is *exactly* the right quantum, morally) will remain whatever we do.

The implications for social policy are clear: we should take steps to alleviate most of the suffering of people even if they have in some sense brought that suffering upon themselves, just so long as that suffering is markedly worse than they would have had, statistically, any reason to expect at the time of their actions.

Significantly, much the same conclusions were reached by much the same route by Winston Churchill, who, as Home Secretary in 1911, found himself arguing for social insurance schemes in the following terms:

> The penalties for misfortune are terrible to-day; they are wholly disproportionate, even when they are brought on by a man's own fault, either through the culpability of the individual or neglect of what is necessary to make him try or to make him take care. A man may have neglected to make provision for unemployment; he may have neglected to make provision for sickness; he may be below the average standard as a workman; he may have contracted illness through his own folly or his own misconduct. No doubt he is a less good citizen for that reason than others who have taken more thought and trouble. But what relation is there between these weaknesses and failings and the appalling catastrophes which occasionally follow in the wake of these failures ? . . . (Churchill 1911: 510)

Hicks (1941). Otherwise people may have to bear far larger costs than they deserve, for far longer than they deserve. Therein lies the fallacy of Hart and Honoré's suggestion (1959: 243) that "the justice of holding me liable, should the harm on that occasion turn out to be extraordinarily grave, must be judged in the light of the hundred other occasions on which, without deserving such luck, I have incurred no liability."

[23] For example, the British Workmen's Compensation Act originally compensated workers for only half the costs of their injuries; now the figure stands at seven-eighths (Atiyah 1970: chap. 14).

This proposition remains as true in our day as it was in the early days of Churchill's paliamentary career.

I I I

To say that P clearly deserves q, even if we are using the notion of positive desert in a truly moralized sense (as my previous arguments suggest is rarely justified), does not necessarily entail that P ought on balance morally to receive q. One reason may be that desert is only one consideration among many others carrying at least as much of a moral charge, and in any particular case those other considerations might outweigh claims of desert. Another more interesting reason—which is particularly applicable to the welfare state, and upon which I shall here concentrate—is that in certain sorts of circumstances questions of personal deserts are simply out of place.

A

Consider first the way in which needs trump deserts. Imagine an automobile accident. The drivers of both cars are brought into the hospital emergency room with identical injuries and identical prognoses. One of them was clearly to blame for the accident: his negligence caused the crash, and the policemen bringing the injured drivers in make sure that the doctors know that fact. The other driver was merely his innocent victim, and the policemen make sure the doctors know that, too.

Now, the innocent victim is clearly less deserving of his fate than the reckless driver is of his. In the normal course of events— i.e., absent the untoward intervention of reckless drivers—he would never have suffered these injuries. Does that, however, mean that emergency room medics should devote substantially greater efforts to treating the innocent victim than the guilty driver, even though their injuries and prognoses are identical? I think not.[24] And I would stick by that judgment even where re-

---

[24] The reason has to do with the deeper duty I discuss under the heading of "protecting the vulnerable" in Goodin (1985b) and in chapters 5 through 7 above. In chapter 3, I argued that *positive* discrimination—discrimination motivated purely by positive feelings of sympathy for someone—might be permissible. But discrimination is permissible only where we can be sure it is positive rather than negative—*for* one person, rather than *against* some other. In the case at hand, the medics could justify treating the innocent victim first if and only if they could be sure that their desire to do so grew out of positive sympathy for him, and not out of negative feelings toward the guilty driver. This is not only uncertain but actually highly un-

sources are desperately scarce, and we have enough to treat only one: flipping a coin rather than examining driving records is the right way to make that sort of tragic medical choice.

Part of the reason is no doubt that the guilty driver, though he may deserve some sort of punishment for his recklessness, does not deserve to suffer nearly as much pain in punishment as the accident has in fact inflicted upon him. Let us suppose he took a 1 in 10 chance of crashing: then he deserves only one tenth of the pain he is now experiencing; the rest we would put down to pure bad luck, which is totally undeserved. And similarly with most welfare claimants, as section II above has argued.

But that cannot be the whole story. If it were, we would reckon the medics right to devote ten percent less time and effort to treating the guilty driver than to treating the innocent driver; or we would think them right in treating the innocent victim first, even though he is less severely injured, just so long as his injuries are at least 90 percent as bad as those of the guilty driver. Both standard intuitions and conventions of medical ethics join in rejecting that sort of conclusion.[25]

Another part of the reason no doubt has to do with the social division of labor. It is the job of the courts, not the hospitals, to punish reckless drivers. Confident though the police may be in assuring doctors that one driver was at fault, the doctors would rightly ignore that information in treating the injured drivers. Their job is merely to patch up the injured, even if that is only so the courts will have a chance to hang them.

The position of social service departments is strictly analgous to that of hospitals in this respect. Both are in the business of providing emergency services to people, some of whom may well cease to exist without such assistance. For both, these urgencies preclude the sort of calm and considered judgment that would be required for a balanced decision on how to allocate credit or blame for what has happened. Both must therefore leave it to other agen-

---

likely. If the choice were between treating the two drivers and another victim of an unrelated and purely accidental event, then medics would presumably be no more sympathetic toward the road victim than toward the victim of the pure accident. Being a victim of another's reckless driving does not make you a *more* sympathetic figure. Rather, being a reckless driver makes the driver a *less* sympathetic figure. It is that sort of impermissible negative discrimination (disguised in the positive terms of "sympathy" for the victim) which any inclination to treat the one first would reflect. I am grateful to David Thame for raising this point.

[25] Officially, at least, "it makes no difference . . . whether a disease is 'deserved' or not" in whether or how physicians should treat it; this, according to Aubert and Messinger (1958) is one crucial difference between "the criminal and the sick."

cies to determine questions of deserts. What those "other agencies" should be might be unclear, especially in the case of the "undeserving poor." Perhaps, just as we allow reckless drivers to be sued in courts of law once doctors have them back on their feet, so too should we allow social service departments to take the "undeserving poor" to court for repayment of benefits, should they ever get sufficiently back on their feet to pay. That we do not do so, I submit, merely reflects the fact that so few of the "undeserving poor" ever get sufficiently back on their feet to make that effort worthwhile.

The latter consideration is important, I think. But more important still is the fact that there are simply some circumstances in which considerations of desert are simply out of place, and this is one of them. A perfectly general characterization of such circumstances remains elusive. But what is going on in this particular sort of case is clear enough. Needs are trumping deserts. If two people's needs are identical and both cannot simultaneously be met, then it might be permissible to decide which to favor on the basis of deserts.[26] But it is never permissible to allow desert-based considerations to outweigh needs-based ones. In the hospital emergency room, it surely *never* is right to treat the less seriously injured before the more seriously injured person with the same prognosis, however little the difference in the seriousness of their injuries or however much the difference in their responsibilities for

---

[26] Notice that I say here that needs enjoy priority over deserts; the argument of chapter 2 was merely that they should enjoy none over "mere wants." David Miller (personal correspondence, 1986) objects that "life-and-death" issues being at stake does not wipe out considerations of desert altogether, offering the following example: "X very stupidly falls into a stormy sea. Y very heroically dives in to rescue him, but also gets into trouble. I'd say we should rescue Y before X, even if X is going to get more badly knocked about. . . ." It is unclear what is meant by this example, however. As phrased, the implication is that we will be able to rescue both X and Y in the end—the question is merely who gets "knocked about" longer. But then their needs (understood in life-or-death terms, at least) would be equally well met no matter which we pulled out first. Thus, it is a tie, on the basis of needs, which we should rescue first—which is precisely the sort of situation in which I concede deserts a tie-breaking role. The hard question is this: Suppose we can rescue only one person, either X or Y: should we attempt to rescue Y rather than X, even if it is less probable that we will succeed in that effort than if we had attempted to rescue X, on account of Y's greater moral deserts? (Alternatively: should we attempt to rescue Y first, thereby accepting a greater probability that X will drown before we reach him than there would have been of Y's drowning had we attempted to save X first?) If, as Miller supposes, deserts retain some residual power, at least at the margins, there must be some probabilities sufficiently close to one another that would lead him to answer yes. For my part, the answer is clearly no: we should take our best shot at saving lives, and reserve recriminations for later.

the accident. And likewise in allocating social assistance to needy clients.

Certainly needs trump deserts in this way where life or death is at stake.[27] But it also seems to happen where the stakes are substantially lower. Suppose neither of the drivers in my earlier example had sustained life-threatening injuries. I think we would still balk at saying that doctors should treat the innocent driver first, even though the guilty driver was in 9.99 percent more pain.[28]

The same principles should apply, for the same reasons, to social welfare policy. It would be clearly wrong (except, perhaps, as a deterrent to others) to deny public housing or unemployment benefits to people who have recklessly vacated one apartment or job without having first arranged for another. In some sense, homelessness or unemployment is something which such people might be said to "have coming" to them in the ordinary course of events; and, on the analysis offered here of "deserts," that might mean that they deserve those outcomes. That is precisely the point

[27] Once again, the notion of deserts in the context of punishment proves to be a special case. There it sometimes is said that people deserve to be put to death for some particularly heinous crime. Even if we dissent from the substance of that judgment, we are nonetheless comfortable talking there in terms of "deserts" even though life-and-death issues are involved.

[28] In practice, it is clear that physicians—especially emergency room medics—do pass "moral judgment" of a kind on their patients. That is partly a matter of blaming them for violating physicians' own norms concerning what sorts of cases should be brought to an emergency room and what sorts should be left to outpatient clinics or private physicians. But that "moral judgment" is at least in part a more general reflection upon the moral character of patients and their actions. It distinguishes especially between patients who are suffering injuries that are "self-inflicted" in some sense and those that are not. On this, see Sudnow (1967: 100–9), Roth (1972), Ghodse (1978), Jeffery (1979), and Dingwall and Murray (1983). While it is clear from all these studies that physicians' opinions of their patients are affected by judgments of their "moral worth," it is far less clear how and to what extent these moral evaluations affect their *treatment* of patients. Certainly they lead to some harmful errors in classification: someone coming into an emergency room comatose, shabbily dressed, and smelling of alcohol, will often be thrown into the drunk tank without much careful investigation; and if, as may happen, his coma is the result of diabetes rather than drink, the consequences of this morally motivated oversight may be disastrous. Physicians' moral evaluations of patients might also affect the way in which they treat—or fail to treat—chronic conditions (such as diabetes), where the treatment requires the active cooperation of patients. And certainly it is clear that "bad" patients get less prompt and polite treatment in emergency rooms. What is also abundantly clear from these studies, however, is that "bad patients" suffering from acute and unambiguous life-threatening conditions receive precisely the same medical treatment as "good" ones. In this case, at least, it seems that morally the emergency room medics behave as this argument suggests they should.

that New Right writers who oppose welfare payments being made to the "undeserving poor" want to make. But there are various reasons to resist the policy implications of their analysis.

Some have to do with considerations raised in section II above. While the undeserving poor might not positively deserve social assistance, neither do they positively deserve in any sense (moral or otherwise) their plight absent assistance. Usually their only sin was recklessness or fecklessness. The most they can be said to deserve, even in purely statistical terms, is therefore some probability of suffering a bad outcome—the statistical expectation, say, of a rather worse job or house. (They might not deserve even that, if their recklessness or fecklessness were itself covered by some further excusing condition.) Complete homelessness or complete joblessness is far worse than the merely reckless or feckless deserve.

Other reasons to resist the policy implications of the New Right's analysis of the "undeserving poor" have to do with considerations raised in section I above. The reckless or feckless may deserve bad outcomes in some *statistical* sense of that being what the consequences of their recklessness or fecklessness would ordinarily be. But such statements about positive deserts are without any *moral* warrant. All such statements tell us is the way the world ordinarily works. Whether it should work that way is an open question. That is in itself quite enough to defeat any suggestion that bad outcomes are positively deserved in any moral sense. At the very least, we must say that those bad outcomes are neither deserved nor undeserved, morally speaking. And insofar as there is a moral case for making the world work some other way—insofar as there is a moral case for the welfare state, e.g.—we can go further still. Then the (morally) normal course of affairs should and hence would be one in which welfare officers stepped in to assist the reckless and the feckless. Those people thus deserve assistance. Failure to render it to them would constitute a morally improper "untoward" intervention in what is morally the normal course of affairs; any suffering that followed from that failure would itself then be seen as undeserved.

Beyond all that, however, is the further question of whether it would be right to let social unfortunates suffer, even if they deserve to suffer and even if the deserts in question are genuinely moral deserts. The argument here has been to suggest that it would not be right, at least where their suffering would be very great.[29] Needs should morally trump deserts, just as surely in the

[29] This may well explain the common view that the welfare state is right to act as

social security office as in the hospital emergency room. Those whose circumstances are rightly described as "desperate" should be given assistance, whether they deserve it or not.

B

There is another class of cases where considerations of deserts (fault, credit, blame, etc.) should be put into abeyance. This, generically, is that class of cases where questions of causation are particularly confused. The paradigm cases tend to arise within the realm of the law of accidents. There, "no-fault" principles have come to enjoy increasing prominence, starting (in common-law jurisdictions, anyway) with the 1897 British Workmen's Compensation Act, then with various no-fault automobile insurance schemes, and now with the far broader New Zealand Accident Compensation Act of 1972 (Palmer 1973).[30]

Of course, the no-fault impulse is motivated largely by economic considerations quite unconnected with any notions of moral deserts (Calabresi 1970). And insofar as there is a moral component to the argument, it derives largely from considerations of proportionality akin to those raised in section II above: whatever fault there may have been on whomsoever's part, the harm suffered is usually wildly out of proportion to that fault.[31]

---

a "safety net": it is right for needs to trump deserts where people's circumstances are truly desperate, but wrong to ignore deserts where they are not. What counts as "desperate" is, in turn, relative to the society in which you find yourself.

[30] Such schemes often purport to be essentially *insurance* schemes, whether voluntary (as automobile insurance still largely is) or compulsory (as Workman's Compensation), and whether underwritten privately (as are both schemes) or publicly (as is the New Zealand Accident Compensation scheme). But notice that, when introducing the no-fault principle, we treat bad risks (faulty parties) and good risks (innocent ones) the same, which of course violates the fundamental actuarial principles that underlie any genuine insurance scheme. This is a characteristic of "social insurance" systems quite generally. See Titmuss 1968: 173–87.

[31] As some early critics of the fault system write, "The findings of the individual psychologists who have studied accident proneness show . . . that there is little correspondence between dangerous conduct and moral fault such as carelessness or recklessness. . . . They point up the emptiness of the arguments, both from morals and expediency, which are currently used to support the fault principle of liability. They represent, in short, a strong further argument for comprehensive social insurance for accidents" (James and Dickinson 1950: 794). Similar arguments against the fault system were offered by the New Zealand Royal Commission leading up to the Comprehensive Accident scheme: the fault principle "stops short of attempting to see that the damages do not become disproportionate to the conduct which is said to justify them. The extent of liability is not measured by the quality of the defendant's conduct, but by its results. Reprehensible conduct can be followed by feather blows while a moment's inadvertence could call down the heavens" (Woodhouse 1967: para. 49).

There is another important source of this no-fault impulse in accident law, however, and this serves to define a separate class of exceptions to desert/fault principles. At least one of the reasons we want to resist the suggestion that liability ought be proportional to fault is that there is just too much fault on the part of too many agents for us to make any nonarbitrary allocations of fault, liability, or blame.

Such considerations were clearly what prompted inclusion of the no-fault principle in workmen's compensation legislation. The injured worker was ordinarily partially at fault, but so, too, were his co-workers, his supervisors, and his employers. Likewise in automobile accidents, fault is ordinarily shared between drivers, auto manufacturers, state highway departments, etc. So, too, New Zealanders have come to appreciate that with most accidents the "background conditions" created by society at large are often inextricably intertwined with personal negligence on the part of both the injurer and the injured. As the royal commission giving rise to this legislation observed:

> People have begun to recognize that the accidents regularly befalling large numbers of their fellow citizens are due not so much to human error as to the complicated and uneasy environment which everybody tolerates for apparent advantages. The risks are the risks of social progress, and if there are instinctive feelings at work today in this general area they are not concerned with the greater or lesser faults of individuals, but with the wider responsibility of the whole community. It is for these reasons that compulsory insurance for highway and industrial accidents is generally acceptable.
>
> Since we all persist in following community activities, which year by year exact a predictable and inevitable price in bodily injury, so should we all share in sustaining those who become the random but statistically necessary victims. The inherent cost of these community purposes should be borne on the basis of equality by the community [as a whole, through general taxation].[32] (Woodhouse 1967: paras. 89 and 56)

[32] Compensating people for accidents but not for diseases is something of an anomaly, as Atiyah (1970: chap. 20) points out. But once we come to recognize the social sources of disease, perhaps that anomaly too will be rectified. Indeed, the New Zealand Royal Commission explicitly recognized the illogic of compensating accidents but not sickness or disease, saying in justification merely that "it might be thought unwise to attempt to take one massive leap when two considered steps can be taken" and that "the proposals now put forward for injury leave the way

The basic principle seems to be this. Notions of personal fault are appropriate only where there is a small set of actors making discrete (separate or easily separable) and readily identifiable causal contributions to the outcome. Where many casual factors are deeply intertwined, any apportionment of fault between them would be arbitrary; and principles of blame, fault, or desert should therefore not apply.[33] As more and more cases are being seen as falling into this class, "the demise of tort law" and its accompanying notions of individual fault "is the inevitable result" (Cane 1982: 62).

Since the paradigm cases all come from accident law, the discussion here is invariably cast in terms of fault and liability for disagreeable outcomes. But the same sort of principle can surely apply, mutatis mutandis, to questions of how to apportion credit for agreeable outcomes.[34] There, too, desert statements only make sense where there are only a few actors who make discrete and readily identifiable causal contributions to the outcome. Where many causal factors are deeply intertwined, any apportionment of credit between them would be arbitrary; and principles of positive entitlement (the converse of fault) should therefore not apply.[35]

---

entirely open for sickness to follow whenever the relevant decision is taken" (Woodhouse 1967: para. 17).

[33] Or at least they should not apply *at this level*. Sometimes causation is unclear in the particular but clear enough in the aggregate. We might not be able to say whether any given worker's cancer was caused by exposure to carcinogens in the workplace, but we certainly can say that on aggregate such exposure increases the risks of such cancers by x percent. In such cases, it would be possible to apply the fault principle at one remove. The basic idea would be to require everyone to contribute to some common fund in proportion to their fault and draw out of it in proportion to their injuries, thus retaining the notion of fault but doing away with any notion of contributory fault for any *particular* accident. For discussion of such schemes see, Feinberg (1970: 215–16), Calabresi (1970: 302, 306), and Coleman (1974).

[34] The symmetry of these cases ordinarily goes unappreciated. That leads some writers on accident law to suggest, as a principle of charity, that we should compensate people for undeserved losses but allow them to enjoy undeserved benefits. That makes good enough sense, perhaps, when the "undeserved benefit" in view is simply not crashing when you have been driving recklessly (although even there some would dissent—see Feinberg 1970: 213–14). But when it is a vast fortune, as it may well be in the positive desert case, that principle of charity is obviously just *too* charitable.

[35] Neoclassical economists might be inclined to reply that, under certain conditions (e.g., continuous constant returns to scale), we can apportion responsibility for marginal products among the various factors of production (Arnold 1986). "But," as Sen (1982: 4) says, "even when all these assumptions have been made— quite a tall order—it is still arbitrary to assert that each resource's earnings reflect the overall contributions made by that resource to the total output. There is nothing in the marginalist logic that establishes such an identification. Marginal product

This, again, obviously has enormous implications for social policy. Cluttered causal histories characterize almost all outcomes of consequence in complex modern societies. There are very few things, indeed, which people can, therefore, be said unequivocally to deserve or not deserve. "Nothing," says Tocqueville (1835/1983: 111), "is so difficult to distinguish as the nuances which separate unmerited misfortune from an adversity produced by vice. How many miseries are simultaneously the result of both these causes!"

There are many possible responses to such a finding. Perhaps the most common is to introduce a presumption that would do all the work that proper analysis cannot. Setting the presumption one way, we might suppose that all the needy are deserving of assistance until proven otherwise; setting it the other way, we might suppose that none of the needy are deserving until proven otherwise. Given the confused causal relations involved, either presumption would prove irrebuttable. So at least these procedures would yield conclusive results to guide social policy.

It would be to misdescribe these results, however, to present them as being conclusions about people's "deserts" in any genuine sense. Such judgments follow from some peculiar facts about their characters and past performances. The policy conclusions here in view follow the presumption, which—because in circumstances of confused causation there is never enough information about people's characters and past performances—cannot be refuted. "Presumed desert" is not desert at all. It is not based on any particular facts about people's characters and performances, but rather on the absence of any such facts.

Thus, the only legitimate response in situations of confused causation would seem to be to put notions of desert (credit, blame, fault, etc.) into abeyance. When considering whether or not to provide aid to some social unfortunate, in circumstances of radically confused causal relations, the appropriate question is not

---

accounting, when consistent, is useful for deciding how to use additional resources so as to maximize profit, but it does not 'show' which resource has 'produced' how much of the total output" (see similarly Harcourt 1972; Nell 1987). Furthermore, marginalist calculations work by taking everything else as given, and computing only the difference made by factor x. Taking everything else as given is itself an arbitrary act. For one thing, the status quo is as arbitrary a baseline as any other (Rae 1975). For another, there is no nonarbitrary way of specifying exactly what each agent should be able to take with him when withdrawing from the production process and hence for deciding how much difference his contribution makes to the end-product (Roemer 1982a, b, c). All this lends credence to my claim that there is no nonarbitrary way to apportion causal responsibility for positive outcomes, at least in ordinary economic circumstances.

"Do they deserve to suffer?" or, "Do they deserve assistance?" but merely, "Is some social interest served by assisting them?"[36] Similarly, when considering whether or not to tax away some of rich people's fortunes, in circumstances of radical confusion about the causal relations that led to their being rich, the appropriate question is not, "Do they deserve their riches?" or, "Do they deserve to have them taken away?" but merely, "Is some social interest served by reallocating these resources?"

I V

The practical question addressed in this chapter concerns the proper role of considerations of personal desert in social policy-making. Here I have offered three independent reasons for supposing that they should have only a very limited role, if any at all. The first has to do with the concept itself: usually desert considerations will provide at most a negative moral warrant for remedying the effects of wrongful interventions in the normal course of events; they will only rarely, and even then only derivatively, provide any positive moral warrant for producing one particular outcome rather than another. The second reason has to do with the relationship between probabilities and deserts: luck largely mitigates deserts. The third has to do with the context in which desert judgments are employed: where causal relationships are complex or considerations of needs are in play, considerations of deserts are simply out of place. All of these characteristics are standardly present in the sorts of circumstances in which the welfare state ordinarily intervenes. The New Right's moralized attack on the welfare state, couched in terms of what people deserve to have happen to them, is therefore unsuccessful.

[36] What Tocqueville (1835/1983: 111–12) says *will* happen if you try to predicate poor relief on judgments of personal deserts in circumstances of confused causation is what I would argue *should* happen; and I think it should happen for precisely the same reasons Tocqueville gives for thinking that it will. Tocqueville asks, "What profound knowledge must be presumed about the character of each man and of the circumstances in which he has lived, what knowledge, what sharp discernment, what cold and inexorable reason. Where will you find the magistrate who will have the conscience, the time, the talent, the means of devoting himself to such an examination. Who would dare to let a poor man die of hunger because it's his own fault that he is dying?" From this, Tocqueville is led to conclude that, while "the laws may declare that only innocent poverty will be relieved, [the] practice will [be to] alleviate all poverty." And so it should, I would argue, if we cannot tell who is deserving and who is not.

ELEVEN

FREEDOM

The New Right's second moralistic challenge to the welfare state is couched in terms of "freedom." Market transfers are, paradigmatically, voluntary exchanges. Welfare state transfers, by definition, are not; they are collective, coerced, one-way transfers. In markets, both parties are notionally "free to choose" whether or not to enter into a transaction. In welfare states, neither is, in one sense or another (Friedman and Friedman 1981; Friedman 1962). By supplanting the market, the welfare state thus allegedly replaces a system of freedom with a system of unfreedom. This provides yet another point of New Right criticism of the welfare state.

Surely, however, the relationship between the welfare state is—at best and at worst—a mixed one. In some ways, the welfare state promotes certain kinds of freedom for certain people. In others, it restricts those or other freedoms, for those or other people. In this chapter, I shall try to assess the overall impact of the welfare state on freedom, taking all those partial influences into account.

After discussing various senses of "freedom" in section I, I shall, in section II, survey nine particular ways in which the welfare state might affect such freedoms. On balance, my findings tend to favor the welfare state. Allegations concerning its negative impact on freedom, where true, are contingently rather than inherently so. The positive impacts are more clearcut and work to the benefit of citizens as a whole in addition to the benefit of welfare recipients themselves.

I

The classical debate over the impact of the welfare state on social freedom turns on the distinction between "positive" and "negative" freedom. Laissez-faire liberals rely on the notion of negative

Material in this chapter is reprinted from Robert E. Goodin, "Freedom and the Welfare State: Theoretical Foundations," *Journal of Social Policy*, 11 (April 1982), 149–76, by permission of the editor and Cambridge University Press.

liberty, understood as "freedom from" the arbitrary will of another (Hayek 1944: 25; 1960: chap. 1). For them the crucial question is, "What is the area within which the subject . . . is or should be left to do what he is able to do, without interference by other persons?" (Berlin 1969: 121–22). By these standards, the meddlesome interferences of the welfare state look like restrictions on people's freedom which come without any compensating gains in terms of (negative) freedom.

On the other side of this set-piece debate, champions of the welfare state use a positive conception analyzing freedom as the "freedom to" do what one wants and accomplish one's goals (Berlin 1969: 131). Whereas their opponents focus narrowly on freedom as "opportunities," advocates of the positive conception also take notice of people's capacity to exercise those options (Taylor 1979; Plant 1985). Freedom, Tawney (1971: 228) insists, "involves a power of choice between alternatives which is real, not merely nominal, between alternatives which exist in fact, not only on paper." The second major difference between these two notions is that negative freedom emphasizes the coerciveness of human agents exclusively, whereas positive freedom also takes note of the coerciveness of social structures and other impersonal forces (Ball 1978). "Oppression . . . is not less oppressive when its strength is derived from superior wealth, than when it relies on a preponderance of physical force" (Tawney 1971: 228). By these standards, any restrictions on freedom necessary for the operation of the welfare state are more than outweighed by the increased freedom of its beneficiaries from poverty and suffering.

That classical debate is dangerously misleading, however, because it poses the issue entirely too starkly. Positive and negative freedom are not, as the labels imply, two absolutely contradictory notions. Indeed, they are not two different notions at all but only incomplete references to the same underlying conception of freedom. MacCallum (1967) has shown that freedom is a triadic notion taking the form "x is (is not) free from y to do (not do, become, not become) z," where:

x   ranges over agents;

y   ranges over such "preventing conditions" as constraints, restrictions, interferences, and barriers; and

z   ranges over actions or conditions of character or circumstance.

Thus, the debate between proponents of positive and negative freedom is not a debate over alternative conceptions but is only a debate over the proper emphasis within one and the same fundamental conception. Negative freedom emphasizes the relationship between x and y, positive freedom that between x and z.

Without getting too deeply embroiled in the positive/negative liberty dispute, I can at least sketch two arguments for thinking that the two notions should be used in tandem. Notice, first, that negative liberty refers to the set of opportunities available to a person, whereas positive liberty refers to his capacity to make use of them. Positive liberty determines, in Rawls's (1971: sec. 32) phrase, the "worth" of negative liberty. Rawls himself takes this as an excuse for ignoring positive liberty, since it is not, strictly speaking, an aspect of liberty at all. But the real effect of this move is surely to upgrade rather than downgrade those things that go into making liberty valuable. I can see no plausible reason for championing or cherishing *worthless* liberties. If you care about liberty, you must also care about those elements that make that liberty practically meaningful.[1] If you do not, I simply have to question the sincerity of your arguments for liberty in the first place.

Perhaps the most poignant example emerges from Ransom and Sutch's (1977: 198) masterful cliometric analysis of the position of the newly liberated slaves in the American South:

> In 1865 emancipation from chattel slavery permitted black Americans one kind of freedom. No one would deny that this freedom was a significant and meaningful one. . . . Yet this freedom was incomplete. . . . Land redistribution was aborted and the blacks were forced to begin their lives as free men and women without money, without tools, without work animals, without assets of any kind. . . . The economic institutions established in the post-emancipation era effectively operated to keep the black population a landless agricultural labor force, operating tenant farms with a backward and unprogressive technology. What little income was generated in excess of the bare essentials of life was exploited by monopolistic merchants.

---

[1] Liberties to do things you do not want to do are also, in some sense, worthless to you. But is would surely count as a restriction on your liberty (understood as your opportunity to exercise effectively your will in the world) to brainwash you so as to make you regard as especially valuable those options that your resources would permit you to pursue successfully.

In the introduction to *Four Essays on Liberty*, Berlin (1969: xlv–xlvi) himself concedes the larger theoretical point, saying,

> I should perhaps have stressed . . . the failure of [laissez-faire] systems to provide the minimum conditions in which alone any degree of significant "negative" liberty can be exercised by individuals or groups, and without which it is of little or no value to those who may theoretically possess it. For what are rights without the power to implement them? . . . The case for social legislation or planning, for the welfare state and socialism, can be constructed with as much validity from considerations of the claims of negative liberty as from those of its positive brother.

Judgments about the effective liberty afforded individuals by any socioeconomic system must combine considerations of both positive and negative liberty. Notional negative liberties—opportunities without the means of making use of them—are worthless. Likewise, increasing positive liberties in the absence of opportunities (negative liberties) to make use of them is to "provide the conditions of freedom, yet withhold freedom itself." (Berlin 1969: lv)

A second reason for considering positive liberties alongside negative ones is that that is the only way to make sense of our desire for "freedom-*maximizing*" institutions or, in Rawls's (1971: sec. 11) terms, ones guaranteeing each person the "*most extensive* basic liberty compatible with a similar liberty for others." Given the enormous difficulties in individuating and counting liberties, such calculations as these phrases imply might prove utterly indeterminate (O'Neill 1979). But insofar as we can do the sums at all, negative liberty—freedom from the interference of other human agents—would seem to be a constant-sum concept. One person is free from the interference of others only insofar as they are not free to interfere with him, and vice versa. This is captured in Tawney's classic phrase, "Freedom for the pike is death for the minnows" (1971: 164). Insofar as power is analyzed as power over other men rather than over nature (as in positive liberty), one person's power is predicated on another's powerlessness.[2] In a "po-

---

[2] More precisely, that is to say that for A *necessarily* to be free from B's interference, B must be unfree to interfere with A. It may, of course, be true that B is (morally or legally) free to interfere with A but is contingently unable to do so (owing to lack of resources, etc.). In that latter case, A might be said to be "free" from B's interference in a way that does not correspond to any correlative unfree-

sitional" economy, "what is possible for the single individual is not possible for all individuals" (Hirsch 1976: 6). Or, in Marxian terms, any one member of the proletariat is free to become one of the bourgeoisie, but "each is free only on condition that the others do not exercise their similar freedom" (Cohen 1979: 23; 1983). Where constant-sum games such as these are involved, it makes no sense to talk of maximizing liberties across society as a whole. The total always sums to the same constant. There is nothing to choose between alternative systems on the basis of sum-total liberties that they afford.

A weaker form of the libertarian goal might shift the emphasis to guaranteeing equal distribution of liberties, constant though the sum total may be. This would stress the second half of Rawls's (1971: sec. 11) requirement that social institutions promote the "most extensive basic liberty *compatible with a similar liberty for others.*" This goal at least makes sense in a constant-sum game. But, unlike the first, this form of argument forces us to move beyond the narrow terms of negative liberty to justify the goal in view. As Peter Jones (1982: 233) points out, "To prefer equal liberty to unequal liberty is to prefer equality to inequality rather than freedom to unfreedom." The simple fact that we value liberty, understood in negative terms, can explain why we should wish to *maximize* it. Something else is required to explain why we should want to *equalize* liberty.

There may be other values, having nothing to do with liberty, to which we could appeal to explain our fondness for equalizing liberty. Perhaps the concept of "respect for persons" plays this role in Rawls's (1971) theory. Insofar as we want to trace the value of equal liberty to something about *liberty*, rather than other values, however, we must forsake the negative conception.

If we believe that the goal of maximizing or equalizing liberties is morally important (or, in the former case, even coherent as a goal), we must be talking in terms of a positive-sum concept. In particular, we seem to be distinguishing—as with the positive liberty concept—between liberties according to their worth. Although guaranteeing some liberties always restricts others, liberty on net may be maximized because the more important liberties are secured through the sacrifice of the less important ones (Berlin

---

dom on B's part. But that would be in a much weaker sense of "contingently free" that is much more sensitive to shifting contingent circumstances than the sense of "necessarily free." In that latter sense, freedom is indeed a fixed-sum concept. I am grateful to Michael Saward for calling this point to my attention.

1969: xlvii–xlix). And an egalitarian distribution of liberties accomplishes this most successfully on the plausible assumption that liberties display decreasing marginal utility: someone already rich in opportunities and abilities would derive less satisfaction from an incremental increase in his liberty than would a person with very restricted opportunities and abilities from an increase in his.[3] All this makes perfectly good sense in terms of negative liberty. Hence I deem it particularly important to include the positive conception alongside the negative one when evaluating social institutions.

In addition to these two familiar notions of freedom, I also suggest that we use two other rather less familiar ones in such evaluations. One is "psychological freedom." By this, I do not mean "feeling free," which, of course, has nothing to do with how free one really is. (The slave can feel free even though he is actually in chains, etc.) The phrase refers instead to freedom from internal psychological fetters, i.e., to the subjective capacity to avail oneself of powers and opportunities objectively available (Bay 1961). This might be regarded as merely an aspect of positive freedom. It is, however, a particularly crucial aspect, since the absence of psychological freedom can preclude the exercise of all other types.

The second rather less conventional sense of freedom I shall be using here is "moral freedom." This picks up on the classical idealist argument that how *much* total freedom institutions offer is less important than *which* freedoms they offer. T. H. Green, for example, maintains that

> the mere removal of compulsion, the mere enabling a man to do as he likes, is in itself no contribution to true freedom. . . . The ideal of true freedom is the maximum of power for all members of human society alike to make the best of themselves. (1881: 371–72)

I doubt that it pays to be very dogmatic about what "making the best of themselves" amounts to, especially in the present context. For Rousseau and Kant, "moral freedom" would be equated with an "autonomous will." Others might fill out the phrase differently. Surely, however, all can agree that a wider range of freedoms is less desirable if, as a condition of obtaining the wider choice, the

---

[3] Any fuller argument for equal liberty in terms of diminishing marginal utility would, of course, have to take into account indivisibilities and complementarities. Notice that the same basic model lies unacknowledged behind Rawls's (1971: sec. 82) argument for the "priority of liberty," which seems better interpreted in terms of ordinary-shaped indifference curves displaying decreasing marginal utility.

most morally desirable option is foreclosed (Goodin 1976: 119). This is the more general criterion of moral freedom I shall be using. It consists in the freedom to meet moral demands imposed internally (by an individual's own principles) or externally (by moral truths demonstrable independently of them).

I I

The bulk of this chapter is devoted to a survey of ways in which the welfare state may affect freedom. The baseline against which its performance will be judged will, unless otherwise specified, be the free market laissez-faire state. Naturally, some of the claims will turn out to be ill-founded, and others point in opposite directions: the welfare state increases the freedom of some people while restricting that of others; it imposes certain sorts of constraints in the process of removing others; it frees us to achieve certain sorts of outcomes while preventing us from achieving others. Thus it will be necessary, in the concluding section of this chapter, to try setting losses off against gains. To help make this a more precise and systematic balancing, I shall fully and explicitly specify all three elements of each freedom in question, following Mac-Callum's (1967) format.

A. Infringement of Property Rights

Claim: The welfare state reduces the freedom *of* taxpayers
      from legal obstacles
      to dispose of their property as they please.

What crucially distinguishes private charities from state welfare services is, after all, that the former are financed through voluntary contributions whereas the latter are financed out of coercively extracted tax revenues. Even if we repudiate Nozick's overblown polemic against taxation as "forced labor" (1974: 169), I think we have to concede that it does somehow restrict our freedom to use and abuse our possessions as we please. True, few people actually resist paying their taxes. But that hardly proves that they are uncoerced, since there is (as everyone knows) a coercive machine prepared to enforce tax claims if need be. And, true, many people *might* have contributed happily to the aims of the welfare state without coercive threats. But the point remains that those threats have deprived them of the opportunity of not contributing, were

they so inclined. We cannot say "contributions" to the welfare
state were "freely" given unless people were also free to do otherwise (cf. Cohen 1979).

It is crucial, however, that we apply a common standard across
the board in assessing the coerciveness of alternative social arrangements. If what the rich man loses when his property is redistributed is described as a loss of freedom, then the gain to the poor
must similarly be described as a gain of freedom (Jones 1982). If
what the monopolist does when exercising his overwhelming bargaining power is described as infringing the freedom of others, as
libertarians concede, then they must also concede that any contract predicated on unequal bargaining power (in capitalist employment markets, for example) infringes freedom to some greater
or lesser extent (Miller 1983; Zimmerman 1981; Cohen 1981: 5–6).

To evaluate the restrictions of one regime, we must consider
those that would be imposed under alternative regimes. Much as
any one institution curtails, it might turn out that none can do
better. In the present case, the alternative to coercive taxation is,
presumably, respecting rights to private property. There, however, we find "a hidden presumption . . . that private property
. . . does not itself constitute a barrier to freedom . . ." (Lindblom
1977: 46). That is obviously untrue. The freedoms which property
rights secure for one individual or group always come at the expense of another: the landowner's rights make me a trespasser;
and had I right of way across his land, his liberty to plough as he
pleases would be impaired. The distribution of property rights—
and their redistribution—is necessarily a constant-sum game.
Freedoms that are taken away from one person are given to another; or freedoms taken from a person in one capacity (e.g., landowner) are returned to him in another (e.g., rambler). No net loss
of freedom for society as a whole, as distinct from individuals
within it, is involved in redistributive taxation. Thus, there is no
basis in terms of freedom (as opposed, perhaps, to justice or efficiency) for objecting to it.

A final argument for the noncoerciveness of taxation turns on
the familiar proposition that many of the goods we would like to
have provided come in the form of "public goods," which all must
enjoy if anyone does.[4] Since everyone will enjoy the good equally,

[4] "The most compelling examples of collective public goods have always seemed
to be national defense, law and order, and public health. What is their particular
appeal? Is it that they are collective consumption goods? So is television. It is . . .
rather . . . that they are part of and condition the *environment* of the society. . . .

whoever pays for it, everyone waits for someone else to pay the costs. The "logic of collective action" is such that relying upon purely voluntary provision results in gross undersupply, if not necessarily total nonsupply (M. Taylor 1976), of mutually desired public goods. Seeing that this is the inevitable outcome in systems relying on voluntary provision, all of us would agree to an enforceable contract compelling each of us to contribute to the costs of collective goods. While we would all rather be free riders and let others pay our way, we see that a system of "mutual coercion mutually agreed upon" is preferable to the *real* alternative, viz., going without the goods altogether. Insofar as we can subsume welfare state services under such a model, any coercion entailed in taxing people to pay for them seems on a par with "coercing" people to keep their own contractual commitments. In one sense, "coercion" may be involved, but at another, deeper level there really is none at all (Samuelson 1954; Olson 1965; Schelling 1971; Hardin 1968).

B. Uniformity

Claim: The welfare state reduces the freedom *of* citizens
      from legal regulations
      to display diverse tastes for certain public services.

Universalism is a hallmark of the welfare state. That everyone enjoy a legal guarantee of the same social minimum is the defining feature of the "welfare state" as shown in chapter 1. Libertarians such as Nozick (1974: 93–94) are quick to point out that some people enjoy the public goods in question less than other people do, and it is therefore unfair to tax them the same as we do those with stronger tastes for the goods. But there are solid technical arguments for believing that we cannot levy taxes for public goods in proportion to the benefits people perceive themselves receiving from them. These arguments arise from the problem of securing an honest revelation of people's true preferences: where public

---

Looked at this way they suggest other things that affect the environment and thus create externalities not linked to particular goods: for example, the literacy rate, the level of unemployment, the crime rate, the rate of technological progress, and importantly, the pattern of distribution of income and wealth" (Steiner 1970: 31). Miller (1981: 326) similarly argues that those goods that are necessarily public are so "because they meet desires which are interpersonal in nature. If I gain satisfaction from living in a society which has certain over-all features [e.g., "cooperative modes of organization" or an "egalitarian" distribution of income and wealth], this good necessarily cannot be provided for me without simultaneously being provided for everyone else."

goods are involved, everyone has an incentive for understating his taste, thus minimizing his own tax bill with little reduction in the total amount of the public good society provides to him and everyone else (Samuelson 1954). Any unfairness arising from the disjunction between taxes paid and benefits received is, therefore, inherent in the provision of collective goods.

Why, then, do we insist on offering the goods in question in the form of collective goods? Sometimes it is assumed that goods are provided in the form of public goods because, for some technical reason, that is the only way that they *can* be provided. That supposition is almost always in error. Virtually all public goods are provided in the form they are for reasons of convenience or policy rather than of natural necessity (Margolis 1955). Certainly we could imagine alternative ways of providing welfare services, for example. We might allow people to draw out only so much national insurance as they have paid into their accounts. Or we might allow people to opt out of the public system entirely, making private provision for old-age pensions and medical insurance if they preferred (Hayek 1960: chap. 19; Friedman 1962: chap. 11; cf. Higgins 1982: 186–88). Or, at the very least, we might make levels of welfare payments a matter for local decision, so people who want low welfare and low taxes can sort themselves into one community and those wanting high levels of both can form another (Tiebout 1956). Any of those or various other arrangements would make welfare something less than a full-fledged collective good, equally available to everyone.

While the welfare state goes a fair way toward this collective good "ideal," the extent of the uniformity it imposes must not be exaggerated. For one thing, only a limited range of "essential" goods and services are distributed by the welfare state. For another, the welfare state only sets minima. Substantial variation remains, as many people exceed the bare minimum level of welfare which the state guarantees for all. Nevertheless, the welfare state does impose a certain measure of uniformity and restrict people's freedom to pursue their own tastes to this limited extent. Such restrictions can, however, be justified in terms of freedom itself, as the following two subsections indicate.

C. *Impartiality*

Claim: The welfare state enhances the freedom *of* citizens
from psychological obstacles
to display moral impartiality.

315

One of the greatest advantages of a rule of uniformity is that it precludes partiality, favoritism, and special pleadings. Where people are forced to consume collective goods *as* collective goods, the only way anyone can increase his own allotment is by increasing everyone's: "One cannot work for someone else without also working for oneself" (Rousseau 1762b: bk. 2, chap. 4). If we all must send our children to the same state schools or use the same public health facilities, we will all feel the need to provide a higher-quality service than we would have done had there been the opportunity to opt out of the public sector (Hirschman 1971).

The point is not just that the poor thereby get better medical or educational services. More importantly, everyone is obliged to behave in a more ethical manner. A rule of uniformity prevents people's judgments on the appropriate levels of public services being influenced by particularistic considerations of how likely they are to have to rely on them. Wealthy Californians who vote against property tax levies do so less out of a principled opposition to the welfare state and more out of unprincipled regard for their own personal interests. They know they will not have to go to the public wards of California state hospitals when they are ill, etc. This sort of partiality and favoritism is only natural. But it is, on almost any account, the antithesis of "justice" and, indeed, of "morality" itself.

Not only is this suppression of partiality intrinsically desirable but, more to the present point, it contributes to people's freedom. At first, this claim might seem paradoxical. Restricting people's opportunity sets would ordinarily be thought the opposite of increasing their freedom. The air of paradox dissolves, however, if we see it as a matter of freeing people from psychological fetters. Suppose a person, having firmly resolved to stop smoking, removes all tobacco products from his house. In one sense, this renders him less free than before, by depriving him of the opportunity to sneak a quick smoke. In another far more important sense, however, it frees him from irresistible temptations, induced by his psychological (indeed, physiological) dependence on nicotine, to break his resolution (Elster 1979: chap. 1). A rule of uniformity, by denying people the opportunity to pursue their own interests at the expense of those of others, similarly frees people from ordinary psychological pressures to behave immorally in this way.[5] As

---

[5] Under a rule of uniformity, it is both the selfish and the selfless thing to do to vote for a tax/benefit package that promises each and every person most benefits on net. But that is in itself an argument, addressed to one's compulsively selfish side, to cease thinking in exclusively selfish terms. If there is no longer any prac-

in the case of nicotine, the temptations might otherwise have proven irresistible. But that is all the more reason for people (assuming that they are of good, albeit weak, will) to wish them removed.

By an argument paralleling one offered in chapter 3, it can be shown that temptations toward partiality might be removed either through cleverly designed social institutions or through the workings of uncertainty. The rule of uniformity as enforced (however imperfectly) by the welfare state renders self-serving behavior impossible in terms of the social game. Self-serving behavior can also be rendered impossible by the uncertain nature of the social world: if you do not know what your own future holds, then you will be forced to consider the interests of all "representative individuals" in future societies equally, because you may yourself come to occupy any of those slots (Goodin 1976: chap. 6).

Most of the time that sort of uncertainty is lacking. You can usually make pretty shrewd guesses about your own future, and make selfish choices accordingly (Benn 1978). Occasionally, however, this more radical uncertainty forces impartial choices upon us. Modern war is one of the more important sources of such uncertainties. Notice Titmuss's parallel explanation of the genesis of the modern British welfare state through the exigencies of wartime social services:

> That all were engaged in war whereas only some were afflicted with poverty and disease had much to do with the less constraining, less discriminating scope and quality of the wartime social services. Damage to homes and injuries to persons were not less likely among the rich than the poor and so . . . the assistance provided by the Government to counter the hazards of war carried little social discrimination, and was offered to all groups in the community. The pooling of national resources and the sharing of risks were not always practicable nor always applied; but they were the guiding principles.

And the impartiality that risk-pooling in wartime forces upon us shapes the postwar social institutions as well. "It follows that the acceptance of these social disciplines . . . made necessary by war, by preparations for war, and by the long-run consequences of war,

---

tical difference between selfishness and selflessness in their action-implications, then there is no longer any objective basis for compulsively thinking in selfish rather than selfless terms. One may end up voting for the same policies, but for different reasons. In that way, a rule of uniformity would free people to think moralistically.

must influence the aims and content of social policies not only during the war itself but in peace-time as well" (Titmuss 1976: 85). The impartiality that naturally emerges under certain special circumstances, like wars, is ossified into social engineering arrangements (such as welfare state rules of uniformity) which are to serve as their functional equivalents when the special circumstances have passed (Dryzek and Goodin 1986).

Both historically and analytically, then, the rule of uniformity should be seen as a device for forcing impartiality upon people. Far from constraining their freedom, however, that contributes to it. People are thereby freed from temptations, which may have been psychologically irresistible, to behave in an immorally self-serving fashion.

D. Paternalism

Claim: The welfare state reduces the freedom *of* citizens
　　　 generally, and welfare recipients especially,
　　　 from legal obstacles
　　　 to pursue their own preferences.

The welfare state is widely regarded as a paternalistic institution. The very name gives the game away: a state promoting people's *welfare* is serving their objective interests rather than their subjective preferences. In practice, welfare states often seem to live up to their billing. They prevent people from working under dangerous conditions (Green 1881) or from buying dangerous products (Buchanan 1970). They distribute benefits "in kind," which guarantees that people get the food or medicine they need, rather than passing cash which could be spent instead on things (drink, gambling, etc.) which people prefer (Tobin 1970; Weale 1978). As Hayek (1960: 261) complains,

> If . . . government uses its coercive powers to insure that men are given what some expert thinks they need . . . people thus can no longer exercise any choice in some of the most important matters of their lives, such as health, employment, housing, and provision for old age, but must accept decisions made for them by appointed authority on the basis of its evaluation of their need.

One narrow reply to these criticisms is that people's informed preferences do not really vary all that widely over the limited range of basic goods that the welfare state provides. The fundamental premise of "negative utilitarianism" is that, much as people's tastes for positive goods such as automobiles and dishwashers may vary, they can all agree on what makes them miserable (Acton 1963; Watkins 1963; Moore 1970). Insofar as people seem to disagree, it is only because their preferences on the matter are ill-informed. This is clearest in cases like product safety, where the ignorance in question concerns the probability that the machine will blow up in your face. The argument is less clearcut, but I think equally powerful, in cases where the ignorance surrounds your own future preferences—most particularly, where you are insufficiently sensitive to just how miserable you would be if the accident befell you.

Even if we are willing to respect people's tastes in general, we should draw the line at respecting tastes for risks (cf. Sugden 1982a). People are notoriously bad at assessing the probabilities (and are even worse at anticipating their evaluations of possible outcomes) in "low probability, high risk" ventures. Furthermore, risk markets not only reflect but exaggerate biases in the existing distribution of social resources. Finally, the protection that insurance schemes and tort law ostensibly offers those with no taste for gambling is woefully inadequate (Goodin 1982c: chap. 8).[6]

It has, for example, been argued that "passive restraints" such as automobile air bags (which automatically inflate upon impact) deprive passengers of the freedom to risk a crash unprotected (by, e.g., not fastening their seat belts). (Reppy 1979: 153; Merrill 1978) I simply cannot see this as a serious infringement of the freedom of the ordinary passenger, who may have failed to belt up out of carelessness or haste but not out of a considered preference for death over life (Dworkin 1971: 121). Likewise with people who would "willingly" purchase risky products or do risky jobs, re-

---

[6] Notice that those risks we are most anxious to regulate are those where risk markets fail in one or more of these ways. We make superannuation schemes compulsory because people underestimate how miserable it would be to be old and indigent. Making medical or flood insurance compulsory is justifiable because, although people might intellectually know the risks, they are psychologically incapable of imagining themselves the victims of catastrophic illness or natural disasters. We are much more concerned to legislate against occupational hazards than against analogous consumer ones because economic pressures force people to run enormous risks in the workplace for derisory rewards. And we think government should control the dumping of hazardous chemical wastes and the development of nuclear power plants because no private underwriter would insure such activities (and, in any case, liability would be difficult to establish, since cancers carry no certificates of origin).

stricting their freedom to pursue the risky course may (if the risks are big enough and bad enough) increase their freedom to pursue their ultimate goals. I concede that this argument turns on a reading of "true" rather than "revealed" preferences, much to the dismay of libertarians and liberal economists. But, as the latter well know, choices reveal preferences only very imperfectly (Sen 1973). Often we can indeed surmise people's actual preferences better, and serve them more effectively, by tracing out the practical implications of their own life plans (Weale 1978b: 170–71; Goodin 1982c: chap. 3; 1985a).

E. Red Tape

Claim: The welfare state restricts the freedom *of* welfare
      recipients
      from legal (bureaucratic) obstacles
      to live their lives as they please.

In order to become and stay eligible for certain welfare state services, recipients must comply with more or less demanding regulations imposed by the sponsors of these programs. The Old Age Pension Act of 1908, for example, denied payments to any Briton convicted of drunkenness or any other crime in the previous two decades: people were rendered unfree to drink excessively and to draw a pension simultaneously (Higgins 1982: 180). American recipients of unemployment insurance are not free to loaf: they must demonstrate that they have been trying to find work in order to draw their money. Recipients of Aid to Families with Dependent Children (AFDC) payments were not originally free to cohabit: before the advent of the AFDC-UE program (and still, in states not participating in that program), having an ablebodied man in permanent residence would cause them to forfeit their benefits (Rainwater and Yancey 1967).

There is no point in denying that such strings are attached to welfare-state services, or that these are the cause of real annoyance or humiliation. But it is just worth asking to what extent these constraints are a *necessary* feature of the welfare state. Some of these more authoritarian accompaniments certainly seem to have very little to do with the fundamental goal of providing for people's *welfare*. Instead they are designed to penalize their moral shortcomings, saving the money for the "deserving" poor rather than just giving it to people strictly on account of their poverty, which is what the "welfare" goal would require (Stone 1978; Higgins 1982; Lipsky 1984; Schorr 1985).

In another sense, however, such restrictions *are* implicit in state welfare provision. They follow from the imperatives of administering programs spending other people's money (cf. Higgins 1982: 188–90). Social workers, charged with the responsibility of spending public money, have an obligation to make sure that the money is used as it was intended. Perhaps the intentions were perverse, or perhaps their political masters wrote more restrictions into the law than was strictly required. But even in the best conceivable program, there will have to be some restrictions on the behavior of beneficiaries.

The question remains whether and how badly this constrains their freedom. Here, ironically, it is the spokesman for negative liberty who would (or should) rush to the defense of the welfare state. These restrictions can be represented as conditions of receiving public assistance. In this way, they are not fundamentally different from the conditions set by trading partners for surrendering their commodities in market exchanges ("I will give you some of my cloth if you will give me some of your dye," etc.). Provided the traders/welfare-recipients have not been compelled by any *human* agents to accept offers of trades/welfare; their negative liberty is not infringed by the conditions attached to such trades/payments. Advocates of the positive conception of liberty, however, would see that welfare states

> often supply essential services which citizens cannot obtain elsewhere. Government agencies may have a monopoly on the service, clients may not be able to afford private services, or they may not have ready access to them. Potential welfare recipients in a sense "volunteer" to apply for welfare . . . but their participation in the welfare system is hardly voluntary if they have no income alternatives. (Lipsky 1980: 54)

Just as desperate economic circumstances can "force" people into notionally free market exchanges, so, too, can they force people to submit to notionally voluntary conditions attached to welfare services. Those who impose and administer those conditions on recipients of state services are thus being coercive on this broader understanding.

The solution is, presumably, to establish firm rules so that administrators and caseworkers have no discretion and hence no coercive power to threaten to withhold benefits. This is the generalization, suggested in chapter 7, of the classic case for "welfare rights" (Marshall 1965; 1981: chap. 5). Indeed, Reich (1964) has argued that legal entitlements to state-provided services constitute a "new property" with rights strictly analogous to traditional property rights. Saying that administrators have no discretion in how to treat people falling within a certain class, however, leaves them broad discretion in determining who is indeed within the category. A large part of the social worker's task is in "rationing" services, applying restrictive criteria to determine who is legally entitled to receive the services. These decisions are rarely clearcut (Nelson 1980; Lipsky 1980; Foster 1983). In exercising this sort of discretionary judgment, administrators do make clients subject to their arbitrary will, to some greater or lesser extent.

Although restrictive welfare services necessarily restrict the freedom of recipients, this might be justified in terms of the increased freedom such provisions afford to the rest of society. People care about the nature of their social environment. That is one of the reasons they provide public goods as public goods (Steiner 1970: 31). And that is one of the reasons they impose restrictions on the uses that may be made of public benefices, to the point of insisting on in-kind rather than cash transfers. They do not simply internalize the utility function of a poor person as a whole (cf. Hochman and Rogers 1969). At most, they internalize selected components of the poor person's utility function. Certain dimensions of poverty they regard as an unattractive feature of their social environment, while others they happily ignore. Inequality in general might not bother them, while inequality in certain basic services such as medical care does. "To have equality in the distribution of medical care and still permit inequality in the distribution of other goods and services, it is necessary to provide a voucher or in-kind distribution of medical sevices" (Thurow 1974: 192). Perhaps it is niggardly of people to restrict their concern in this way, but such constrained benevolence is what the welfare state is all about—restricting the scope of inequality rather than eliminating it altogether. If people are to be free to act upon such sentiments, restrictions on welfare recipients are necessary.

F. Dependency

Claim: The welfare state reduces the freedom *of* welfare
recipients
from psychological and economic pressures
to pursue alternative social and political arrangements.

A closely related criticism is that the welfare recipients become virtual slaves of the state. They become dependent, both economically and psychologically, upon the welfare services of the state, and are unable to contemplate (or, at any rate, to pursue) a range of social and political alternatives that would otherwise be available and attractive to them (cf. Campbell 1981; Higgins 1982). There are various ways to make this connection. One is the traditional conservative claim that the spirit of the welfare recipient is broken, that he becomes a slovenly lout who cannot imagine making a living in any other way. Another is the anarchist claim that living under any state—but especially a welfare state—causes traditional "mutual aid" mechanisms to atrophy (M. Taylor 1976: chap. 7; 1982). Another still comes from disappointed revolutionaries, who see social welfare as a method of buying off potentially disaffected classes: they are given a stake in the existing regime, and are naturally reluctant to bite the hand that feeds them (Cloward and Piven 1971; Higgins 1978; 1980).

The first of these claims is discussed more fully in chapter 12. Suffice it to say, for now, that I there find it without any substantial theoretical or empirical merit.

As regards the anarchist version of this argument, conclusions must be rather more tentative. Certainly it is true that state institutions can take the place of old networks, which then fall into disuse and eventually break down altogether. At that point, people are unfree to use institutions that no longer exist, and are dependent upon the state instead. No doubt this has happened in some places and to some extent. The question is simply whether it *must* happen. Obler's (1981) case study of one East Anglian village suggests otherwise: mutual aid practices coexist alongside the welfare state, particularly to provide services (e.g., of a social or recreational kind) unavailable from the state social services.

The welfare state might encourage the growth of these social networks by doing its work *through* them, reinforcing mutual aid institutions rather than supplanting them. Dutch and Belgian welfare states, for example, rely upon the ancient religious and linguistic communities for front-line administration of state welfare services (Brenton 1982; Kramer 1985). Such tribalism can, of course, be opposed in the name of national integration and sometimes even in the name of freedom itself—people can become far more dependent, materially as well as psychologically, upon their traditional communities than they ever could upon the welfare state. Be that as it may, the present point is merely that if we want to encourage the growth of mutual aid institutions the welfare state can be arranged to do so.

In assessing the third (cooptation) version of the welfare-dependency argument, we must bear our present focus firmly in mind. The question is whether the welfare state infringes people's freedom. In answering this question, the intentions of the founders of the welfare state are irrelevant. All that matters are the effects of the institutions. (The founders may have intended to coopt workers, but failed; or the real effect of welfare provision may be to reduce the freedom of workers to rebel, although the intent was purely humanitarian.) Furthermore, what workers actually do in reaction is beside the point. Even if they do, in the end, rebel against welfare states, all that proves is that their freedom was not eliminated altogether. It does not prove that it was not restricted, perhaps severely.

The question must, instead, be addressed philosophically. Champions of negative freedom, looking only at the number of options notionally available to people, would see no loss of freedom: welfare recipients are formally as free or unfree to rebel now as before, unless perhaps they were required to swear a loyalty oath as a condition of receiving welfare payments. (Even then, advocates of negative liberty would say that they are not forced by any human agents—which are the only forces they count—to accept the payment and the associated strings.) Advocates of positive liberty would, however, go on to consider the relative "eligibility" of the various options that are notionally available. By these standards, which I regard as clearly more appropriate, the welfare recipient is indisputably less free to rebel. The more of a stake he has in the existing arrangements, the more constraints there are preventing him from overthrowing it. The option is formally still open to him, but it is considerably less eligible than it once was.[7] I am not persuaded that this is an important criticism of the welfare state: the better off a state makes people, and the more it increases their freedom from natural constraints, the less free they are to rebel against it; which merely proves to me that the latter freedom

[7] Here I am assuming that how "eligible" an option is—and hence how "free" you are to pursue it—is in part a function of the costs that you will incur in the course of pursuing it. I am further assuming that among the costs to be reckoned here are "opportunity costs," i.e., the value of the best option that you forgo in the course of pursuing the one you do. Then cooption, by having made one option more eligible/free, really has made another (viz., revolution) less eligible/free.

is of strictly limited value. But I see no point in denying the obvious, viz., that it has decreased in this respect, at least.

G. Irreversibility

Claim: The welfare state reduces the freedom *of* citizens
   from bureaucratic and political obstacles
   to pursue alternative social and political arrangements.

The previous argument considered economic and psychological barriers preventing welfare recipients from rejecting the welfare state. This one points to political and bureaucratic obstacles to citizens more generally repudiating and dismantling the welfare state apparatus once it is in place. Kaufman (1977), asking *Are Government Organizations Immortal?*, concludes that that description exaggerates the truth only slightly (cf. Casstevens 1980). The American horse cavalry, useful though it had been in chasing Indians, had clearly outlived its usefulness long before it was eventually disbanded in the mid-twentieth century. It may be marginally easier to pull the plug on a particular program than on an entire agency. But Behn and Clark (1979), studying one of the rare success stories, found that a beach erosion control project was terminated only after: (1) a persistent critic demonstrated beyond a reasonable doubt that the project caused actual harm, increasing rather than reducing erosion; and (2) a larger national environmentalist constituency was activated to overcome entrenched local and agency interests; and (3) it became clear that there were no halfway measures between complete termination and continuing as before. All that was required to terminate one modest beach erosion project at one site. Terminating nationwide whole classes of activities (like "public housing") looks, from that, to be next to impossible.

Once the welfare state is in place, then, about all opponents can hope to do is curtail its expenditures. Both Thatcher and Reagan have favored this tactic. But even this is no simple task. A large portion of the budget is relatively "uncontrollable": existing statutes, for example, require the government to pay out unemployment benefits to every qualified citizen who claims them. Even if the statutes were altered so as to remove all obstacles to the readjustment of budgets (ranging, in America, from trust funds and permanent and indefinite appropriations to fixed charges and matching formulae—see Weidenbaum 1970: 232–33)—there would still be great bureaucratic pressure against big budget cuts. One of the strongest correlations political scientists have discovered is between an agency's budget from year to year: next year's budget is just this year's plus (or, in really dire times, minus) some tiny increment (Cutright 1965; Wildavsky 1975; Wilensky 1975: chap. 2). Bureaucrats, threatened with a new budget-cutting regime, usually just shuffle accounting categories, dip into slush funds, and generally evade and obstruct any efforts at imposing real economies. There is already evidence of this happening to Thatcher's cuts in British public expenditure (Hood and Wright 1981); and to hear Stockman tell the tale, Reagan's much-heralded cuts in the U.S. federal budget have met the same fate (Greider 1982). Many suppose it would take an amendment to the American Constitution to limit growth in federal spending (Moore and Penner 1980; Wildavsky 1980). Some of Reagan's more wild-eyed supporters suppose that nothing less than the so-called Liberty Amendment, ending the federal income tax, would suffice. Obviously, neither is politically likely.

All of this leads me to the conclusion that critics of the welfare state are probably right in their factual claim that it is next to impossible to dismantle the welfare state, and hence that adopting such institutions restricts people's future freedom of choice of political and social institutions. The question remains whether this is praise or criticism. Reversibility is not always a desirable feature, in social policies or in social institutions either. Ordinarily we want to avoid getting locked into programs that might not turn out as we had hoped. But if we are considering a policy guaranteed to do good, then we count it as an advantage that it is irreversible and will carry on doing good forever. Take the smallpox innoculation program, for instance: if the bacterium is eradicated forever from the world, we would consider ourselves fortunate (Goodin 1982c: chap. 2). How well this applies to the welfare state depends, of course, on how strong a do-good guarantee we can provide, and on how strong a one we require. Precision seems impossible in such matters, but my own hunch is that it is sufficiently superior to the one political form it absolutely precludes (the laissez-faire state) for us to welcome an irreversible shift. Freedom may have been lost, but in a good cause.

A second line of reply, for those whose hunches differ from my own, is that where an irreversible shift is being contemplated, freedom is sacrificed either way we turn. On freedom-maximizing grounds, we are most naturally drawn to a rule that we must not make irreversible changes. They would obviously deprive us of future freedom of choice. But notice that that same rule (no irreversible choices) makes us unfree to pursue *that* option. Which unfreedom is to be preferred depends, presumably, upon which option looks most attractive. But neither is to be preferred on grounds of freedom alone.

H. Poverty

Claim: The welfare state increases the freedom *of* welfare
   recipients
   from social and economic obstacles
   to live their lives as they please.

I have saved what I regard as the two most powerful arguments for the welfare state for last. This particular one is too familiar to belabor. The welfare state frees many people from the debilitating poverty that they would otherwise suffer (Danziger, Haveman, and Plotnick 1981); and in this way, it serves the high-priority moral goal of protecting people's autonomy (Weale 1982: chaps. 3 and 4). How efficiently it serves this goal, whether all the money gets spent on the right people and the right things, whether there are alternative ways of accomplishing the same goals—all these are open questions. Be the precise parameters as they may, however, I doubt that anyone can seriously deny that the welfare state makes a substantial contribution to freedom in this way.

I. Moralizing

Claim: The welfare state increases the freedom *of* citizens
   from practical/psychological constraints
   to act upon seriously held moral principles in public
   affairs.

This argument needs rather more discussion than the last, but in the end I consider it at least as important. Let me begin by pointing directly to the greatest puzzle surrounding the welfare state, which is, *why stop there*? I have described the welfare state as being characterized by its modest task of limiting the scope of inequality (chapter 1). But if limiting inequality is good, then eliminating it altogether surely must be better. Some supporters of the welfare state may be closet radicals, secretly looking upon it as the most effective practical means to that larger ultimate goal. Many,

327

however, suppose that only certain inequalities merit state attention. There is a strong streak of what Tobin (1970) calls "specific egalitarianism," which he describes as "the view that certain specific scarce commodities should be distributed less unequally than the ability to pay for them." We are regularly provided with a list of such things. Food, shelter, medical care, education, and rights to vote, bear children, and die for one's country figure prominently on Tobin's. But what makes these things so special remains something of a mystery.

The usual explanation is couched in terms of the distinction between "needs" and "mere wants." I have discussed various problems with any such distinction in chapter 2. Here let me focus on just two. First is that of explaining the universality of needs in a way that is consistent with the wide variability of tastes. Here contemporary social philosophers successfully piggy-back on the Rawlsian analysis of "primary goods," construing "needs" as "basic resources" instrumental to any and all life plans people may choose. Whatever particular things people may want, they need roughly the same things in order to get them. The second problem is that of justifying an absolute priority of "needs" over "mere wants." This is crucial not only to our concept of needs but, more to the point, to the argument for requiring the welfare state to attend to one to the absolute exclusion of the other. Notions of absolute priority are, in the wake of discussions of Rawlsian maximin and lexicographical orderings, in utter disrepute (Arrow 1973; Harsanyi 1975; Barry 1973). Besides, if anything, the primary goods analogy undercuts the argument for priority. Primary goods, recall, are of no ultimate, intrinsic value. They are "needed" and valued only as instruments to other more basic objectives. If we construe "needs" merely as "universal means," then it is hard to see we should, either as individuals or as a society, give the means absolute (or any) priority over the ends they are to serve.[8]

What seems curious is not that the welfare state serves needs but that it serves them exclusively—not its egalitarianism but

[8] An obvious reply is that needs are basic resources, which we should try to equalize in order to guarantee a fair start to the social race. But this argument falls afoul of similar objections as Rawlsian primary goods. To say that the same primary goods are useful in all life plans is not to say that each primary good is *equally* useful in each plan. The ingredients may be the same, but the proportions vary. Which mix of primary goods you want depends on what you propose to do with them (Arrow 1973; Barry 1973). Likewise, presumably, with "needs": everyone needs health, regardless of his particular plans; but just *how* healthy he needs to be depends on what he wants to do.

rather its single-minded concern with an equal distribution of certain goods and not others. The best way to explain this peculiar behavior is not, I suggest, to engage in a futile search for some peculiar objective features in the goods themselves but is, instead, in terms of moral psychology. Elsewhere I have argued that our most deeply held moral principles are extraordinarily sensitive to contamination. What it means to "take something seriously" is to think of it as something special, set apart from the mundane world (Goodin 1982c: chap. 6). The clearest cases are those things that we think "money cannot buy," and the way that those things are profoundly debased when they are bought and sold: bought sex is not the same (Hirsch 1976: chap. 6); bought blood is not the same (Titmuss 1971a); war bonds promoted as good investments rather than as patriotic contributions to the war effort are not the same; etc. So, too, with moral principles. Part of what it is to take them seriously is to see them as something special and apart. This is why we give needs absolute priority over ordinary wants and why we restrict the welfare state to serving only this elevated set of concerns.[9] In that way, and only in that way, can we be free to play our most seriously held moral principles.

The moral indignation that people display toward illicit trading in controlled commodities suggests that moral principles have been contaminated rather than just compromised. Consider the case of housing in Oslo. Prices were officially set very low, on the grounds that no one should be denied this most basic necessity. People were initially glad to act on this noble principle: it was a matter of pride that market considerations should not enter into trading in basic commodities. Once a black market arose, and it became common practice to make a side-payment several times the official price to induce the owner to part with his house, people promptly set aside seriously held moral principles and "played the game" according to more ordinary commercial rules. Yet they were "morally indignant" that they had been deprived of the opportunity to act on their moral principles by the intrusion of these mundane market forces (Gulbrandsen and Torgersen 1974). On a more modest scale, the surprisingly strong reaction of supporters of the welfare state to reports of "welfare cheats" might have roughly the same explanation.

It is indeed a form of freedom that is at stake here. People are

[9] Even if this partitioning off of "needs" is theoretically untenable, people with such a vested psychological interest in the distinction may never notice, owing to the enormous power of self-deception (Goodin 1982c: chap. 6; Elster 1979: 172–79).

psychologically free to act on seriously held moral principles only if they are free from forces that would contaminate them. Here as elsewhere, one freedom comes at the cost of others. We gain the opportunity to act on morally serious principles by closing off opportunities to behave in ways that would undermine them. But the chance to act on such principles is, for anyone who internalizes some such principles, indisputably the more valuable.

III

Such discussions ordinarily conclude that the welfare state is a good thing from the point of view of positive freedom but not so good from the point of view of negative freedom. I have intentionally arranged my discussion in this chapter to avoid that conclusion, partly because I see no theoretical justification for championing one variety to the exclusion of the other, but mostly because I take MacCallum's (1967) point that it is worse than useless to talk about freedom in such unspecified terms. I have, therefore, explicitly nominated agents, obstacles, and actions/conditions for each of the alleged interconnections between freedom and the welfare state in section II above. These reappear in summary fashion in Table 11.1.

The overall pattern of allegations is largely as expected. As regards *obstacles*, the welfare state is said to buy freedom from psychological and economic/social obstacles at the price of reducing freedom from legal and political/bureaucratic ones. As regards *actions* we are free to do and *conditions* we are free to enjoy, the allegation is that the welfare state trades political for moral freedom, while having a mixed effect on the freedom to live our lives as we please. Only as concerns *agents* does anything very novel emerge: whereas the ordinary presumption is that the welfare state sacrifices the freedom of citizens for that of welfare recipients, the present analysis suggests that some of the most important gains (c and i) fall to citizens.

How you evaluate the impact of the welfare state on freedom depends, naturally, on which of these allegations you take most seriously. On my analysis, all the alleged negative effects are equivocal at best. The unfreedoms invariably turn out to be necessary conditions for the existence of other equally important freedoms, either for the same people or for other people. Three of the positive effects (claims c, h, and i), on the other hand, seem un-

Table 11.1 Summary of Alleged Effects of Welfare State on Freedom

Argument	Effect on freedom	Of (agent)	From (obstacles)	To (actions/ conditions)
a. property	reduces	citizens cum taxpayers	legal obstacles	dispose of property as they please
b. uniformity	reduces	citizens	legal obstacles	display diverse tastes for public services
c. impartiality	enhances	citizens	psychological obstacles	display moral impartiality
d. paternalism	reduces	welfare recipients	legal obstacles	pursue their own preferences
e. red tape	reduces	welfare recipients	legal and bureaucratic obstacles	live their lives as they please
f. dependency	reduces	welfare recipients	psychological and economic obstacles	pursue alternative social and political arrangements
g. irreversibility	reduces	citizens	bureaucratic and political obstacles	pursue alternative social and political arrangements
h. poverty	enhances	welfare recipients	social and economic obstacles	live their lives as they please
i. moralizing	enhances	citizens	psychological obstacles	act upon seriously held moral principles

equivocal and quite important. My conclusion would, therefore, be that the gains to freedom outweigh the losses.

There are many other ways of arguing *for* the welfare state, of course. Freedom is only one among many values it serves. Most of the arguments *against* the welfare state, however, turn largely on its alleged harm to freedom—allegations which here have been largely dismissed.

T W E L V E

SELF-RELIANCE

A final New Right critique of the welfare state is basically social-psychological, though with moralistic overtones and economic implications. This is the argument that welfare programs have done more to create dependency than to cure it. The government, the New Right maintains, should therefore reduce its role in promoting social welfare, and leave many (maybe most) of the social problems it currently tackles to be resolved instead by the individuals most directly concerned. Thus, the doctrine of "self-reliance" has once again become a—perhaps *the*—dominant theme in shaping American social policy.

The aim of this chapter is to show that those arguments are morally flawed. Relying upon state assistance is importantly different from merely receiving it, as I shall show in section II. Furthermore, "self-reliance" as it is currently advocated amounts to reliance upon one's family (section III). But the family must necessarily have discretionary control over needed resources in a way that state officials need not, making dependence upon one's family for needed resources morally more objectionable than equally heavy reliance upon state services (section IV). Finally, there seems to be little empirical support for the hypothesis that the welfare state has the deleterious effects upon people's characters that advocates of self-reliance suppose it does (section V).

In short, enforcing "self-reliance," as construed by the New Right, would amount to shirking our collective moral responsibilities for vulnerable members of our communities. It would also, all too often, unnecessarily exacerbate dependencies of the most morally objectionable sort. The doctrine of "self-reliance" would have us neither protect the vulnerable nor reduce vulnerability. Thus we would be violating what seem to be some of our very strongest

Material in this chapter is reprinted from Robert E. Goodin, "Self-Reliance versus the Welfare State," *Journal of Social Policy*, 14 (January 1985), 25–47, by permission of the editor and Cambridge University Press.

moral responsibilities (Goodin 1985b; and chapters 5 through 7 above).

I

The goal of self-reliance has a long and honorable history. Certainly it has long been held up as an ideal in our individualistic societies. But it is just worth noting that it was embraced in qualified form by the Greeks (Nussbaum 1986), and in fairly unqualified form by medieval moralists such as Maimonides (1168: bk. 7, treatise 2, chap. 10, sec. 18).

While no recent invention, then, the real heyday of the notion undoubtedly came in the nineteenth century. And, for once, literature was a broadly accurate reflection of existing social realities. In one of the best-selling British books of the period, Samuel Smiles (1859) extoles the virtues of *Self-Help*, and in one of the most famous American essays of the era, Ralph Waldo Emerson (1841) enters a fervent plea for "Self-reliance." One modern commentator reports that, for example, "The engineer Brunel, who built the Great Western Railway from London to Bristol, surveyed almost every inch of the line himself." Reflecting upon this case, and the plight of nineteenth-century businessmen more generally, Atiyah (1979: 279) concludes that "these men practised self-reliance because it was the only way they could do what they wanted; to them, self-reliance was not so much a moral principle, as a plain necessity of circumstance."

Self-reliance remains an influential ideal down to our own day. American social legislation regularly proclaims goals such as "to help individuals . . . to attain or retain capability for self-care" (42 USCA sec. 301) and "achieving or maintaining self-sufficiency, including reduction or prevention of dependency" (42 USCA sec. 2001). In Australia, " 'thrift,' 'self-help' and 'self-reliance' are terms which have been running through official income security policy statements . . . since the inception of the scheme in 1908" (Lewis 1975: 28). In Britain, Canon Blackley (1878: 835) justified his initial proposal for "National Insurance" by appeal to "a simple axiom that to make a reasonable provision against occasional sickness and the inevitable feebleness and infirmity of old age is the duty of every man gifted with health and strength"; and among the three guiding principles in Sir William Beveridge's (1942: para. 9) blueprint for the postwar British welfare state is the proposition that "the state in organizing security should not stifle incentive, opportunity, responsibility; in establishing a national minimum, it should leave room and encouragement for voluntary action by each individual to provide more than that minimum for himself and his family."

The implications of this ideal for social policy would appear to be relatively straightforward. Herbert Spencer (1894: 345–46) spells them out fairly genteelly when writing, "Each shall so live as neither to burden his fellows nor to injure his fellows." The point is put more sharply in William Graham Sumner's remarkably nasty little essay on *What Social Classes Owe to Each Other*:

> In a free state every man is held and expected to take care of himself and his family, to make no trouble for his neighbor, and to contribute his full share to public interests and common necessities. . . . The only help which is generally expedient, even within the limits of the private and personal relations of two persons to each other, is that which consists in helping a man to help himself. . . . [Under] the schemes for improving the conditions of the working classes . . . the friends of humanity once more appear, in their zeal to help somebody, to be trampling on those who are trying to help themselves. (1883: 39–40, 165, 128)

Social welfare legislation has long been attacked for inhibiting self-reliance. Malthus's *Essay on the Principle of Population*, which so deeply influenced the 1834 revisions in the British Poor Law, argues that "the poor laws are strongly calculated to eradicate the spirit . . . of independence among the peasantry," and that already "they have succeeded in part" in that task (1826: bk. 3, chap. 6). Moralists (Emerson 1841: 44–45) and economists, right to the end of the century, were constantly bemoaning the way in which the poor laws tend to "perpetuate many of the worst evils of dependence" (Freemantle 1892: 431); and opponents of Asquith's 1908 plan for very limited forms of old-age pensions regarded as among their strongest arguments against the plan the detrimental effect it would presumably have upon "self-help," in the form of private thrift (Hannah 1986: chap. 2). Even the great economist Alfred Marshall, in the Royal Statistical Society discussion of Charles Booth's influential paper on "The Enumeration of Paupers," is found to be remarking that self-respect and independence of character were "of far more real value to the English working classes than all the money they had received in poor relief" (1892: 62; see similarly Mill 1869: chap. 4).

Such complaints carry over into our own day, as the American experience with welfare reform bears abundant witness. For Daniel Patrick Moynihan, the architect of President Nixon's unsuccessful proposal for a nationally guaranteed income, "The issue of welfare is," quite simply, "the issue of dependency"; and this is a theme Nixon himself picked up in proposing the scheme (Moynihan 1973: 17, 226). Similarly, Ronald Reagan's California policies were deeply influenced by Cornuelle's (1965) plea for *Reclaiming the American Dream* through a reemphasis upon "voluntarism" (a combination of self-help and mutual aid) as an alternative to state welfare services. Upon reaching the White House, Reagan himself appointed a domestic policy adviser famous for arguing that welfare programs

> have created a new caste of Americans—perhaps as much as one tenth of this nation—almost totally dependent on the State, with little hope . . . of breaking free. . . . Practical welfare reform . . . requires that we reaffirm our commitment to the philosophical approach of giving aid only to those who cannot help themselves.[1] (Anderson 1978: 153)

In his influential book, *Losing Ground*, Charles Murray (1984: 180, 65) describes "self-sufficiency" as "a precondition for being a member of society in good standing" and "an intrinsic obligation of healthy adults," and he indicts the Great Society welfare programs for increasing "latent poverty" by undermining people's "economic independence." These sorts of views have clearly made their mark on President Reagan's policies, to judge from his 1986 State of the Union message to Congress:

> After hundreds of billions of dollars in poverty programs, the plight of the poor grows more painful. But the waste in dollars and cents pales before the most tragic loss—the sinful waste of human spirit and potential. We can ignore this terrible truth no longer. As Franklin Roosevelt warned 57 years ago standing before this chamber . . . welfare is "a narcotic, a subtle destroyer of the human spirit." And we must now escape the spider's web of dependency. . . . I am talking about real and lasting emancipation, because the success of welfare should be judged by how many of its recipients become independent of welfare. (Reagan 1986)

[1] See similarly Rimlinger (1961), Glazer (1971; 1983), Berger (1976), Berger and Neuhaus (1977), and Berger and Berger (1983: chap. 9).

In Britain, too, notions of "self-reliance" loom large in the Tory threat to dismantle the welfare state. The 1979 Conservative Party Manifesto on which Margaret Thatcher won office reads in part, "We want to work with the grain of human nature, helping people to help themselves—and others. This is the way to restore that self-reliance and self-confidence which are the basis of personal responsibility and national success" (quoted in Dean 1983a). The Prime Minister's Policy Unit has been exploring some more-or-less draconian methods of implementing that promise by curtailing the state's social services (Dean 1983a, b). In the meanwhile, Smiles' *Self-Help* has been reissued, over an introduction signed by Thatcher's Secretary of State for Education, Sir Keith Joseph, in a bowdlerized edition presenting the doctrine in even more vicious terms than in the full original (Sage 1986).

Similar trends are afoot in the antipodes as well. The New Zealand Planning Council's report on *The Welfare State? Social Policy in the 1980s* (1979: 28) "calls for a fundamental change in political and social philosophy." Exploring the fine print, it becomes clear that the centerpiece of this reformulation is the proposition that "the real need . . . is for the state to do *less*, and at the same time assist *people* to do more for themselves."

I I

These arguments in favor of self-reliance crucially refer to two central concepts. One is the notion of "reliance"; the other is that of "the self." I shall critically consider each of these component notions in turn in the next two sections, in order to reveal the hidden flaws in these larger arguments.

Let us consider first the notion of "reliance." There, the first thing to be noticed here is that the objection is not to people *receiving* assistance from others. It is not even to their *coming to need* it—not even through some *fault* of their own. The objection is much narrower than that. It is merely to their *relying* on such assistance. John Stuart Mill's *Principles of Political Economy* makes this abundantly clear:

> In all cases of helping, there are two sets of consequences to be considered; the consequences of the assistance itself, and the consequences of relying on the assistance. The former are generally beneficial, but the latter, for the most part, injurious; so much so, in many cases, as greatly to outweigh the value

of the benefit. And this is never more likely to happen than in the very cases where the need of help is the most intense. There are few things for which it is more mischievous that people should rely on the habitual aid of others, than for the means of subsistence. . . . The problem to be solved is therefore . . . how to give the greatest amount of needful help with the smallest encouragement to undue reliance on it. (1848: bk. 5, chap. 11)

Nor is this just an economist's view of the world. An 1876 report of a district committee of the Charity Organisation Society voices almost identical concerns (Mowat 1961: 42). And even the great turn-of-the-century social reformer Charles Booth alludes to "the curse of relief *expected* and *relied upon*" (1892: 182, emphasis added).

The classical utilitarians themselves acknowledged an important distinction between relying on public assistance and merely receiving it. But they evoked that distinction primarily in order to justify emergency relief in cases of natural disaster, and no more. Among Victorian economists it was a pretty standard point that public relief should be "confined mainly to casual and extraordinary causes of distress," on the grounds that that "does not establish any resource on which the poor can rely, so as to dispense with ordinary and necessary prudence on their part" (Neaves 1871: 475); and that was explicitly why the Charity Organisation Society confined its relief to cases of "protracted sickness, or some special infirmity" (Mowat 1961: 42). Such reasoning is also arguably what led Bentham (1789: 292–93) himself to suggest that the "duty of rescue" should be restricted to situations of emergency (Weinrib 1980: 283). Certainly it weighed heavily in the thinking on this matter of Sidgwick (1874: bk. 4, chap. 3) and, later, Pigou (1902).

The implications of this line of reasoning extend far more widely than the classical utilitarians ever realized, however. The basic principle seems to be that any public relief measure would be permissible, just so long as it did not alter the behavior of recipients. The demand is not so much that people should be self-reliant, in the sense of prudently planning for their own future. Imprudence is perfectly permissible. All we insist upon is that people should not *count on* the help of others, i.e., that they should not *plan* to rely upon others for support.

This more general principle is implicit in the operation of all the ordinary "emergency relief" programs which were the focus of the more restrictive utilitarians themselves. After all, few natural disasters come as complete surprises. Someone who lives on a fault line should expect earthquakes; someone who lives on a flood plain should expect high water; someone who builds a house in dense Australian bush should expect a bushfire; and so on. Yet when these perfectly predictable calamities do occur, governments dub them "disasters" and offer public relief. That they will do so is as near to a sure thing as there can be in politics.

So why is this disaster relief not criticized for discouraging self-reliance? The answer is simple: people, for the most part and in the usual sorts of cases, would not have done anything to protect themselves even in the absence of these programs. Of course, there was plenty they *could* have done, starting with choosing another site on which to build their houses in the first place, to insuring themselves against the disasters in question. No doubt they are guilty of negligence of some sort in not anticipating these disasters and protecting or insuring against them. But whatever the measure of "fault" involved in such negligence, making people bear the full brunt of the disastrous outcomes themselves is clearly too high a penalty to make them pay (Goodin 1985b: chap. 5; chapter 10 above; cf. Sugden 1982a).

The reason we do not worry about disaster relief programs discouraging self-reliance is, thus, not that people *could not* have protected or insured themselves but rather that they *would not* have done so, even if the government made it absolutely clear that post-disaster relief would not be forthcoming. People know that disasters happen, but they seem psychologically incapable of imagining that the disaster will ever happen to *them* (Kunreuther 1978; Goodin 1982c: chap. 8). Hence we can safely offer public relief, knowing that people will not rely on it in the special sense of "reliance" that matters morally. They will do no less to protect themselves with the government guarantee; they would do no more if it were withdrawn.

All this has potentially important implications for social welfare policy. It suggests that objections to such policies predicated on notions of self-reliance should drop away if it can be shown that all talk of reliance (whether on oneself or on others, either) implies more planning and foresight than is ordinarily exercised by those desperately poor individuals most likely to be most in need of public assistance. This, ironically, is a theme dear to the hearts of right-wing commentators. Banfield (1970: chap. 4), for example, identifies "present-orientedness" as a character flaw that consti-

tutes the defining feature of the lower classes. And even left-wing-
ers concede this, emphasizing, however, that it is perfectly rational that people with pressing short-term concerns should not
devote too much attention to the long term (Portes 1972). But both
sides tend to agree, albeit on the basis mostly of anecdote and casual empiricism, that the poor do not—and probably cannot, in
some sense or another—plan very far into the future. And if the
poor are not planners, then "reliance" (being quintessentially a
planning notion) would be inappropriate as applied to them. People with no plans one way or the other can hardly be said to be
"relying" on state aid.

There are two more formal kinds of evidence that can be
brought to bear on such questions. First is the large and growing
body of econometric work, such as that surveyed in chapter 8, on
the labor supply effects of cash transfer payments. We must, of
course, be cautious in our inferences here, partly because different
studies so often tend to contradict one another in these fields but
more importantly because those studies were all done with somewhat different questions in mind from what is before us here.
("Reliance" is an intentional notion, which may or may not mani-
fest itself in "labor supply changes" as its behavioral consequence.) One interesting generalization that does seem to emerge
from the wide variety of studies surveyed by Danziger, Haveman,
and Plotnick (1981), however, is that the programs upon which
recipients might be more inclined to rely are the ones most like
genuine insurance programs (e.g., retirement, unemployment insurance, disability insurance, workmen's compensation); "social
assistance" programs targeted more tightly on the poor generally
seem to have much weaker incentive effects upon recipients (see
also Judge 1981; Gruen 1982; Mitchell and Fields 1982). Similar
findings emerge from experiments with a negative income tax.
Overall, beneficiaries seem to reduce labor supply only slightly
(by, perhaps, five percent), while those in the very poorest households sometimes actually increase it (Brown 1980: chap. 6; Ferber
and Hirsch 1978). In short, the poor—and the poorest of the poor,
most especially—tend not, for the most part, to work less hard
when they know that they can rely on state support. That is, if
anything, a vice of the middle classes, who do tend to rely upon
social security to provide a large component of their old-age income and to save less themselves in consequence. If we want to
eliminate such reliance, then our attacks should concentrate upon

reducing various forms of state subsidy to the middle classes rather than upon reducing programs targeted on the poor.

A second and more direct form of evidence might come from examining the welfare rolls themselves. First we might argue, with Moynihan (1986: 136, 140–41), that if people were intentionally relying upon state assistance, then more people would rely upon it more heavily the more generous and certain it was. There is, within the U.S., considerable interstate variation in this matter. But those variations do not seem to correlate with any corresponding differences in claim rates. Second, we might look directly at rates of "welfare recidivism"—i.e., the rate at which people on the welfare rolls stay on the welfare rolls from one year to the next. This is a less than perfect indicator of the phenomenon we want to investigate: presumably welfare recidivism often merely betokens a continuing objective circumstance that is beyond the recipient's power to alter; so these statistics inevitably overstate (perhaps badly) the extent of intentional, willful reliance. In that light, the modest rates of recidivism are truly impressive. Consider first the program of Aid to Families with Dependent Children. These recipients, among all welfare beneficiaries, have among the fewest opportunities for altering their circumstances through their own efforts. But even in that program, only a third of beneficiaries receive continuous aid for three or more years (Rydell et al. 1974: 15–21; Lyon 1975: 4–12); and only about a fifth of recipients depend on the program for more than half their income for more than four years (Rein and Rainwater 1978). Evidence on the extent of reliance upon welfare payments of any sort is even more scarce. The University of Michigan Panel Study of Income Dynamics from 1969 to 1978 concludes, bluntly, "The current system does not foster large-scale dependency," offering in evidence such facts as these:

> One-half of the persons who lived in families where welfare benefits were received at least once in a decade did not receive it more than two of the ten years. . . . Even in the year they receive it, most welfare recipients are not *dependent* on welfare income. Although one out of four Americans were in households that received welfare at some time in a ten-year period, fewer than one in ten was ever in a household in which more than half of the annual income of the head and wife came from welfare sources. . . . Furthermore, even among those people who were dependent on welfare at some time [for

more than half their household's income], nearly half were dependent in only one or two years of the ten-year period. Eventually they find other sources of incomes, in amounts sufficient to enable them either to leave the welfare rolls altogether or at least to greatly reduce their reliance on welfare income. Thus, *dependency* is the exception rather than the rule among welfare recipients, and only about 2 percent of the entire population could be characterized as *persistently* dependent upon welfare income [i.e., dependent upon it in at least 8 out of 10 years for at least half their household's income] during the late 1960s and 1970s.[2] (Duncan 1984: 90–91)

What such findings seem clearly to suggest is that most people tend to use public assistance only to help tide them over temporary emergencies. They are not, for the most part, "relying" upon it in any willful, intentional way for long-term support.

All these results are, I emphasize, equivocal at best. But such evidence as we do have tends to support the conclusion that the poor do not rearrange their affairs intentionally and willfully with a view to relying upon state support. Indeed, insofar as they "plan" at all, they seem to try to avoid such outcomes.

I I I

Next we must ask, with Emerson (1841: 37), "What is the aboriginal Self on which a universal reliance may be grounded?" The "self" to which advocates of self-reliance refer is obviously not any ordinary notion of the self, naively understood as, for example, a

---

[2] This may underestimate the *level* of people's dependency on welfare, since it excludes "housing assistance, Medicaid, child nutrition, and unemployment payments," as Murray (1985a: 429) points out. But its estimate of the *persistence* of people's reliance on welfare is not disputed by Murray; all he says on that point is that intermittent claimants over a long period should be considered as "dependent," too. That, however, would require reconceptualization of the New Right's view of what is wrong, morally, with welfare dependence. The standard story, as discussed in section V below, is in terms of "bad habits" and "character defects"; and people who claim welfare intermittently, whatever else you say about them, clearly cannot be said to be claiming it habitually. Even if intermittent claimants were included among the persistently dependent, that would not increase their numbers all that dramatically. The Duncan (1984: 75) findings suggest that only 8.3 percent of the population receives welfare in 5 out of the 10 years and only 3.5 percent receives more than half the household income from welfare in 5 or more years out of the 10. So if 2 percent is the lower bound for the "persistently dependent," as Murray claims, 8.3 percent bids fair to constitute an upper bound. Either number is impressively small, compared to the rhetorical burden the New Right puts upon this claim.

natural individual. It is simply impossible for anyone ever to be completely self-reliant in that sense. Even the most extravagant champion of self-help, Samuel Smiles (1859: chap. 1), has to concede that "the help which we derive from others in the journey of life is of very great importance. . . . From infancy to old age, all are more or less indebted to others for nurture and culture; and the best and the strongest are usually found the readiest to acknowledge such help." Advocates of self-reliance not only acknowledge these forms of dependency but actually *celebrate* them. Martin Rein (1965: 85, 87) observes this anomaly clearly:

> All of us are dependent during major and important periods of our lives. . . . Childhood, schooling, illness, old age, pregnancy, childbirth, and early child-rearing include periods of dependency. . . . No one finds this strange or reprehensible. What does cause great and rising concern is *public* dependency.

The New Right seems to be dedicated to a policy of "self-reliance" which would, in effect, force people to rely upon family and friends rather than the state as the basic source of support. No one could be more forthright in support of such a proposition than Charles Murray (1984: 228), who describes the broad implications of his basic policy proposal in *Losing Ground* in these terms:

> It would leave the working-aged person with no recourse whatsoever except the job market, family members, friends, and public or private locally funded services. . . . Sons and daughters who fail to find work [would] continue to live with their parents or relatives or friends [until they do]. Teenaged mothers [would] have to rely on support from their parents or the father of the child and perhaps work as well. People laid off from work [would] have to use their own savings or borrow from others to make do until the next job is found.

Outrageous though that may seem, it clearly was not meant as a throw-away line. Murray (1985b: 32) returns to that theme in a subsequent *Commentary* article, where he once again says that the "residual problems" left over after the welfare state as we know it has been abolished "can safely be left to the . . . natural responses of relatives helping relatives, friends helping friends, and communities protecting communities."

That may or may not be an appealing vision. The curious thing about it, however, is that it is being promoted under the name of "self-sufficiency" and "self-reliance." This way of construing self-reliance is plainly bizarre. Surely no one is *self*-reliant when he has to rely for support on others, whether they be family, friends, or state officials. The only way to make any sense at all of this otherwise perplexing notion is to understand that, for purposes of this argument, the boundaries of the "self" have been extended to include one's household (or extended family, or social network) as a whole. Whatever its political appeal, such an expanded notion of the self is philosophically preposterous.

Shunting the welfare burden off onto families is, of course, a familiar trick. The Elizabethan Poor Law stipulated that "every poor, old, blind, lame, and impotent or other poor person not able to work" must be maintained by his parents, grandparents, or children, so far as they are able.[3] Those charged with the administration of the British poor law continued to insist upon this principle, right into the present century. The Majority Report of the Royal Commission on the Poor Laws of 1909, for example, argued that the state ought not show itself "willing to make provision and even lavish provision for parents whose sons fail to support them," and expressed the hope that "if the position is clearly defined and a consistent policy laid down both as to pensions and Poor Relief, the natural feeling between parents and children will again assert itself" (quoted in Collins 1965: 249; see also Bosanquet 1909: 3).

To this day, many politicians continue to cherish this goal. Long before joining Margaret Thatcher's Cabinet, Sir Keith Joseph had proclaimed in a Conservative Political Centre pamphlet on *Social Security: The New Priorities*,

> The Tory approach is both more selective and less dependent on the State. . . . To us self-help and voluntary action are more desirable and more likely where practicable to be effective than State intervention. We can state our objectives: to strengthen the family, thrift and self-reliance; to remove

[3] That is the phrasing of the 1601 Act for the Relief of the Poor, 43 Elizabeth I, c.2, sec.7. Interestingly, the first such law, enacted in 1572, contains no provision at all for family responsibility (14 Elizabeth I, c.5) while the second, enacted in 1597, stops short of imposing it on grandparents (39 Elizabeth I, c.3, sec.5). Speculating on why these provisions were included at all, Abbott (1940: 163) offers a most intriguing suggestion: since women in this period had no legal identity independent of their husbands, "the only way a wife could secure support from the husband who had deserted her or ill-treated her was thought to be prosecution under the poor law." If so, these provisions of the Elizabethan Poor Law were no more than a pragmatic response to legal rules that have long since altered.

crutches from those who can walk; to strengthen the social network; . . . (quoted in Pope, Pratt, and Hoyle 1986: 215)

The proclamation of the Minister for Social Security in one recent right-wing Australian government was even less coded:

My personal preference would be to see a higher level of personal independence and family interdependence . . . with young people living at home and receiving support from their families, with husbands and wives recognizing their obligations of mutual support, with families committing themselves to the care of their aged members and parents accepting their primary responsibility for the care of their own children. (Chaney 1983: 4–5)

But Sir Keith and Senator Chaney are hardly alone in these sentiments. The Archbishop of Canterbury opened a recent debate in the House of Lords on the subject of "The Family in Britain Today" by arguing that the family—being "the bulwark of a stable society"—should be "a first line of defence in times of crisis or strain," be it economic or spiritual (Coggan 1976: cols. 1259–60; see similarly Land 1978: 1979). The same goal is endorsed, in somewhat more circumspect language, by various contributors to the 1980 OECD symposium on "The Welfare State in Crisis," from the Secretary-General (van Lennep 1981: 2) and Secretariat (1981: 80-81) on down (e.g., Schreiner 1981: 117), and by the New Zealand Planning Council (1981: 20–23). Something similar is clearly contemplated in the social policies of both Thatcher (Dean 1983a, b; Loney 1986: 30–32, 130–39) and Reagan (Eisenstein 1982). In Britain, at least, there has been substantial movement in the direction of implementing those plans: the new Social Security Act creates a Social Fund to provide discretionary assistance to needy people with things like furniture, heating, funeral, and maternity expenses; the rules governing administration of that fund, however, formalize the long-standing informal practices among DHSS officers in administering analogous provisions of the Supplementary Benefits scheme in requiring that claimants first seek assistance with those expenses from relatives, friends, and charities before coming to claim state assistance (Hencke 1986).

The most common practical manifestation of such a principle is, as in the Elizabethan Poor Law itself, a legal duty on families to support needy members. The requirement of filial responsibility to support indigent parents, though until recently a firm and widespread demand (Abbott 1940, 155–76; Burns 1956, chap. 5; Schorr 1960), had been thought to be disappearing from social welfare law. Although the rule remains in force in France and several Eastern European countries to this day, it was officially abolished in Britain in 1948, in Norway in 1964 and in Sweden in 1979.[4] In the U.S., while it remains true that in practice "the low-income aged and disabled . . . often substitute family for public support" owing to fear of stigma or ignorance about available public assistance (Menefee, Edwards, and Schieber 1981: 18), the official scope of relative responsibility for the aged, blind, and disabled was substantially limited by federal legislation in 1974 (Hagen 1982: 114). But against all this, we must set various counter trends. In the U.S., for example, those who are not old, blind, or disabled must rely upon states rather than the federal government for assistance; and laws in many states continue to hold adult children (and sometimes even siblings, grandparents, and grandchildren) responsible for the financial support of indigent relatives. So the principle of requiring needy elders to seek assistance from their families, rather than from the state, is far from dead.

The policy of attempting to force parents to support dependent children is particularly thriving. Enforcement of maintenance orders against noncustodial parents, in cases of divorce or separation, is an increasing concern across a wide range of countries (Griffiths, Cooper, and McVicar 1986). There are various ways of enforcing this obligation (Chambers 1979; Garfinkel, and Uhr 1984). Where the noncustodial parent's failure to pay maintenance forces the custodial parent to seek public assistance, the typical pattern is for the state to provide such assistance, but then to attempt to extract reimbursement from the delinquent parent. One particularly striking example of this is in the U.S. Social Security

[4] For details, see Burns (1956: 85), Land (1979: 142), and Sundstrom (1982: 22). The French practice is to lay upon "children . . . an obligation to provide sustenance to their father and mother or other forbears who are in need" under Article 205 of the *Code Civil* (an obligation extended to sons-in-law and daughters-in-law under Article 26). "The law requires that, when an application for *aide sociale* (social assistance) is made, any relatives who are liable for the support of the applicant be asked to indicate what contribution they can make. . . . The local committee . . . dealing with the application then decides what proportion of the sums required should be provided out of public funds, leaving the applicant to recover the remainder from the liable relatives. . . . It may . . . happen that an application is refused or a reduced grant awarded on the grounds that there are children who can afford to support the applicant, even though they are not in fact doing so." *Préfects* are empowered, and in ministerial circulars encouraged, to take legal action on an applicant's behalf against defaulting relatives; but such actions apparently continue to be rare (Lynes 1967: 113–14).

Amendments of 1974 (PL 93–647, 88 Stat. 2337). They make it a condition of eligibility for Aid to Families with Dependent Children that every applicant must assign support rights to the state, and must cooperate with the state in proving paternity and securing child support payments from the defaulting spouse. That law further requires states to establish programs to utilize information from Department of Health and Human Services and Internal Revenue Service files in locating absent spouses and in enforcing child-support orders against them.[5] This practice was extended to non-AFDC families, with 1981 legislation requiring "the IRS to withhold tax refunds in cases when states certified that the individual had an overdue child support obligation" (Garfinkel 1986: 76). Antipodean practice is much the same. The Australian Social Security Act of 1947 (s. 62 and 83 AAD) provides that "a woman with children in her care who applies for a pension or benefit must take all available maintenance proceedings for the support of herself and the children" against the noncustodial parent; this "universal feature of Australian social welfare law" was relaxed only at the margins by the policy, adopted by the Department of Social Security in mid-1983, to exempt sole parents from this requirement where the income of the noncustodial parent is "not substantial" (Sackville 1975: 183, Edwards 1986: 6). Similar practice prevails in New Zealand (Petre 1978), France (Lynes 1967), Britain, Canada, and Denmark (Griffiths, Cooper, and McVicar 1986).

In practice, family members have rarely been pursued very vigorously for support of indigent relatives. In Britain, the poor law commissioners were complaining as early as 1834 that "the clause of [the Poor Law] which directs the parents and children of the impotent to be assessed for their support is very seldom [later in the Report they say "scarcely ever"] enforced" (Blomfield 1834: 115; see similarly Fremantle 1892: 431 and Anderson 1977: 54). Much the same seems long to have been true in the U.S. An interwar survey of county attorneys in Illinois found that only one in eight of them had, over the entire year, initiated so much as a single legal action under the family responsibility provisions of the state poor law (Abbott 1940: 165–66). A recent U.S. Senate committee investigation found that the total revenues raised by all child support enforcement programs in 17 states ranged from $179 in West Virginia to $53,000 in California; the mean state collection

<hr />

[5] See Mondale, Bentsen, and Ribicoff (1974), Steiner (1981: 119), Bernstein (1982), Hagen (1982: 114) and Garfinkel (1986: 76).

was $10,927, the median merely $8,000. These paltry sums led the committee to conclude that "most states have not implemented in a meaningful way the provision of the present law relating to the enforcement of child support. . . ." (Mondale, Bentsen, and Ribicoff 1974: 8149).

The reasons for this failure to enforce family responsibility have always been largely pragmatic. Family ties "cannot be maintained or strengthened by statutory enactments. . . . Litigation . . . is often very painful to those in need of help, . . . does not yield any returns in family solidarity, and . . . yields monetary returns which are far below the expense of litigation" (Abbott 1934: 15).[6]

As for the first point of criticism, it certainly is true that there are certain sorts of affective support that only the family can provide.[7] But if the families are unwilling to provide such support, it will do no good to try to compel it. Although we might be able to extract the material component, the affective component will still be missing (Blau 1964: 17). As Gilbert Steiner (1981: 128) says, "A broken family supported by a reluctant father is no stronger than a broken family supported by public assistance" (cf. Bernstein, 1982; Blomfield 1834: 115).

As for the second pragmatic criticism of proposals to enforce family responsibility, the basic point is that poor people are usually found in poor families (Keniston et al. 1977). Those families are not ordinarily in a much better position to provide assistance than is the individual in need of it. One California study showed that, "even in a county outstanding for the vigor with which it administered its relative's responsibility requirement, only fifteen percent of relatives were found to have some measure of [financial] ability" to support indigent relations (Burns 1956: 83). Another study of the extent to which Connecticut grandparents could be made to support grandchildren then receiving public relief found that in only 4 out of 108 cases studied could grandparents be expected to make any contribution at all (Beyrer and Tevald 1956). As with grandparents so, too, with parents: trying to extract child support payments from parents is rightly likened to "efforts to squeeze water from a stone. Nonsupporting fathers . . . either work irregularly or support a second family that would become

[6] See similarly Abbot (1940: 167–68), ten Broek and Wilson (1954: 270–71), Schorr (1980: 25–31), Anderson (1977); cf. Burns (1956: chap. 5), and Bond et al (1954: 315–20).
[7] Litwak (1965), Pinker (1979: chap. 2), Rothman (1976: 59), and Tulloch (1984) emphasize this point.

dependent if the father's income were diverted to his first family" (Steiner 1981: 114).[8]

Finally, and paradoxically, in encouraging "self-reliance" on the part of recipients of family benefices we may be *dis*couraging self-reliance on the part of intrafamily benefactors. The doctrine of "self-reliance" asks two contradictory things of people: on the one hand, "prudential regard to their own future"; and on the other, "effacement of self in response to the claims of helpless relatives." But in practice, "those who are the most ready with help for others are probably by disposition least likely to save money for their own old age. The lavish may have the virtue of generosity, and the close-fisted that of prudence; but we cannot often expect to find all these qualities at once in any one person." Booth (1892: 178–79) therefore criticizes the doctrine that people should be made to rely on their family and friends for support on the grounds that "its efficacy in relieving the [tax] rates today may be only a cause of their being required tomorrow." Booth found psychological reasons for supposing that to be true, but there are economic ones, as well. "Family care" policies typically require some (usually female) members of the family to abandon paid employment to care for needy relatives; and by abandoning paid employment, they compromise their capacity, economically, to take care of themselves (Sapiro 1986). For that reason, too, policies of "self-reliance," thus construed, are likely to prove counterproductive.

All of these pragmatic points are true and important. My own objection to family responsibility provisions is, however, a principled one. It is not just that they are inefficient or counterproduc-

---

[8] Mondale, Bentsen, and Ribicoff (1974: 8146–49) report that states presently collect $5 of child support for every $1 of enforcement costs. But since the states make few collections—and presumably only the easiest—there is every reason to suppose that the rate of return would decrease dramatically with any serious effort at widespread collection. There is scant evidence of any kind for the central hypothesis underlying these 1974 social security amendments. Mondale, Bentsen, and Ribicoff's (1974) Senate report on the legislation relies heavily upon what must be one of the flimsiest papers ever prepared at the RAND Corporation. The only direct evidence Winston and Forsher (1971: 15–16) offer for their hypothesis (i.e., that "welfare dependence" is largely caused by "nonsupport of legitimate children by affluent fathers") is a survey of child support cases arising over eleven days in five California counties, involving 630 fathers. Winston and Forsher report that the nonsupporting fathers thus identified were not particularly poor nor unemployed, and conclude from that that nonsupporting fathers as a whole could reasonably be made to support their children. But of course this is a biased sample: presumably it is not worth a woman's while bringing a child-support action against a penniless father; and, as Mondale, Bentsen, and Ribicoff (1974) bemoan, welfare agencies tended not to insist upon this as a precondition of public assistance, either.

tive. It is not even that they are inequitable, forcing as they do the burden of "family care" upon female members of the family (Land 1978; 1979; Sundstrom 1982; Sapiro 1986). That is certainly true, and it certainly is a serious moral objection. Here, however, I shall focus on another, viz., that such programs reduce public dependency only by increasing private dependency. People are made less dependent upon state aid by being made more dependent on family assistance.

Much in the public record suggests that increasing intrafamily dependency is seen by champions of "self-reliance" as a goal positively to be desired. The Australian Minister for Social Security quoted above was quite explicit in his desire for "a higher level of family interdependence" (Chaney 1983: 4). Land (1975: 227, 159) reports that one of the strongest objections to early British proposals for a family allowance was that it would "interfere with prevailing patterns of family responsibility, thus reducing the dependency of wives on husbands and children on parents"; even Ramsay MacDonald seems to have taken that objection very seriously indeed. Similar objections have been offered to child allowances in the U.S. (Burns 1956: 92), and to welfare programs more generally throughout Scandinavia (Sundstrom 1982). The Australian tax system actually provides positive inducements—in the form of the Dependent Spouse Rebate—for one spouse (ordinarily but not necessarily the wife) to renounce the financial independence that comes with employment outside the home, and to rely instead upon the other spouse for support (Edwards 1980; Cass 1981). In Britain, too, regulations governing payment of a Dependency Benefit under Supplementary Benefits provide disincentives to working wives (Land 1979: 144–45). And on present reports, Thatcher's plan for further dismantling the welfare state includes yet more "proposals to encourage mothers to stay at home"— backed up by a "re-examination of the Equal Opportunities Commission," presumably with a view to undermining its efforts to help them get jobs outside the home (Dean 1983b). All of this betrays a pretty clear desire actually to *increase* dependency within the family, whether or not it is strictly necessary, as a means of reinforcing traditional ties and values.[9]

[9] This goal is often quite explicit. Various Victorians suggested explicitly that elderly paupers whose families refused to support them should be forced into the workhouse in an effort "to restore relationships to the condition which God intended for them" (Anderson 1977: 55). In postwar America, "fears have been expressed" that social security programs, by narrowing the "economic responsibili-

I V

Having critically examined the two component notions contained within references to "self-reliance," let us now consider what exactly it is that is so morally worrisome about states of dependency. Here I shall argue that forcing people to rely upon support from family or friends (which is what, in practice, "self-reliance" as advocated by the New Right amounts to) exacerbates what is morally worrisome about dependency, whereas allowing people to rely upon state officials for obligatory provision of welfare services alleviates it.

The naive view of dependencies as entirely naturally induced might lead us to suppose that the total quanta of dependency is naturally fixed, and that alternative policies can only shift the locus of that dependency. Early opponents of old-age pensions, for example, asserted that "such pensions would be no *cure* of pauperism but only *pauperism in a new dress*" (cf. Booth 1892: 217). On this view, our choice is not whether a person will be dependent, or even how dependent he will be, but merely upon whom he will depend.

Dependency, however, is variable rather than fixed. Some ways of "helping people help themselves" may make them more dependent (upon, e.g., their families); others may make them less dependent upon anyone else. The same is true of state aid. Some forms reduce dependency, while others induce it.[10] Considerations relating to the *quantity* of dependency, then, do not systematically favor either self-help or state aid.

Considerations relating to the *quality* of the dependency relationship do, however, systematically favor state assistance. Ethnographers join sociologists in reporting that people earnestly hope to avoid unilateral dependency on their families.[11] Charles

---

ties of the family," may "destroy the cohesion of one of society's most important institutions" (Burns 1956: 80; Schorr 1960: 27). Contemporary essayists in the neoconservative journal *The Public Interest* ask, "Is the welfare state replacing the family?" fearing that those institutions might "reduce social integration and the sense of responsibility that people in the society feel for each other" (Bane 1983: 93). This theme is echoed by the Archbishop of Canterbury (Coggan 1976) and the Norwegian Director of Long-Term Planning and Coordination (Schreiner 1981: 117). Indeed, even the Aid to Families with Dependent Children program in America declares that "to help maintain and strengthen family life" is one of its goals, which is ironic, given its actual effects (42 USCA sec. 601).

[10] Burns (1956: 86–89), Titmuss (1976: chap. 2), Rainwater and Yancey (1967), Schorr (1960: 20–22), and Passmore (1981: 34–35) make this point in various ways.

[11] Among the former, see Goode (1963); among the latter, see Townsend (1957:

Booth's (1894: 169, 295) surveys poignantly illustrate this theme. Time and again he was told that "parents are unwilling to ask help from children and expect little," and that the "aged prefer a pittance from the parish, regarded as their due, to compulsory maintenance by children" (see similarly Anderson 1977: 50). Relieving this sense of dependency upon the family has been one of the major accomplishments of old-age pensions, and social security schemes more generally (Anderson 1977: 51–53; Kreps 1977: 22; Sundstrom 1982).

Now, there is undeniably something prima facie odd about the fact that "old people don't want to be dependent on their children, but they don't mind being dependent on the state" (Bond et al. 1954: 317). But there is an easy explanation for this near-universal preference among recipients for public over private sources of assistance. The first step is to recognize that the relationship between those in need of such assistance and those providing it (whether officers of the state or members of the family) is ordinarily an *asymmetrical* one. This fact is crucial in Townsend's (1957: 56) explanation, for example: "Some old people can no longer reciprocate the services performed for them [by their children] and this seems to make them less willing to accept help" from them (see similarly Schorr 1980: 19–20 and Litwak 1965: 310).

Asymmetry per se, however, is not objectionable—from the philosopher's point of view, or from the recipient's either. What makes it objectionable is the addition of another crucial element, discretion. Depending upon their families for assistance subjects beneficiaries to the "arbitrary will of another." Families, by their nature, must enjoy substantial discretionary control over the disposition of family resources. Those dependent upon those resources must, in some real sense, "beg" those with discretion to supply them. Under state systems of aid, the old and young still depend on the middle generation for support; but the effect of public welfare schemes is to "remove intergenerational support from the family unit basis, making it mandatory that persons with income from work or other sources provide support for both young adults and the aged. . . ." (Kreps 1965: 287).

Depriving families of discretion over needed resources is only the first step, however. We must guarantee that the discretion is not just passed on to state officials, as so often it is (Gummer 1983;

chaps. 3 and 5), Shanas and Streib (1965), Bond et al. (1954: 297), Burns (1956: 84–85), and Schorr (1960: 4–5).

chapter 7 above). Here what is crucial is that state officials be under strong legal obligations to provide public assistance to claimants. Then state officials have no choice but to supply claimants with what they need. As Charles Booth (1892: 213–34) emphasized in the early British debates over the old-age pension, "There is no parallel in feeling between the taking of a sum of money to which a man is legally entitled and the suing *in forma pauperis* for a benefit which may be granted or postponed or withheld, and the granting of which must, in the public interest, be protected by preliminary suspicion and searching inquiry."

Families must have substantial discretion; public officials may, by law, be deprived of it. That goes some considerable distance toward explaining why state aid is preferable to relying upon families for support. Dependency itself is not eliminated—recipients depend just as heavily upon their welfare check as they would formerly have depended upon their families' benefice (Nelson 1981: 176–77; cf. Steiner 1981: 89). But our moral objection to it is substantially mitigated (Goodin 1985b, chap. 7). And so, too, are the objections of recipients. That is why, for example, the aged poor were so much less hesitant to apply for pensions than for Supplementary Benefits, in the days when those were dispensed largely at the discretion of caseworkers. As one of Townsend's (1957: 162) informants explained, "Your pension, now, you have a right to that. . . . The Supplementary Benefit is not like something you're entitled to." Of course, some element of discretion must always remain, insofar as caseworkers will always have to decide whether or not any particular case falls under the general rule governing entitlements (Lipsky 1980; Nelson 1981; and chapter 7 above). But this is a lesser form of discretion, and our objections to it are correspondingly reduced.

The role of formally codified rights and obligations in overcoming our objections to welfare dependency was recognized first and perhaps most clearly by an attorney with the U.S. Department of Health, Education and Welfare, A. Delafield Smith. He observes,

> We are criticized for stimulating the sense of dependency. Are we not properly criticized for so doing? There is only one proven method for avoiding the growth of the sense of dependency in company with any increased reliance upon proffered services. That method is to make him who is dependent the legal master of that on which he depends. The will retains its natural prerogatives when its needs are met through the

exercise of a legal right. . . . Independence results from the fact that the person or thing upon which we depend can do nought but serve our need. (Smith 1955: 3, 17; see similarly Smith 1946; 1949: 288; and Rousseau 1762a: bk. 2)

Once we have institutionalized a "right to welfare," Smith argues, welfare recipients would be dependent upon state aid in no more worrying a way than we all are on a train service. You are "dependent on it because you may have no alternative but to use it, [but] independent of it because all that it is capable of doing is at your command in the fulfillment of your own chosen aims" (Smith 1955: 50). Others have since taken up this argument (Reich 1964; Marshall 1965; 1981: chap. 5; cf. Titmuss 1971). But none have seen more clearly how welfare rights—or, in light of my arguments in chapter 7, at least welfare obligations on the part of state officials—can constitute the solution to the problem of dependency.[12]

The upshot of all this is that it is morally undesirable to insist upon "self-reliance," if the boundaries of the "self" for these purposes are expanded to include the family but to exclude the state. The sorts of dependencies that occur within the family are morally more objectionable than the dependencies that occur between citizen and state, at least insofar as the citizen's entitlements come in the form of rights which state officials have no choice but to honor.

V

What is it that makes "self-reliance" such an appealing value? Surely it is not *just* that, by reinforcing family ties, these policies strengthen traditional mechanisms of social control. Nor is it *just* a

[12] Early theorists of the welfare state appreciated this point in some inchoate way. Canon Blackley (1878) and Sir William Beveridge (1942: para. 9) in Britain, and the architects of the New Deal in America (Brown 1956; 1960) all do obeisance to the ideal of self-reliance and all offer insurance schemes as being perfectly suited to its realization. The valid point lying behind that claim is that demanding your due under an insurance policy is a matter of right: when one of the contingencies against which you are insured occurs, the insurer has no discretion in deciding whether or not to pay you. Blackley (1878: 850) likens filing an insurance claim to a millionaire's "drawing a cheque on the bank where he had lodged his wealth. Such a one surely would never fancy that he was receiving a dole from the cashier!" Though compulsory state insurance removes you from control by the arbitrary will of others in honoring insurance claims, however, it is not truly a form of self-reliance in the sense which all these writers evoke. They tend to offer social insurance as "a mechanism whereby the individual could prevent dependency through his own efforts" (Brown 1956: 3) in purchasing insurance. But those "efforts" were far from voluntary: *compulsory* social insurance can therefore hardly count as *self*-reliance, in the sense in which those arguments require.

matter of reducing public expenditures, or of increasing gross national product. All those ends certainly sometimes are in view.[13] But surely there is some larger matter of principle at stake as well.

Self-reliance is valued most highly as a character trait, desirable quite apart from any material benefits it might happen to bring to either the individual or the larger society (Galtung 1980b: 21). Emerson's plea for self-reliance was, after all, principally a plea for an independent and nonconforming spirit, as Updike's (1984) brilliant essay makes plain; it was only secondarily, and very incidentally, an argument against public relief of paupers. "The real objection" to early proposals for an old-age pension must similarly "be sought in the effect on the character [of the poor] . . . , in the extent to which bad habits are encouraged or discouraged" (Booth 1892: 217, 220).

This emphasis on character is also betrayed by our choice of *which* dependencies we find offensive. "When we think of . . . dependency . . . , we neglect the student preparing for a socially useful occupation, the mother caring for children, the aged who have earned retirement, the workers who are forced out of the labor force by technological change . . . [Instead] our attention is rigidly fixed on those who should be working and are not," and whose dependency therefore would seem to betray a flaw in character (Rein 1965: 97).[14] On this point, Moynihan (1973: 17–18) is admirably explicit:

> To be poor is an objective condition; to be dependent, a subjective one as well. . . . Being poor is often associated with considerable personal qualities; being dependent rarely so. . . . Concern for the poor . . . does not necessarily or even commonly extend to those who are dependent, that is to say, those who own nothing and earn nothing and depend on society for their livelihood. When such persons are very young or very old, allowances are made. But when they are of the age when other persons work to earn their way and, further, if they are dependent during periods when work is to be had, dependency becomes a stigma.

Assuming that our concern with self-reliance is essentially a concern for people's character, the crucial question is whether and what way public welfare payments might alter the character of re-

---

[13] Cf. Emerson (1841: 43), Sumner (1883: 165–66), and Galtung (1980b).
[14] See similarly Titmuss (1958), Land (1979), and Tulloch (1983).

cipients. Certain psychological studies reported to a 1972 conference under the title "The Pigeon in a Welfare State" talk in terms
of "learned laziness"—pigeons who have learned that they will be
fed regardless of what they do will refuse to perform any tricks at
all for the experimenter.[15] But these studies have been widely criticized, both for misunderstanding what makes pigeons peck and
for inferring improperly from pigeon studies conclusions about
human behavior (Gamzu and Williams 1973; Seligman 1975).

Where humans are concerned, there are strong a priori reasons
for doubting that receiving state assistance will have much effect
on self-reliance. Psychologists tell us that character traits such as
this are acquired principally in childhood, in early interactions
with our families and friends (Bowlby 1973; Whiting 1978). And
even those, such as Seligman (1975: 55–56) who offer cognitive
theories of "learned helplessness" agree that lessons, once
learned, are difficult to unlearn: people whose previous experiences have led them to be self-confident will be little affected by
subsequent discouraging experiences, and vice versa. Hence, from
both developmental and cognitive psychological perspectives, it
seems highly unlikely that later adult experiences (with the welfare state or anything else) can reshape very dramatically the character that was formed early in life.[16]

Even if adult experiences can in principle reshape a person's
character, it seems unlikely that interactions with the welfare state
will in practice be of a sort to compromise recipients' self-reliance.
Charity is not all of a cloth so far as its impact on the recipient's
character is concerned. At the one extreme, such unilateral charity
as is given by the lord of the manor to indigent villagers is soul-
destroying indeed. At the other extreme, completely reciprocal
"mutual aid" such as "the kindly action of co-workers, neighbors
or friends, who . . . subscribe to help the widow to make a fresh
start, in this doing only as they would be done by, . . . is mani-
festly more humane and less degrading . . ." (Booth 1892: 156).
The impersonal (and often, in the long run, reciprocal) transfers
effected by the welfare state are much nearer the latter pole. Psy-

[15] This study, originally presented to the Psychonomic Society Conference, St.
Louis, Mo., 1972, was subsequently published under the less provocative title,
"Acquisition of Key-pecking via Auto Shaping as a Function of Prior Experience:
'Learned Laziness'?" (Engberg et al. 1974).

[16] Furthermore, there is no evidence of intergenerational transmission of welfare
dependency: children growing up in families in receipt of welfare benefits are not
significantly more likely to receive welfare benefits themselves once they are grown
(Weissberg 1970–1971).

chological studies show that aid which is given anonymously, which protects the autonomy of the recipient, and which allows him opportunities to reciprocate all have positive rather than negative effects upon the recipient—among them, encouraging subsequent attempts at self-help on his part (Fisher, DePaulo, and Nadler 1981; Fisher, Nadler, and Whitcher-Alanga 1982). These findings are verified cross-culturally (Gergen and Gergen 1971) and in ethnographic reports on attitudes in a modern English village (Obler 1981). In the end, we are left believing T. H. Marshall (1981: 114) to have been right to say that it is simply "absurd to argue that free medical care and free schooling undermine the sense of personal responsibility for the health and education of oneself and one's family"—and likewise the various other activities of the modern welfare state.

A case can be made for supposing that the welfare state actually has precisely the opposite effect to that alleged by advocates of self-reliance. By offering encouragement to people who would otherwise regard themselves as utterly helpless and their plight as utterly hopeless, the welfare state might actually *promote* self-reliance on the part of its beneficiaries.[17] This is John Stuart Mill's argument:

> Energy and self-dependence are . . . liable to be impaired by the absence of help, as well as by its excess. It is even more fatal to exertion to have no hope of succeeding by it, than to be assured of succeeding without it. When the condition of any one is so disastrous that his energies are paralyzed by discouragement, assistance is a tonic, not a sedative. (1848: bk. 5, chap. 11, sec. 13; see similarly ten Broek and Wilson 1954: 268–69 and Lane 1981)

Ultimately, what (if any) impact the welfare state has on the character of recipients is an empirical question, and can only be answered conclusively with direct empirical evidence. Some evidence points to a deleterious effect: ill-health, arguably associated with psychological stress, seems to result when AFDC payments are terminated to long-term recipients, for example (Berlin and

[17] There is some psychological evidence of an inverse relationship between the impact of aid on a recipient's self-esteem and his efforts at self-help: the more "self-threatening" the help, the more a recipient will try to help himself, to prove that implication incorrect (Fisher and Nadler 1976). It should be emphasized, however, that these studies were conducted as one-off experiments. It seems a priori unlikely that a steady stream of self-threats will continue having that stimulating effect for long.

Jones 1983). But the bulk of the evidence seems to point in the opposite direction. Surveys show that a vast majority of people who have, in the past, received public assistance nonetheless believe that they should, in the future, try to help themselves instead of relying on yet more public aid (Sniderman and Brody 1977). There is also the evidence from the welfare rolls, discussed above, that only a minority of recipients tend to make heavy and protracted use of public assistance; and presumably only in a minority of those cases does that reflect more on the recipients' character than their objective circumstances. In short, it seems that in most cases the effect of public assistance upon the character of those receiving it is negligible.

VI

The overall conclusion is that self-reliance, in the form in which it is advocated by opponents of the welfare state, is a pernicious doctrine. It does nothing to prevent vulnerability and dependency. Quite the contrary, it exacerbates the worst kind of dependency. Neither does this doctrine do anything to protect those who are vulnerable and dependent. Quite the contrary, it insists that those most in need rely upon those who generally have fewest resources to help them. I have argued that protecting the vulnerable and reducing certain sorts of vulnerabilities are prime moral imperatives (Goodin 1985b and chapters 5–7 above). On both counts, the doctrine of "self-reliance" as currently cast is a moral abomination.

This is not to say that the welfare state as currently organized is an unqualified success. Some studies suggest that the net effect of direct income transfer programs is indeed to reduce both poverty and overall income inequality (Danzinger, Haveman, and Plotnick 1981). But other commentators insist that, whatever the redistributive gains in this sphere, they are more than counterbalanced by the regressive impact of various other government activities (Page 1983). Still others suggest that, even within the social services sector itself, many of the universalistic services are decidedly not pro-poor in their impacts (Le Grand 1982). All this may well be true; and if it truly is a necessary rather than merely an incidental feature of public programs, this may well provide good grounds for rejecting the welfare state in favor of some more robustly redistributive mechanism. That is obviously another even larger question, to be addressed on some other occasion. My argument here is merely that, if the welfare state is to be rejected, it should not be in favor of "self-reliance" as currently conceptualized.

Neither does my argument that the policies presently being peddled under the name of "self-reliance" suggest that it is impossible for governments to pursue policies which *genuinely* promote self-reliance. There are a great many things the state can do to encourage independence in otherwise dependent people.[18] Roughly speaking, this just amounts to following through on the promises contained in President Kennedy's 1962 proposals for welfare reform, which seem geniunely to have aimed at "prevention and rehabilitation."

Among his various more particular proposals for attaining those goals, undoubtedly the most important was that for job training. Finding exactly the right administrative shell is, of course, enormously difficult. But a humanely administered "workfare" program—such as ET in Massachusetts, or perhaps even GAIN in California (Kirp 1986)—has much to recommend it in terms of promoting genuine self-reliance. For evidence of this, consider the results of a demonstration project conducted in the late 1970s:

> For twenty-seven months an experimental group of 1,600 AFDC mothers received jobs, training, and special supervision—"supported work environments"—funded by the Department of Labor and the Ford Foundation. Their progress was measured against a control group that continued only to get AFDC. The women in the supported work program naturally enough worked more and earned more than the control group during the experiment, but these differences remained significant after the program ended. The program reduced welfare dependency: by the last nine months of the program, participants were twice as likely to have left the welfare rolls as those in the control group. Those who needed the most help made the most gains—older AFDC women (aged 36–44), those with no previous work histories, and those with the longest AFDC histories. (Moynihan 1986: 165–66)

[18] John Passmore (1981: 34–35) provides a slightly eccentric list of measures that nonetheless serves to make the general point. The state, he suggests, "can, for example, abolish the disgracefully immoral practice of compulsory retirement. It can be more interested in encouraging the handicapped, the elderly, the chronically ill, the unemployed, to earn what little income they can. . . . More positively, a government can encourage the elderly, the chronically ill, the handicapped to maintain their independence by household aids, training in skills, the provision of public transportation, and the like" (see similarly Kane and Kane 1979; Gibson 1985; Hannah 1986: chap. 9; cf. Lazear 1979).

If self-reliance really is a morally important goal, then this is the sort of thing that should be done to promote it. But all of that has very little indeed to do with the main thrust of the New Right's attack on the welfare state that is presently proceeding under the banner of "self-reliance." That is, essentially, an attempt to force the welfare burden back upon the family; and that is the very antithesis of self-reliance, properly understood.

Part IV

CONCLUSION

T H I R T E E N

CONCLUSION

In an insightful recent essay, Hugh Heclo (1986, 182–83) shows that "the American political tradition embraces two competing concepts of the general welfare," which he characterizes in the following terms:

> The first concept might be called "welfare as self-sufficiency."
> It is a conception of well-being that is supremely individualistic, for it has to do with the capacity of an individual to get his own way, to enjoy the fruits of his own labor, to be unbeholden, unentangled, able to make it on his own. To paraphrase President Reagan in a recent Fourth of July speech, we Americans do not get together to celebrate Dependence Day.
> . . . The second concept might be termed "welfare as mutual dependence." If the first concept is tied to individualistic economic rationality, the second has to do with a social or group-oriented rationality. . . . This is not a question of asking us to choose between rational individualism and all other behavior that is somehow irrational. It is . . . asking us to apply rational criteria to the self-in-group rather than to the self-in-isolation as the point of reference.

The once—and, judging from present indications, possibly future—conventional wisdom elevates the ideal of self-sufficiency above almost all else. Dependency is held to be an unfit state for a human being, and dependency upon public authorities for basic subsistence doubly so. Tocqueville's (1835/1983: 113) prose is particularly purple, but his conclusions are nowise peculiar to him:

> The right of the poor to obtain society's help is unique in that instead of elevating the heart of the man who exercises it, it lowers him. . . . Ordinary rights are conferred on men by reason of some personal advantage acquired by them over their fellow men. This other kind [a right to poor relief] is accorded by reason of a recognized inferiority. The first is a clear state-

ment of superiority; the second publicizes inferiority and le-
galizes it. The more extensive and the more secure ordinary
rights are, the more honor they confer; the more permanent
and extended the right to relief is, the more it degrades. (See
similarly Moon 1986)

Such sentiments have never died out altogether. "A hand, not a
handout" was the recurring theme of U.S. social policy right
through the 1960s. One commentator goes so far as to describe
that slogan as a veritable "rallying cry for the War on Poverty"
(Murray 1984: 23). President Kennedy (1962) himself announced
as the central goal of his proposed welfare reforms to "help our
less fortunate citizens help themselves."

During that era, of course, there were other overlays as well.
Increasing recognition of the structural basis of poverty left more
room for a "mutual dependence" model of welfare to operate, too.
But with the resurgence of the rhetoric of "self-reliance," traced in
chapter 12, this threatens once again to become the one overriding
theme of social policy, not only in the U.S. but throughout the
English-speaking world.

There are problems with the current welfare system. Of that
there can be no doubt. But the vision of "welfare as self-sufficiency" misdiagnoses the causes of those problems, and mispre-
scribes the cure. Surely it is obvious that there is nothing necessarily wrong with people depending upon one another, in various
respects and under various circumstances. All relationships of
trust are grounded in conditions of dependence and interdependence. Most would suppose that it is highly desirable, morally, to
be in a situation such that you may—indeed, must—trust a friend
or loved one. Similarly with the state: many modern social scientists suppose that the health of a "civic culture" is best assessed by
the extent to which people feel that they can place "trust" in their
public institutions (Almond and Verba 1963; Parry 1976).[1] Most of
us depend heavily upon the state, for everything from our salaries
to our physical security (Titmuss 1976: chap. 2). Few of us think
ourselves any the worse, morally, for that dependency.

If mutual dependence or dependence upon mutually shared institutions is morally innocuous in general, then what is it about

---

[1] Woodrow Wilson (1887: 213) similarly holds that "suspicion . . . is never health-
ful either in the private or in the public mind. *Trust is strength* in all relations of life;
and, as it is the office of the constitutional reformer to create conditions of trustful-
ness, so it is the office of the administrative organizer to fit administration with
conditions of clear-cut responsibility which shall insure trustworthiness."

welfare dependence in particular that might make it so morally obnoxious? Perhaps some would say that it is something peculiar to the nature of welfare services that makes dependence upon the state for *their* provision so very undesirable. Perhaps, where welfare is concerned, there is an important difference between depending upon particular individuals who truly care about us, on the one hand, and upon uncaring agents of an impersonal state, on the other. No doubt it is better to get needed commodities with love attached. But that is not an argument against depending upon the state for those needed commodities when there is no other source of supply (Goodin 1985b: chap. 6; 1985c: 785; 1986a).

Perhaps it is permissible to depend upon the state for goods and services if—but only if—those goods and services cannot, by their very nature, be procured privately. In the Preamble to the U.S. Constitution, one of the goals of the Union is "to promote the general welfare." But perhaps welfare provision is a fit area for state action only insofar as it is "general," i.e., necessarily a public good. Otherwise, perhaps, people should take private action to promote their own welfare.

That would seem too strong, however. There are various things that private individuals can do, through the good offices of Pinkerton's and the Mafia, to protect themselves and their property. Private justice is, indeed, one form of "self-help." Morally, though, it is a fairly unattractive one. We think that the state should take a role in promoting people's welfare in this regard, even though individual efforts might not be logically impossible.

Similarly, certain aspects of air pollution can be handled privately. Particulate matter in the Pittsburgh air, back in the days when steel was still being produced in that city, was for many years removed primarily (if at all) by filters attached to one's own window air conditioners. Modern-day arguments for public air-quality control measures do not hinge crucially on the proposition that private action is literally impossible. They hinge instead upon the proposition that it should not be necessary. Promoting people's welfare in these respects should be the job of the state, even if there were something that private individuals could themselves do.

Perhaps it is permissible to depend upon the state for certain aspects of our welfare, but not others. Perhaps the point is that, in a market society, you should be able to provide basic food, clothing, and shelter for yourself and your family through your own efforts. That explains why it is deemed shameful to depend upon the state to do so on your behalf: it constitutes an admission of inadequacy, "a notarized manifestation of misery, of weakness, of misconduct on the part of the recipient" (Tocqueville 1835/1983: 113).

Sometimes, however, it is simply untrue that you can provide for your family's basic welfare needs through your own efforts. Perhaps you cannot do so because you are old or disabled, for example—there would be no shame in that. Furthermore, saying that the able-bodied members of the working-age population "should be able to provide" for themselves is a double-edged sword. One way, it cuts as an indictment of the worker for failing to find work; the other way, it cuts as an indictment of "the system" (of education, macroeconomic management, or whatever) for failing to provide it. The classic case for the social safety net has always rested on the first of these propositions; that for the expansion of the welfare state beyond the safety-net function (as in the Kennedy-Johnson War on Poverty) on the indictment of the "system" contained in the second (Murray 1984: chap. 2).

None of these variations on the theme of "self-sufficiency" seem particularly plausible. It is not just that the ideal of self-reliance is unrealistic: it is not just that "the norm of self-sufficiency is more and more running up against the reality of mutual dependence . . . because of many complex changes in our economy and the nation's position in the world," as Heclo (1986: 192) intimates. There is substantial evidence that that is true, of course. One recent study revealed that "one out of four Americans were in households that received welfare at some time in a ten-year period" (Duncan 1984: 90). But the problem with the model of "welfare as self-sufficiency" is not just that it is an unrealizable ideal for all too many people in the modern world. The problem runs deeper than that.

The problem is that "self-sufficiency" is not necessarily an ideal at all. For a variety of reasons, alluded to here and elaborated elsewhere (chapters 6 and 12 above; see further Goodin 1985b), the widespread worry about "welfare dependency" per se is *morally* misplaced. Morally, there is nothing necessarily wrong with dependency in general, with depending on the state in particular, or with depending upon the state for provision of basic welfare supports more particularly still.

There is a potential problem with welfare dependency, to be sure. But the problem does not lie, morally, with the sheer existence of dependency but rather with the risk of its corruption through exploitation. We have strong special responsibilities to protect those who are particularly vulnerable to our actions and choices, as I argue elsewhere (Goodin 1985b).[2] Exploitation consists in the flagrant violation of that responsibility—taking special advantage of those whom we have special responsibilities to protect.

If the problem, morally, lies with the risk of exploitation of dependencies rather than with the mere existence of dependencies per se, however, then the form of solution required is not the elimination of dependencies but rather their protection from exploitation. What we have to prevent is not people depending upon one another, individually or collectively; rather, we need merely to prevent them from being in a relationship of peonage to those upon whom they depend.

Mutuality is one way of solving that problem. If each depends upon the other, then neither has any power to exploit the other. To some extent—and, in some times and places, to a large extent—public welfare programs can be justified in precisely these terms: we never know when we will need them ourselves (Dryzek and Goodin 1986). But that cannot be universally true. And nowhere is mutuality and reciprocity more absent than in relations between welfare recipients and welfare officers: the former need and want things from the latter; the converse is not true, or anyway not true to anything like the same extent. Hence the model of "welfare as mutual dependence" constitutes only a partial solution to the general problem.

Welfare recipients, as long as they are in receipt of welfare benefits, are necessarily "clients" in the sense of being "persons using services of a professional"—in this case, a welfare officer. There is nothing necessarily wrong, morally, with clientelism of this sort. All that we must morally prevent is their becoming, as well, "clients" in the old Roman sense of "plebeians under the protection of a patrician; dependent, hangers-on" (*Oxford English Diction-*

---

[2] President Kennedy (1962), in his message to Congress on welfare reform, similarly invoked the language of "protecting the vulnerable." But he did so as much to argue for programs rendering people invulnerable as to argue for programs to protect those who are and will inevitably remain vulnerable from threats of exploitation. "The goals of our public welfare programs must be positive and constructive—to create economic and social opportunities for the less fortunate—to help find them productive, happy and independent lives. It must stress the integrity and preservation of the family unit. It must contribute to the attack on dependency, juvenile delinquency, family breakdown, illegitimacy, ill health and disability. It must reduce the incidence of these problems, prevent their occurrence and recurrence, and strengthen and protect the vulnerable in a highly competitive world."

ary). That is to say, the task is not to eliminate dependencies, and not even to make them mutual, but merely to make them unexploitable.

It is the characteristic function of the welfare state to protect persons who are "abjectly dependent," i.e., who are wholly outside the bounds of relationships of mutual dependence. That is not the only function it discharges; to protect all abjectly dependent persons adequately, it is often necessary to extend similar protections to many others as well. Nor is that the only sort of social welfare program that might be justified; there may be many other reasons, equally compelling as the reasons that can be offered for that program, for moving beyond those minimal tasks. Still, that is the characteristic, defining feature of the welfare state, as it has been presented in chapter 1.

The way the welfare state protects the abjectly dependent from exploitation, in the absence of mutuality and the power it brings, is through the device of legally codified rules governing entitlements. ("Welfare rights" is the standard phrase; but as I showed in chapter 7, legally codified duties laid upon officials to provide the benefits are actually of more importance.) No matter how nonmutual their dependence, dependent persons cannot be manipulated or exploited by those upon whom they depend for needed resources if those people do not themselves enjoy any discretion in whether to give or to withhold those resources.

On the analysis offered here, what was crucial in the shift from the old poor law state to the modern welfare state was the move (coming in 1911 in Britain, and in 1935 in the United States) away from discretionary public charity and toward nondiscretionary entitlement rules. It is these nondiscretionary entitlement rules, more than anything else, that give the welfare state its peculiar moral flavor. It is upon the peculiar properties and consequences of them that the moral case for the welfare state must ultimately—and can most successfully—rest.

To end this book where I began it, I should emphasize once again that the arguments presented here show why, morally, we must *at the very least* make some sort of "minimal" welfare state provision, of a collective, nondiscretionary kind, to meet people's basic needs. But the arguments I have offered for going at least that far certainly do not contain anything to prohibit us from going farther.

Of course, to justify moving "beyond the welfare state," thus construed and thus legitimized, we will require other, different arguments. Perhaps arguments in terms of risk-sharing and mutual dependence could provide the impetus for moving "beyond" minimal welfare state provision of social assistance to meet basic needs, and toward programs of social insurance and of categorical assistance (at least in its quasi-insurance, contributory form, and perhaps even in its noncontributory form as well). More importantly, such arguments might help us move "beyond" the welfare state's focus upon succoring the needy and dependent, and reveal to us ways in which it might actually be desirable to create amongst ourselves new dependencies, and with them new needs and new vulnerabilities. Arguments sketched here, in previous chapters, and elsewhere (Goodin 1985b: esp. chap. 7) suggest that that is both morally permissible and socially potentially highly desirable. At that point, though, a different argument truly has begun.

REFERENCES

Abbott, E. 1934. Abolish the pauper laws. *Social Service Review* 8: 1–16.

———. 1940. *Public assistance.* Chicago: University of Chicago Press.

Ackerman, B. A. 1980. *Social justice in the liberal state.* New Haven: Yale University Press.

Ackerman, B. A., and Hassler, W. T. 1981. *Clean coal/dirty air.* New Haven: Yale University Press.

Acton, H. B. 1963. Negative utilitarianism. *Proceedings of the Aristotelian Society (Supplement)* 37: 83–94.

Albert, L. A. 1974. Standing to challenge administrative action: an inadequate surrogate for claims for relief. *Yale Law Journal* 83: 425–97.

Allardt, E. 1976. Dimensions of welfare in a comparative Scandinavian study. *Acta Sociologica* 19: 227–39.

———. 1977. On welfare, happiness and discontent in the Scandinavian countries. In *Scandinavia at the polls,* ed. K. H. Cerny, Washington, D.C.: American Enterprise Institute, pp. 155–80.

Almond, G. A., and Verba, S. 1963. *The civic culture.* Princeton: Princeton University Press.

Anderson, M. 1964. *The federal bulldozer: a critical analysis of urban renewal, 1949–1962.* Cambridge, Mass.: MIT Press.

———. 1977. The impact on the family relationships of the elderly of changes since Victorian times in governmental income-maintenance provision. In *Family, bureaucracy and the elderly,* ed. E. Shanas and M. B. Sussman. Durham, N.C.: Duke University Press, pp. 35–69.

———. 1978. *Welfare.* Stanford, Calif.: Hoover Institution Press.

Anon. 1969. Note: Scarce medical resources. *Columbia Law Review* 69: 620–92.

Anscombe, G.E.M. 1958. Modern moral philosophy. *Philosophy* 33: 1–19.

Arneson, R. J. 1981. What's wrong with exploitation? *Ethics* 91: 202–27.

Arnold, N. S. 1987. Why profits are deserved. *Ethics* 97: 387–402.

Arrow, K. J. 1963. Uncertainty and the welfare economics of medical care. *American Economic Review* 53: 941–73.

———. 1972. Gifts and exchanges. *Philosophy & Public Affairs* 1: 343–62.

———. 1973. Some ordinalist-utilitarian notes on Rawls. *Journal of Philosophy* 70: 245–63.

Arrow, K. J., and Hahn, F. H. 1971. *General competitive analysis*. San Francisco: Holden-Day.

Atiyah, P. S. 1970. *Accidents, compensation and the law*. 2d ed. London: Weidenfeld & Nicholson.

———. 1978. *From principles to pragmatism*. Oxford: Clarendon Press.

———. 1979. *The rise and fall of freedom of contract*. Oxford: Clarendon Press.

Atkinson, A. B., and Stiglitz, J. E. 1980. *Lectures on public economics*. Maidenhead, Berks.: McGraw-Hill.

Aubert, V., and Messinger, S. L. 1958. The criminal and the sick. *Inquiry* 1: 137–60.

Austin, J. L. 1956. Ifs and cans. *Proceedings of the British Academy* 42: 109–32.

Baer, J. A. 1983. *Equality under the Constitution*. Ithaca, N.Y.: Cornell University Press.

Baldwin, D. A. 1980. Interdependence and power: a conceptual analysis. *International Organization* 34: 471–506.

Baldwin, R., and Houghton, J. 1986. Circular arguments: the status and legitimacy of administrative rules. *Public Law* 239–84.

Ball, T. 1978. Two concepts of coercion. *Theory and Society* 5: 97–112.

Bane, M. J. 1983. Is the welfare state replacing the family? *Public Interest* 70: 91–101.

Banfield, E. C. 1970. *The unheavenly city*. Boston: Little, Brown.

Barber, B. R. 1984. *Strong democracy*. Berkeley: University of California Press.

Barclay, P. M., chairman. 1982. *Social workers: their role and tasks*. Report of a Working Party of the National Institute for Social Work. London: Bedford Square Press/NCVO for National Institute for Social Work.

Bardach, E., and Kagan, R. A. 1982. *Going by the book*. Philadelphia, Pa.: Temple University Press.

Barlow, R., Brazer, H. E., and Morgan, J. N. 1966. *Economic behavior of the affluent*. Washington, D.C.: Brookings Institution.

Barnett, S. A. 1912/1986. Charity up to date. *Contemporary Review*

(February). Reprinted in part in Pope, Pratt, and Hoyle 1986: 69–74.

Barry, B. M. 1965. *Political Argument*. London: Routledge and Kegan Paul.

———. 1973. *The liberal theory of justice*. Oxford: Clarendon Press.

———. 1980. Review of J. M. Buchanan, *Limits of liberty. Theory and Decision* 12: 94–106.

Bator, F. M. 1958. The anatomy of market failure. *Quarterly Journal of Economics* 72: 351–79.

Bay, C. 1961. *The structure of freedom*. Stanford, Calif.: Stanford University Press.

———. 1968. Needs, wants and political legitimacy. *Canadian Journal of Political Science* 1: 241–60.

Beales, H. L. 1946. *The making of social policy*. Hobhouse Memorial Trust Lecture, no. 15. London: Oxford University Press.

Behn, R. D., and Clark, M. A. 1979. The termination of beach erosion controls at Cape Hatteras. *Public Policy* 27: 99–127.

Beltram, G. 1984. *Testing the safety net: an enquiry into the reformed supplementary benefit scheme*. Occasional Papers on Social Administration, no. 74. London: Bedford Square Press/NCVO.

Bendix, R., and Rokkan, S. 1964. The extension of citizenship to the lower classes. In R. Bendix, *Nation-building and citizenship*. New York: Wiley, pp. 74–104.

Benn, S. I. 1967. Egalitarianism and the equal consideration of interests. In *Nomos IX: equality*, ed. J. R. Pennock and J. W. Chapman. New York: Atherton, pp. 61–78.

———. 1978. The rationality of political man. *American Journal of Sociology* 83: 1271–76.

———. 1982. Individuality, autonomy and community. In *Community as a social ideal*, ed. E. Kamenka. London: Edward Arnold, pp. 43–62.

Bennett, J. 1983. Positive and negative relevance. *American Philosophical Quarterly* 20: 185–94.

Bentham, J. 1789. *An introduction to the principles of morals and legislation*. London: Athlone Press, 1970.

Berger, B., and Berger, P. 1983. *The war over the family*. New York: Doubleday.

Berger, P. L. 1976. In praise of particularity: the concept of mediating structures. *Review of Politics* 38: 399–410.

Berger, P. L., and Neuhaus, R. J. 1977. *To empower people*. Washington, D.C.: American Enterprise Institute.

Berlin, I. 1969. *Four essays on liberty*. Oxford: Clarendon Press.

———. 1978. *Concepts and categories*. London: Hogarth.

Berlin, S. B., and Jones, L. E. 1983. Life after welfare: AFDC termination among long-term recipients. *Social Service Review* 57: 378–402.

Bernstein, B. 1982. Shouldn't low-income fathers support their children? *Public Interest* 66: 55–71.

Beveridge, W. H. 1942. *Social insurance and allied services*. Cmd. 6404. London: His Majesty's Stationery Office.

Beyrer, J. B., and Tevald, E. 1956. Responsibility of grandparents of children receiving aid to dependent children. *Social Service Review* 30: 428–35.

Black, D. J., and Rees, A. 1967. Patterns of behavior in police and citizen transactions. In *Studies in crime and law enforcement in major metropolitan areas*. President's Commission on Law Enforcement and the Administration of Justice, Field Studies 3, vol. 2, sec. 1. Washington, D.C.: Government Printing Office.

Blackley, W. L. 1878. National insurance: a cheap, practical and popular means of abolishing poor rates. *The Nineteenth Century* 4: 834–57.

Blackmun, H. A. 1971. Opinion of the U.S. Supreme Court. *Graham v. Richardson*, 403 US 366–82.

Blackstone, W. 1783. *Commentaries on the laws of England*. London: Strahan.

Blau, P. M. 1963. *The dynamics of bureaucracy*. Revised ed. Chicago: University of Chicago Press.

———. 1964. *Exchange and power in social life*. New York: Wiley.

Blaug, M. 1963. The myth of the old poor law and the making of the new. *Journal of Economic History* 23: 151–84.

Blomfield, C., chairman. 1834. *The poor law report of 1834*. Harmondsworth, Mddx.: Penguin.

Bloom, G. F. 1940. A reconsideration of the theory of exploitation. *Quarterly Journal of Economics* 55: 413–42.

Blum, L. A. 1973. Deceiving, hurting and using. In *Philosophy and personal relations*, ed. A. Montefiore. London: Routledge and Kegan Paul, pp. 34–61.

———. 1980. *Friendship, altruism and morality*. London: Routledge and Kegan Paul.

Bogart, J. H. 1985. Lockean provisos and state of nature theories. *Ethics* 95: 828–36.

Bohlen, F. H. 1910. The rule in *Rylands and Fletcher*. *University of Pennsylvania Law Review* 59: 298–326, 423–53.

Bond, F. A.; Baber, R. E.; Vieg, J. A.; Perry, L. B.; Schaff, A. H.; and Lee, L. J., Jr. 1954. *Our needy aged*. New York: Holt.

Bond, N. 1975. Knowledge of rights. In *Social welfare in modern Britain*, ed. E. Butterworth and R. Holman. Glasgow: Fontana, pp. 134–40.

Booth, C. 1891. Enumeration and classification of paupers, and state pensions for the aged. *Journal of the Royal Statistical Society*, Series A 54: 600–34.

————. 1892. *Pauperism and the endowment of old age*. London: Macmillan.

————. 1894. *The aged poor in England and Wales*. London: Macmillan.

Bosanquet, H. 1909. *The poor law report of 1909*. London: Macmillan.

Boudon, R. 1974. *Education, opportunity and social inequality*. New York: Wiley.

Bowlby, J. 1973. Self-reliance and some conditions that promote it. In *Support, innovation and autonomy*, ed. R. Gosing. London: Tavistock, pp. 23–48.

Bradley, A. 1975. National Assistance Appeal Tribunals and the Franks Report. In *Justice, discretion and poverty*, ed. M. Adler and A. Bradley. London: Professional Books, pp. 33–54.

Brandt, R. B. 1976. The psychology of benevolence and its implications for philosophy. *Journal of Philosophy* 73: 429–53.

Braybrooke, D. 1968. Let needs diminish that preferences may prosper. *American Philosophical Quarterly Monographs* 1: 86–107.

Brennan, G., and Buchanan, J. M. 1986. *The reason of rules*. Cambridge: Cambridge University Press.

Brennan, W. J. 1970. Opinion of the U.S. Supreme Court. *Goldberg v. Kelly*. 397 US 255–71.

Brennan, W. J.; White, B. R.; Marshall, T.; and Blackmun, H. A. 1978. Concurring opinion. *University of California Regents v. Bakke*. 438 US 265, 324–79.

Brenton, M. 1982. Changing relationships in Dutch social services. *Journal of Social Policy* 11: 59–80.

Brewer, D. J. 1875. Opinion of the Kansas Supreme Court. *Griffith v. Osawkee Township*. 14 Kansas 418. Reprinted in Abbott 1940, 73–80.

Briar, S. 1966. Welfare from below: recipients' views of the public welfare system. *California Law Review* 54: 370–85. Reprinted in ten Broek 1966: 45–61.

Briggs, A. 1961. The welfare state in historical perspective. *Archives Européennes de Sociologie* 2: 221–58.

Briggs, E., and Rees, A. M. 1980. *Supplementary Benefits and the consumer.* Occasional Papers on Social Administration, no. 65. London: Bedford Square Press/NCVO.

Brilmayer, L; Hekeler, R. W.; Laycock, D.; and Sullivan, T. A. 1980. Sex discrimination in employer-sponsored insurance plans: a legal and demographic analysis. *University of Chicago Law Review* 47: 505–61.

Broad, C. D. 1916. On the function of false hypotheses in ethics. *International Journal of Ethics [Ethics]* 26: 377–97.

Broddason, T., and Webb, K. 1975. On the myth of social equality in Iceland. *Acta Sociologica* 19: 49–61.

Brodkin, E., and Lipsky, M. 1983. Quality control in AFDC as an administrative strategy. *Social Service Review* 57: 1–33.

Bronfenbrenner, M. 1971. *Income distribution theory.* New York: Aldine-Atherton.

Broome, J. 1984. Selecting people randomly. *Ethics* 95: 39–55.

Brown, C. V. 1980. *Taxation and the incentive to work.* Oxford: Clarendon Press.

Brown, J. D. 1956. The American philosophy of social insurance. *Social Service Review* 39: 1–8.

———. 1960. The role of social insurance in the United States. *Industrial and Labour Relations Review* 14: 107–12.

Brown, L. D., and Frieden, B. J. 1976. Rulemaking by improvisation: guidelines in the Model Cities Program. *Policy Sciences* 7: 455–88.

Brown, M. K. 1981a. The allocation of justice and police-citizen encounters. In *The public encounter,* ed. C. T. Goodsell. Bloomington: Indiana University Press, pp. 102–25.

———. 1981b. *Working the street.* New York: Russell Sage Foundation.

Browning, E. K. 1975. The externality argument for in-kind transfers: some critical remarks. *Kyklos* 28: 526–44.

Buchanan, A. E. 1979. Exploitation, alienation and injustice. *Canadian Journal of Philosophy* 9: 121–39.

———. 1984a. The right to a decent minimum of health care. *Philosophy and Public Affairs* 13: 55–78.

———. 1984b. What's so special about rights? *Social Philosophy and Policy* 2: 61–83.

———. 1985. *Ethics, efficiency and the market.* Totowa, N.J.: Rowman and Allanheld.

Buchanan, J. M. 1970. In defense of caveat emptor. *University of Chicago Law Review* 38: 64–73.

Bull, D. 1970. Action for welfare rights. In *The fifth social service*, ed. P. Townsend et al. London: Fabian Society.

Burns, E. M. 1956. *Social security and public policy*. New York: McGraw-Hill.

Calabresi, G. 1965. The decision for accidents. *Harvard Law Review* 78: 713–45.

———. 1970. *The costs of accidents*. New Haven: Yale University Press.

Calabresi, G., and Bobbitt, P. 1979. *Tragic choices*. New York: Norton.

Calabresi, G., and Hirschoff, J. T. 1972. Toward a test for strict liability in torts. *Yale Law Journal* 81: 1055–85.

Campbell, T. D. 1974. Humanity before justice. *British Journal of Political Science* 4: 1–16.

———. 1978. Discretionary "rights." In *Philosophy in social work*, ed. N. Timms and D. Watson. London: Routledge and Kegan Paul, pp. 50–77.

———. 1981. Counterproductive welfare law. *British Journal of Political Science* 11: 331–50.

———. 1983. *The left and rights*. London: Routledge and Kegan Paul.

Cane, P. 1982. Justice and justification for tort liability. *Oxford Journal of Legal Studies* 2: 30–62.

Carlin, J. E.; Howard, J.; and Messinger, S. C. 1966. Civil justice and the poor. *Law and Society Review* 1: 9–89.

Cass, B. 1981. Wages, women and children. In *The welfare stakes: strategies for Australian social policy*, ed. R. F. Henderson. Melbourne: Institute of Applied Economic and Social Research, University of Melbourne, pp. 45–83.

Casstevens, T. W. 1980. Birth and death processes of governmental bureaus in the United States. *Behavioral Science* 25: 161–65.

Cerny, K. H., ed. 1977. *Scandinavia at the polls*. Washington, D.C.: American Enterprise Institute.

Chambers, D. L. 1979. *Making fathers pay: enforcement of child support*. Chicago: University of Chicago Press.

Chaney, F. M. 1983. Opening address. In *Social policy in the 1980s*, ed. J. Dixon and D. L. Jayasuriya. Canberra: Canberra College of Advanced Education, pp. 1–6.

Christensen, C. 1978. World hunger: a structural approach. *International Organization* 32: 745–74.

Churchill, W. 1911. Speech on the National Insurance Bill. *Hansard's Parliamentary Debates (Commons)*, 5th series, 26: 493–510.

Clark, D. B. 1973. The concept of community: a re-examination. *Sociological Review* 21: 397–413.

Cloward, R. A., and Piven, F. F. 1971. *Regulating the poor*. New York: Random House.

Coggan, F. D. 1976. The family in Britain today. *Hansard's Parliamentary Debates (Lords)*, 5th series, 371: 1257–68.

Cohen, G. A. 1978. *Karl Marx's theory of history*. Oxford: Clarendon Press.

———. 1979. Capitalism, freedom and the proletariat. In *The idea of freedom*, ed. A. Ryan. Oxford: Clarendon Press, pp. 9–25.

———. 1979. The labor theory of value and the concept of exploitation. *Philosophy and Public Affairs* 8: 338–60.

———. 1981. Freedom, justice and capitalism. *New Left Review* 126: 3–16.

———. 1982. Reply to Elster (1982a). *Theory and Society* 11: 483–95.

———. 1983. The structure of proletarian unfreedom. *Philosophy and Public Affairs* 12: 3–33.

Cole, G.D.H. 1975. What is socialism? In *Ideologies of politics*, ed. A. de Crespigny and J. Cronin. Capetown, S.A.: Oxford University Press, pp. 79–105.

Coleman, J. L. 1974. On the moral argument for the fault system. *Journal of Philosophy* 71: 473–90.

———. 1983. Liberalism, unfair advantage and the volunteer armed forces. In *Conscripts and volunteers*, ed. R. K. Fullinwider. Totowa, N.J.: Rowman and Allanheld, pp. 109–25.

Coleman, J. S., et al. 1966. *Equality of educational opportunity*. Washington, D.C.: Government Printing Office.

Coleman, J. S.; Kelley, S. D.; and Moore, J. A. 1975. *Trends in school segregation, 1968–73*. Washington, D.C.: Urban Institute.

Collins, D. 1965. The introduction of old age pensions in Great Britain. *Historical Journal* 8: 246–59.

Comte, A. 1848/1953. *General view of positivism*, trans. J. H. Bridges. Stanford, Calif.: Academic Reprints.

Cornuelle, R. C. 1965. *Reclaiming the American dream*. New York: Random House.

Coser, L. A. 1965. The sociology of poverty. *Social Problems* 13: 140–48.

Cowles, G., ed. 1958. *Problems of United States economic development*. New York: Committee for Economic Development.

Craven-Ellis, W. 1940. Debate on the War Damage Insurance Act.

Hansard's Parliamentary Debates (Commons), 5th series, 367: 1290–2.

Creedy, J., and Disney, R. 1985. *Social insurance in transition: an economic analysis*. Oxford: Clarendon Press.

Crick, B. 1984. *Socialist values and time*. Fabian Tract 495. London: Fabian Society.

Crocker, L. 1972. Marx's concept of exploitation. *Social Theory and Practice* 1: 201–15.

Crosland, C.A.R. 1952. The transition from capitalism. In *New Fabian essays*, ed. R.H.S. Crossman. London: Turnstile Press, pp. 33–68.

———. 1956. *The future of socialism*. London: Jonathan Cape.

Cutright, P. 1965. Political structure, economic development and national social security programs. *American Journal of Sociology* 70: 537–50.

D'Agostino, F. 1981. The ethos of games. *Journal of the Philosophy of Sport* 8: 7–15.

D'Amato, A. 1983. Legal uncertainty. *California Law Review* 71: 1–55.

Daniels, N. 1985. *Just health care*. Cambridge: Cambridge University Press.

Danziger, S.; Haveman, R.; and Plotnick, R. 1981. How income transfer programs affect work, savings and income distribution. *Journal of Economic Literature* 19: 975–1028.

Davis, K. C. 1969. *Discretionary justice*. Baton Rouge: Louisiana State University Press.

———. 1970. The liberalized law of standing. *University of Chicago Law Review* 37: 450–73.

Day, J. P. 1977. Fairness and fortune. *Ratio* 19: 70–84.

———. 1981. Compensatory discrimination. *Philosophy* 56: 55–72.

Deacon, A. 1976. *In search of the scrounger: the administration of unemployment insurance in Britain 1920–1931*. Occasional Papers on Social Administration, no. 60. London: G. Bell.

Deacon, A., and Bradshaw, J. 1983. *Reserved for the poor*. Oxford: Blackwell/Martin Robertson.

Deacon, B. 1983. *Social policy and socialism*. London: Pluto Press.

Dean, M. 1983a. Ministers plan to reshape the welfare state. *Guardian Weekly* 128 (no. 9): 5.

———. 1983b. The Cabinet's secret brainchild. *Guardian Weekly* 128 (no. 9): 5.

Derthick, M. 1976. Guidelines for social service grants. *Policy Sciences* 7: 489–504.

Deutsch, K. W. 1957. *The political community and the North Atlantic area*. Princeton, N.J.: Princeton University Press.

Devlin, P. 1965. *The enforcement of morals*. Oxford: Clarendon Press.

Dewey, J. 1927. *The public and its problems*. New York: Holt.

Dicey, A. V. 1908. *The law of the constitution*. 7th ed. London: Macmillan.

Dingwall, R., and Murray, T. 1983. Categorization in accident departments: "good" patients, "bad" patients and "children." *Sociology of Health and Illness* 5: 127–48.

Donnison, D. 1976. Supplementary Benefits: dilemmas and priorities. *Journal of Social Policy* 5: 337–58.

————. 1977. Against discretion. *New Society* 41 (no. 780): 534–36.

Douglas, M., and Isherwood, B. 1979. *The world of goods*. London: Allen Lane.

Douglas, W. O. 1974. Dissenting opinion. *De Funis v. Odegaard*. 416 US 312, 321–48.

Downs, A. 1967. *Inside bureaucracy*. Boston: Little Brown.

Doyal, L., and Gough, I. 1984. A theory of human needs. *Critical Social Policy* 4 (1): 6–38.

Dryzek, J., and Goodin, R. E. 1986. Risk-sharing and social justice: the motivational foundations of the post-war welfare state. *British Journal of Political Science* 16: 1–34.

Duncan, G. J. 1984. *Years of poverty, years of plenty*. Ann Arbor, Mich.: Institute for Social Research, University of Michigan.

Dunleavy, P. 1981. *The politics of mass housing in Britain, 1945–1975*. Oxford: Clarendon Press.

————. 1985. Bureaucrats, budgets and the growth of the state. *British Journal of Political Science* 15: 299–329.

Durkheim, E. 1925/1961. *Moral education*, trans. E. K. Wilson and H. Schnurer. New York: Free Press.

Dworkin, G. 1971. Paternalism. In *Morality and the law*, ed. R. A. Wasserstrom. Belmont, Calif.: Wadsworth, pp. 107–26.

Dworkin, R. M. 1963. Judicial discretion. *Journal of Philosophy* 60: 624–38.

————. 1977. *Taking rights seriously*. Cambridge, Mass.: Harvard University Press.

————. 1978. Liberalism. In *Public and private morality*, ed. S. Hampshire. Cambridge: Cambridge University Press, pp. 113–43.

————. 1981. What is equality? *Philosophy and Public Affairs* 10: 185–246, 283–345.

————. 1983. Neutrality, equality and liberalism. In *Liberalism re-*

considered, ed. D. MacLean and C. Mills. Totowa, N.J.: Rowman and Allanheld, pp. 1–11.

———. 1985. *A matter of principle*. Cambridge, Mass.: Harvard University Press.

Eckstein, H. 1966. *Division and cohesion in democracy: a study of Norway*. Princeton, N.J.: Princeton University Press.

Edwards, M. 1980. Social effects of taxation. In *The politics of taxation*, ed. J. Wilkes. Sydney: Hodder and Stoughton.

———. 1986. Child support. In *Child support*. Canberra: Social Justice Project, RSSS, Australian National University, pp. 1–42.

Eisenberg, P., and Lazarsfeld, P. 1938. The psychological effects of unemployment. *Psychological Bulletin* 35: 358–90.

Eisenstein, Z. R. 1982. The sexual politics of the New Right. *Signs* 7: 567–88.

Ellis, A., and Kumar, K., eds. 1983. *Dilemmas of liberal democracies*. London: Tavistock.

Elster, J. 1978a. Exploring exploitation. *Journal of Peace Research* 15: 3–17.

———. 1978b. The labor theory of value: a reinterpretation of Marxist economics. *Marxist Perspectives* 1: 70–101.

———. 1979. *Ulysses and the sirens*. Cambridge: Cambridge University Press.

———. 1982a. Marxism, functionalism and game theory. *Theory and Society* 11: 453–82.

———. 1982b. Roemer versus Roemer: a comment on Roemer (1982c). *Politics and Society* 11: 363–73.

———. 1983. Exploitation, freedom and justice. In *Nomos XXVI: Marxism*, ed. J. R. Pennock and J. W. Chapman. New York: New York University Press, pp. 277–304.

Ely, J. H. 1974. The constitutionality of reverse discrimination. *University of Chicago Law Review* 41: 723–41.

Emerson, R. W. 1841. Self-reliance. In *The collected works of Ralph Waldo Emerson*, ed. J. Slater, A. R. Ferguson and J. F. Carr. Cambridge, Mass.: Harvard University Press, vol. 2, pp. 25–51.

Engberg, L. A.; Hansen, G.; Welker, R. L.; and Thomas, D. R. 1974. Acquisition of key-pecking via auto shaping as a function of prior experience: "learned laziness"? *Science* 178: 1002–4.

Epstein, R. A. 1985. Products liability as an insurance market. *Journal of Legal Studies* 14: 645–69.

Feinberg, J. 1970. *Doing and deserving*. Princeton, N.J.: Princeton University Press.

———. 1973. *Social philosophy*. Englewood Cliffs, N.J.: Prentice-Hall.

———. 1980. *Rights, justice and the bounds of liberty*. Princeton, N.J.: Princeton University Press.

———. 1983. Noncoercive exploitation. In *Paternalism*, ed. R. Sartorious. Minneapolis: University of Minnesota Press, pp. 201–35.

Ferber, R., and Hirsch, W. Z. 1978. Social experimentation and economic policy. *Journal of Economic Literature* 16: 1379–414.

Fienberg, S. E. 1971. Randomization and social affairs: the 1970 draft lottery. *Science* 171: 255–61.

Finnis, J. 1980. *Natural law and natural rights*. Oxford: Clarendon Press.

Fiorina, M., and Noll, R. 1978. Voters, bureaucrats and legislators: a rational choice perspective on the growth of government. *Journal of Public Economics* 9: 239–54.

Fisher, J. D.; DePaulo, B. M.; and Nadler, A. 1981. Extending altruism beyond the altruistic act: the mixed effects of aid on the help recipient. In *Altruism and helping behavior*, ed. J. P. Rushton and R. M. Sorrentino. Hillsdale, N.J.: Lawrence Erlbaum Associates, pp. 367–422.

Fisher, J. D., and Nadler, A. 1976. Effect of donor resources on recipient self-esteem and self-help. *Journal of Experimental and Social Psychology* 12: 139–50.

Fisher, J. D.; Nadler, A.; and Whitcher-Alanga, S. 1982. Recipient reactions to aid: a conceptual review. *Psychological Bulletin* 91: 27–59.

Flemming, J. S. 1978. Aspects of optimal unemployment insurance. *Journal of Public Economics* 10: 403–25.

Foster, P. 1983. *Access to welfare*. London: Macmillan.

Frankfather, D. L.; Smith, M. J.; and Caro, F. G. 1981. *Family care of the elderly*. Lexington, Mass.: Lexington Books, D. C. Heath.

Frankfurt, H. 1973. Coercion and moral responsibility. In *Essays on freedom of action*, ed. T. Honderich. London: Routledge and Kegan Paul, pp. 63–86.

———. 1984. Necessity and desire. *Philosophy and Phenomenological Research* 45: 1–13.

Franks, O. S. 1957. *Report of the Commission on Administrative Tribunals and Enquiries*. Cmnd. 218. London: Her Majesty's Stationery Office.

Freeden, M. 1978. *The new liberalism*. Oxford: Clarendon Press.

Freemantle, C. W. 1892. Opening address of the president of section F (economic science and statistics) of the British Association for the Advancement of Science. *Journal of the Royal Statistical Society*, Series A, 55: 415–36.

Freund, E. 1921. The use of indefinite terms in statutes. *Yale Law Journal* 30: 437–55.

Fried, C. 1969. The value of life. *Harvard Law Review* 82: 1415–37.

———. 1970. *An anatomy of values*. Cambridge, Mass.: Harvard University Press.

———. 1975. Rights and health care. *New England Journal of Medicine* 293 (June): 241–45.

———. 1978. *Right and wrong*. Cambridge, Mass.: Harvard University Press.

Friedman, L. M. 1969. Social welfare legislation: an introduction. *Stanford Law Review* 21: 217–47.

Friedman, M. 1947. Lerner on the economics of control. *Journal of Political Economy* 55: 310–11.

———. 1962. *Capitalism and freedom*. Chicago: University of Chicago Press.

Friedman, M. and R. 1981. *Free to choose*. New York: Avon.

Friedrich, C. J. 1959. The concept of community in the history of political and legal philosophy. In *Nomos II: community*, ed. C. J. Friedrich. New York: Liberal Arts Press, pp. 3–24.

Fuller, L. 1964. *The morality of the law*. New Haven: Yale University Press.

Furniss, N., and Mitchell, N. 1984. Social welfare provisions in Western Europe: current status and future possibilities. In *Public policy and social institutions*, ed. H. R. Rogers, Jr. Greenwich, Conn.: JAI Press, pp. 15–54.

Furniss, N., and Tilton, T. 1977. *The case for the welfare state*. Bloomington: Indiana University Press.

Galston, W. A. 1980. *Justice and the human good*. Chicago: University of Chicago Press.

Galtung, J. 1980a. The basic needs approach. In *Human needs*, ed. K. Lederer. Cambridge, Mass.: Oelgeschlager, Gunn, and Hain, pp. 55–130.

———. 1980b. Self-reliance: concept, practice and rationale. In *Self-reliance: a strategy for development*, ed. J. Galtung, P. O'Brien and R. Preiswerk. London: Bogle-L'Ouverture for Institute of Development Studies, pp. 19–44.

Gamzu, E., and Williams, D. A. 1973. Pitfalls of organismic concepts: "learned laziness." *Science* 181: 367–68.

Gardner, M. 1981. Mathematical games: the Laffer curve and other laughs in current economics. *Scientific American* 245 (December): 16–20.

Garfinkel, I. 1986. Child support assurance. In *Child support*. Canberra: Social Justice Project, RSSS, Australian National University, pp. 74–86.

Garfinkel, I., and Uhr, E. 1984. A new approach to child support. *Public Interest* 75: 111–22.

Gaus, G. F. 1983. *The modern liberal theory of man*. London: Croom Helm.

Gergen, K. and M. 1971. International assistance in psychological perspective. *Yearbook of World Affairs* 25: 87–103.

Ghodse, A. H. 1978. The attitudes of casualty staff and ambulance personnel towards patients who take drug overdoses. *Social Science and Medicine* 12: 341–46.

Gibson, D. M. 1985. The doormouse syndrome: restructuring the dependency of the elderly. *Australian and New Zealand Journal of Sociology* 21: 44–63.

Gibson, D. M.; Goodin, R. E.; and Le Grand, J. 1985. "Come and get it": distributional biases in social service delivery systems. *Policy and Politics* 13: 109–25.

Gilder, G. 1981. *Wealth and plenty*. New York: Basic Books.

Ginzberg, E. 1966. The case for a lottery. *Public Interest* 5: 83–89.

Glazer, N. 1971. The limits of social policy. *Commentary* 52 (September): 51–58.

———. 1983. Towards a self-service society? *Public Interest* 70: 66–90.

Goggin, M. L. 1984. Social policy as theory: Reagan's public philosophy. In *Public policy and social institutions*, ed. H. R. Rogers, Jr. Greenwich, Conn.: JAI Press, pp. 55–96.

Goldthorpe, J. H. 1964. The development of social policy in England, 1800–1914. *Transactions of the fifth World Congress of Sociology, Washington, D.C., September 1962*. Paris: International Sociological Association, vol. 4, pp. 41–56.

———. 1978. The current inflation: towards a sociological account. In *The political economy of inflation*, ed. F. Hirsch and J. H. Goldthorpe. London: Martin Robertson, pp. 186–214.

Goode, W. J. 1963. *World revolution and family patterns*. Glencoe, Ill.: Free Press.

Goodin, R. E. 1976. *The politics of rational man*. London: Wiley.

———. 1979. The development-rights tradeoff: some unwarranted political and economic assumptions. *Universal Human Rights [Human Rights Quarterly]* 1: 31–42.

———. 1980. *Manipulatory politics*. New Haven: Yale University Press.

———. 1982a. Banana time in British politics. *Political Studies* 30: 42–58.

———. 1982b. Discounting discounting. *Journal of Public Policy* 2: 53–72.

———. 1982c. *Political theory and public policy*. Chicago: University of Chicago Press.

———. 1982d. Rational politicians and rational bureaucrats in Washington and Whitehall. *Public Administration* (London) 60: 23–41.

———. 1983. The ethics of destroying irreplaceable assets. *International Journal of Environmental Studies* 21: 55–66.

———. 1985a. Erring on the side of kindness in social welfare policy. *Policy Sciences* 18: 141–56.

———. 1985b. *Protecting the vulnerable: a re-analysis of our social responsibilities*. Chicago: University of Chicago Press.

———. 1985c. Vulnerabilities and responsibilities: an ethical defense of the welfare state. *American Political Science Review* 79: 775–87.

———. 1986a. Defending the welfare state. *American Political Science Review* 80: 952–54.

———. 1986b. Laundering preferences. In *Foundations of social choice theory*, ed. J. Elster and A. Hylland. Cambridge: Cambridge University Press, pp. 75–101.

———. 1986c. Responsibilities. *Philosophical Quarterly* 36: 50–56.

Goodin, R. E., and Dryzek, J. 1980. Rational participation: the politics of relative power. *British Journal of Political Science* 10: 273–92.

Goodin, R. E., and Le Grand, J., et al. 1987. *Not only the poor: the middle classes and the welfare state*. London: Allen and Unwin.

Goodsell, C. 1981. Looking once again at human service bureaucracy. *Journal of Politics* 43: 763–78.

Graham, K. 1986. Terrorists need the press, but so does a free society. *Washington Post National Weekly Edition*, May 5, pp. 24–25.

Green, T. H. 1881. Liberal legislation and freedom of contract. In *Green's works*, ed. R. L. Nettleship. London: Longmans, Green, vol. 3, pp. 365–86.

Greider, W. 1982. *The education of David Stockman and other Americans*. New York: Dutton.

Grier, E., and Grier, G. 1965. Equality and beyond: housing segregation in the Great Society. In *The negro American*, ed. T. Parsons and K. B. Clark. Boston: Houghton Mifflin, pp. 525–54.

Griffiths, B.; Cooper, S.; and McVicar, N. 1986. *Overseas countries' maintenance provisions*. Background/Discussion Paper no. 13, Social Security Review. Canberra: Department of Social Security, Commonwealth of Australia.

Grote, J. 1870. *An examination of the utilitarian philosophy*. Cambridge, England: Deighton, Bell.

Grotius, H. 1625. *On the law of war and peace*, trans. F. W. Kelsey. Oxford: Clarendon Press, 1925.

Gruen, F. H. 1983. The welfare expenditure debate. *Economic Record* 58: 207–23.

Gulbrandsen, L., and Torgersen, U. 1974. Market interests and moral indignation: the political psychology of housing price regulation in postwar Oslo. *Scandinavian Political Studies* 9: 75–101.

Gummer, B. 1979. On helping and helplessness: the structure of discretion in the American welfare system. *Social Service Review* 53: 214–28.

Gurr, T. R. 1970. *Why men rebel*. Princeton, N.J.: Princeton University Press.

Hadley, R., and Hatch, S. 1981. *Social welfare and the failure of the state*. London: Allen and Unwin.

Hagen, J. L. 1982. Whatever happened to 43 Elizabeth I, c.2? *Social Service Review* 56: 108–19.

Haksar, V. 1976. Coercive proposals. *Political Theory* 4: 65–79.

Hall, A. S. 1974. *The point of entry*. London: Allen and Unwin.

Hall, P. 1980. *Great planning disasters*. London: Weidenfeld, Nicholson.

Handler, J. F. 1966. Controlling official behavior in welfare administration. *California Law Review* 54: 479–510. Reprinted in ten Broek 1966, 155–86.

———. 1968. The coercive children's officer. *New Society* 12: 485–87.

———. 1969. Justice for the welfare recipient: fair hearings in AFDC—the Wisconsin experience. *Social Service Review* 43: 12–34.

———. 1973. *The coercive social worker*. Chicago: Rand McNally.

———. 1979. *Protecting the social service client: legal and structural controls on official discretion.* New York: Academic Press.

Handler, J. F., and Hollingsworth, E. J. 1969. Stigma, privacy and other attitudes of welfare recipients. *Stanford Law Review* 22: 1–69.

———. 1970. Reforming welfare: the constraints of the bureaucracy and the clients. *University of Pennsylvania Law Review* 118: 1167–87.

———. 1971. *The "deserving poor."* Chicago: Markham/Rand McNally.

Handler, J. F., and Sosin, M. 1983. *Last resorts: emergency assistance and special needs programs in public welfare.* New York: Academic Press.

Hannah, L. 1986. *Inventing retirement.* Cambridge: Cambridge University Press.

Harcourt, G. C. 1972. *Some Cambridge controversies in the theory of capital.* Cambridge: Cambridge University Press.

Hardin, G. 1980. *Promethean ethics.* Seattle: University of Washington Press.

Hardin, R. 1982. *Collective action.* Baltimore, Md.: Johns Hopkins University Press/RFF.

Hare, R. M. 1957. Reasons of state. In R. M. Hare, *Applications of moral philosophy.* London: Macmillan, 1972, pp. 9–23.

Harrington, M. 1962. *The other America.* New York: Macmillan.

Harrod, R. F. 1958. The possibility of economic satiety. In Cowles 1958, vol. 1, pp. 207–14.

Harsanyi, J. C. 1975. Can the maximin principle serve as a basis for morality? *American Political Science Review* 69: 594–606.

Hart, H.L.A. 1955. Are there any natural rights? *Philosophical Review* 64: 175–91.

———. 1961. *The concept of law.* Oxford: Clarendon Press.

———. 1967. Social solidarity and the enforcement of morality. *University of Chicago Law Review* 35: 1–13.

———. 1983. *Essays in jurisprudence and philosophy.* Oxford: Clarendon Press.

Hart, H.L.A., and Honoré, A. M. 1959. *Causation in the law.* Oxford: Clarendon Press.

Hauser, P. M. 1965. Demographic factors in the integration of the negro. In *The negro American,* ed. T. Parsons and K. B. Clark. Boston: Houghton Mifflin, pp. 71–101.

Hay, D. 1975. Property, authority and crime. In *Albion's fatal tree,* ed. D. Hay et al. London: Allen and Unwin, pp. 17–63.

Hayek, F. A. 1944. *The road to serfdom*. London: Routledge.

———. 1958. Inflation resulting from downward inflexibility of wages. In Cowles 1958, vol. 1, pp. 147–52.

———. 1960. *The constitution of liberty*. London: Routledge and Kegan Paul.

Hayter, T. 1971. *Aid as imperialism*. Harmondsworth, Mddx.: Penguin.

Hayward, J. E. S. 1959. Solidarity: the social history of an idea in nineteenth century France. *International Journal of Social History* 4: 261–84.

Heckscher, A. 1963. *The public happiness*. London: Hutchinson.

Heclo, H. 1974. *Modern social policies in Britain and Sweden*. New Haven, Conn.: Yale University Press.

———. 1981. Toward a new welfare state? In *The development of welfare states in Europe and America*, ed. P. Flora and A. Heidenheimer. New Brunswick, N.J.: Transaction Books, pp. 383–406.

———. 1986. General welfare and two American political traditions. *Political Science Quarterly* 101: 179–96.

Hencke, D. 1986. Families could be asked to help needy. *Guardian*, March 12, p. 32.

Herman, M. 1972. *Administrative justice and Supplementary Benefits*. Occasional Papers on Social Administration, no. 47. London: G. Bell.

Hibbs, D. A. 1973. *Mass political violence*. New York: Wiley.

Hicks, J. R. 1941. The rehabilitation of consumers' surplus. *Review of Economic Studies* 8: 108–16.

Higgins, J. 1978. Regulating the poor revisited. *Journal of Social Policy* 7: 189–98.

———. 1980. Social control theories of social policy. *Journal of Social Policy* 9: 1–23.

———. 1982. Public welfare: the road to freedom? *Journal of Social Policy* 11: 177–99.

Hill, M. J. 1969. The exercise of discretion in the National Assistance Board. *Public Administration* 47: 75–90.

Hill, T. E., Jr. 1973. Servility and self-respect. *Monist* 57: 87–104.

Hillery, G. A. 1955. Definitions of community: areas of agreement. *Rural Sociology* 20: 111–23.

Himmelfarb, G. 1984. *The idea of poverty: England in the early industrial age*. London: Faber and Faber.

Hirsch, F. 1976. *Social limits to growth*. Cambridge, Mass.: Harvard University Press.

Hirschman, A. O. 1971. *Exit, voice and loyalty*. Cambridge, Mass.: Harvard University Press.

Hobbes, T. 1651. *Leviathan*. London: Andrew Crooke.

Hobhouse, L. T. 1911. *Liberalism*. London: Oxford University Press, 1964.

Hobsbawm, E. J. 1975. Fraternity. *New Society*, 34 (no. 686): 471–3.

Hochman, H. M., and Rogers, J. D. 1969. Pareto optimal redistribution. *American Economic Review* 59: 542–57.

Hochschild, J. L. 1984. *The new American dilemma: liberal democracy and school desegregation*. New Haven, Conn.: Yale University Press.

Hodgkinson, C. 1978. *Towards a philosophy of administration*. Oxford: Blackwell.

Hodgson, D. H. 1967. *Consequences of utilitarianism*. Oxford: Clarendon Press.

Holmstrom, N. 1977. Exploitation. *Canadian Journal of Philosophy* 7: 353–69.

Holt, J. 1975. The New Deal and the American anti-statist tradition. In *The New Deal: the national level*, ed. J. Braeman, R. H. Bremner and D. Brody. Columbus, Ohio: Ohio State University Press, pp. 27–49.

Hood, C., and Wright, M., eds. 1981. *Big government in hard times*. Oxford: Martin Robertson.

Hudson, W. H. 1921. *A traveller in little things*. London: Dent.

Hume, D. 1777. *An enquiry concerning the principles of morals*. London: T. Cadell.

Ignatieff, M. 1984. *The needs of strangers*. London: Chatto and Windus.

Jackson, R. 1949. Concurring opinion. *Railway Express Agency v. New York*. 336 US 106.

Jacob, P. E., and Toscano, J. V., eds. 1964. *The integration of political communities*. Philadelphia: Lippincott.

Jaffe, L. L. 1961. Standing to secure judicial review. *Harvard Law Review* 74: 1265–314 and 75: 255–305.

Jahoda, M. 1979. The psychological meanings of unemployment. *New Society* 49: 492–95.

———. 1982. *Employment and unemployment*. Cambridge: Cambridge University Press.

Jahoda, M.; Lazarsfeld, P. F.; and Zeisel, H. 1933/1972. *Marienthal*. London: Tavistock.

James, F., Jr., and Dickinson, J. J. 1950. Accident proneness and accident law. *Harvard Law Review* 63: 769–95.

Jefferson, T. 1785. *Notes on Virginia*. New York: Harper & Row, 1964.

Jeffery, R. 1979. Normal rubbish: deviant patients in casualty departments. *Sociology of Health and Illness* 1: 90–107.

Jencks, C. 1979. The social basis of unselfishness. In *On the making of Americans*, ed. H. J. Gans. Philadelphia, Pa.: University of Pennsylvania Press, pp. 63–86.

Johnson, S. L. 1983. Race and the decision to detain a suspect. *Yale Law Journal* 93: 214–58.

Jones, P. 1982. Freedom and the redistribution of resources. *Journal of Social Policy* 11: 217–38.

Jouvenel, B. de, 1960. Toward a "communist welfare state": the logic of economics. *Problems of Communism* 9: 13–16.

Jowell, J. 1973. The legal control of administrative discretion. *Public Law* 1973: 178–220.

Judge, K. 1981. State pensions and the growth of social welfare expenditures. *Journal of Social Policy* 10: 503–30.

Judge, K., and Matthews, J. 1980. *Charging for social care*. London: Allen and Unwin.

Kadish, S. H. 1962. Legal norm and discretion in the police and sentencing process. *Harvard Law Review* 75: 904–31.

Kahn, A. J. 1976. Service delivery at the neighborhood level: experience, theory and fads. *Social Service Review* 50: 23–56.

Kahn, R. L. 1972. The meaning of work. In *The human meaning of social change*, ed. A. Campbell and P. E. Converse. New York: Russell Sage Foundation, pp. 159–203.

Kahneman, D., Slovic, P., and Tversky, A., eds. 1982. *Judgment under uncertainty: heuristics and biases*. Cambridge: Cambridge University Press.

Kane, R. L. and R. A. 1979. *Alternatives to institutional care of the elderly*. RAND Paper P-6256. Santa Monica, Calif.: RAND Corporation.

Karst, K. L. 1977. Equal citizenship under the Fourteenth Amendment. *Harvard Law Review* 91: 1–68.

Kasarda, J. D., and Janowitz, M. 1974. Community attachment in mass society. *American Sociological Review* 39: 328–39.

Kaufman, H. A. 1977. *Are government organizations immortal?* Washington, D.C.: Brookings Institution.

Kearns, T. R. 1970. On de-moralizing due process. In *Nomos XVIII: due process*, ed. J. R. Pennock and J. W. Chapman. New York: New York University Press, pp. 229–56.

Keith-Lucas, A. 1953. Political theory implicit in social case-work theory. *American Political Science Review* 47: 1076–91.

Kemeny, J. 1983. Professional ideologies and organizational structure: tanks and the military. *Archives Européennes de Sociologie* 24: 223–40.

Keniston, K., et al. 1977. *All our children*. New York: Harcourt, Brace, Jovanovich.

Kennedy, J. F. 1962. Text of President's message to Congress seeking reforms in welfare program. *New York Times* 111 (no. 37, 995; February 2): 10.

King, J. H., Jr. 1981. Causation, valuation and chance in personal injury torts involving preexisting conditions and future consequences. *Yale Law Journal* 90: 1353–97.

Kirp, D. L. 1986. The California work/welfare scheme. *Public Interest* 83: 34–48.

Kleinig, J. 1971. The concept of desert. *American Philosophical Quarterly* 8: 71–8.

———. 1982. The ethics of consent. In *New essays in ethics and public policy*, ed. K. Nielsen and S. C. Patten. *Canadian Journal of Philosophy*, supplementary vol. no. 8. Guelph, Ont.: Canadian Association for Publishing in Philosophy, pp. 91–118.

Kousser, J. M. 1983. Suffrage and political participation. Social Science Working Paper no. 471, California Institute of Technology, Pasadena, Calif. Forthcoming in *Encyclopedia of American political history*, ed. J. P. Greene. New York: Scribner.

Kramer, R. M. 1985. The welfare state and the voluntary sector: the case of the personal social services. In *The welfare state and its aftermath*, ed. S. N. Eisenstadt and O. Ahimeir. London: Croom Helm, pp. 132–40.

Krepps, J. M. 1965. The economics of intergenerational relationships. In Shanas and Streib 1965, pp. 267–88.

———. 1977. Intergenerational transfer and the bureaucracy. In Shanas and Sussman 1977, pp. 21–34.

Kronman, A. T. 1980. Contract law and distributive justice. *Yale Law Journal* 89: 472–511.

———. 1983. Paternalism and the law of contracts. *Yale Law Journal* 92: 763–98.

Kropotkin, P. 1914. *Mutual aid*. Boston: Extending Horizons Books, n.d.

Kunreuther, H. 1978. *Disaster insurance protection*. New York: Wiley.

Kydland, F. E., and Prescott, E. C. 1977. Rules rather than discretion: the inconsistency of optimal plans. *Journal of Political Economy* 85: 473–92.

Labour Party, U.K. 1952. *The welfare state*. London: Labour Party. Reprinted in part in Pope, Pratt, and Hoyle 1986, 169–73.

Lamb, J. 1986. Limited gains as welfare rules move onto disk. *The Observer*. London: October 19, p. 44.

Land, H. 1975. The introduction of family allowances: an act of historical justice? In *Change, choice and conflict in social policy*, ed. P. Hall. London: Heinemann, pp. 157–230.

———. 1978. Who cares for the family? *Journal of Social Policy* 7: 257–84.

———. 1979. The boundaries between the state and the family. In *The sociology of the family*, ed. C. Harris. *Sociological Review Monograph* no. 28. Keele: Sociological Review, pp. 141–59.

Lane, R. E. 1981. Markets and politics: the human product. *British Journal of Political Science* 11: 1–16.

———. 1982. Government and self-esteem. *Political Theory* 10: 5–31.

Lange, O. 1936–1937. On the economic theory of socialism. *Review of Economic Studies* 4: 53–71 and 123–42.

Laumann, E. O. 1973. *Bonds of pluralism: the form and substance of urban social networks*. New York: Wiley.

Lazear, E. P. 1979. Why is there mandatory retirement? *Journal of Political Economy* 87: 1261–84.

Le Grand, J. 1982. *The strategy of equality*. London: Allen and Unwin.

Le Grand, J., and Robinson, R. 1984. *The economics of social problems*. 2nd ed. London: Macmillan.

Leman, C. 1979. How to get there from here: the grandfather effect and public policy. *Policy Analysis* 6: 99–116.

Levine, A. 1981. *Liberal democracy*. New York: Columbia University Press.

Lewis, M. T. 1975. *Values in Australian income security policies*. Australian Government Commission of Inquiry into Poverty, Research Report, series 4. Canberra: Australian Government Printing Service.

Lightman, E. S. 1981. Continuity in social policy behaviours: the case of voluntary blood donorship. *Journal of Social Policy* 10: 53–79.

Lindblom, C. E. 1977. *Politics and markets*. New York: Basic Books.

Lipsey, R. G., and Lancaster, K. 1956. The general theory of second best. *Review of Economic Studies* 24: 11–33.

Lipsky, M. 1980. *Street-level bureaucracy*. New York: Russell Sage Foundation.

———. 1984. Bureaucratic disentitlement in social welfare programs. *Social Service Review* 58: 3–27.

Litwak, E. 1965. Extended kin relations in an industrial democratic society. In Shanas and Streib 1965, pp. 290–323.

Lloyd-George, D. 1908/1986. Speech on old-age pensions. *Hansard's Parliamentary Debates (Commons)*, 4th series 140: 565–86. Reprinted in part in Pope, Pratt, and Hoyle 1986, 53–55.

Lockwood, D. 1974. For T. H. Marshall. *Sociology* 8: 363–67.

Loney, M. 1986. *The politics of greed*. London: Pluto Press.

Lowenthal, R. 1960. Toward a "communist welfare state": ideology, power and welfare. *Problems of Communism* 9: 18–21.

Lynes, T. 1967. *French pensions*. Occasional Papers in Social Administration no. 21. London: G. Bell.

———. 1979. Welfare rights. In *The fifth social service*, ed. P. Townsend et al. London: Fabian Society, pp. 120–30.

Lyon, D. W. 1976. *The dynamics of welfare dependency: a survey*. RAND Paper P-5769. Santa Monica, Calif.: RAND Corporation.

Lyons, D. 1975. Welcome threats and coercive offers. *Philosophy* 50: 427–36.

McBride, J. P.; Moore, R. E.; Witherspoon, J. P.; and Blanco, R. E. 1978. Radiological impact of airborne effluents from coal and nuclear plants. *Science* 202: 1045–51.

MacCallum, G. 1966. Legislative intent. *Yale Law Journal* 75: 754–87.

———. 1967. Negative and positive freedom. *Philosophical Review* 76: 312–45.

MacDonagh, O. 1958a. Delegated legislation and administrative discretions in the 1850s. *Victorian Studies* 2 (no. 1): 29–44.

———. 1958b. The nineteenth-century revolution in government: a reappraisal. *Historical Journal* 1: 52–67.

———. 1961. *A pattern of government growth, 1800–1860*. London: MacGibbon and Kee.

MacIntyre, A. 1968. Egoism and altruism. In *Encyclopedia of philosophy*, ed. P. Edwards. London: Collier Macmillan, vol. 2, pp. 462–66.

Mackie, J. L. 1955. Responsibility and language. *Australasian Journal of Philosophy* 33: 143–59.

———. 1965. Causes and conditions. *American Philosophical Quarterly* 2: 115–25.

Macpherson, C. B. 1962. *The political theory of possessive individualism*. Oxford: Clarendon Press.

———. 1973. *Democratic theory*. Oxford: Clarendon Press.

———. 1985. *The rise and fall of economic justice*. Oxford: Oxford University Press.

Maimonides, M. 1168. *The code of Maimonides (Misheneh Torah)*, trans. I. Klein. New Haven, Conn.: Yale University Press.

Maine, H. S. 1871. *Village-communities in the East and West*. London: J. Murray.

Malthus, T. R. 1826. *An essay on the principles of population*. 6th ed. London: J. Murray.

Mann, M. 1985. *Socialism can survive: social change and the Labour Party*. Fabian Tract no. 502. London: Fabian Society.

Manser, A. R. 1962. It serves you right. *Philosophy* 37: 293–306.

Margolis, J. 1955. A comment on the pure theory of public expenditure. *Review of Economics and Statistics* 37: 347–49.

———. 1975. Bureaucrats and politicians. *Journal of Law and Economics* 18: 645–59.

Marsden, D. 1982. *Workless*, revised ed. London: Croom Helm.

Marshall, A. 1892. Discussion of Mr. Booth's (1891) paper. *Journal of the Royal Statistical Society*, Series A, 55: 60–63.

Marshall, G. 1984. *Constitutional conventions*. Oxford: Clarendon Press.

Marshall, T. H. 1949. *Citizenship and social class*. The Marshall Lectures, Cambridge University. Cambridge: Cambridge University Press. Reprinted in Marshall 1963, 70–134.

———. 1963. *Class, citizenship and social development*. Chicago: University of Chicago Press.

———. 1965. The right to welfare. *Sociological Review* 13: 261–72.

———. 1981. *The right of welfare and other essays*. London: Heinemann.

Marx, K. 1843. On the Jewish question. In Tucker 1972, 24–51.

Mashaw, J. L. 1983. *Bureaucratic justice: managing social security disability claims*. New Haven, Conn.: Yale University Press.

Mazrui, A. 1972. *Cultural engineering and nation-building in East Africa*. Evanston, Ill.: Northwestern University Press.

Mead, L. M. 1982. Social programs and social obligations. *Public Interest* 69: 17–32.

Mechanic, D. 1962. Sources of power of lower participants in complex organizations. *Administrative Science Quarterly* 7: 341–64.

Menefee, J. A.; Edwards, B.; Schieber, S. J. 1981. Analysis of non-participation in the SSI program. *Social Security Bulletin* 44 (6): 3–21.

Merrill, S. A. 1978. The politics of passenger protection: behavioral versus environmental control. In *The policy cycle*, ed. A. B. Wildavsky and J. V. May. Beverly Hills, Calif.: Sage, pp. 89–107.

Merton, R. K. 1936. The unintended consequences of purposive social action. *American Sociological Review* 1: 894–904.

———. 1946. *Mass persuasion: the social psychology of a war bond drive*. New York: Harper and Brothers.

Meyerson, M., and Banfield, E. C. 1955. *Politics, planning and the public interest: the case of public housing in Chicago*. Glencoe, Ill.: Free Press.

Michelman, F. I. 1969. On protecting the poor through the Fourteenth Amendment. *Harvard Law Review* 83: 7–59.

Mill, J. S. 1848. *The principles of political economy*. London: Parker and Son.

———. 1863. *Utilitarianism*. London: Parker and Son.

———. 1869. *The subjection of women*. Oxford: Oxford University Press, 1975.

Miller, D. 1976. *Social justice*. Oxford: Clarendon Press.

———. 1978. Democracy and social justice. *British Journal of Political Science* 8: 1–19.

———. 1980. Social justice and the principle of need. In *The frontiers of political theory*, ed. M. Freeman and D. Robertson. Brighton: Harvester Press, pp. 173–97.

———. 1981. Market neutrality and the failure of cooperatives. *British Journal of Political Science* 11: 309–29.

———. 1982. Arguments for equality. *Midwest Studies in Philosophy* 7: 73–88.

———. 1983. Constraints on Freedom. *Ethics* 94: 66–86.

———. 1986. Altruism and the welfare state. Paper presented to Conference for the Study of Political Thought conference on "Poverty, charity and welfare," New Orleans. Forthcoming in Moon 1988.

Mirrlees, J. A. 1981. The economic uses of utilitarianism. In *Utilitarianism and beyond*, ed. A. Sen and B. Williams. Cambridge: Cambridge University Press, pp. 63–84.

Mitchell, O. S., and Fields, G. S. 1982. The effects of pensions and earnings on retirement: a review essay. *Research in Labor Economics* 5: 115–55.

Mondale, W. F.; Bentsen, L.; and Ribicoff, A. 1974. Senate report no. 93-1356: social security amendments of 1974. *United States*

Code: Congressional and Administrative News, 93rd Congress, 2nd Session, vol. 4, pp. 8133–60.

Montefiore, A. 1975. *Neutrality and impartiality*. Cambridge: Cambridge University Press.

Moon, J. D. 1986. The moral basis of the democratic welfare state. Mimeo., Wesleyan University, Middleton, Conn. Forthcoming in Moon 1988.

Moon, J. D., ed. 1988. *Responsibility, rights and welfare: essays on the welfare state*. Westport, Conn.: Greenwood Press.

Moore, B., Jr. 1970. *Reflections on the causes of human misery*. Boston: Beacon Press.

Moore, W. S., and Penner, R. G., eds. 1980. *The constitution and the budget*. Washington, D.C.: American Enterprise Institute.

Mosteller, F., and Moynihan, D. P., eds. 1972. *On equality of educational opportunity*. New York: Random House.

Mowat, C. L. 1961. *The Charity Organisation Society*. London: Methuen.

Moynihan, D. P. 1973. *The politics of a guaranteed national income*. New York: Random House.

———. 1986. *Family and nation*. San Diego, Calif.: Harcourt, Brace, Jovanovich.

Murray, C. A. 1982. The two wars against poverty: economic growth and the Great Society. *Public Interest* 69: 3–16.

———. 1984. *Losing ground: American social policy, 1950–1980*. New York: Basic Books.

———. 1985a. Have the poor been "losing ground?" *Political Science Quarterly* 100: 427–45.

———. 1985b. Helping the poor: a few modest proposals. *Commentary* 79 (5): 27–34.

Musgrave, R. A. 1983. A reappraisal of Social Security and its financing. In *Public expenditure and policy analysis*, ed. R. H. Haveman and J. Margolis. 3rd ed. Boston: Houghton Mifflin, pp. 369–97.

Myrdal, G. 1932. Socialpolitikens dilemma. *Spektrum* 2(3): 1–13 and 2(4): 13–31.

———. 1960. *Beyond the welfare state*. New Haven, Conn.: Yale University Press.

Nagel, E., and Newman, J. R. 1959. *Gödel's proof*. London: Routledge and Kegan Paul.

Neaves, C. 1871. Opening address of the president of section F (economic science and statistics) of the British Association for the Advancement of Science. *Journal of the Royal Statistical Society*, Series A, 34: 461–75.

Nell, E. J. 1987. On deserving profits. *Ethics*. 97: 403–10.

Nelson, B. 1980. Help-seeking from public authorities: who arrives at the agency door? *Policy Sciences* 12: 175–92.

Newman, F. M., and Oliver, D. W. 1967. Education and community. *Harvard Educational Review* 37: 61–106.

New Zealand Planning Council (NZPC). 1979. *The welfare state? Social policy in the 1980s.* NZPC no. 12. Wellington, N.Z.: NZPC.

———. 1981. *Directions.* NZPC no. 18. Wellington, N.Z.: NZPC.

Ng, Y.-K. 1978. Economic growth and social welfare: the need for a complete study of happiness. *Kyklos* 31: 575–87.

Nielsen, K. 1969. Morality and needs. In *The business of reason,* ed. J. J. MacIntosh and S. Coval. London: Routledge and Kegan Paul, pp. 186–206.

Niskanen, W. A., Jr. 1971. *Bureaucracy and representative government.* Chicago: Aldine-Atherton.

———. 1975. Bureaucrats and politicians. *Journal of Law and Economics* 18: 617–43.

Nordhaus, W. 1981a. The new brand of economics. *New York Times,* February 22: sec. 3, p. 2.

———. 1981b. Reagan's dubious tax revolution. *New York Times,* August 9: sec. 3, p. 3.

Nove, A. 1960. Toward a "communist welfare state": social welfare in the USSR. *Problems of Communism* 9: 1–10.

Nozick, R. 1972. Coercion. In *Philosophy, politics and society,* ed. P. Laslett, W. G. Runciman, and Q. Skinner. 4th series. Oxford: Blackwell, pp. 101–35.

———. 1974. *Anarchy, state and utopia.* Oxford: Blackwell.

Nussbaum, M. C. 1986. *The fragility of goodness: luck and rational self-sufficiency in Greek ethical thought.* Cambridge: Cambridge University Press.

Obler, J. 1981. Private giving in the welfare state. *British Journal of Political Science* 11: 17–48.

———. 1986. Moral duty and the welfare state. *Western Political Quarterly* 39: 213–35.

Offe, C. 1984. *Contradictions of the welfare state,* ed. J. Keane. London: Hutchinson.

Okun, A. 1975. *Equality and efficiency: the big tradeoff.* Washington, D.C.: Brookings Institution.

Olson, M., Jr. 1965. *The logic of collective action.* Cambridge, Mass.: Harvard University Press.

O'Neil, R. M. 1970. *The price of dependency*. New York: Dutton.

O'Neill, O. 1979. The most extensive liberty. *Proceedings of the Aristotelian Society (Supplement)* 53: 49–59.

Organisation for Economic Cooperation and Development (OECD). 1981. *The welfare state in crisis*. Paris: OECD.

Page, B. I. 1983. *Who gets what from government?* Berkeley: University of California Press.

Paine, R. 1969. In search of friendship. *Man* 4: 505–24.

Palmer, G.W.R. 1973. Compensation for personal injury: a requiem for the common law in New Zealand. *American Journal of Comparative Law* 21: 1–44.

Panichas, G. E. 1981. Vampires, werewolves and economic exploitation. *Social Theory and Practice* 7: 223–42.

Parry, G. 1976. Trust, distrust and consensus. *British Journal of Political Science* 6: 129–42.

Parsons, T. 1965. Full citizenship for the negro American? A sociological problem. In *The negro American*, ed. T. Parsons and K. B. Clark. Boston: Houghton Mifflin, pp. 709–54.

Passmore, J. A. 1979. Civil justice and its rivals. In *Justice*, ed. E. Kamenka and A. E-S. Tay. London: Edward Arnold, pp. 25–49.

———. 1981. *The limits of government*. Sydney: Australian Broadcasting Commission.

Pauley, M. V., and Wilcott, T. D. 1968. Who "should" bear the burden of national defense? In *Why the draft?*, ed. J. C. Miller, III. Baltimore, Md.: Penguin, pp. 58–68.

Petre, C. 1978. Maintenance default or maintenance at fault? *Australian Journal of Social Issues* 13: 314–18.

Piachaud, D. 1981. Peter Townsend and the Holy Grail. *New Society* 57 (no. 982): 419–21.

Pigou, A. C. 1902. Some aspects of the problem of charity. In *The heart of the Empire*, ed. C.F.G. Masterman. London: T. Fisher Unwin, pp. 236–61.

———. 1932. *The economics of welfare*. 4th ed. London: Macmillan.

Pinker, R. A. 1971. *Social theory and social policy*. London: Heinemann.

———. 1979. *The idea of welfare*. London: Heinemann.

———. 1982. An alternative view. In Barclay 1982, Appendix B: 236–62.

———. 1983. Traditions of social welfare. In Dixon and Jayasuriya 1983, 7–22.

Piven, F. F., and Cloward, R. 1971. *Regulating the poor*. New York: Random House.

Plamenatz, J. P. 1967. Diversity of rights and kinds of equality. In *Nomos IX: equality*, ed. J. R. Pennock and J. W. Chapman. New York: Atherton, pp. 79–98.

Plant, R. 1978. Community: concept, conception and ideology. *Politics and Society* 8: 79–107.

———. 1985. Welfare and the value of liberty. *Government and Opposition* 20: 297–314.

———. 1986. Needs, agency and rights. Paper presented to the Conference for the Study of Political Thought conference on "Poverty, charity and welfare," New Orleans. Forthcoming in Moon 1988.

Plant, R.; Lesser, H.; and Taylor-Gooby, P. 1980. *Political philosophy and social welfare*. London: Routledge and Kegan Paul.

Pocock, J.G.A. 1975. *The Machiavellian moment*. Princeton, N.J.: Princeton University Press.

———. 1985. *Virtue, commerce and history*. Cambridge: Cambridge University Press.

Pope, R.; Pratt, A.; Hoyle, B., eds. 1986. *Social welfare in Britain, 1885–1985*. London: Croom Helm.

Portes, A. 1972. Rationality in the slum. *Comparative Studies in Society and History* 14: 268–86.

Postow, B. C. 1978–1979. Economic dependence and self-respect. *Philosophical Forum* 10: 181–205.

Powell, L. F. 1978. Opinion of the U.S. Supreme Court. *University of California Regents v. Bakke*. 438 US 265, 269–328.

Prosser, T. 1981. The politics of discretion: aspects of discretionary power in the Supplementary Benefits scheme. In *Discretion and welfare*, ed. M. Adler and S. Asquith. London: Heinemann, pp. 148–70.

Prosser, W. L. 1971. *Handbook of the law of torts*. 4th ed. St. Paul, Minn.: West.

Pryor, F. 1968. *Public expenditures in communist and capitalist nations*. London: Allen and Unwin.

Rae, D. 1975. The limits of consensual decision. *American Political Science Review* 69: 1270–94.

———. 1981. *Equalities*. Cambridge, Mass.: Harvard University Press.

Rainwater, L. 1982. Stigma in income-tested programs. In *Income-tested transfer programs: the case for and against*, ed. I. Garfinkel. New York: Academic Press, pp. 19–46.

Rainwater, L., and Yancey, W. L., eds. 1967. *The Moynihan Report and the politics of controversy.* Cambridge, Mass.: MIT Press.

Ransom, R. L., and Sutch, R. 1977. *One kind of freedom: the economic consequences of emancipation.* Cambridge: Cambridge University Press.

Raphael, D. D., ed. 1967. *Political theory and the rights of man.* Bloomington: Indiana University Press.

Ravitch, D. 1978. The "white flight" controversy. *Public Interest* 51: 135–49.

Rawls, J. 1958. Justice as fairness. *Philosophical Review* 67: 164–94.

———. 1971. *A theory of justice.* Cambridge, Mass.: Harvard University Press.

———. 1980. Kantian constructivism in moral theory. *Journal of Philosophy* 77: 515–72.

———. 1982. Social unity and primary goods. In *Utilitarianism and beyond,* ed. A. Sen and B. Williams. Cambridge: Cambridge University Press, pp. 159–86.

Raz, J. 1978. Principles of equality. *Mind* 87: 321–42.

Reagan, R. 1981. Budget proposals: a program for economic recovery. *Congressional Quarterly Weekly Report* 39 (February 21): 360–63.

———. 1986. State of the Union message. *New York Times* 135 (no. 46, 676): A 20.

Reeve, A., ed. 1987. *Modern theories of exploitation.* London: Sage.

Reich, C. A. 1963. Midnight welfare searches and the Social Security Act. *Yale Law Journal* 72: 1347–60.

———. 1964. The new property. *Yale Law Journal* 73: 733–87.

———. 1965. Individual rights and social welfare: the emerging legal issues. *Yale Law Journal* 74: 1245–57.

Reiman, J. H. 1986. Law, rights, community and the structure of liberal justification. In *Nomos XXVIII: justification,* ed. J. R. Pennock and J. W. Chapman. New York: New York University Press, pp. 178–203.

Rein, M. 1965. *Social policy.* New York: Random House.

Rein, M., and Rainwater, L. 1978. Patterns of welfare use. *Social Service Review* 53: 511–34.

Reppy, J. 1979. The automobile airbag. In *Controversy,* ed. D. Nelkin. Beverly Hills, Calif.: Sage, pp. 145–58.

Rettig, R. A. 1975. The policy debate on patient care financing for victims of end-stage renal disease. *Law and Contemporary Problems* 40 (Autumn): 196–230.

Rimlinger, G. V. 1961. Social security, incentives and controls in the U.S. and U.S.S.R. *Contemporary Studies in Society and History* 4: 104–24.

Riskin, C. 1975. Maoism and motivation: work incentives in China. In *China's uninterrupted revolution,* ed. V. Nee and J. Peck. New York: Pantheon.

Roback, J. 1984. Southern labor law in the Jim Crow era. *University of Chicago Law Review* 51: 1161–92.

Robinson, J. 1933/1969. *The economics of imperfect competition.* 2nd ed. London: Macmillan.

———. 1980. Time in economic theory. *Kyklos* 33: 219–29.

Robson, W. A. 1976. *Welfare state and welfare society.* London: Allen and Unwin.

Roemer, J. E. 1982a. Exploitation, alternatives and socialism. *Economic Journal* 92: 87–107.

———. 1982b. *A general theory of exploitation and class.* Cambridge, Mass.: Harvard University Press.

———. 1982c. New directions in the Marxian theory of exploitation and class. *Politics and Society* 11: 253–87. Reprinted in part as: Property relations versus surplus value in Marxian exploitation. *Philosophy and Public Affairs* 11: 281–313.

———. 1985a. Equality of talent. *Economics and Philosophy* 1: 151–88.

———. 1985b. Should Marxists be interested in exploitation? *Philosophy and Public Affairs* 14: 30–65.

Roos, J. P., ed. 1978. The Nordic welfare states. *Acta Sociologica* 21 (Supplement).

Rose, R. 1971. *Governing without consensus.* London: Faber and Faber.

———. 1986. Learning to understand democratic government better. Paper presented to Tenth Annual Conference of Civitas on "Individual Liberty and Democratic Decision Making," Herdecke, Federal Republic of Germany, October 22–25.

Rose, R., and Peters, B. G. 1978. *Can government go bankrupt?* New York: Basic Books.

Rosen, H. S. 1976a. Taxes in a labor supply model with joint wage-hours determination. *Econometrica* 44: 485–507.

———. 1976b. Tax illusion and the labor supply of married women. *Review of Economics and Statistics* 58: 167–72.

Roth, J. A. 1972. Some contingencies of the moral evaluation and control of the clientele: the case of the hospital emergency service. *American Journal of Sociology* 77: 839–56.

Rothman, S. M. 1976. "Rights" versus "needs": American attitudes toward women, children and family. In *The Americans: 1976*, ed. I. Kristol and P. Weaver. Lexington, Mass.: Lexington Books, D. C. Heath, pp. 51–85.

Rousseau, J.-J. 1762a. *Emile*, trans. B. Foxley. London: Dent, 1911.

———. 1762b. *Social contract*, trans. J. R. and R. D. Masters. New York: St. Martin's, 1978.

Rydell, C. P.; Palmerio, T.; Blais, G.; and Brown, D. 1974. *Welfare caseload dynamics in New York City.* RAND Report R-1441-NYC. New York: New York City RAND Institute.

Sackville, R. 1975. *Law and poverty in Australia.* Australian Government Commission of Inquiry into Poverty, Second Main Report. Canberra: Australian Government Printing Service.

Safire, W. 1972. *The new language of politics*, rev. ed. New York: Macmillan.

Sage, L. 1986. A book for our times? *The Observer.* London. April 20, p. 25.

Samuelson, P. A. 1954. The pure theory of public expenditure. *Review of Economics and Statistics* 36: 387–89.

Sandel, M. J. 1982. *Liberalism and the limits of justice.* Cambridge: Cambridge University Press.

Scanlon, T. M. 1975. Preference and urgency. *Journal of Philosophy* 77: 655–69.

Scheingold, S. A. 1974. *The politics of rights.* New Haven, Conn.: Yale University Press.

Schelling, T. C. 1968. The life you save may be your own. In *Problems in public expenditure analysis*, ed. S. P. Chase. Washington, D.C.: Brookings Institution, pp. 127–62.

———. 1971. On the ecology of micromotives. *Public Interest* 25: 61–98.

Scholzman, K. L. 1976. Coping with the American dream: maintaining self-respect in an achieving society. *Politics and Society* 6: 241–63.

Schorr, A. L. 1960. *Filial responsibility in the modern American family.* U.S. Department of Health, Education and Welfare, Division of Program Research. Washington, D.C.: Government Printing Office.

———. 1980. "*. . . Thy father and thy mother . . .*" *A second look at filial responsibility and family policy.* U.S. Department of Health and Human Services, Social Security Administration Publication no. 13–11953. Washington, D.C.: Government Printing Office.

———. 1985. Professional practice as policy. *Social Service Review* 59: 178–96.

———. 1986. *Common decency: domestic politics after Reagan.* New Haven: Yale University Press.

Schreiner, P. 1981. Economic prospects and some implications for social policies development. In OECD 1981, pp. 110–19.

Schuck, P. H. 1980. Suing our servants: the Court, Congress and the liability of public officials for damages. *Supreme Court Review* 1980: 281–368.

———. 1983. *Suing government.* New Haven, Conn.: Yale University Press.

Schultze, C. L. 1977. *The public uses of private interest.* Washington, D.C.: Brookings Institution.

Schumpeter, J. A. 1950. *Capitalism, socialism and democracy.* 3rd ed. New York: Harper and Brothers.

Scott, J. C. 1975. Exploitation in rural class relations: a victim's perspective. *Comparative Politics* 7: 489–532.

———. 1976. *The moral economy of the peasant.* New Haven, Conn.: Yale University Press.

Seligman, M.E.P. 1975. *Helplessness.* San Francisco: Freeman.

Sen, A. K. 1970. *Collective choice and social welfare.* San Francisco: Holden-Day.

———. 1973. Behaviour and the concept of preference. *Economica* 40: 241–59.

———. 1977. Starvation and exchange entitlements: a general approach and its application to the Great Bengal Famine. *Cambridge Journal of Economics* 1: 33–59.

———. 1980. Equality of what? In *Tanner lectures on human values*, ed. S. McMurrin. Cambridge: Cambridge University Press, vol. 1, pp. 195–220.

———. 1981a. Ingredients of famine analysis: availability and entitlements. *Quarterly Journal of Economics* 95: 433–64.

———. 1981b. *Poverty and famines.* Oxford: Clarendon Press.

———. 1982. Just deserts. *New York Review of Books* 29 (no. 3): 3–6.

———. 1983. Poor, relatively speaking. *Oxford Economic Papers* 35: 153–69.

———. 1985a. *Commodities and capabilities.* Amsterdam: North-Holland.

———. 1985b. Well-being, agency and freedom. *Journal of Philosophy* 82: 169–221.

Sen, A. K., and Williams, B., eds. 1982. *Utilitarianism and beyond.* Cambridge: Cambridge University Press.

Sensat, J. 1984. Exploitation. *Noûs* 18: 21–38.

Shanas, E., and Streib, G. F., eds. 1965. *Social structure and the family: generational relations.* Englewood Cliffs, N.J.: Prentice-Hall.

Shanas, E., and Sussman, M. B., eds. 1977. *Family, bureaucracy and the elderly.* Durham, N.C.: Duke University Press.

Shapley, L., and Shubik, M. 1967. Ownership and the production function. *Quarterly Journal of Economics* 81: 88–111.

Shonfield, A. 1965. *Modern capitalism.* London: Oxford University Press.

Shrader-Frechette, K. S. 1980. *Nuclear power and public policy.* Dordrecht, Holland: D. Reidel.

Shue, H. 1980. *Basic rights.* Princeton, N.J.: Princeton University Press.

Shue, V. 1980. *Peasant China in transition.* Berkeley: University of California Press.

Sidgwick, H. 1874. *The methods of ethics.* 7th ed. London: Macmillan.

Simon, R. L. 1978–1979. An indirect defense of the merit principle. *Philosophical Forum* 10: 224–41.

Simon, W. H. 1983. Legality, bureaucracy and class in the welfare system. *Yale Law Journal* 92: 1198–269.

Singer, P. 1973. Altruism and commerce: a defense of Titmuss against Arrow (1972). *Philosophy and Public Affairs* 2: 312–20.

Skolnick, J. H. 1966. *Justice without trial.* New York: Wiley.

Smith, A. 1776. *The wealth of nations.* Oxford: Clarendon Press, 1976.

Smith, A. D. 1946. Community prerogative and the legal rights and freedom of the individual. *Social Security Bulletin* 9 (pt. 8): 6–10.

———. 1949. Public assistance as a social obligation. *Harvard Law Review* 63: 266–88.

———. 1955. *The right to life.* Chapel Hill: University of North Carolina Press.

Smith, L. 1986. The Democrats' desperate search for the big idea. *Fortune* (September 29): 108–16.

Sniderman, P. M., and Brody, R. A. 1977. Coping: the ethics of self-reliance. *American Journal of Political Science* 21: 501–21.

Spencer, H. 1884. *Man versus the state.* London: Williams and Norgate.

———. 1894. *The study of sociology.* London: Williams and Norgate.

Spender, H. 1982. *Worktown people: photographs from Northern England 1937–38,* ed. J. Mulford. Bristol: Falling Wall Press.

Spicker, P. 1984. *Stigma and social welfare*. London: Croom Helm.

Sprizak, E. 1973. African traditional socialism—a semantic analysis of political ideology. *Journal of Modern African Studies* 11: 629–47.

Sraffa, P. 1926. The laws of returns under competitive conditions. *Economic Journal* 36: 535–50.

Steiner, G. Y. 1981. *The futility of family policy*. Washington, D.C.: Brookings Institution.

Steiner, H. 1984. A liberal theory of exploitation. *Ethics* 94: 225–41.

———. 1987. Exploitation: a liberal theory amended, defended and extended. In Reeve 1987: 132–48.

Steiner, P. O. 1970. The public sector and the public interest. In *Public expenditures and policy analysis*, ed. R. H. Haveman and J. Margolis. Chicago: Markham, pp. 21–58.

Stevens, J. P. 1978. Opinion of the U.S. Supreme Court. *City of Los Angeles Department of Water and Power v. Manhart*. 435 US 702, 704–23.

Stewart, R. B. 1975. The reformation of American administrative law. *Harvard Law Review* 88: 1669–1813.

Stigler, G. J. 1975. *The citizen and the state*. Chicago: University of Chicago Press.

Stone, D. A. 1978. The deserving poor: income-maintenance policy towards the ill and disabled. *Policy Sciences* 10: 133–55.

———. 1984. *The disabled state*. London: Macmillan.

Sudnow, D. 1967. *Passing on*. Englewood Cliffs, N.J.: Prentice-Hall.

Sugden, R. 1982a. Hard luck stories: the problem of the uninsured in a laissez-faire society. *Journal of Social Policy* 11: 201–16.

———. 1982b. On the economics of philanthropy. *Economic Journal* 92: 341–50.

Sumner, W. G. 1883. *What social classes owe to each other*. New York: Harper and Brothers.

Sundstrom, G. 1982. The elderly, women's work and social security costs. *Acta Sociologica* 25: 21–38.

Tawney, R. H. 1932/1971. *Equality*. 4th ed. London: Unwin.

Taylor, C. 1976. Responsibility for self. In *The identities of persons*, ed. A. O. Rorty. Berkeley: University of California Press, pp. 281–99.

———. 1979. What's wrong with negative liberty? In *The idea of freedom*, ed. A. Ryan. Oxford: Clarendon Press, pp. 175–94.

Taylor, M. 1976. *Anarchy and cooperation*. London: Wiley.

Taylor, M. 1982. *Community, anarchy and liberty*. Cambridge: Cambridge University Press.

ten Broek, J., ed. 1966. *The law of the poor*. San Francisco: Chandler.

Thompson, E. P. 1968. *The making of the English working class*. Harmondsworth, Mddx.: Penguin.

———. 1971. The moral economy of the English crowd in the eighteenth century. *Past and Present* 50: 76–136.

Thurow, L. C. 1974. Cash versus in-kind transfers. *American Economic Review (Papers and Proceedings)* 64: 190–95.

———. 1980. *Zero-sum society*. New York: Basic Books.

Tiebout, C. M. 1956. A pure theory of local expenditure. *Journal of Political Economy* 64: 416–24.

Tilton, T. A. 1986. Alva and Gunnar Myrdal: equality and efficiency. Mimeo.: Indiana University, Bloomington, Ind.

Titmuss, R. M. 1950. *Problems of social policy*. London: Longmans, Green and HMSO.

———. 1958/1976. *Essays on "the welfare state."* 3rd ed. London: Allen and Unwin, 1976.

———. 1968. *Commitment to welfare*. London: Allen and Unwin.

———. 1970. Equity, adequacy and innovation in social security. *International Social Security Review* 23: 259–67.

———. 1971a. *The gift relationship*. London: Allen and Unwin.

———. 1971b. Welfare "rights," law and discretion. *Political Quarterly* 42: 113–32.

———. 1974. *Social policy*. London: Allen and Unwin.

Tobin, J. 1970. On limiting the domain of inequality. *Journal of Law and Economics* 13: 363–78.

Tocqueville, A. de. 1835/1983. Memoir on pauperism. *Public Interest* 70: 102–20.

———. 1840. *Democracy in America*, trans. G. Lawrence, ed. J. P. Mayer and M. Lerner. New York: Harper & Row, 1966.

Tormey, J. F. 1973. Exploitation, oppression and self-sacrifice. *Philosophical Forum* 5: 206–21.

Törnblom, K. Y., and Foa, U. G. 1983. Choice of a distribution principle: cross-cultural evidence on the effects of resources. *Acta Sociologica* 26: 161–73.

Townsend, P. 1954. Measuring poverty. *British Journal of Sociology* 5: 130–37.

———. 1957. *The family life of old people*. London: Routledge and Kegan Paul.

———. 1962. The meaning of poverty. *British Journal of Sociology* 13: 210–19.

————. 1979. *Poverty in the United Kingdom*. Harmondsworth, Mddx.: Penguin.

Tribe, L. H. 1975. Childhood, suspect classifications and conclusive presumptions. *Law and Contemporary Problems* 39 (Summer): 8–37.

Trollope, A. 1883. *Mr. Scarborough's family*. London: Oxford University Press, 1973.

Tucker, R. C., ed. 1972. *The Marx-Engels reader*. New York: Norton.

Tulloch, P. 1983. Workforce exclusion and dependency. In Dixon and Jayasuriya 1983, pp. 23–27.

————. 1984. Gender and dependency. In *Unfinished business: social justice for women in Australia*, ed. D. Broom. Sydney: Allen and Unwin, pp. 19–37.

Tussman, J., and ten Broek, J. 1949. The equal protection of the laws. *California Law Review* 37: 341–81.

Tversky, A., and Kahneman, D. 1981. The framing of decisions and the psychology of choice. *Science* 211: 453–58.

Unger, R. M. 1975. *Knowledge and politics*. New York: Free Press.

United Kingdom. Department of Health and Social Security (UK DHSS). 1978. *Social assistance: a review of the Supplementary Benefits scheme in Great Britain*. London: UK DHSS.

————. Royal Commission on the Aged Poor. 1895/1985. *Report*. Cmd. 1684. London: HMSO. Reprinted in part in Pope, Pratt, and Hoyle 1986, 51–52.

————. Supplementary Benefits Commission (UK SBC). 1976. *Annual report 1975*. Cmnd. 6615. London: Her Majesty's Stationery Office.

————. Supplementary Benefits Commission (UK SBC). 1977. *Annual report 1976*. Cmnd. 6910. London: Her Majesty's Stationery Office.

Updike, J. 1984. Emersonianism. *New Yorker* 60 (no. 23): 112–32.

Urmson, J. O. 1950. On grading. *Mind* 59: 145–69.

————. 1958. Saints and heroes. In *Essays in moral philosophy*, ed. A. I. Melden. Seattle: University of Washington Press, pp. 198–216.

van der Veen, R. J. 1978. Property, exploitation, justice. *Acta Politica* 13: 433–65.

van Gunsteren, H. 1976. *The quest for control*. London: Wiley.

————. 1978. Notes on a theory of citizenship. In *Democracy, consensus and social contract*, ed. P. Birnbaum, J. Lively, and G. Parry. London: Sage, pp. 9–35.

van Krieken, R. 1986. Social theory and child welfare: beyond social control. *Theory and Society* 15: 401–29.

van Lennep, E. 1981. Opening address. In OECD 1981, 9–11.

Vincent, A. and R. Plant, 1984. *Philosophy, politics and citizenship.* Oxford: Blackwell.

Vlastos, G. 1962. Justice and equality. In *Social justice*, ed. R. B. Brandt. Englewood Cliffs, N. J.: Prentice-Hall, pp. 31–72.

Wade, H.W.R. 1982. *Administrative law.* 5th ed. Oxford: Clarendon Press.

Waldron, J., ed. 1984. *Theories of rights.* Oxford: Oxford University Press.

Waldron, J. 1986. Welfare and the images of charity. *Philosophical Quarterly* 36: 463–82.

Walt, S. 1984. Comment on Steiner's (1984) liberal theory of exploitation. *Ethics* 94: 242–47.

Walzer, M. 1968. *Obligations.* Cambridge, Mass.: Harvard University Press.

———. 1980. *Radical principles.* New York: Basic Books.

———. 1982. The community. *New Republic* 3507 (March 31): 11–14.

———. 1983. *Spheres of justice.* Oxford: Martin Robertson.

Wamsley, G. L. 1969. Decision-making in local boards: a case study. In *Selective service and American society*, ed. R. W. Little. New York: Russell Sage Foundation, pp. 83–106.

Warwick, D. P. 1981. The ethics of administrative discretion. In *Public duties*, ed. J. L. Fleishman, L. Liebman, and M. H. Moore. Cambridge, Mass.: Harvard University Press, pp. 93–127.

Wasserstrom, R. A. 1977. Racism, sexism and preferential treatment. *UCLA Law Review* 24: 581–622.

———. 1980. *Philosophy and social issues.* Notre Dame, Ind.: Notre Dame University Press.

Watkins, J.W.N. 1963. Negative utilitarianism. *Proceedings of the Aristotelian Society (Supplement)* 37: 95–114.

Weale, A. 1978a. *Equality and social policy.* London: Routledge and Kegan Paul.

———. 1978b. Paternalism and social policy. *Journal of Social Policy* 7: 157–72.

———. 1982. *Political theory and social policy.* London: Macmillan.

Weidenbaum, M. L. 1970. Institutional obstacles to reallocating government expenditures. In *Public expenditures and policy analysis*, ed. R. H. Haveman and J. Margolis. Chicago: Markham, pp. 232–45.

Weinrib, E. J. 1980. The case for a duty to rescue. *Yale Law Journal* 90: 247–93.

Weisbrod, B. A. 1968. Income redistribution effects and benefit-cost analysis. In *Problems in public expenditures*, ed. S. B. Chase, Jr. Washington, D.C.: Brookings Institution, pp. 177–209.

Weissberg, N. C. 1970. Intergenerational welfare dependency: a critical review. *Social Problems* 18: 257–74.

Weitzman, M. L. 1977. Is the price system or rationing more effective in getting a commodity to those who need it most? *Bell Journal of Economics* 8: 517–24.

Weizsäcker, C. C. von. 1973. Modern capital theory and the concept of exploitation. *Kyklos* 26: 245–81.

Westen, P. 1982. The empty idea of equality. *Harvard Law Review* 95: 537–96.

White, A. R. 1971. *Modal thinking*. Oxford: Blackwell.

Whiting, B. B. 1978. The dependency hang-up and experiments in alternative life-styles. In *Major social issues*, ed. J. M. Yinger and S. J. Cutler. New York: Free Press, pp. 217–36.

Wiggins, D. 1985. Claims of need. In *Morality and objectivity*, ed. T. Honderich. London: Routledge and Kegan Paul, pp. 149–203.

Wildavsky, A. 1966. The political economy of efficiency. *Public Administration Review* 26: 292–301.

———. 1975. *Budgeting*. Boston: Little, Brown.

———. 1979. *Speaking the truth to power*. Boston: Little, Brown.

———. 1980. *How to limit government spending*. Berkeley: University of California Press.

Wilenski, P. 1980–1981. Equity or efficiency: competing values in administration. *Policy Studies Journal* 9: 1239–49.

Wilensky, H. L. 1975. *The welfare state and equality*. Berkeley: University of California Press.

Wilensky, H. L. and C. N. Lebeaux. 1958. *Industrial society and social welfare*. New York: Russell Sage Foundation.

Williams, G. 1954. Blackmail. *Criminal Law Review* 1954: 79–92, 162–72, and 240–46.

Williams, G., and Hepple, B. A. 1984. *Foundations of the law of torts*. 2nd ed. London: Butterworth.

Wilson, J. Q. 1968. *Varieties of police behavior*. Cambridge, Mass.: Harvard University Press.

Wilson, J.R.S. 1978. In one another's power. *Ethics* 88: 299–315.

Wilson, W. 1887. The study of administration. *Political Science Quarterly* 2: 197–222.

Winston, M. P., and Forsher, T. 1971. *Nonsupport of legitimate chil-*

dren by affluent fathers as a cause of poverty and welfare dependence. RAND Paper P-4665. Santa Monica, Calif.: RAND Corporation.

Wolf, C., Jr. 1979. A theory of non-market failure. *Journal of Law and Economics* 22: 107–40.

Wolff, R. P. 1974. There's nobody here but us persons. *Philosophical Forum* 5: 128–44.

Wood, A. W. 1972. The Marxian critique of justice. *Philosophy and Public Affairs* 1: 244–82.

Woodham-Smith, C. 1975. *The greater hunger: Ireland 1845–9.* London: New English Library.

Woodhouse, A. O., chairman. 1967. *Report of the Royal Commission of Inquiry on Compensation for Personal Injury in New Zealand.* Wellington, N.Z.: Government Printer.

Woodhouse, A.S.P., ed. 1951. *Puritanism and liberty.* London: Dent.

Wright, A. 1984. Tawneyism revisited: equality, welfare and socialism. In *Fabian essays in socialist thought*, ed. B. Pimlott. London: Heinemann, pp. 81–100.

Wright, E. O. 1984. A general framework for the analysis of class structure. *Politics and Society* 13: 383–423.

Wright, J. S. 1980. Color-blind theories and color-conscious remedies. *University of Chicago Law Review* 47: 213–45.

Zeckhauser, R. J. 1973a. Coverage for catastrophic illness. *Public Policy* 21: 149–72.

———. 1973b. Time as the ultimate source of utility. *Quarterly Journal of Economics* 87: 668–75.

Zelizer, V. A. 1978. Human values and the market: the case of life insurance and death in nineteenth-century America. *American Journal of Sociology* 84: 591–610.

Zimmerman, D. 1981. Coercive wage offers. *Philosophy and Public Affairs* 10: 121–45.

Zimmerman, D. H. 1971. The practicalities of rule use. In *Understanding everyday life*, ed. J. D. Douglas. London: Routledge and Kegan Paul, pp. 221–38.

INDEX

absolute needs, 30n, 31n

abuse: claims difficulties, 214–15; exploitation and, 150–51

abuse of discretion, concept of, 198n

abuse of process: and discretionary powers, 198; exploitation, 144

accidents: compensation for, 302; fault system, 294n

activist welfare state, ix–x

act/omission doctrine, 138; needs justification, 32–35

actuarial studies: contingency prediction, 158n; retirement plan equalization, 53n

administration of welfare: community enhancement, 101–2; discretion, 190–91; rule making, 222n

Administrative Procedure Act (U.S.), 200

advantage and exploitation, 124–27, 130–31

adverse selection, 157–58

affectionate relationships and exploitation, 136–38, 140

affirmative action, 65–66

Aid to Families with Dependent Children (AFDC): eligibility requirements, 188, 204, 320–21; investment aspects, 238–39; noncustodial spouses, 346; recidivism, 340–41; as social control, 195

air bags, 319–20

air pollution, 365

allocation efficiency, 168–69; and impartiality, 60–61

alterability of needs, 40–41

altruism: and charity, 156; and communitarianism, 76–78, 100–102, 113–18; and egoism, 79n; institutionalization of, 115–16; value of, 78–79

Anderson, Martin, 230

apartheid policies, 69

appeals procedures, 199–200

appropriateness of moral deserts, 287n

"approximate equality," 58n

arbitrariness and discretion, 198–201, 204–5; reform of, 208; supply-side policies, 268–69

Are Government Organizations Immortal, 325

asymmetrical relationships: dependency as, 175–78; welfare service as, 351

Athenian concept of community, 90–91; and welfare rights, 93

Austin, J. L., 281–82

Australia and welfare state: families as support, 344; self-reliance concept, 333

autonomy: community, 76–77; dependency, 183n; freedom, 311–12; needs vs. wants satisfaction, 46–48; poverty, 327

backlash, state government, 118–19

bargaining power: exploitation, 145–46; freedom, 313–14; in market place, 165–66; no reasonable choice standard, 180–81

behavior standards: and discretionary powers, 197–98; exploitation, 147–48

benefactor-beneficiary relationship, 19, 116–18; exploitation, 126–27

Benefit (Interest) Theory of rights, 212–13

benefits: needs justification, 32–35; upward adjustments for special groups, 64–65; whole-person exploitation, 131

Bentham, Jeremy, 337

Beveridge, Sir William, 4, 333–34, 353n

bias and impartiality, 57

Blackley, Canon, 280n; self-reliance concept, 333, 353n

blackmail: as abuse of process, 144; as exploitation, 134n

Blacks: police treatment of, 65n; reverse discrimination, 65–66; voting rights for, 84–85

Booth, Charles, 101n, 334, 337; family interdependency, 350–51

bottoms-up welfare administration, 211n

"breaks," and moral deserts, 291n

British National Blood Transfusion Service, 116

411

British War Damage Insurance Act, 272–73

British Workmen's Compensation Act, 295n, 301

Bryan, William Jennings, 268n

bureaucracy: discretionary control of, 172n; disentitlement, 210; dynamics of, 243–45; economic theory of, 242–44; freedom from red tape, 320–22; irreversibility of, 325–27

capital distribution, 9

Capitalists, moral deserts of, 278

carcinogen exposure, 302n

caseworkers: discretionary powers, 192–93; overload, 221–22; social control, 195

cash transfer programs, 5; and economies of scale, 240–41; vs. in-kind benefits, 219n; labor market, 339; manipulation of, 220n

caste society, and dependency, 182–83

Catholic Benevolent Fund, 11

character traits: dependency, 341n; and deserts, 285; self-reliance as, 354–57

charity, 11; as Assurance Game, 155n; benefactor-beneficiary relationship, 116–17; division of labor, 67n; as public good, 12, 155–57; self-reliance, 355; state coordination, 155; undeserved losses, 303n; unreliability, 202

Charity Organisation Society (Great Britain), 337

child allowances, 349

children: as future investment, 238–39; impartiality toward, 59–60, 62–63; negative attitudes toward, 63n; as noncitizens, 86–87

Children's Officers (Great Britain), 195

choice: freedom as, 307; needs satisfaction, 37n; vs. preferences, 319–20

Churchill, Winston, 295–96

citizenship: benefits, 83–91; and economic security, 183n; and equality, 111–13; rights of, 88, 184–85

"Citizenship and Social Class," 83–84, 184

Civil Rights Act of 1964 (Title VI), 65n

class structure: conflict among, 112–13; in community, 99–100; education, 260–61; and self-reliance, 334; social solidarity, 110n; and supply-side policies, 275–76; welfare rights, 216n

"clean hands" principles and exploitation, 151

client overload, 221–22

clientelism in welfare, 367–68

closet altruism, 156–57

coalition politics: supply-side policies, 275–77; and welfare policy, 13

coercion: drowning millionaire analogy, 145–46, 165–66; exploitation, 13–34; freedom, 313–14; lifestyles (social control), 57; unfairness of, 132–34

cohabitation prohibitions, 204; and freedom, 320–21

Coleman Report, 260

collective conscience, 100n

collective consumption, 101

collective goods: economic efficiency, 238–39; and freedom, 314–15

"color-blind" discrimination theories, 66n

"color-conscious" discrimination remedies," 66n

command economy, 31–32; value skepticism, 45

commerce and dependency, 171n

commercialization and services, 166

commodities: exploitation, 124; illicit trading, 329–30; needs satisfaction, 48–49; nonmarket distribution, 166

community: Athenian concept, 90–91; charity, 117n; cultural policy, 104–5; defined, 71–79; equalization, 53; exploitation, 151n; full participation concept, 89–90, 109–13; hierarchical, 110–11; justification for welfare state, x, 70–118; membership, 80–96; as moral ideal, 93–94; and mutual aid, 323–24; nationalistic, 87; networking within, 100–108; single-status ideal, 73–75; solidarity in, 93–95; state as, 87n; village society, 75–76; welfare attachments, 98–108; welfare rights, 82–91, 96–98

community service, national conscription, 61n

competition: dependency, 167; solidarity, 112

compulsory insurance programs, 158–59

computerized decision making. See decision making

conditional needs, 30n

confiscation vs. distribution, 9n

conscience and moral deserts, 286–87

constant-sum concept: and freedom, 310; and property rights, 313; supply-side policies, 276–77

constitutional aspects of welfare, 16n

constrained benevolence of welfare, 322

consumer: and education, 241n; exploitation of, 135n

consumption: and income level, 109n; vs. production, 9n

contingencies, prediction of, 158n

contingent freedom, 310

contributory insurance programs, 278–79

controls of welfare administration, 211–12

conventional intentions in welfare state, 14

cost-benefit analysis, 246–47

credential inflation, 270

criminals: compensation, 216n; and freedom, 320–22; medical ethics, 297n

Crosland, Anthony, 104–5

"Cross of Gold" speech, 268n

culpability and moral deserts, 294n

cultural policy and community, 104–5

culture of poverty, 195

death, identifiable vs. statistical, 58–59

deception: and exploitation, 138–39; in games, 143n; using people as, 140n

decision making: allocative, 60–61; communitarian ideal, 114–18; computerized, 211n; consensual, 269; criteria, 191–92; discretionary powers, 191–92, 205; efficiency, 248–49

Declaration of the Rights of Man, 95n

defense contracts, 127n

definition of welfare state, 3–12; political history and institutional structure, 13

delayed benefits, 272–73

Democratic process: and dependency, 170n; and efficiency, 248n

dependency in welfare state, 153–83, 340–41; discretionary power, 216–18; and exploitation, 21–22, 121–22, 173–78; and freedom, 322–24; intergenerational transmission, 355n; levels of assessment, 341n; shifted on families, 174–75, 350–51; on state services, 364–65; particular vs. multiple providers, 176; politics, 170–71; public vs. private, 349; self-reliance, 332–59, 366–69; and suffrage, 171–72; variability of, 350–53

Dependent Spouse Rebate, 349

deserts. See moral deserts

"deserving poor" concept, 279–81; fallacy of, 283

desires: and needs, 27; nonvolitional needs, 31n; urgency of needs, 35–36; volitional needs, 30

desperation bidding, 168–70; supply-side policies, 276–77

despoiling, exploitation as, 130n

Dewey, John, 75–76

diminishing marginal utilities, 32–33

direct vs. indirect welfare measures, 10–11

disability insurance, 233

disaster relief: discretionary powers during, 190–91; exploitation of, 147–48; and moral deserts, 295–96; reliance on, 337–41; spontaneity, 249n

discretionary powers, 184–223; appeals procedures, 199–200; arbitrariness, 198–201, 204–5; circumvention of, 220; defined, 186; dependency, 176–77, 216–18; eligibility requirements, 368–69; exploitation, 185, 193–98, 206; family interdependency, 351–53; historical context, 193–94; illicit power, 194; insecurity, 201–3, 205–6; limits of, 206n, 219–20; manipulation, 185, 193–98, 206; meta-rules for, 191–93; necessity of, 190–93, 219; positive vs. negative, 185–90; privacy, 203–4, 206–7; relief allocations, 172–73; rules and, 207–11; structuring of, 205; types of, 186–89; voluntary welfare, 11–12. See also types of discretion

disease: moral desert, 297n; vs. accidents, 302n

distress: direct vs. indirect approach, 10; as welfare function, 10

distribution: housing problems, 261–62; income and equality, 8–9, 113; of liberties, 310; supply-side policies, 263–64

distributional weights concept, 251

distribution-side welfare solution, 257

divorced parents' maintenance orders, 345–46

drowning millionaire analogy, 145–46, 165–66

drug addicts, exploitation of, 145–46

due process and discretionary powers, 205n

duty, and welfare state: protection of dependents, 16; and welfare administration, 217–19

duty of care concept, 147–50

duty of fair play concept, 142–48
"duty of rescue," 337
duty to protect: and exploitation, 125; vulnerability and, 149n

earnings, and labor supply, 233
economic efficiency, 237–39, 256. *See* efficiency
economic exploitation, 123–24; and manipulation, 137–39
economic growth: as benefit for poor, 229n; relative shares in, 270–71; and welfare state, 154–55, 257–77
economic justice, 166n
economic theory of bureaucracy, 242–45
education: efficiency of social services, 241n; historical context, 4; supply-side policies, 259–60; welfare, 105–6
effectiveness and efficiency, 247n
efficiency and welfare state, 229–56; bureaucracy, 243–45; desirability, 245–47; market vs. non-market failure, 243–45; moral value of, 227; P-level principles, 253–56; relative aspects of, 246n; vs. social equity, 235; want-satisfaction, 247–51
egalitarianism: and communitarianism, 110–13; specific, 156n, 328; in welfare state, 52–55
egoism, and altruism, 79n
eligibility requirements: and discretionary powers, 188–89; exploitation, 368; freedom, 320–22
emergency relief, reliance on, 337–41. *See also* disaster relief
Emerson, Ralph Waldo, 333–34
emigration policies: discretionary powers and, 200; officials' powers, 189n
employer-sponsored retirement plans, 53n
end-goods, supply-side policies, 264–65
entailed estates, 272–73
entitlements vs. deserts concept, 291n
equality: "approximate," 58n; baseline for, 64–65; community spirit, 108–13; consumption of goods and services, 8–9; efficiency and, 248–49; excesses of, 56–57; of freedom, 310–11; income distribution, 113; justification for welfare state, x, 51–69; social solidarity and, 111–13; uncertainty, 58–60; value of, 67–69
equal protection vs. minimal protection, 16–19

Equal Protection Clause (U.S. Constitution), 55
equity vs. efficiency, 235–36
Essay on the Principle of Population, 334
ethics, 121–22; in defense of welfare state, 15–16; emergency-room practice, 296–98; of games, 143n; minimal welfare, 20–21
ethics and the welfare state, 121–22
ET program (Massachusetts), 358
exchange relationships, 135n
expectation preserving insurance, 159–60
expectations and moral deserts, 288–89, 293–94
exploitation: awareness, 143n; beneficiaries, 138n; confrontation with, 9n; cooperation, 133–34; defined, 124–25; dependency, 121–22, 173–78, 366–67; discretionary powers, 185, 193–98, 206, 210; freedom, 308; frequency, 129–30; human character trait, 125–30; manipulation, 137–39; moral ambivalence, 132; needs, 175n; opportunity, 127–28; prevention, xi, 21–22, 123–52; reciprocity, 132n, 134–37; self-generated, 133; social control, 197–98; state charities, 12n
extortion as exploitation, 134n
extraction as exploitation, 133–34
extra-market allocation, 181–83

Factory Acts (Great Britain), 86
fairness: efficiency, 248–49; exploitation, 137–39, 142–48; moral deserts, 285–87
families as welfare substitute, 117n, 332, 342–49; enforcement of support payments, 346–48; interdependency, 349–50. *See also* filial responsibility
family structure: preservation of, 367n; welfare as threat, 349–50
famine: and food availability, 258–60; supply-side policies, 263–64
farm relief, 182n
fault concept, moral deserts, 294n, 302–3
Federal Housing Administration, 103
filial responsibility, 344–46
flagrant violation concept, 150
food availability during famines, 258–60
food distribution: as direct or indirect measure, 10; impartiality and equality in, 68–69; supply-side policies, 263–64

force: discretionary power and, 196–97; unfairness of, 132–34. *See also* coercion

foreign aid, and exploitation, 127n

formal discretion, 188

France, welfare responsibilities, 345

fraternal organizations, 75

fraternity: community and, 75–78, 95; and decision making, 114; equality, 108n; value of, 78–79

fraud, and needs justification, 29

freedom in welfare state, 306–31; bureaucracy, 320–22, 325–27; dependency, 322–24; impartiality, 315–18; morality, 327–30; and needs satisfaction, 37n; New Right interpretation, 227–28; occupational hazards, 319n; paternalism, 318–20; positive vs. negative freedom, 306–12; poverty, 327; priority, 311n; property rights, 312–14; triadic notion, 307–8; uniformity, 314–15

freedom-maximizing institutions, 309

Friedman, Milton: charity as public good, 156–57; progressive taxation, 55

"friendly societies" (Great Britain), 55; and communitarianism, 77; insurance programs, 159n

"fundamental rights," in market economy, 7n

GAIN program (California), 358

Galbraith, John Kenneth, 266

gambling, as nonvolitional need, 41n

games: of advantage, 146–47; exploitation and unfairness, 143–48; rules as exploitation, 137–39

generosity, 221–22

gift relationship: altruism, 78, 116–17; community attachment, 78, 99–100; exploitation and, 135–36

Gift Relationship, The, 99

Gilder, George, 230

Gini coefficient of income equality, 235, 239

Godel's theorem, 191

good as least common denominator, 44

goodness, variations in standards, 289n

grandfather clauses, 271–72

gratuity, welfare as, 12, 172

Great Bengal famine of 1943, 258–60; supply-side policies, 263

Green, T. H., 311

Gross National Product (GNP), 257n

guaranteed income. *See* income

handicapped: as criminals, 64; equalization, 52n; exploitation, 62–64, 145–47, 163; noncontributory social assistance benefits, 157n; self-reliance, 358n; special treatment for, 62–65. *See also* mentally handicapped

harmfulness: definition of, 34; and needs justification, 32–35

"harmful use" test of exploitation, 141–42

Harrington, Michael, 17

hazardous working conditions. *See* occupational hazards

Hayek, F. A., 18n

hazardous wastes, 319n

health: and disease, 297n, 302n; and moral deserts, 294–95; as need, 39

health care: consumer's role in, 241n; efficiency principles in, 249–50; historical context, 4; privatization of, 315; as public good, 239, 313n

Heckscher, August, 104n

Heclo, Hugh, 363

hierarchy in community, 110–11

"hold harmless" clause, 166; supply-side policies, 269

housing: arbitrary evictions, 199n; density patterns, 261–62; interpersonal interactions and networks, 103; moral deserts, 299–300; in Norway, 329–30; supply-side policies, 260–61

human capital: supply-side policies, 265; welfare as investment, 154–55, 237–39

humanism, and dependency, 170n

identifiable deaths, 58–59

"Ifs and Cans" (Austin), 281–82

ignorance, and judgment, 242

impartiality: vs. equality, 54–58; freedom, 315–18; military conscription, 61; negative discrimination, 63–64; probabilistic reasoning, 59; uncertainty, 58–61; unsympathetic clients, 64–65

"inappropriate use" concept, 147n

incentives: disincentives, 230–31; supply-side policies and, 268–69

income: consumption, 109n; distribution and equality, 113; effects on labor supply, 232; guarantees, 8n; self-reliance, 335; transfer programs, 233–34. *See also* pensions

increasing returns to scale, 239–41
independence: and market, 167–68; and suffrage, 171–72
individuality and community, 76–77
"indoor relief," 4
inequality, limiting, 8–9, 327–30; permissibility of, 58–59; as positive discrimination, 64–65
inflation, 270
informal discretion, 188
information management, and efficiency, 241–42
informed preferences, 318–19
in-kind benefits, 318–19
insecurity and discretion, 201–5 reform, 208–9
institutionalized altruism, 78
"institutionalized" deserts, 284–85
instrumental needs, 30n
insurance: compulsoriness of, 319n; model of welfare, 155–60; private programs for, 157–58; self-reliance, 353n
integration: neighborhoods, 102–3; schools, 106
intentional discrimination, 65–66
interdependent relationships, 175
intergenerational reliance on welfare, 355n
intermediate goods, supply-side policies, 264–65
"internal logic" of market societies, 153; extra-market allocation, 181–83
interpersonal communication, 100–108
intervention, exploitation as, 139n
intrinsic needs, 30n
intrusiveness, and discretionary powers, 204, 206–7, 209–10
investment: pensions on, 233–34; welfare as human investment, 237–39
"invidious intent" to discriminate, 62n
involuntary needs, 42
irrationality and risk assessment, 59n
irreversibility of welfare state, 325–27

Jackson (Justice), 55
job training: cost effectiveness of, 250–51; education, 260–61; and self-reliance, 358–59
Johnson, Lyndon Baines, 70
"joint first" concept of positional goods, 266
Joseph, Sir Keith, 336, 343–44
Journal of Economic Literature, 233
judges in welfare administration, 192

justice: communitarianism and, 82n; and efficiency, 248–49
justification-dependent definitions of welfare, 5n
justifications of welfare, x–xi; community, 71–118, 255; equality, 51–69; ethical grounds for, 20–21; fraternity, 255; needs satisfaction, 27–50; social equality, 25; social minimum and needs, 25
"just wants" in market economy, 7n

Kant, Immanuel: autonomous will, 311–12; egalitarianism, 61n
Kennedy, John F., 367n
Keynesianism, 270n
kidney dialysis: impartial allocation, 60–61; and needs justification, 40–41; supply-side and policies, 262

labor: exploitation, 132–36; reduction in as result of welfare, 233; transfer payments and labor supply, 230–32; and welfare policy, 4, 339
Laffer curve, 266
laissez-faire, 312–30
land-use planning, 103
law enforcement: equality, 53n; handicapped criminals, 64; impartiality, 57; as public good, 313n; racial prejudice, 65n; and social morality, 89–91
law of anticipated reactions, 138n
learned helplessness, 357–59
learned laziness, 355–57
least common denominator, needs satisfaction, 44
Le Chapelier, 54
legal rights, unawareness of, 214–15
legislation and welfare administration, 178–81, 192; rule-making discretions, 192–93; social control riders on welfare law, 194
liability: hazardous materials, 319n; moral deserts and, 294n; no-fault principles, 301–5
Liberty Amendment, 326
lifestyles: bias against, 57, 62–63; and dependency, 180–81; and socialism, 71
literacy, 314n
Lloyd-George, David, 73
logic of collective action, 314
Losing Ground, 230–31, 280–81; impact on rollback legislation, 17; reliance on family advocated, 342; self-reliance, 335

pluralism and welfare state, 15, 220n
police. *See* law enforcement
politics, welfare beneficiaries and, 177n
poor laws (Great Britain): Amendment Act of 1834, 230; disenfranchisement, 182–83; family support procedures, 343–46; formal organization, 11n; and inefficiency, 229–30; less eligibility principle, 230; New Right proposals resemble, 19; self-reliance, 334; as welfare state, 6
positional economy, 310
positional goods, 264–67
positive deserts, 281–83
positive discretion, 185–90
positive discrimination, 296n
positive-sum concept of freedom, 306–12; and dependency, 324–25
post-obit bond device, 169n, 272–73
poverty: basic necessities, 109–10; freedom, 321–22, 327; incidence of, 178; inter-family and intergenerational, 347–48; lack of resources, 215; morality, 195; property rights, 162–63; relativity of, 269–71; social control, 197–98; uncertainty, 202–3
Poverty and Famines, 258–64
power: exploitation, 144–45; freedom, 308–10
Power Theory of rights, 212–13
"pragmatic consensus," 18n
preconditions and needs analysis, 36–40
preschool programs for disadvantaged children, 4
"present-orientedness," as character flaw, 338–39
presumed moral desert, 304–5
price discrimination (monopolistic), 167–70
principle of precedence, 28–29; nonvolitional needs, 31; objective needs, 31n; personal autonomy, 47–48; priority of needs, 37; resources, 39–40; value theories on, 42–44
Principle of Political Economy, 336–37
priorities: avoiding harm, 33–34; and autonomy, 47–48; efficiency, 250–51; of freedom, 311n; needs, 28–29
privacy and welfare, 203–4
privatization: private insurance programs, 157–58; of public goods, 315; social services, 154–55; of welfare services, 11, 365–66
probability: impartiality, 59; moral deserts, 292–93
procedures and efficiency vs. spontaneity, 248–49
production vs. consumption, 9n
product safety, 319–20
property rights: enforcement mechanisms, 164–65; morality, 144n; welfare, 161–64, 312–14
prostitution, as exploitation, 131n
protected choices, rights as, 212
protecting the vulnerable, 147–50
protest, and social solidarity, 112
provisional discretionary power, 189
psychological aspects of welfare, 355–57
psychological freedom, 311
Public and Its Problems, The, 75–76
public charity, 12
public goods: and freedom, 313–14; and privatization, 314–15; supply, 155–56; types of, 313–14; welfare as, 238–39
Public Interest, The, 74n
punishment: and moral deserts, 283n, 299n
punitive relief policies, 230

quality control, 246n
queuing for benefits as interpersonal interaction, 100–103

racial integration and welfare, 106–7
radioactivity, susceptibility/impartiality, 59–60, 62–63
random selection, impartiality of, 61
Rawls, John: equality of opportunity, 61n; moral deserts, 289n; positive liberty, 308–9; primary goods and basic resources, 328
Reagan, Ronald: families as welfare source, 344; reduction of welfare, 325–26; safety net, 16; supply-side policies, 266; voluntarism, 335
reasonableness concept, 205
recidivism of welfare, 340
reciprocity: altruism, 77–78; exploitation, 132n, 134–37; vulnerabilities, 149n
reckless drivers, moral deserts of, 296–98
Reclaiming the American Dream, 335
rectification of needs, 34n
red tape, and freedom, 320–22
relativity: supply-side policies, 269–70; and unfairness, 143–44
relevance, and equalization, 53–54
reliance on social assistance, 336–41. *See also* self-reliance
relief of distress concept, 6–7

resident aliens, welfare for, 86–87
residential patterns, 102–3
residualism definition of welfare, 5–6
resources, distribution of: equality, 51–52, 56–57; exploitation, 128–29; insurance plans, 159–60; and market failure, 166–70; needs and satisfaction, 38–40, 48–49, 328n; vs. supply-side policies, 271–73; transfer of, 177–78
respect, equality of, 52
responsibility: community, 73–75, 92–93; discretionary power based on, 185, 211–12; human actions, 230; moral deserts, 303n; and risk assessment, 59n; welfare administration, 217–19
result-based welfare controls, 218–19; equalization of, 60–61
retirement, abolishment of compulsory, 358n
reverse discrimination, 65–67
revolution of rising expectations, 111–13; and property rights, 162
revulsion as bias, 57, 63–64
rights-based welfare administration, 210–12, 213–17; citizenship, 83–85; claiming of, 214–15; discretionary powers, 212–17; moral deserts, 290n; natural rights, 36n; private property, 163–64
right to life, 213–14
risk assessment: low-probability risks, 59n; and mutual aid, 99n; uncertainty, 59–60
risks: dependency and, 369; freedom to take, 319–20; moral deserts, 294–96
role playing, 67
rollback of welfare: New Right advocacy of, 18–19; political tolerance for, 17–18
Roman law and community, 75
Roosevelt, Franklin, 70
Rousseau, Jean-Jacques: autonomous will, 311–12; on equality, 54–55
Royal Commission on the Aged Poor, 280n
rule-based welfare administration, 220–21, 284–85
rules: discretionary powers, 191–93, 207–11; regulatory unreasonableness, 208n; relativity of, 209–10; social deserts, 290–91

safety net, 16; moral deserts, 280–81, 301n; as welfare minimum program, 366–67

Salvation Army, 11
savings patterns: impact of pensions on, 233–34; pay-as-you-go vs. reserve funds, 234n
Scandinavia: child allowance programs, 349; communities in, 87n; public housing in, 103n. See also Norway
"Seattle God Committee," 262
security and poverty, 202–3
segregated neighborhoods, 103n
"seizing opportunities," as exploitation, 127n
self-development, 341–49; and altruism, 79n; and community solidarity, 76n
self-esteem, and self-reliance, 356
self-exploitation, 133, 142
Self-Help, 333, 336
self-help, 365
selfishness, and freedom, 316–17
selflessness, and freedom, 316–17
self-preservation, and property rights, 163
self-referring laws, 191n
self-reliance: as character trait, 354–57; and dependency, 332–59; family, 342–49; historical context of, 333–34; New Right interpretation, 228; psychological aspects, 355–57; sacrifice of future benefits, 348–49; vs. self-sufficiency, 365–69; welfare state promotes, 356–57
self-respect: and dependency, 183n; and self-reliance, 334–35; want-satisfaction, 253; welfare beneficiaries, 217n
self-sufficiency, welfare as, 363–69
Sen, Amartya, 258–64
sick people, equality for, 54–55
single status moral community, 73–75
slavery, exclusion from labor market, 135n; as exploitation, 132; and freedom, 308–9
Smiles, Samuel, 333, 336, 342
Smith, Adam, 109
social assistance: community solidarity, 76n; as core of welfare state, 4; historical background, 3
social control: discretionary power, 194–95; exploitation, 197–98; family interdependency, 349; freedom, 320–22; moral desert, 287–88; welfare as, 172–73
social insurance: impact on labor supply, 233; incentive effects of, 339; vs. private insurance, 159; welfare state as, 4

socialism: eradication of status, 71; view of welfare state, 4–5

social rules, discretionary powers and, 191–92

social security: discretionary powers, 206–7; private savings' patterns, 234–35; self-reliance, 339–40; U.S./U.S.S.R. expenditures compared, 8n

Social Security Act (Great Britain), 344

Social Security Amendments of 1972, 262

Social Security: The New Priorities, 343

Social Security (U.S.) Amendment of 1974, 345–46

social services, planned vs. market economies, 8

social workers: bias in, 57; moral desert, 297–301; exploitation by, 152; monitoring, 198–99; moral responsibilities of, 321–22

solidarity, 70–71; class differences, 110n; and community, 72–73; equality, 108–9, 111–13; populist vision of, 75

sovereignty, and dependency, 170–71

specific egalitarianism, 10–11, 156n, 328; needs satisfaction, 46–48

Spencer, Herbert, 279n; self-reliance concept, 334

squandering, exploitation as, 130n

squatters movements, 261

standard of living, 181n. *See also* lifestyles

starvation, 259–60

state administration of welfare: altruism, 118–19; citizenship, 85–86; coordination, 7–12, 155, 211–12; community image, 87n; discretionary powers, 192–93; exploitation, 12n, 177–78; interpersonal interactions and networks, 102–3; reform, 214–15; value skepticism, 45–46

statistical deaths, 58–59

statistical expectations and moral deserts, 293–94

status: community, 71, 73, 99–100; education, 260; equality, 52; noncitizens, 87; poverty, 216n; solidarity, 112; welfare rights, 85, 92–93, 216n

stigma-avoidance, communitarianism, 73–74

strong discretion, 187

subjectivism, and unfairness, 143–44

suffrage, and community membership, 84–85. *See also* voting rights

Sumner, William Graham, 280n, 334

Supplementary Benefits (Great Britain): allocation decisions, 64n; Appeals Tribunal, 199n, 200–201; case overload, 222n; complexity of, 209n; Dependency Benefit, 349; discretionary powers, 195–96, 352; "exceptional needs" criteria, 57, 188; Form A124, 209n; interpersonal communication, 101; privacy and intrusiveness, 204; voluntary savings schemes, 204

supply-side policies, 222–23, 257–77; arbitrariness, 268–69; criticism, 266–67; and famines, 258–60; fixed vs. limitless supplies, 266; flaws, 263–64; insolubility of, 267–68; partial optimization of, 264–65; and relative wealth, 269–70; slowness, 271–74

symmetrical relationships, and equality, 65–66

sympathy: community, 77–79, 93–94; and equality, 54, 63–67; medical ethics, 297n; moral deserts concept, 279–80; mutual aid, 66–68, 114–15; negative discrimination, 63–64

"taking advantage" concept, 124–27, 144–48

targeting welfare benefits, 19

taxation: charitable donations, 156n; equality, 55–57; for farmers, 129; freedom, 312–14; moral deserts, 279; work incentive, 231–32

Thatcher, Margaret: families welfare resource, 344; self-reliance concepts, 336; welfare reductions, 325–26

theft: exploitation as, 133

theory-dependent definitions of welfare, 5n

Third World: exploitation of, 134–35; and price manipulation, 137

time: standards of living, 180–81; supply-side policies, 271–74

Title i of Elementary and Secondary Education Act of 1965, 259–60

Titmuss, Richard, 99–100

Tocqueville, Alexis de, 304, 305n

top-down approach to bureaucracy, 211n

Townsend, Joseph, 229

tradeoffs in welfare principles, 254–55

transfer payments, 5; and labor supply, 230–33; poverty reduction, 113

tribalism, and mutual aid, 323–24

trickle-down theories, 257n, 268–69; slowness of, 271–72. *See also* supply-side policies

trust in public institutions, 364–65

ultimate discretionary power, 189
uncertainty: bias and impartiality, 62; and discretionary powers, 201–3; and equality, 54, 58–61
unconscionable contracts, 144n, 170
"undeserving poor," 279–83; needs legitimacy of, 298–301
unemployment, isolation of, 103–4
Unemployment Assistance Board (Great Britain), 65n
unemployment benefits: actuarial studies, 158–59; directness, 10; importance, 4; moral deserts, 299–300; and welfare reform, 17
unequal exchange concept, 134–35
unfairness concept: abuse of process, 198; dependency, 174n; desperation bidding, 170; exploitation, 124–25, 142–48; morality of, 132–34; whole-person exploitation, 130–31
uniformity: and equality, 54–58; impartiality, 316–18
United Fruit Company, 146
United Fund, 11, 155
universal fungibility, 273–74
universalism, 55–56; freedom, 314–15; impartiality and, 68–69; vs. selectivity of benefits, 73
universal national service, 61n
universal necessary instruments: autonomy, 49; needs analysis, 36–37
University of Michigan Panel Study of Income Dynamics, 340–41
unsympathetic clients, impartiality toward, 65
"untoward interventions," 286–87
unusual vs. exploitable advantages, 128–29
urgency of needs, 35–36
U.S. Economic Opportunity Act of 1964, 194
U.S. Housing Act of 1949, 260–62
using concept: consent to using, 141; vs. exploitation, 139–42; harmful, 141
utilitarianism: discretionary powers, 201–2; fallacies of, 247n; inequality of wants, 251; negative, 319–20; self-reliance, 337–41

vagueness in welfare requirements, 188–89
values and welfare state, 15–16; command economy, 45; market's effect on, 166; moral deserts, 290–91; skepticism, 43–46
"vending machine society," 166

veteran's benefits: housing aid, 103; selectivity in awarding, 73–74
"victims of misfortune" fallacy, 294n
village society: as ideal community, 75, 87n; and self-reliance, 356–57
virtues, social institutions and, 289–90
volitional needs, 29–30; priority of, 39n
voluntarism, 11; benefactor-beneficiary relationship, 117–18; nonvolitional needs, 40–41; self-reliance, 335
volunteer army, inequality of, 61n
"voodoo economics," 266
voting rights: community membership, 84–85; independence, 171–72; welfare rights, 87–88, 173n
vulnerability: dependency, 165–83, 174n; as end-state notion, 150; moral deserts, 296n; and property rights protection, 162–63; protection against, 16, 125, 147–48, 166, 367n reciprocal, 149n; self-reliance, 357–58; variations in, 148n

wants: freedom, 328–30; inequality, 250–51; moral deserts, 298n; needs, 27; satisfaction, 247–53
wartime services: community altruism, 78; and freedom, 317–18
weak discretion, 187–88
weekend farmers as exploiters, 128–29
welfare rights, 6–7; community membership, 80–83, 91–96; conflicts among, 177n; defined, 178–81; dependency, 353; justification, 184–85; noncitizens, 86–88; voting rights, 88–89
welfare state: benefactor-beneficiary, 116–18; business investment, 236n; coercion, 8, 12, 306; community and, 107–8; core features, 3, 7, 9–10, 12; culture and arts in, 104–5; defined, 3–12; educational policy, 105–6; exploitation, 21–22; family replaced by, 350n; freedom, 8, 312–31; functions, 7; historical background, 3–4; intentions, 14; irreversibility, 325–27; legal rights, 22; mutual aid and, 323–24; policy options, 10–11; political history and structure, 3, 13–16; vs. self-reliance, 357–59
Welfare State? Social Policy in the 1980s, 336
What Social Classes Owe to Each Other, 334
whole-person exploitation, 130–31
will, freedom and, 311

Wolf, C., Jr., 242–43
women in welfare state: dependency vs. self-reliance, 343n, 348–49; family care provisions, 348–49; as noncitizens, 86–87; taxation and married women, 232n; as unpaid caregivers, 133n
workfare, 74n

work hours, 233
workmen's compensation, 302–4
workplace, 103–4
worthless freedoms, 308

Zero-Sum Society, 267